Dealing with Disaster

Dealing with Disaster
Public Management in Crisis Situations

SECOND EDITION

Saundra K. Schneider

Routledge
Taylor & Francis Group

LONDON AND NEW YORK

First published 2011 by M.E. Sharpe

Published 2015 by Routledge
2 Park Square, Milton Park, Abingdon, Oxon OX14 4RN
711 Third Avenue, New York, NY 10017, USA

Routledge is an imprint of the Taylor & Francis Group, an informa business

Library of Congress Cataloging-in-Publication Data

Schneider, Saundra K., 1952–
  Dealing with disaster : public management in crisis situations /
by Saundra K. Schneider. — 2nd ed.
      p. cm.
Includes bibliographical references and index.
ISBN 978-0-7656-2242-6 (hardcover : alk. paper)—ISBN 978-0-7656-2243-3 (pbk. : alk. paper)
1. Emergency management—United States. 2. Crisis management in government—United States.
I. Title.

  HV551.3.S38 2011
  363.34′560973—dc22   2011006578

ISBN 13: 9780765622433 (pbk)
ISBN 13: 9780765622426 (hbk)

The first edition of this book, entitled *Flirting with Disaster*, was dedicated to my father, Jacob W. Schneider. I would like to dedicate this second edition, *Dealing with Disaster*, to my mother, Helen M. Schneider.

Contents

Preface to the First Edition

There is nothing like personal experience to spark one's interest in a topic. That is certainly the case with this study, which began and ended in the midst of natural disasters. I started to think about the main ideas presented in this book shortly after sitting through Hurricane Hugo's onslaught of the southeastern states in September of 1989. Having just moved to South Carolina one month prior to this time, I was struck by the government's apparent inability to respond to the needs and demands of the hurricane victims. So I began investigating the causes and consequences of governmental actions during these traumatic times, as well as the kinds of dilemmas that naturally arise when public officials try to restore order in the aftermath of natural catastrophes.

Like most other research projects, this one turned out to be larger than I originally anticipated. I spent the next five years collecting information on a variety of natural disasters and the governmental actions that took place in each one. As my research proceeded, I was increasingly impressed with the enormity of the problem, the pressures faced by virtually everyone involved in the disaster relief process, and the seemingly constant criticism of the governmental response system. Juxtaposed against these pressure-ridden aspects of the subject matter, I was also pushed toward a fairly clear conclusion: the system usually does work quite well.

Then, just as I was about to complete the manuscript for this book in January 1995, I had another firsthand experience with a natural disaster. This time, a small and compact, but nevertheless violent, tornado touched down in my own backyard (literally). Thankfully, my own home was largely spared, but the brief storm left a swath of damage clearly visible through my neighborhood. It toppled dozens of tall loblolly pine trees, tore the roofs off of several houses, and rearranged just about everything that happened to get in its path. To say the least, this provided me with a potent reminder about the forms of human behavior that occur whenever a disaster strikes. The tornado vividly demonstrated just how unsettling and traumatic even a small natural disaster can be, particularly for those who experience it directly. It also reinforced in my mind the difficulties faced by the relief organizations that are responsible for addressing the concerns, problems, and demands of disaster victims. In short, my research both began and ended with opportunities to observe directly the conceptual principles that I develop in this book.

The central question of this study is a straightforward one: why does the government handle some natural disasters successfully, but seem to fail miserably in other cases? The answer to this question does not really lie in the factors that most people would identify: the magnitude of the disaster and the amount of governmental resources spent on relief efforts. Instead, the success or failure of an emergency response is dependent upon the size of the inevitable gap between the collective behavior of response victims and the bureaucratic procedures of public officials. The case studies presented in this study demonstrate that this relatively simple principle appears again and again in a wide variety of natural disaster situations.

I believe that the topic of this book is both interesting and intrinsically important. Of course, natural disasters do attract a great deal of attention from both journalists and scholars. However, most of the journalist accounts are descriptive and anecdotal in nature, containing little systematic or comprehensive coverage of the topic. And the scholarly treatments have been segmented by academic discipline; thus, the emergency management studies in public administration and the collective behavior field in sociology remain largely separate and distinct research traditions. Moreover, there has been little, if any, attempt to integrate broader principles of bureaucratic behavior and policymaking into research on disaster relief. My purpose in this book is to overcome these limitations. I employ information from journalistic and scholarly sources, along with my own original research, in order to develop a general theoretical framework for analyzing governmental performance in disaster situations.

This book is intended to be a research monograph contributing to our understanding of disaster management in the United States. Although the subject matter may appear to be somewhat narrow, the content of the study should appeal to a broad audience beyond American scholars and practitioners in the field of emergency management. First, the basic principles espoused in this study should be applicable to disaster relief in other nations.

For example, two disasters that occurred when I was completing this study—a major earthquake in Kobe, Japan, and massive flooding in the Netherlands—clearly demonstrate the relevance of the gap between victim's expectations and bureaucratic performance. Consider the Kobe Earthquake of January 17, 1995: the Japanese have a well-developed administrative structure for dealing with emergency situations, but it failed miserably, at least in the initial periods after the disaster struck. Accordingly, the Japanese press, public, and governmental officials have criticized their own system for being slow, ineffective, and nonresponsive to offers of outside help. The floods in the Netherlands represent a somewhat different situation. The Dutch are all too familiar with flooding, and they have routinized procedures for dealing with these situations. However, the floods that occurred in early February 1995 were so massive and widespread that the nation was caught off guard; the preparations and response procedures that had worked so well in the past simply failed in this case. Once again, the Dutch public officials charged with emergency management responsibilities were subjected to intense criticism. Both of these situations, along with literally hundreds of others throughout the world, illustrate the importance of the gap between collective behavior and bureaucratic norms for understanding the success or failure of governmental responses to natural disasters.

Second, the findings of this study may also provide insights into public policymaking during other types of stressful situations. A natural disaster is certainly not the only type of event or problem that can generate a conflict between governmental planning and public expectations. For example, environmental protection agencies at both the national and state levels monitor air and water quality, issue regulations to maintain environmental standards, and oversee compliance with many kinds of environmental protection laws. Most of the time, these agencies carry out their responsibilities in a routine manner, attracting little if any public attention. Occasionally, however, they come into direct conflict with the public and/or powerful interests who become incensed when economic development is halted because of factors such as endangered species, wetlands, and pollution control standards. As another example, consider the state and local social services agencies that are responsible for placing children in foster care homes. Usually, their activities proceed smoothly and the results provide positive benefits for everyone considered. Occasionally, however, foster children suffer injuries, abuse, and even death; when this occurs the agencies that place and protect the children come under intense public scrutiny and criticism. These two examples represent very different substantive policy situations, and they affect very different population groups.

But both of them provide perfect illustrations of a gap between the standard operating procedures of governmental bureaucracies and the norms and expectations of the general public. Thus, the explanatory factor that accounts for governmental responses to natural disasters is also directly applicable to policy performance in other areas as well.

Third, the findings of this study should have broad relevance to the general fields of public policy and public administration. Although the book is focused specifically on disaster relief, it still addresses such general issues as policy implementation, program evaluation, bureaucratic politics, and public management. The study also deals with some of the central features of American policymaking—that is, intergovernmental relations, governmental accountability, and public-private sector interactions. Therefore, it should be useful to political scientists in many of the subfields associated with American government, as well as to scholars in other disciplines, particularly sociology and economics. Finally, and most obviously, this book should be relevant to scholars and practitioners in the field of emergency management. After all, these are the individuals who focus directly on the governmental response to disasters.

I am grateful to the many people who have assisted throughout this project. Kenneth Meier provided helpful comments and suggestions on an earlier draft of the manuscript. In addition, his continuous support of the project over the past three years has been invaluable. Indeed, he convinced me that the study was worthwhile and encouraged me to carry it on to a successful completion.

Several graduate students at the University of South Carolina helped collect important and voluminous information about the natural disasters that are discussed in this study. In this respect, I would particularly like to thank Sherral Brown Guinyard, Shawn Benzinger, and Teresa Spires.

It is also appropriate that I acknowledge the invaluable assistance provided to me by dozens of national, state, and local disaster relief officials. The information and materials that they supplied comprise much of the raw material and data upon which this study is constructed. I would also like to thank B. D. Publishing Company for their generous permission to use photographs of Hurricane Hugo's destruction in Charleston, South Carolina.

At M.E. Sharpe, Inc., I would like to acknowledge my appreciation to Michael Weber, who has helped me get the book into print.

Finally, a special thanks goes to William G. Jacoby who provided me with insightful comments, invaluable support, and continuous help throughout the entire time I worked on this book. Without his assistance and encouragement, I would not have been able to undertake or complete this study. I deeply appreciative all of his efforts.

Preface to the Second Edition

When I finished the first edition of this book—which was published under the title *Flirting with Disaster*—I was hopeful that the nation's emergency management system would be strengthened. I was encouraged that such changes had taken place during the mid to late 1990s. The Federal Emergency Management Agency (FEMA) was transformed from one of the worst federal agencies to one of the best, and the entire disaster response system seemed to be more directly focused on dealing with emergencies. Perhaps even more encouraging was the performance of the governmental response system during this period. Although there were problems during some relief efforts, the government handled most of the disasters that occurred in this period fairly smoothly and effectively.

In the aftermath of the September 11, 2001, terrorist attacks, the nation's emergency management system was restructured. A new organizational framework was created, and the focus of disaster relief was expanded to include a wider array of events. But we seemed to forget what we had learned from previous disaster relief operations. Instead, we set our sights on building a new, bigger, and "better" framework that could deal with any type of crisis event. Unfortunately, however, some of the best aspects of the previous system were revised, eliminated, or lost in the transition.

Hurricane Katrina in 2005 reminded us of the importance of focusing on emergency response activities. The storm revealed serious deficiencies in the nation's disaster management operations at all levels of government. And it led many Americans to question the ability of public institutions to address other types of disasters, as well as the role of government in solving major societal problems.

The public's skepticism about governmental performance developed, at least in part, because of the media's intense coverage of the problematic elements of the response to Katrina during and following the storm. There were numerous reports of breakdowns in social conditions and lines of communication, halting or nonexistent rescue operations, the seeming incompetence of public officials, partisan bickering between political leaders, the wasteful allocation of essential resources, and the slowness of the entire recovery effort. Many commentators, analysts, and scholars said that the real disaster was not Katrina, but rather the government response to it.

But it is important to place the governmental response to Hurricane Katrina in perspective. Katrina is only one of a number of natural disasters that have occurred in recent years. Indeed, the frequency and severity of such events are increasing at a fairly constant pace. In 2010, the federal government declared eighty-one natural disaster situations in the United States alone. This sets the record as the worst year for natural disasters since the declaration of such events became commonplace. Adding to this, other types of emergencies have also been on the rise—such as the 2010 BP Deepwater Horizon oil spill in the Gulf Coast. Governmental agencies are now called upon to play a key role in addressing these situations. For the vast majority of disasters, public institutions respond fairly well. But in some cases, the emergency response process seems to operate too slowly and haphazardly, or breaks down almost completely as it did during Hurricane Katrina.

Worldwide, the situation is even more alarming. During 2010, over two hundred natural disasters occurred in areas around the world: these events have caused massive levels of destruction, unprecedented levels of damages, and hundreds of thousands of deaths. Several of these events—like the earthquake that occurred in Haiti on January 15, 2010—have received fairly widespread attention, and they have triggered unprecedented international relief efforts. Unfortunately, they have also renewed fundamental questions about the capability of emergency response organizations to provide aid to the victims of natural disasters in a swift and effective manner.

The goal of this new edition of the book, now titled *Dealing with Disaster*, is to place the governmental response to natural disasters in a broader perspective. More specifically, my objective is to compare how the emergency management system in the United States has operated across a variety of natural disaster situations over the past twenty years. By using a comparative approach, I believe that we can acquire a better understanding of what public agencies are capable of doing, as well as the constraints and limitations on their operations.

The material presented here reinforces and reiterates the basic premise of the first edition. I argue, once again, that it is the "match" or "mismatch" between bureaucratic behavior and citizens' expectations that explains governmental performance in disaster relief. When governmental preparations match the expectations of the disaster-stricken population, the response process works well. However, when there is a mismatch, discrepancy, or gap between these two important sets of norms, the governmental response process stalls, stumbles, or breaks down completely. Therefore, it is the size of the gap between bureaucratic activity and citizen behavior that determines the success or failure of governmental disaster relief efforts.

In this new edition, I also show how public policy itself can affect the relationship between governmental actions and citizens' expectations. When the intergovernmental response framework is squarely focused on disasters, particularly natural disasters, and when it develops policies and procedures to address these types of situations, the government is able to respond fairly quickly and effectively. This leads to a much better impression of the government's disaster relief capabilities. Moreover, it also contributes to more positive citizen assessments of the overall capabilities and performance of governmental institutions during extremely stressful crisis situations. Hence, the material in this edition provides additional insights into, and recommendations for, improving the governmental response framework.

I hope that the United States does not experience another catastrophic event like Hurricane Katrina. But if we do, I also hope that the governmental response process is better equipped to handle such a disaster. It would be nice to think that we have learned from our past mistakes, incorporated the lessons learned from previous relief efforts, and designed a stronger, more adaptable system. If that is the case, then some good will have emerged from major catastrophes like Katrina.

I am grateful to everyone who has helped and supported me on this project. Several graduate students at Michigan State University collected invaluable information about the natural disasters that are discussed in this edition of the book. I would particularly like to thank Daniel C. Lewis and Daniel O'Connor for their efforts.

I would also like to acknowledge my appreciation to Patricia Kolb, Makiko Parsons, Angela Piliouras, and Kimberly Giambattisto at M.E. Sharpe for their editorial help. Pat played a key role in convincing me to undertake a second edition of the book; she and her staff provided an amazing amount of support as I completed necessary revisions.

Once again, a special thanks goes to William G. Jacoby. Without his encouragement, assistance, and guidance, I might have become another disaster-related casualty. I cannot adequately express my sincere gratitude and appreciation for his continuous support and reassurance.

Part One

Analytical and Theoretical Frameworks

1

The Varied Success of the Governmental Response to Natural Disasters

Over the last two decades, a sizable number of major natural disasters have struck the United States. For example, on September 17, 1989, a massive hurricane named Hugo blasted the U.S. Virgin Islands at full force. Then, on the following day, the storm ripped its way across the northeast portion of Puerto Rico. After a brief respite in the Atlantic Ocean, Hugo hit the U.S. mainland about forty miles northeast of Charleston, South Carolina. The huge storm pounded the coastal areas for several hours; then it moved quickly and violently in a northwesterly direction, carving a destructive path across half the state of South Carolina. Hugo made one last stop at Charlotte, North Carolina, before it finally turned north and diminished in strength. During its brief but violent life, Hugo left thousands of people without shelter, water, food, sewer facilities, electricity, or telephone services. Overall, it was responsible for fifty-six deaths and damages estimated at more than $11 billion. Hurricane Hugo was clearly one of the most destructive storms of the twentieth century.

Less than a month later, on October 17, 1989, a major earthquake rocked the San Francisco Bay area. The quake, called Loma Prieta by geologists, shook the earth for about fifteen seconds with a force measuring 7.1 on the Richter scale. Severe damage was reported within a hundred-mile radius around the quake's epicenter (located eight miles northeast of Santa Cruz). Tremors were felt several hundred miles beyond that point in all directions. The earthquake destroyed or damaged thousands of buildings. Roads cracked open and bridges crumbled. Natural gas and power lines snapped apart, and water pipes exploded. In all, the quake caused more than sixty deaths, thousands of injuries, and an estimated $7.1 billion in damages. The Loma Prieta Earthquake was the largest earthquake to occur along the San Andreas Fault since the 1906 San Francisco Earthquake (U.S. Geological Survey 1990), and it served as a wakeup call for the rest of the nation (U.S. Geological Survey 2010).

Almost three years after these incidents a major hurricane called Andrew smacked into the U.S. coastline about thirty-five miles south of Miami, Florida. On August 23, 1992, Andrew blasted the southern tip of Florida with sustained winds of 140 miles per hour and gusts of up to 164 miles per hour. The storm traveled quickly across the Florida peninsula, leveling virtually everything in its path. It continued to move in a west-northwesterly direction over the Gulf of Mexico. Early on August 25, Andrew made landfall again. This time it hit a sparsely populated section of southern Louisiana. Later that same day, the hurricane finally lost its punch as it moved northward, up through the south-central section of the United States. In its wake, Hurricane Andrew left hundreds of thousands of people homeless, and thousands more without power, water, communications, and sewer facilities. This compact, but extremely fierce, storm caused at least forty deaths and over $26 billion in property damages. Hurricane Andrew was one of the most destructive and expensive natural disasters to strike the U.S. mainland.

In 1993, another type of natural disaster hit the central portion of the United States. From April 1 to July 31, ten times the normal amount of rain fell in the central section of the nation, completely saturating the entire area. There was so much water that the Mississippi and Missouri Rivers were simply overwhelmed. The excess spilled over onto the surrounding land, creating enormous new lakes, rivers, and inland seas. Severe flooding was reported in nine states, stretching from Minnesota in the north to southeastern Missouri. The scope of the flooding was immense. Millions of acres of farmland were completely submerged; hundreds of highways, levees, and dams were washed away; thousands of residents were forced to leave their homes and farms. In all, the flooding caused forty deaths, and $10–15 billion in damages. The devastating overflow of the Mississippi and the Missouri Rivers has been referred to as the Great Midwest Flood of 1993.[1]

A year after the 1993 floods, Mother Nature struck again—this time on the west coast. On January 17, 1994, an earthquake jolted the Los Angeles, California, area at 4:21 in the morning. The tremors lasted for about forty seconds, reaching a level of 6.6 on the Richter scale. Ironically, the quake occurred along a little known, unnamed fault, in the northwestern section of the city. Nevertheless, it inflicted severe damage on one of the nation's most populated urban areas. Major freeways, bridges, and buildings crumbled into pieces; water pipes burst open; and electric wires snapped apart. The quake severed natural gas lines that, in turn, set off a number of serious fires throughout the surrounding neighborhoods. Thousands of residents lost their homes and personal belongings. The damages to property, buildings, highways, and so on, have been estimated at more than $30 billion. In addition, the quake killed sixty-one people and injured hundreds more. Experts say that this earthquake was not fierce enough to qualify as "The Big One." But it definitely sent a wake-up call to the citizens of the city of Los Angeles, the state of California, and the rest of the nation. This disaster was the most costly earthquake to occur in the United States.

Then, in the summer of 2005, a massive storm called Hurricane Katrina slammed into the Gulf Coast region of the United States. Katrina first made landfall on the southeastern tip of Florida near the Broward-Dade county line as a Category One hurricane with winds measured at eighty miles per hour. Then, the storm moved toward the southwest through the unpopulated Everglades National Park, exiting the state on the southwestern tip of mainland Florida. For the next few days, Katrina stayed put in the waters of the Gulf of Mexico where it continued to build strength, intensify, and expand in size, becoming a Category Five hurricane. Then, it turned and began moving in a north, north-westerly direction toward the Gulf Coast states. Hurricane Katrina came ashore for a second time on Monday, August 29, near Buras, Louisiana. The huge storm continued to move over land in a north-northeasterly direction, bringing hurricane-force winds and rain to portions of Louisiana, Mississippi, and Alabama. Finally, the storm lost its strength in the Tennessee Valley and eventually died out over the eastern Great Lakes (U.S. Department of Commerce 2005b).

During its lifespan, Katrina caused an unimaginable amount of destruction. In Louisiana, the city of New Orleans sustained extensive damage. Storm surges (extreme rain and high winds) stressed the city's levee system and several of the flood walls were overtopped or breached.

In turn, this led to catastrophic flooding. At one point, approximately 80 percent of the city of New Orleans was filled with water up to twenty feet deep. But this was not the only community affected by Katrina. The storm had an impact on large parts of the coastal areas across Louisiana, Mississippi, and Alabama, affecting nearly 93,000 square miles over 138 counties and parishes. Katrina devastated far more residential property than had any other recent hurricane. It destroyed many homes, buildings, forests, and vegetation and left behind an unprecedented amount of debris. Katrina was also responsible for broader demographic transformations. Over two million people were displaced from their homes; many were relocated to other places across the United States far away from the area. Although the storm hit in August 2005, disaster assistance funds are still flowing to the Gulf Coast (in 2011) to help communities and families recover. Hurricane Katrina has the dubious distinction of being the most disruptive, damaging, and costly natural disaster in American history.[2]

Major natural disasters, such as Hurricane Hugo, the Loma Prieta Earthquake, Hurricane Andrew, the Great Flood of 1993, the 1994 Los Angeles Earthquake, and Hurricane Katrina, place enormous and extraordinary burdens on the people who experience them. They generate problems and conditions that are difficult to anticipate, comprehend, and address. Individuals, families, and private organizations try to help citizens deal with the chaos and disruption. Their efforts are extremely important, but often woefully inadequate for disasters of these magnitudes. As a result, people turn naturally to the public sector for assistance. Government is the only institution with the resources and authority to help citizens cope with such cataclysmic events.

In the United States, the government has developed a formal system to deal with major disasters. This system is designed to guide official activity before, during, and after a disaster situation occurs. It identifies the basic objectives of governmental activity, as well as the policies and procedures that should be used to achieve these goals. The system also ties together the activities of all three levels of government, and coordinates the operations of various public and private organizations. Overall, this governmental response system strives to provide the most effective and efficient utilization of available resources.

The government relies upon this basic apparatus whenever and wherever a disaster strikes. In general, the system appears to work quite well. For the vast majority of disasters, the government is able to respond in a fairly routine manner. Public institutions use standard operating procedures to step in and provide relief to stricken areas.

Little fanfare, commotion, or publicity surrounds these activities. In these situations, the governmental response is viewed as timely, appropriate, and successful.

Unfortunately, however, the governmental response does not always operate so smoothly or effectively. As Hurricane Hugo, the Loma Prieta Earthquake, Hurricane Andrew, and Hurricane Katrina demonstrated, some natural disasters generate severe environmental and societal disruptions. Public institutions find it extremely difficult to handle such situations. So, the government appears to react too slowly and haphazardly. In other instances, it mobilizes quickly, but subsequently cannot direct available resources to those who are truly in need. And in a few rare cases, the governmental response appears to be completely misguided. Public agencies fail to react swiftly or appropriately for the disaster situation at hand. In sum, the overall effectiveness of governmental efforts in dealing with major natural disasters is highly variable. This raises an interesting and important question: why is governmental performance in the area of disaster response so inconsistent? This book addresses precisely that question.

I argue that the answer does not lie solely in the structure of the governmental response system or in the nature of the disaster. Rather, it is the combination of these two factors. More specifically, the key to a successful governmental response depends upon the extent to which post-disaster human behavior corresponds to prior governmental expectations and planning. On the one hand, public organizations develop standard operating procedures, routine policies, and institutionalized processes that are supposed to address every possible contingency. These bureaucratic norms provide the foundation for the governmental response system. On the other hand, some disasters generate conditions that are unusually difficult, complicated, or stressful. During these situations, bureaucratic norms and institutionalized patterns of behavior simply do not seem to apply. Therefore, new or emergent norms develop to provide guidance and meaning to the affected population.

When the gap between these emergent norms and the pre-existing bureaucratic norms of the governmental system is quite large, the response process breaks down. This leads to widespread dissatisfaction with and criticism of governmental activities. However, when the disaster situation conforms to prior governmental expectations and planning, the gap between bureaucratic and emergent norms is relatively small. In these cases, public organizations are able to cope effectively with the disaster. Response and recovery operations proceed smoothly; little media or public attention is focused on these activities; and the entire governmental effort is perceived as successful. Thus, it is the size of the gap between the bureaucratic norms guiding governmental activity and the emergent norms arising within the affected population that determines the variability in governmental performance.

Varying sizes of the gap correspond to three alternative patterns of policy implementation. First, when the gap between emergent and bureaucratic norms is relatively small, governmental policies and procedures provide an appropriate guide to human behavior. Little confusion or delay occurs, and the government is able to react to the disaster situation in a relatively routine, straightforward manner. All relevant emergency management officials work together and perform their previously defined responsibilities. Governmental activity flows from the "bottom-up," precisely as it was intended. The response "bubbles" up from the local level to the state and ultimately to the national government.

Second, other disasters produce a moderately-sized gap. Bureaucratic and emergent norms do not exactly agree with each other, but they are not entirely contradictory either. This leads to a situation in which no clear guidance for, or support of, governmental activities exists. A number of different actors and agencies at each level of government may try to take action. However, there is little or no coordination to these efforts, and it is difficult to tell exactly which (if any) level of government is responsible for the various relief and recovery operations. The result is a "confused" pattern of governmental activity.

Third, in some situations, bureaucratic procedures and patterns of human behavior diverge entirely from one another; consequently, the gap is extremely wide. In these disasters, the government simply cannot follow its standard operating procedures. The pre-established intergovernmental response framework is incapable of administering disaster relief. Local and state governments may be unable or unwilling to handle the crisis; the national government has to step in and take control of the entire effort. The normal bottom-up intergovernmental response pattern is supplanted by a top-down implementation process.

These three patterns of policy implementation for disaster relief—bottom-up, confused, and top-down—are extremely important. Although the details of specific natural disasters vary widely, almost all response efforts conform to one of these patterns. These three models provide clear illustrations of the government's overall performance in this policy area. More specifically, the three patterns reveal the extent to which governmental plans match the needs and expectations of the affected population. Governmental responses that conform to the bottom-up process are most likely to be labeled successes, those that proceed in a confused, disorganized manner are usually viewed with mixed reactions, and those that follow the top-down pattern are generally perceived to be failures. Consequently, these three implementation patterns are used here to construct a framework for understanding the success or failure of the government's natural disaster relief efforts.

The rest of the book is organized as follows: in Part One, I present the fundamental theoretical and analytical frameworks of the study. Chapter One examines two basic questions: (1) why are disasters viewed as legitimate public problems, requiring governmental action? and (2) what role should the government play in disaster-related activities? In order to answer these questions, Chapter Two compares disasters to other types of public problems and issues. Unlike situations in many other policy areas, citizens expect government to act when disaster strikes, and public beliefs about governmental intervention have had a significant influence on the development of disaster relief policy in the United States. Chapter Three examines the basic governmental approach to disasters in the United States, and it provides a brief overview of the historical development of governmental activity in this area. Then, I discuss the basic framework and structure of the current governmental disaster assistance system, looking at both the strengths and weaknesses of the government's policy approach.

Chapter Four examines the two sets of norms that exist in every disaster situation: the bureaucratic norms that guide the governmental response process and the emergent norms that develop within the disaster-stricken population. Chapter Five uses these two sets of norms to construct a general framework for explaining the government's disaster assistance efforts. Here, I focus on the key concept of the study. I argue that it is the size of the gap between bureaucratic norms and emergent norms that determines the predominant policy implementation pattern for emergency relief. More importantly, it is the size of the gap that accounts for the success or failure of the entire governmental relief effort.

In Part Two of the book, I provide detailed examples of eight natural disasters that have occurred over the past twenty years. These case studies illustrate the extreme variability of governmental activity in this policy area, including differences that arise when the same type of natural disaster successively strikes in different locations. In addition, they also show quite clearly the importance of the size of the gap in explaining the success or failure of the governmental response to natural disasters.

Part Three of the book summarizes and expands upon key points made earlier. Chapter Fourteen discusses the fundamental paradox of public policymaking in emergency management. When the government responds to disasters smoothly and effectively, its efforts receive little attention. However, when the response breaks down, governmental activity is highly publicized. Finally, Chapter Fifteen examines the most popular recommendations for improving the government's disaster relief operations. In addition, it emphasizes the broader implications of this study. Governmental operations during natural disasters help us to understand the general limitations of public-sector activity during extraordinarily stressful conditions. And they also show the impact that bureaucratic actions, or inactions, during crisis situations can have on broader perceptions of governmental performance.

Notes

1. For additional summary information on the Midwest Floods of 1993, see the Federal Emergency Management Agency (2003); U.S. Department of Commerce (1994); U.S. Senate (1994a); and U.S. Senate (1993a). There are also a number of excellent sources for more detailed, day-by-day accounts of the flooding; see *New York Times*, *Washington Post*, and *St. Louis Post Dispatch* during the months of July and August, 1993.

2. Hurricane Hugo, the Loma Prieta Earthquake, Hurricane Andrew, the Los Angeles Earthquake, and Hurricane Katrina are used as case studies in this book. Additional references for each of these situations are provided in later chapters.

2

Natural Disasters as Public Policy Issues

When a natural disaster occurs, few people stop to ask if the government *should* intervene. Instead, citizens automatically tend to view the situation as a serious *public* problem, requiring immediate *governmental* action. Part of this perception is inevitable. Government has a basic responsibility to restore public safety, utilities, and so on. However, popular expectations go far beyond this to a widespread belief that government should take an active, positive role by helping private individuals and businesses in their recovery efforts. But this raises an interesting question: Why are natural disasters perceived to be *public* problems? After all, many private institutions, such as insurance companies, relief agencies, and charity organizations, could help resolve the kinds of disruptions caused by natural disasters. So, why do these situations produce an almost automatic expectation of a *governmental* response?

The answer to this question is extremely important. Many social problems are never elevated to the status of political issues. Likewise, many political issues are never addressed by meaningful public policies. This is simply not the case with natural disasters, which garner immediate public attention and almost invariably become the target of large-scale governmental activity. Therefore, it is essential that we determine why natural disasters seem to move through this usually slow, difficult policy process in a speedy and almost automatic manner.

Theoretical Perspectives on Agenda Building

The process through which social problems evolve into public and governmental concerns is called agenda building.[1] The notion of an agenda-building process is an abstraction. It does not exist in any concrete or officially designated form; certainly no statutes or regulations guide the evolution of problems into issues. Instead, this concept is useful because it explains why certain problems become the focus of public attention, and why they become matters for governmental action. More broadly, the agenda-building process identifies how collective judgments are made about ideas, events, and activities. Therefore, it reveals a great deal about the values, priorities, and commitments that exist within a political system.

The agenda-building process has received a great deal of attention in the scholarly literature (Eyestone 1978; Cobb and Elder 1983a; Kingdon 1994; Baumgartner and Jones 1993, 2009). Researchers have devised many different explanations of how the process works, and they have identified different types of factors that affect an issue's placement onto the policy agenda. Several of these factors have particular relevance for natural disasters:

- The objective dimensions of the problem
- The political aspects of the situation
- The symbolic elements of the issue
- The lack of private-sector solutions.[2]

Taken together, these factors help explain why natural disasters are considered to be legitimate public problems requiring governmental solutions. Let us take a closer look at each one.

Objective Dimensions

Certain problems are so large and salient that they almost automatically attract public attention. Analysts have referred to such problems as "triggering mechanisms" (Cobb and Elder 1983a) or "focusing events" (Kingdon 1994). Some triggering mechanisms develop gradually over time. A series of technological breakthroughs might eventually create new situations and problems for governmental action. The industrial revolution and the attendant problems of urbanization and economic change illustrate this kind of triggering mechanism. Others can erupt instantaneously and unexpectedly. For example, an act of international aggression will almost certainly become an immediate policy issue.

By definition, all triggering mechanisms convert routine problems into important policy issues. But when does a problem become a triggering mechanism? Two basic factors determine this transformation from the mundane to the extraordinary: (1) the number of people affected by the situation; and (2) public perceptions of the event's importance.

The significance of triggering mechanisms is widely recognized in the agenda-building literature (Eyestone 1978; Cobb and Elder 1983a; Baumgartner and Jones 1993), and their role is perhaps most clearly explained by Anthony Downs (1972). He describes agenda building as a dynamic, highly unstable process which follows an "issue attention cycle." According to Downs, a triggering mechanism initiates the cycle: A dramatic event is responsible for catapulting an issue onto the agenda almost instantaneously. Once it is on the agenda, the issue receives intense public and governmental attention, but only for a brief period of time. As the public begins to realize the costs of addressing the problem, it loses interest in the issue and shifts its focus to other situations and problem areas. Governmental decision makers usually follow suit. So, issues tend to "fall off" the agenda almost as quickly as they ascend to prominence.

Not all social problems will go through this issue-attention cycle. But the cycle is more likely to occur if: (1) the problem affects a sizable, noticeable minority of the public; (2) the underlying causes of the problem actually benefit certain powerful groups within society; and (3) the problem initially appears to be "new" and/or "different," but it does not have long-lasting appeal. Thus, the nature of the social problem itself—its objective dimensions as well as the manner in which these characteristics are transmitted across a society—determines public and governmental involvement in any particular policy area.[3]

Baumgartner and Jones (1993, 2009) also emphasize the role of triggering events in the agenda-building process. Dramatic events shake up the policymaking system. They disrupt the political status or policy equilibrium that normally exists, forcing the members of policy subsystems and coalitions to re-evaluate their ideas about acceptable/unacceptable governmental activity. To Baumgartner and Jones, triggering mechanisms are one of the major precipitants of change in the American policymaking process.

Political Factors

Political forces also play a key role in pushing issues onto, or off, the policy agenda. Here, there are many different kinds of factors to consider. Some scholars focus on the general impact of public opinion (Key 1961; Page and Shapiro 1983; Wright, Erikson, and McIver 1987; Erikson, MacKuen, and Stimson 2002; Stimson 2004). Others emphasize the role of political parties, interest groups, the media, issue networks, or subsystems in shaping policy preferences (Ginsberg 1976; Sinclair 1977; Walker 1977; Heclo 1978; Sabatier 1986; and Iyengar 1991; Sabatier and Jenkins-Smith 1993). Still others look more directly at the individual motivations of political leaders or policy entrepreneurs (Light 1982; Riker 1986; Schneider, Teske, and Mintrom 1995; Mintrom 2000; Jones and Baumgartner 2005). Taken together, it is extremely difficult to deny the impact of political variables during the agenda-building process.

John Kingdon (1984) groups all of these forces into one general category and calls it the "political stream." According to Kingdon, an issue becomes a prominent item on the policy agenda when a "policy window" opens in the political environment. Policy windows open when: (1) a shift in public opinion occurs; (2) pressures within the political system organize; or (3) administrative changes bring about personnel and procedural changes within government. These conditions allow policy advocates to push their preferred ideas and issues onto the policy agenda. However, if policy entrepreneurs do not take advantage of these opportune situations, the policy window closes and the issue will not gain prominence on the policy agenda. Kingdon and others certainly view agenda building as an intensely *political* activity in which partisan and/or ideological forces play a decisive role in the agenda-building phase of public policy development.

Deborah Stone (2002) takes this argument one step further. She states that it is simply impossible to think about policymaking without considering the role of politics. Public policies are generated in political communities, and they represent the struggle over political values and ideas. Issues are crafted images of political problems. They get placed on the policy agenda because individuals or groups of individuals are actively trying to define the boundaries of acceptable governmental activity. In this view, agenda building is not a rational, straightforward process of orderly governmental efforts to meet pressing social needs. Instead, it is an inherently irrational and unpredictable process—one that is always shaped by political preferences and values.

Symbolic Aspects

Some scholars (for example, Edelman 1964, 1977, 1989 and Cobb and Elder 1983b) have argued that the symbolic aspects of an issue are the most important elements of agenda building. A symbol can be anything—a word, a phrase, a gesture, an object, a person, an event—that gives meaning or value to an issue beyond the objective content that is inherent in the issue itself (Cobb and Elder 1983b). Some symbols seem to emerge almost spontaneously. For example, the term "Watergate" was coined to indicate a specific political event (the illegal wiretapping of the Democratic National Party headquarters during the 1972 elections), but it quickly became a shorthand way of communicating more general concerns about governmental corruption and dishonesty. Other symbols seem to be more deliberately and carefully crafted. Presidential programs are given labels, such as Woodrow Wilson's "New Freedom," Lyndon Johnson's "Great Society," Ronald Reagan's "New Beginning," George H. W. Bush's "Thousand Points of Light," and George W. Bush's "War on Terror" in order to describe their focus and to garner public and governmental support. Given the subjectivity of these phenomena, it is virtually impossible to predict precisely when a particular type of symbol will emerge. However, it is possible to identify the circumstances that contribute to the use of symbolism in the policy process.

Symbols are human inventions. They are created and used to impart varying degrees of significance to social problems. On the one hand, if a new issue can be tied to an enduring, acceptable societal value (e.g., freedom, liberty, or self-sufficiency in the American context), it is much more likely to receive serious attention by the general public and by governmental officials (Edelman 1977; De Neufville and Barton 1987; Weiss 1989). For example, President Kennedy succeeded in making poverty a major issue in the 1960s by appealing to a traditional notion about "America, the land of opportunity": The poor were pictured as unable to pursue the American dream, and it was society's responsibility to help them. On the other hand, proponents of the status quo can also employ symbols to block the emergence of new issues (Schattschneider 1960; Baratz and Bachrach 1963; L. Bennett 1988). The health care reform debate in the United States illustrates this point quite clearly. Opponents of more comprehensive, universal plans with greater governmental involvement contend that such a system would violate the freedom of choice enjoyed by American citizens—their right to select their own health care providers and their own form of medical treatment (Johnson and Broder 1997; Cohn 2007). In both of these cases, symbols are used to link social problems to enduring values and beliefs. This can, in turn, either propel or deter the placement of issues on the policy agenda. And it can affect what, if any, type of governmental response will occur. This makes symbolism a vitally important component of the agenda-building phase in public policy development. [4]

Prevailing Beliefs About Legitimate Governmental Action

Closely related to the symbolic interpretation is the belief that certain types of issues systematically get mobilized into the policy process while others do not. Here, there are really two separate, but related, arguments to consider. First, some scholars contend that a set of prevailing values and beliefs within every political community shapes the scope and content of the policy agenda. If a new issue coincides with the prevailing values of the community it has an excellent chance of getting onto the agenda. However, if the issue conflicts with prevailing values, it is likely to become a "nondecision" or a non-agenda item—it will never be taken up for serious public consideration (Baratz and Bachrach 1963). This screen of bias works to the advantage of old agenda items. In many cases, governmental officials and the general public already know something about these issues, and they can rely upon past governmental activities to guide their responses. This makes old issues both easier and safer to address; hence, they tend to dominate policy agendas. At the same time, the screen of bias works against the emergence of new issues that have not been addressed previously. These new issues may affect groups in society whose members lack status or access in the community, such as the poor, the mentally ill, or convicted criminals. Alternatively, these new issues may be dismissed because they simply are not viewed as legitimate topics for governmental discussion or action. For example, outright governmental ownership of corporations and businesses is often not considered as a viable policy option in American politics, even though it is widely used in other political systems. And when the U.S. government does assume greater control over private companies—as it did in 2008 with the economic "bailout" of the auto industry—it is done with a great deal of trepidation and under intense criticism.[5]

Second, certain types of issues—for example, maintaining a sound economy and promoting national defense—are widely accepted as being particularly appropriate, legitimate foci for governmental action. These kinds of items are often called "public goods" or "collective goods." Such goods are indivisible—that is the consumption by one individual does not interfere with the consumption by another individual (Donahue 1989). Public goods are also nonexclusive, meaning that nobody can be excluded from the use and benefits of a public good (Savas 1982, 1987, 2000; Wolf 1988). Consequently, every individual has an economic incentive to become a "free rider"—to take advantage of public goods without paying for them (Savas 1987). In order to counter the free-rider problem, collective action is necessary (M. Olson 1965). More specifically, governmental involvement is usually considered justifiable when it is addressing issues that involve public goods. So, citizens accept governmental regulations on highways and roadways (for example, traffic signals and speed limits) because all motorists benefit from them, but no one would volunteer to provide them in every location or across all jurisdictions.

Specific Characteristics of Natural Disasters

As we have just seen, there are many different ideas about how the agenda-building process works. Analysts have identified several important factors that make it more likely that a particular problem will develop into a prominent policy issue. The agenda-building literature says that any *one* of these factors should be sufficient to propel an issue onto the policy agenda. Natural disasters present a relatively unusual situation because they possess all four of the characteristics necessary to attain immediate agenda status. Let us consider each one in turn.

Objective Dimensions

Natural disasters easily qualify as triggering mechanisms. They are, by definition, severe events (Silverstein 1992). When a tornado tears through a community, it can completely uplift homes, farms, and businesses. When excessive rains cause normally quiet, serene rivers to overflow their banks, buildings, roads, highways, and bridges can be completely washed away. The severity of these events is easy to calculate both in terms of the amount of physical destruction incurred and the economic costs involved. Since 1980, the United States has experienced ninety-nine "weather-related disasters . . . in which overall damages/costs reached or exceeded $1 billion." Collectively, these ninety-nine events have been responsible for over $725 billion in losses (U.S. Department of Commerce 2011). Natural disasters can also cause serious physical injuries, psychological trauma, and even death. The World Health Organization estimates that between 1964 and 1978, natural disasters killed nearly 2.5 million people and left an additional 750 million injured or harmed throughout the world. The number of deaths caused by extreme weather events increased about 50 percent during every decade from 1890 to 1950. There have been even more dramatic increases in fatality rates since the 1950s (Kreimer and Munasinghe 1990).

Second, natural disasters encompass an incredible range of sizes, circumstances, and effects (Fritz 1957; Drabek 1970; Dynes 1970; Kreps 1989). On the one hand, they can cause widespread destruction, affecting large numbers of people across an extensive geographic area. For example, droughts in the United States have destroyed thousands of acres of crops in states spanning the entire width of the country. On the other hand, they can strike in one small, isolated area. A tornado may touch down in a neighborhood and destroy a single house, leaving all others completely undamaged. Thus, natural disasters can inflict far-reaching damages on extensive sections of the population and the nation, or they can have a limited, concentrated impact on small numbers of people.

Third, natural disasters are highly visible problems. They can generate conditions that are difficult, and often impossible, for citizens to ignore (Hodgkinson and Stewart 1990). When an ice storm knocks out the electricity in a community, the people living in the affected area are definitely aware of the situation. When high winds tear the roofs off buildings and scatter personal belongings, the inhabitants of those buildings clearly recognize the existence of a problem. Furthermore, information about these kinds of situations is easily and readily transmitted by the news media (Norris, Just, and Kern 2003; Haider-Markel, Delehanty, and Beverlin 2007). Natural disasters are exactly the type of events that the media like to spotlight (Barsky, Trainor, and Torres 2006; Iyengar and McGrady 2007). They are unusual, different, spectacular, and at times even horrific. They also provide compelling visual images for mass circulation (Nimmo and Combs 1985; Adams 1986; Benthall 1993; Deppa 1993; Singer 1993; Ploughman 1995; Barsky, Trainor, and Torres 2006; Rodriquez and Dynes 2006; Maestas, Atkeson, Croom, and Bryant 2008; Scanlon 2008). So, the problem is visible not only to those who are immediately affected by it, but to the vast majority of the American population as well (Quarantelli 1991c).

Each of these objective characteristics—severity, range, and visibility—affects how natural disasters are identified and described. Taken together, these attributes facilitate our general awareness of such situations. However, several other important aspects must also be considered in order to understand completely why natural catastrophes are viewed as public issues and legitimate "targets" of governmental action.

Political Factors

Disaster situations possess several significant political components. When a natural catastrophe occurs, the public's attention is riveted on that event. In Kingdon's (1984) terms, a natural disaster provides a window of opportunity for political action. Public officials can use a natural disaster to demonstrate their leadership abilities and willingness to tackle tough, difficult problems (Boin, Hart, Stern, and Sundelius 2005; Smith 2007). Their actions will almost always receive instant public consideration and media publicity. Moreover, it is virtually impossible to oppose or criticize an official who steps in and takes charge of the situation in order to help disaster-stricken citizens.

Natural disasters also produce conditions that allow political leaders to show their concern for citizens' needs and demands. Disaster victims often encounter problems that they have never before experienced. They may be unprepared or unequipped to handle these difficulties on their own. Public officials are simply in a much better position to channel necessary resources to help those who are truly in distress. Thus, they have a perfect opportunity to demonstrate their responsiveness to the needs of the people. Political leaders who successfully address disaster-related problems are rewarded. They can dispense particularized benefits to constituents and use these as a resource to facilitate their re-election efforts (Mayhew 1974; Fenno 1978; Sylves 2006).

In contrast, leaders who are unwilling or unable to act during a disaster situation can suffer negative political repercussions. If they hesitate or delay to act when an emergency erupts, they may be depicted as being unresponsive to the needs of their constituents (Abney and Hill 1966; R. Wolensky and Miller 1981; S. Schneider 2005; Waugh 2006a; Sylves 2007).[6] If they are bewildered or confused by the situation that develops, they may appear to be unprepared and out-of-touch, or even incompetent and uncaring ("Anatomy of a Disaster" 2005; Connolly 2005; Lipton, Drew, Shane, and Rohde 2005; W. Schneider 2005; Steinhauer and Lipton 2005;

Waugh 2006a). These negative images of political leadership—actually, the lack of political leadership—are extremely difficult to change and overcome.

Symbolic Aspects

The issues surrounding natural disasters are imbued with highly symbolic content (Brown 1990). When an occurrence is identified as a "disaster," the term itself immediately signals that something terrible and calamitous has occurred. The urgency and severity of the situation is automatically understood. In addition, "disaster" implies an unusual, extraordinary event that private individuals cannot handle on their own. It represents a situation that will almost inevitably require broader public attention and action. Thus, the term "disaster" is a strong metaphor.[7] Not only does it describe a complex, unusual event, but the word also carries the symbolic connotation that collective action is warranted (Ibarra and Kitsuse 1993; Rochefort and Cobb 1994).

In addition, natural disasters can occur without warning (Drabek 1986). They can strike at virtually any time (that is., in any season, any month, or any time of day) and in a variety of different forms (for example, as the consequence of too little rain—droughts—or too much rain—floods). The unpredictable and highly variable nature of such weather-related events contributes further to their symbolic appeal. More specifically, it provides additional justification for governmental intervention. Individuals simply may not know how to handle such unusual circumstances because they have never experienced them before. Hence, governmental intervention is warranted when unexpected, unpredictable situations develop.

Finally, it is important to note that natural disasters can, and often do, hit innocent citizens. Some public problems develop because of the actions or inactions of the victims themselves. For example, teenage pregnancy, delinquency, and drug addiction are primarily the result of teen behavior and decisions. In most instances, teenagers are not forced to engage in sex, experiment with drugs, or get involved in criminal or illegal activity. Thus, they are at least partially to blame for the consequences of their actions. But the victims of disasters do not cause the natural occurrence. In many situations, they have virtually no control over the scope or severity of the event. Disaster victims are the innocent, helpless, and blameless targets of a natural catastrophe, and for that reason alone, they deserve to be helped.

Thus, natural disasters easily invoke all of the symbolic elements that readily propel events onto the governmental agenda for action. Natural disasters are, by definition, unsettling, problematic situations; they are often almost impossible to predict with any accuracy (such as the timing of an earthquake or the path of a hurricane); they can affect innocent, blameless citizens; and they all seem to be extremely difficult to manage.

Absence of Private-Sector Solutions

Finally, natural disasters create problems that can only realistically be addressed and managed by government (Perry and Mushkatel 1984). When a severe thunderstorm causes massive damage in an area, private utility companies can repair broken electrical lines and (eventually) restore power. But they cannot deal with contaminated water supplies, massive communication system outages, or severe disruptions in sewer services. Similarly, when a fire destroys homes and property, private volunteer groups can effectively distribute clothing and food to fire victims. But they do not have the authority to tell local citizens to evacuate before the fire spreads or the resources to help people rebuild after the disaster occurs. Only the government has the technical capability, the appropriate resources, and the authority to coordinate a range of disaster-related responses. Thus a natural disaster situation tends to be viewed as a "public" responsibility because the private sector offers no feasible alternatives (Kingdon 1984; Majone 1989). Natural disasters inevitably involve problems that cannot be adequately addressed by private market activities.

Another argument holds that the policies and procedures needed to address natural disaster situations can only be produced by the public sector. Everyone in society—regardless of age, sex, income, or occupation—could be affected by a natural catastrophe. And theoretically all citizens will benefit from the goods and services that decrease the impact of these occurrences. But individual citizens have no incentive to pay voluntarily for these services through the private sector because they will still reap the benefits in any case. Stated simply, the policies and procedures required to address disaster situations qualify as nearly perfect examples of public goods (Downs 1957; Arrow 1963). And like other public goods, they certainly fall within the purview of governmental responsibility.

In sum, the government becomes involved in disaster situations for a variety of reasons. First, they can cause extraordinarily severe and patently obvious societal problems. The economic, physical, and emotional costs of these events can reach such high levels that they cannot be ignored or overlooked. Second, disaster situations can become highly politicized issues: they reveal the extent to which public figures are willing and able to respond to citizens' needs. Natural disasters also contain extremely important symbolic elements: individual people tend to view these events as cataclysmic, life-threatening, and beyond their own control. Finally, many natural disasters, particularly larger, cataclysmic events, generate problems that the private sector simply cannot or will not handle: Efforts to deal with these events fit the characteristics of a public or collective good.

As in any policy area, the definition of natural disasters is extremely important. It affects the level of attention that these events receive. The definition also determines the range and type of responses that are presented to address the problem. In theory, natural disasters could be described as individual-level problems requiring private-sector solutions. In fact, this was precisely the definition of natural disasters that was used in the early days of the American republic. Today, however, disasters are perceived quite differently. For all the reasons discussed above, natural disasters are now viewed as critical *policy* issues that require *governmental* attention.

Governmental Involvement in Disasters

If natural disasters are, in fact, policy issues, then this raises several further questions: How have public institutions in the United States dealt with disaster situations? When did the government first become involved in this policy area? Has the government's involvement changed over the years? What factors affect the nature and direction of governmental policy? How does governmental activity in disaster situations compare to governmental involvement in other policy areas?

Brief History of Governmental Disaster Assistance Policy

It is impossible to say exactly when the American government first became involved in disaster issues. Even before the United States existed, public institutions in this country were providing assistance to the victims of natural catastrophes. For example, local officials helped Boston residents who were affected by a major earthquake that struck the area in 1755. Disaster relief, however, was historically considered to be primarily a local responsibility (Bourgin 1983; Popkin 1990). When a natural catastrophe occurred, city and county officials were expected to help those in need. The actions of local governments were often supplemented by the efforts of private relief agencies, such as religious organizations and the American Red Cross. By and large, however, there was no expectation that higher levels of government would become directly involved in disaster situations.

State governments could be called in to help if local resources were exhausted. But most state-level organizations were ill-equipped, unprepared, and even unwilling to intervene. They did not have the resources, capabilities, or inclination to supplement local efforts (Stratton 1989). Disaster assistance simply was not considered a top priority among state governments.

Similarly, the federal government played a very limited role in early recovery efforts. Whenever events exceeded the capacities of subnational authorities, the federal government *could* be asked to step in and help. The U.S. Congress established the legal basis for federal intervention in 1803 when it granted special allowances to the victims of a devastating fire in Portsmouth, New Hampshire (Bourgin 1983; National Emergency Management Association 2008a). From 1803 to 1947, the federal government provided aid to the victims of some 128 disasters (Popkin 1990). In each instance, specific legislation was passed to deal with a particular situation (May 1985b). But it is important to note, that the government did *not* establish general procedures to deal with different types of disasters in different areas and locations.

Early federal disaster assistance was often uncertain and uncoordinated. There were no general policies or guidelines to shape governmental intervention, and it was never clear whether the federal government would intervene at all. Basically, it responded to each disaster on a piecemeal, case-by-case basis. Furthermore, federal intervention was often politically motivated as elected officials pushed through relief proposals in order to alleviate specific disaster-related conditions in their own states and congressional districts.

During this early period (pre-1950), governmental activities were primarily reactive in nature (May 1985b). Public institutions only provided relief in the aftermath of truly major disasters. The situation did change somewhat in the 1920s and 1930s when the government initiated some preventive measures. For example, Congress passed a series of flood control acts which authorized the financing, construction, and maintenance of thousands of miles of levees, flood walls, and channels throughout the nation. These initial proactive efforts were often passed for political reasons, as the result of logrolling and pork-barrel tactics carried out by members of Congress. In addition, these early measures stressed structural solutions to disaster-related issues. The emphasis was on building physical barriers (such as dams and other flood control measures) to contain disastrous situations and limit the scope of disaster-related problems. Little, if any, attention was given to other, non-structural types of programs that would actually encourage citizens and communities to prepare for emergencies before they occurred.

The nature of government involvement in natural disasters changed dramatically during the middle decades of the twentieth century. This was partially due to a much broader trend: After the 1930s, the national government assumed more responsibility for a wide variety of domestic policy concerns. Federal agencies were given greater authority to help individuals, families, and businesses recover from economic losses. As part of this general trend, specific legislation was passed making grants and loans available to industries and public facilities that incurred disaster-related damages (May 1985b). In 1950, Congress enacted legislation that made federal assistance even more readily available to disaster-stricken communities. The Disaster Relief Act of 1950 stated that federal resources could and should be used to supplement state and local efforts when necessary. In addition, the Act specified a standard process by which local and state authorities could request federal assistance. In sum, it changed the entire tone and structure of disaster relief in the United States by bringing the national government into the process on a regular basis.

It is important to emphasize that the precedent-setting nature of the Disaster Relief Act of 1950 was not immediately recognized. The legislation was passed as another limited response by the national government to a particular disaster situation—severe flooding in the upper portions of the Midwest. The Act was not originally intended to surpass the scope or intent of earlier efforts, and it received little attention or fanfare at the time (Bourgin 1983). But the 1950 Disaster Relief Act followed a series of other congressional provisions that identified the responsibilities of various federal agencies and established the intergovernmental context of disaster relief. Perhaps more important, congressional leaders themselves soon began to regard the Act as a precedent-setting piece of legislation.

The 1950 Disaster Relief Act delineated the first general, national-level policy for providing emergency relief (Bourgin 1983). As a result, it established a framework for governmental disaster assistance that has essentially remained in place since that time.

This Act's provisions have had a tremendous impact on all subsequent governmental activity in this policy area—for better or worse.

Throughout the 1950s, 1960s, and 1970s, Congress passed a series of laws that expanded the scope of national governmental responsibility in disasters. Federal assistance was extended to additional population groups (such as farmers living in rural areas and disaster victims living in the U.S. territories). Legislation also made new types of relief available, including temporary housing, emergency shelters, legal services, unemployment insurance, food coupons, small business loans, and so on.[8] In addition, the basic governmental approach to natural disasters shifted away from its earlier emphasis on "structural" controls to "nonstructural" measures. So, instead of funding construction projects, such as strengthening or rebuilding physical barriers and frameworks through dams, levees, and sea walls (that is, structural improvements), a greater emphasis was placed on keeping people out of hazard-prone, high-risk areas through zoning laws, building codes, and land use regulations (that is, nonstructural limitations on behavior). By the late 1960s, public policies forced individuals to assume more responsibility for where and how they lived, thereby making nonstructural policy elements more salient than structural improvements.

The shift in governmental policy was consolidated in the 1970s. Congress passed several major pieces of legislation that integrated earlier efforts and expanded the scope of the government's responsibilities. In particular, the Disaster Relief Act of 1974, along with subsequent amendments, established the precedent for a new wave of federal policy. The 1974 Act institutionalized efforts to mitigate against, instead of simply to respond to, major disaster events. It also contained provisions requiring local, state, and federal agencies to develop strategies aimed at preventing future catastrophes. Furthermore, it stressed a "multihazard" approach to disasters. The latter perspective holds that instead of designing different policies for each particular kind of disaster, governmental efforts should be capable of handling *all* kinds of hazards— both natural and manmade.

By the late 1970s, there existed a fairly comprehensive set of public disaster assistance programs. However, the very number of programs was problematic, because administrative responsibilities were divided among a variety of different departments and governmental entities. This was particularly true at the national level, where many federal agencies were involved, at least in part, in some type of disaster-relief activity (Popkin 1990). Criticisms of the existing system were common: there seemed to be little, if any, coordination of governmental efforts. In addition, it was also extremely difficult to determine exactly who was in charge of disaster relief. This was compounded by the fact that the responsibility for disaster relief at the national level had repeatedly shifted from one agency to the next. For example, in 1950 the Housing and Home Finance Administration was placed in charge of disaster assistance; in 1953 disaster-relief activities were reassigned to the Federal Civil Defense Administration; in 1958 the Office of Civil and Defense Mobilization was created to handle the nation's emergency relief and response functions; in 1961 the Office of Emergency Planning (later renamed the Office of Emergency Preparedness) was established in the

Executive Office of the President to coordinate the nation's civil defense and natural disaster efforts. Then, in 1973, major disaster-related responsibilities were divided up and distributed among three agencies—the Federal Disaster Assistance Administration, the Defense Civil Preparedness Agency, and the Federal Preparedness Agency (May 1985b). At this time, there was widespread support for developing a more organized, cohesive emergency management process (Stratton 1989).

Consequently, the Carter administration issued Reorganization Plan #3 in 1978. This directive focused explicitly on the structure, management, and operations of the government's disaster-relief programs. It created an entirely new administrative body, the Federal Emergency Management Agency (FEMA), to lead the governmental effort. FEMA was given the primary responsibility for: (1) mobilizing federal resources; (2) coordinating federal efforts with those of state and local governments; and (3) managing the efforts of the public and private sectors in disaster responses. For the first time, emergency management functions at the national level were centralized in one governmental agency.

Ten years later, in 1988, Congress passed the Robert T. Stafford Disaster Relief and Emergency Assistance Act. The Stafford Act clarified inconsistencies in past policies; for example, it refined the definition of an "emergency" situation, and it further expanded the responsibilities and obligations of public institutions during natural emergencies. It emphasized the importance of mitigation and preparedness activities that would occur before a disaster struck, as well as the more traditional response and relief functions of governmental agencies that unfold after a disaster has occurred. In addition, the Stafford Act established a process to guide when and how the government would become involved in disaster situations. It also delineated how the response would move from the local level, through the state, up to the national government.

For the next ten years, there were no major legislative or statutory revisions in governmental policy.[9] However, several important administrative elaborations and additions were made to the Stafford Act. Reacting to intense criticism of the governmental response to Hurricane Hugo in the late 1980s, the Federal Emergency Management Agency began working on a new set of guidelines and directives for the federal government. The guidelines, called the Federal Response Plan, were completed in April 1992 and presented as a cooperative agreement between twenty-six federal agencies and the American Red Cross.

The Federal Response Plan was a blueprint for coordinating and mobilizing federal resources in disaster situations. It provided more detail on the functions and activities of various federal agencies during large-scale natural disasters (Federal Emergency Management Agency 1992b). It also grouped together the various types of emergency assistance available to public organizations and private citizens, and it identified a lead federal agency for each of these areas. Moreover, it specified a process whereby the resources of the federal government could be deployed more quickly and efficiently, particularly during large-scale natural disasters. Overall, the Federal Response Plan delineated the national government's roles and responsibilities when responding to any type of disaster or emergency.

The terrorist attacks of September 11, 2001, reopened the discussion about the focus, structure, and impact of the nation's disaster-response system (Kettl 2004). Although emergency management agencies performed fairly well in this situation, there were noticeable problems of intergovernmental coordination and communication. And there was an overarching concern that the nation was not adequately prepared to handle the next catastrophic event. Consequently, a number of steps were taken to strengthen the government's disaster-response capabilities (Birkland 1997, 2007; Harrald 2007; Sylves 2008).

In October 2001, President Bush created the White House Office of Homeland Security and the Homeland Security Council. Then, in July 2002, the Office of Homeland Security released a national strategy to guide the future development of the nation's emergency management operations. A central component of the plan was the integration of all the various federal response plans into a single, nationwide incident management system. This system would cover all types of disasters, no matter where, when, or how they occurred. But it was argued that a new federal entity was needed to lead such a comprehensive initiative and to coordinate the national government's efforts.

Congress followed through on this recommendation and passed the Homeland Security Act of 2002. This Act authorized the creation of a new cabinet-level Department of Homeland Security (DHS). By January 2003, DHS was operating as the lead agency for the nation's emergency management system. In order to coordinate governmental operations, the Department of Homeland Security assumed control of almost 180,000 employees from twenty-two previously existing departments, agencies, and offices. For the most part, the reorganization of the nation's disaster-response system proceeded fairly quietly and smoothly.

But the formation of the Department of Homeland Security ushered in major changes for the Federal Emergency Management Agency. FEMA lost its status as a free-standing, independent agency: It was moved into the Department of Homeland Security where it, along with several other agencies, became DHS's Emergency Preparedness and Response Directorate. Although FEMA could now draw upon the resources of a much larger federal department, it was also forced to compete with other governmental units for funding, influence, access, and clout.

President Bush solidified the reorganization and redirection of the nation's response system in Homeland Security Presidential Directive 5 (HSPD-5), issued in February 2003. This Directive designated the Secretary of the Department of Homeland of Security as the principal federal coordinating official for domestic incident management involving terrorist attacks, natural disasters, and other major emergencies. This is a responsibility that had previously been given to the Director of the Federal Emergency Management Agency. HSPD-5 also instructed the Secretary of the Department of Homeland Security to develop a system that would enable the nation "to prepare for, respond to, and recover from terrorist attacks, major disasters, and other emergencies" (White House 2003).

As a consequence, the Secretary of the DHS issued guidelines that officially established the Nationwide Incident Management System (NIMS). The NIMS embodies a set of principles, policies, and organizational processes that are designed to enhance the activities of emergency management organizations at all jurisdictional levels (Sylves 2008). One of the core features of NIMS is the establishment of a unified command team immediately at the onset of a major disaster in order to manage and coordinate the actions of multiple agencies. Unified command teams had long been used by firefighters as a way of mobilizing and coordinating the activities of various organizations. Now, they were a required element of every governmental response. All emergency management organizations throughout the governmental system were required to comply with the provisions of NIMS in order to obtain federal funds (Federal Emergency Management Agency 2004).

In December 2004, a new federal response plan was approved. The protocols and procedures of the new plan were signed by twenty-eight federal agencies, the American Red Cross, the Postmaster General, the Corporation for National and Community Services, and the National Voluntary Organizations Active in Disaster. This framework—called the National Response Plan—replaced the Federal Response Plan that had been in existence since 1992. The National Response Plan reinforced the goals of unification and command-and-control networks by requiring all federal agencies to become compliant with the provisions of NIMS (U.S. Department of Homeland Security 2004a).

In addition, the 2004 National Response Plan also established a new set of protocols to guide the government's response to extraordinarily severe events. More specifically, it described how federal resources would be deployed before, during, and after an "incident of national significance." Incidents of national significance were identified as catastrophic events that overwhelm or exceed the capacities of local and state jurisdictions (U.S. Department of Homeland Security 2004a). During such extreme situations, the national response plan would be activated and the federal government would have the ability to initiate a response prior to an official declaration of a "major disaster." This would enable federal resources to be deployed before, during, and after the incident. It would also put the federal government at the helm of the relief effort for catastrophic emergency situations.

Because of the problems that developed following Hurricane Katrina, changes were once again made in the governmental response process. Congress passed several statutes that altered the overall administration and implementation of the nation's emergency management system. The most significant provisions were included in the "Post-Katrina Emergency Management Reform Act of 2006," Title VI of the Department of Homeland Security Appropriations Act (Pub. Law No. 109-295, 120 Stat. 1355, 2006). The Post-Katrina Reform Act changed the organizational structure and operations of the Department of Homeland Security, with a special focus on the role and functions of the Federal Emergency Management Agency. Perhaps, most importantly, it reinstated FEMA as the lead federal agency in charge of the nation's preparations for, and response to, all disaster situations. Specifically, the Act consolidated emergency management activities under FEMA (for instance, moving the Preparedness Directorate back under FEMA's jurisdiction and expanding FEMA's activities to include catastrophic incidents in addition to other types of disasters). It elevated FEMA's status and autonomy within DHS: FEMA would now be classified as a distinct entity within DHS; its resources and functions could not be transferred to other units within the Department. And the Act would allow the president to have the FEMA Administrator serve in the Cabinet when a major disaster occurs (National Academy of Public Administration 2009).

The 2006 Post-Katrina Emergency Management Reform Act also established new requirements for FEMA personnel: The FEMA Administrator must have a background in emergency management and experience with executive leadership and management (Bea 2006). Other top FEMA officials must have knowledge of, and familiarity with, emergency management practices. And the rest of the agency's workforce must be given the necessary training and preparation to enhance their emergency management competencies (Bea 2006). Although there had been other efforts to improve the capabilities of emergency management officials, this was the first time that specific requirements had been established to guide the recruitment, promotion, and retention of federal-level personnel.

The Post-Katrina Reform Act restored many of FEMA's original functions, and it added additional responsibilities to the agency. FEMA is now authorized to implement "new types of assistance for those adversely affected by a major disaster" (for example, providing housing and transportation for individuals with disabilities, low-income populations, and those with limited English proficiency); to develop information and logistics systems that facilitate the distribution of disaster relief through the intergovernmental system (Suburban Emergency Management Project 2008); to strengthen the development of mutual-aid agreements between states; and to increase financial support so that states that have experienced major disasters can enhance their own emergency management capabilities.

Overall, the Post-Katrina Emergency Reform Act enhanced FEMA's position in the nation's disaster-response process. But FEMA was not returned to its earlier status as a freestanding federal agency. FEMA remains a relatively small unit within a much larger Department of Homeland Security, and the FEMA Administrator reports to the Secretary of the Department of Homeland Security. Moreover, several important components of emergency preparedness were *not* transferred into the "new" FEMA; these include the Office of Infrastructure Development, the National Communications System, the National Cybersecurity Division, and the Office of the Chief Medical Officer (Suburban Emergency Management Project 2008). Hence, the newly configured FEMA has more responsibility and clout than it did, but it is still not in charge of many elements of the federal response.

In order to codify these legislative changes, the Department of Homeland Security developed a new response plan, called the National Response Framework, which was put into place in January 2008. This plan, like those that preceded it, emphasizes a single, comprehensive, coordinated approach for handling all emergency situations. It also continues to rely heavily upon the traditional bottom-up approach for disaster management: "The responsibility for responding to incidents, both natural and manmade, begins at the local level . . . ." (U.S. Department of Homeland Security 2008b, 15).

The fundamental assumption of the current system is that most emergencies should be handled at the lowest governmental level possible, with higher levels of government only serving in more supportive and supplementary roles (Sylves 2008). The National Response Framework states that governmental emergency management activities are "rooted in America's federal system and the Constitution's division of responsibilities between federal and state governments" (U.S. Department of Homeland Security 2008b, 8).

But the National Response Framework does indicate the need for more immediate and direct federal involvement during extremely rare, catastrophic situations: The national government can take proactive steps to "mobilize and deploy assets in anticipation of a formal request from the state for federal assistance" (U.S. Department of Homeland Security 2008b, 42), and "in extraordinary circumstances, the President may unilaterally declare a major disaster or emergency" before the governor of the affected state requests such a declaration (U.S. Department of Homeland Security 2008b, 41). Hence, the National Response Framework makes provisions for accelerated federal involvement—or a "top-down" type of governmental response process—when a major incident occurs (or is likely to occur). But a federally-initiated response is still assumed to be needed only in extremely rare, unusual circumstances.

The National Response Framework also helps to clarify some of the ambiguities found in earlier federal policies. For example, it eliminates the term "incident of national significance" (replacing it with more general terminology that would cover all types of disasters) and it indicates that the Federal Coordinating Officer (FCO) is the primary coordinator for major disaster assistance and that this individual's authority cannot be replaced or superseded by the Principal Federal Official (PFO) who may be designated as the Secretary of the Department of Homeland Security's chief representative to the disaster-stricken area (U.S. Department of Homeland Security 2008b).

All in all, the current governmental strategy for handling disasters is the outgrowth of past governmental plans and previous response efforts. It demonstrates the critical role that public institutions at the local, state, and national levels play in helping Americans prepare for and respond to emergency situations. The government provides a host of services and benefits so that public institutions, private companies, and individuals can cope with natural disasters along with other, man-made threats. A standard set of policies and procedures has been developed to enable the government to deal with any type of disaster, no matter where or when it occurs. Efforts have been made to establish a single, comprehensive approach to emergency management in order to facilitate better coordination, cooperation, and communication across the multitude of public and private organizations involved in emergency relief. And steps have been taken to determine how the intergovernmental response process will operate depending upon the severity and magnitude of the threat. Clearly, both the level and scope of governmental activity in this policy area have increased dramatically over the years.

Parallels Between Disaster Policy and Other Policy Areas

The government's involvement in disaster relief parallels several broader trends in American politics and policymaking. Although we tend to think of natural disasters as unusual and unique events, they do have a lot in common with other public policy issues. This is true both in terms of the nature of the events and the development of governmental actions intended to deal with them. The United States has unquestionably undergone a tremendous growth in the size and scope of government. In 1960, government expenditures totaled $62 billion; in 1990, public outlays exceeded $1,800 billion; by 2007, this figure had jumped to more than $4,320 billion (U.S. Office of Management and Budget 2009). Not only does the government spend significantly more today than it did at the midpoint of the twentieth century, it also allocates money toward a much wider variety of issues and problems. For example, it is now heavily involved in developing and maintaining environmental protection programs (Vig and Kraft 2009), and it is the major financier of health care for elderly, disabled, and low-income American families (D. Barr 2007). Consequently, one could argue that the government's growing involvement in disasters is simply a manifestation of the larger trend toward greater public sector responsibilities and obligations.

Another common feature of both disaster-assistance policy and other public activities is the trend toward greater involvement by the national government, relative to the state and local levels. As explained earlier, the federal government began to play a more active role in disaster-relief and recovery efforts during the 1930s. In 1950, a basic framework for public activity was established; as part of this, the federal government was allowed to direct and coordinate assistance efforts in extraordinarily severe disaster situations. By the late 1970s, it was necessary to consolidate and coordinate the national government's actions; in response, the Federal Emergency Management Agency was established in 1979. When the federal government creates a new administrative unit designed to deal with a particular kind of problem, it is a sign that the issue has become a permanent addition of the federal government's policy agenda (Seidman and Gilmour 1986). Therefore, the creation of FEMA revealed the extent to which national-level organizations were becoming more involved in disaster situations. And the establishment of the cabinet-level Department of Homeland Security in 2003 demonstrated the importance of the national government in emergency preparedness and response activities. Clearly, the focus of public policy in this area has shifted away from subnational authorities to the federal government. This mirrors similar trends in other policy areas: For example, the federal government has taken on more and more responsibility to establish nationwide standards and protocols for teachers and school children (Ravitch 1995; Lewin 2010). And, the national government has assumed major responsibility for stabilizing the investment market and stimulating the national economy (Davis, Obey, and TheCapitol.Net 2009; Dinan, and Gamkhar 2009).

The history of governmental involvement in disasters also reveals the highly reactive nature of American public policymaking. Throughout American history, major disasters have been the prime stimulants of governmental relief activity. This was certainly the case during the early years of the United States when disaster assistance legislation was tied directly to specific disaster-related events. Funds and technical assistance were provided to the victims of a particular hurricane, flood, or tornado, and the programs disappeared as soon as their immediate mission was accomplished. Recent policy expansions and additions in this area have had more general objectives, but they still tend to be enacted following major natural disasters. For example, Congress passed PL 89-339 in 1965, which was commonly known as the Hurricane Betsy relief program. Similarly, PL 92-385, commonly referred to as the Hurricane Agnes relief program, was enacted in 1972 (May 1985b), and the Homeland Security Act of 2002 (PL 107-296) was created in direct response to the September 11, 2001, terrorist attacks. More recently, the Post-Katrina Emergency Management Reform Act of 2006 (PL 109-205) was designed to address the problems and shortcomings of the governmental response to Hurricane Katrina (U.S. Government Accountability Office 2008a). Despite their names, all of these statutes established ongoing procedures and broader principles for the governmental response process. They lead to the development of standard operating procedures, which remain in effect long after the disaster situations that create them have faded. Even though the specific content of federal disaster policy has broadened in scope, the evolution of these policies occurs in reaction to particular disaster events (Birkland 2007; Rubin 2007; Sylves 2008).

It is perfectly understandable that disaster-relief policy has developed in this manner. Events like hurricanes, floods, tornadoes, and earthquakes often receive a great deal of media attention. And they produce exactly the kind of problems, issues, and conditions that are likely to prompt an immediate public-sector response. In sum, they easily qualify as "crisis" situations. The policy literature is filled with instances where a specific crisis has triggered a governmental action. For example, a crisis in the late 1950s, the Soviet's orbiting of the first space satellite, Sputnik, led to the passage of the National Defense Education Act in 1958. Similarly, the Love Canal crisis in the late 1970s prompted the enactment of the Compensation and Liability Act (the Superfund Program) in 1980. And the severe economic crisis of 2008 certainly spurred the enactment of a number of governmental policies, including the Economic Stimulus Act of 2008 and the much larger American Recovery and Reinvestment Act of 2009. Unfortunately, however, crisis situations usually do not sustain long-term public and governmental interest.

This is certainly the case with natural disasters. After the immediate problems and disruptions are resolved, the political system moves on to address different, more pressing concerns. Hence, few demands or pressures are placed on public officials to maintain ongoing relief programs.

In fact, natural disasters are precisely the type of issues that are likely to go through the kind of issue-attention cycle identified by Anthony Downs some time ago (1972). They do not usually affect a majority of the population; they require substantial financial and physical resources in order to deal with them effectively; and they lose their fascination, uniqueness, and charm very quickly. Moreover, most people simply do not like to think about these events unless they are directly confronted with them.

When a disaster occurs, the public wants "something" done immediately. But once action is taken, these problems are set aside in order to deal with other more tangible and less troubling situations.

Finally, the government's fundamental approach to disaster situations has evolved over the years. Initially, the content and objectives of policy were strictly reactive in nature; the government only took action after a disaster occurred, and its involvement was highly limited in scope and time. Current governmental policies place much greater emphasis on proactive measures—such as preparing American society and specific local communities for emergencies before they arise (Comfort 1988; Sylves 2008). In particular, the government tries to emphasize policies and procedures that will prevent or mitigate against the occurrence of severe disaster situations. Again, other public policy areas have shown comparable trends. For example, public health care programs currently stress measures intended to prevent unnecessary and costly medical problems from ever developing. Similarly, many of the government's environmental policies aim to protect wildlife, plantlife, and public lands, so that they do not become endangered in the first place.

As is the case with all public policy areas, the government finds it extremely difficult to shift its focus in disaster-relief activities. To begin, the ever-present pressure of incrementalism on governmental decision making is part of the problem. Past policy responses become entrenched, and they provide the firm basis for subsequent governmental activity (Lindblom 1959; Wildavsky 1964). Incrementalism is a pervasive conservative force on governmental disaster-relief policymaking, as it is on virtually every type of public policymaking. In addition, public sentiment may deter governmental officials from pursuing alternative, more preventative strategies for emergency management. Citizens may not want the government to enact stronger zoning laws or building codes if these measures prohibit them from living or working in desirable, but hazard-prone, areas. Finally, natural disasters produce the kinds of situations that inhibit policy change. Disaster-stricken populations want the government to respond immediately to their conditions. No time exists to consider new or different policy alternatives. Consequently, public officials find it more expedient to pursue "old" policies which enable them to make quick, almost automatic, decisions.

Nevertheless, a shift in the governmental approach to natural disasters has occurred across all governmental levels within the United States. This is true for two basic reasons. First, it is simply more cost effective to prevent a natural catastrophe from occurring than it is to deal with its consequences. Although mitigation programs require time, money, and resources, they can produce substantial economic payoffs. For example, the establishment of stricter building codes and regulations in disaster-prone areas has saved millions of dollars in property damages. Warning and evacuation procedures have also prevented the unnecessary loss of human life in a number of disaster situations. Thus the benefits of preventive measures—measured in both economic and physical terms—clearly outweigh their costs.

A second reason for the shift in governmental policy stems from changes in the definition of what constitutes a *disaster* situation. Events such as oil spills (the 1989

Exxon Valdez incident), toxic waste mishaps (the dumping of toxic chemicals into the Love Canal neighborhood of Buffalo, New York), chemical plant fires (the 1984 explosion of the Union Carbide Pesticide Plant in Bhopal, India), and terrorist attacks (in New York and Washington, D.C. on September 11, 2001) are man-made situations: They are not the products of uncontrollable natural phenomena. In the past, human beings were simply incapable of causing situations comparable in scope and magnitude to natural catastrophes. As the previously mentioned events illustrate, however, this is no longer the case. Thus, modern relief efforts must anticipate such "new" disasters as well as more traditional problems like floods, droughts, and hurricanes (Sylves 2008). This, in turn, has placed new demands on the governmental agencies responsible for dealing with emergency situations (Kasperson and Pijawka 1985). Indeed, over the last decade, public expectations about what government should do in a disaster have increased markedly (S. Schneider 2008a). A majority of Americans believe that the government is in the best position to handle major disaster situations (AP/Ipsos 2005a; CBS News 2005; Pew Research Center 2005b; Saad 2005). Consequently, public agencies have developed more extensive plans and procedures for handling a wider variety of these problems (Sylves 2008).

Government's Role in Addressing Natural Disasters

This chapter has addressed two major topics. First, natural disasters are discussed as major issues that are legitimate components of the policy agenda in the United States. Superficially, classifying natural disasters as "political" phenomena may seem strange, since their origins usually lie outside the realm of human capacity. Nevertheless, they share virtually all the characteristics of more traditionally recognized political issues. As a result, citizens naturally look to government for assistance when natural disasters strike.

The second topic addressed in this chapter has been the evolution of governmental disaster-response efforts. There have been two major trends in this area. One is the shift from limited, reactive relief programs to more comprehensive, proactive hazard mitigation policies. The other is the expansion of the federal government's role relative to states and localities. Both of these trends are fully consistent with more general principles and patterns of governmental decision making.

The major conclusion to be drawn from this chapter is a relatively simple one. Natural disasters can be viewed as public policy issues. As such, they can be treated much like any other issue. In order to understand their effects on American society, it is necessary to pinpoint the particular problems that arise with natural disasters as well as the administrative structures designed to deal with them. This, in turn, helps explain how, why, and when governments become involved in disaster-relief efforts. Ultimately, this background information will also help account for the success and failure of various governmental responses. In the next chapter, I will begin to investigate these factors by examining the formal structure of the governmental response system for natural disasters in the United States.

Notes

1. "Agenda building" is sometimes called "agenda setting" in the public policy literature. Both terms represent the same process; therefore, they are used interchangeably in this study.

2. Peters (2009a) identifies these four factors as the most important in the agenda-building process.

3. Downs (1972) shows how public attitudes toward the environment during the 1960s and 1970s went through an issue-attention cycle. Subsequently, Peters and Hogwood (1985) trace the rise and fall of a number of other policy issues through this same cycle.

4. This is sometimes referred to as the "social construction" of problems (Berger and Luckmann 1967; Best 1989; Northcott 1992; A. Schneider and Ingraham 1993), "issue framing" (Iyengar 1991; Schon and Rein 1994), or heresthetical political manipulation (Riker 1986).

5. There is a wealth of material on the U.S. government's "bailout" of the auto industry, banks, and insurance companies due to the economic recession of 2008. For an up-to-date summary of these actions, as well as links to other discussions, see the *New York Times* website, http://topics.nytimes.com/top/reference/timestopics/subjects/c/credit_crisis/index.htm.

6. The political repercussions of failing to deal successfully with a crisis have been documented in other, man-made situations as well. For example, Apple (1992), Mathews (1992), and Pear (1992) provide discussions of the political fallout from the Los Angeles Riots of 1991.

7. The word "disaster" is so powerful that it can be, and is, used to identify a situation that does not technically meet the strict definition of a crisis or an emergency. When a situation is described as a "disaster" it is viewed with more urgency and significance.

8. For more complete accounts of disaster-relief legislation during this time period, see Bourgin (1983) and Popkin (1990).

9. Over the past twenty years, there have been serious discussions about the focus and impact of the government's disaster-relief policy. See, for example, the reports of the National Academy of Public Administration (1993), the U.S. General Accounting Office (1993b), the U.S. Senate (2006a, 2006b, 2006c, 2006d), the U.S. Government Accountability Office (2006a, 2006b, 2006c), and the U.S. House of Representatives (2006).

3

The Governmental Response System

Every year hundreds of natural disasters occur in the United States. Governmental institutions are called upon to respond in virtually every case. The vast majority of these emergencies are handled primarily at the local level, with only minimal involvement from state or federal governments. Indeed, this is precisely how the disaster response process is supposed to work—local governments should provide the first response with limited assistance from higher-level authorities.

But the severity of the situation is sometimes beyond the capabilities of local officials. During these situations, state and national governments play a more prominent role in the disaster assistance process. And in some rare circumstances, the federal government becomes the focal point for almost all response and recovery activities, superseding the actions of subnational emergency response units. Thus, the scope and nature of governmental activity varies greatly from one disaster to the next.

Nevertheless, all governmental disaster relief policies are supposedly guided by a single, overarching structure. This chapter examines the basic components and underlying assumptions of the emergency response system in the United States. A detailed understanding of this system is necessary before we can try to account for governmental efforts in specific disaster situations.

How the System Is Supposed to Work

The United States has an ongoing system that is intended to guide the governmental response to all natural disasters. The process works from the "bottom up." It begins at the local level and follows a series of pre-specified steps up through the state and ultimately the national government. Local, state, and national governments are supposed to share their emergency management responsibilities (May and Williams 1986; Carson and MacManus 2006; Comfort 2007; Scavo, Kearney, and Kilroy 2007). The higher levels of government are not intended to supersede or replace the activities of the lower levels. All three levels of government are supposed to develop coordinated, integrated emergency management procedures, and they should all participate in the process of implementing disaster relief policies.

Formal Structure of the Governmental Response

Municipal and county governments are the first link in the chain. Their job is to deal with emergencies that occur within their jurisdictions (Federal Emergency Management Agency 2011b). The basic assumption is that disaster response will be handled primarily by local emergency management agencies, and related organizations, such as law enforcement units, fire departments, ambulance services, civil defense coordinators, and so on (Bea 2005a; Col 2007). But natural disasters place exceptionally large burdens on these local officials; therefore, they are usually forced to look elsewhere for guidance and assistance with their response procedures.

In most cases, this outside assistance comes from the state and federal governments, which can provide disaster preparedness funds to local units. In doing so, most states require, or at least encourage, the towns, cities, and counties to establish and support local emergency preparedness agencies (Mushkatel and Weschler 1985; National Emergency Management Association 2006). This requirement is intended to impose some degree of regularity and structure on the first line of defense against natural disasters.

Emergency preparedness agencies are supposed to make sure that local communities are ready for disaster situations. Their most tangible product is a plan identifying the duties and responsibilities of all local officials during emergency situations. These plans are prepared by local officials to meet the needs, conditions, and situations of particular areas. But they also usually conform to certain guidelines imposed by the state and federal governments. After all, higher governmental levels often provide money and technical advice to help local officials prepare and maintain their emergency management plans (Rossi, Wright, and Weber-Burdin 1982; Rubin, Saperstein, and Barbee 1985; National Emergency Management Association 2004). In return, they expect local governments to establish basic preparedness and response procedures (Waugh 1990). Most local-level plans describe how citizens will be alerted to, or warned about, potential hazards. They include procedures for evacuating or relocating the local populations in the event of an actual disaster. And local plans usually specify how emergency rescue and response activities will be conducted by, and coordinated across, local organizations, as well as how local governments will obtain assistance from higher authorities if events exceed their capacity (Drabek and Hoetmer 1991; Sylves 2008; U.S. Department of Homeland Security 2008b).

A fundamental assumption of the overall system is that many, if not most, disasters can and will be handled at the local level (Col 2007; Federal Emergency Management Agency 2011a). Even if the capabilities of one community are overwhelmed, local officials can seek help from other neighboring jurisdictions. Over the last decade, a number of city and county governments have developed regional compacts and cooperative agreements in order to facilitate the flow of aid from one community to another (National Emergency Management Association 2006; Col 2007). However, local governments can also turn to higher governmental levels if their resources are totally exhausted. Specifically, they can ask state officials and organizations for additional guidance and assistance.

State governments have the ability to mobilize extra assets and larger-scale organizations to deal with situations that local officials cannot handle on their own. The responsibilities and obligations of each state government are set forth in that state's emergency preparedness/response plan (National Emergency Management Association 2004, 2006, 2008b). These state plans have a number of common elements. They specify a framework to guide the deployment of statewide resources and to guide the support for local disaster relief operations. In addition, state-level plans describe the responsibilities of various state officials for example, the governor, emergency preparedness personnel, and law enforcement officials) in disaster situations. Similarly, they identify the conditions under which the state's National Guard can be mobilized, and they specify how important resources (such as utility-repair services, power generators, and water supplies) can be reallocated to affected areas of the state. Each plan strives to provide an effective system for coordinating and supporting all emergency relief efforts within the state (Waugh 2000).

Every state is responsible for developing its own separate plan that spells out a response system tailored to best address state-specific needs and priorities. Such flexibility is absolutely necessary in order to deal with the diverse kinds of disasters that occur throughout the United States. The response mechanisms that seem to be most effective for dealing with hurricanes are not necessarily those that are best suited for earthquakes, volcanic eruptions, or blizzards. But this flexibility also contributes to variability across states in the quality of the respective emergency management systems.

In order to provide a degree of uniformity across the nation, the federal government imposes some conditions on all state systems. These requirements are not always strictly enforced. But they do establish certain preconditions to which a state must conform in order to receive federal financial assistance. Therefore, all states abide by these guidelines in organizing their disaster response systems (Rossi, Wright, and Weber-Burdin 1982; National Emergency Management Agency 2004, 2006, 2008; U.S. Department of Homeland Security 2008c).

The most prominent federal requirement on the states is intended to maximize the efficiency of the system. Within each state, a single agency must be placed in charge of emergency preparedness and relief (National Emergency Management Agency 2004). The federal government imposes an identical requirement in other policy areas; for example, a single agency must be responsible for administering each state's Medicaid program and each state's cash assistance program for low-income families, that is, Temporary Assistance for Needy Families. This gives the federal government one point of contact within every state, and it clarifies the intergovernmental structure of program development and implementation.

The exact names and organizational placements of these state agencies vary. In some states, emergency management functions are housed in separate administrative divisions or in units within the governor's office. Most states have located these operations within larger departments of public safety or military affairs, such as the Office of Adjutant General (National Emergency Management Association 2008). Regardless, these state organizations play a critical role in the response process. They are responsible for coordinating all state-level activities and ensuring that the state maintains a coherent and effective system for dealing with disasters (National Emergency

Management Association 2006). These state agencies also serve as the main liaisons between local jurisdictions and federal relief efforts. Indeed, one of the major tasks of a state emergency management agency is to coordinate the actions of local governments with state-level efforts, while also serving as the intermediary between national and subnational organizations. State emergency management organizations are involved in funding and dispensing disaster relief operations. They distribute financial aid to local governments for emergency preparedness and response; they negotiate mutual aid agreements with other states in order to consolidate and mobilize their resources; and they are the conduit through which federal funds can be channeled to local communities (National Emergency Management Association 2008; U.S. Department of Homeland Security 2008b).

In addition to the state emergency management agency, the governor plays a key role in disaster preparedness and response at the state level. Some variation from state to state can be found, but in general, most state governors have fairly expansive powers during emergency situations (National Emergency Management Association 2004, 2006; National Governor's Association 2007; U.S. Department of Homeland Security 2008b). They can declare a "state of emergency" either through executive order or by proclamation; identify the conditions under which the state's National Guard can be mobilized; and specify how important resources will be reallocated to affected areas. Governors can also request assistance from other states. Once an emergency has been declared, a governor can ask other states to send personnel, equipment, and emergency supplies. Such requests are usually channeled through mutual aid agreements, which are voluntarily established between state governments. One of the most visible and successful of these interstate systems is the Emergency Management Assistance Compact (EMAC).

EMAC has its origins in a regional compact of mutual emergency aid—called the Southern Regional Emergency Management Association Compact—created by the Southern Governors' Association in 1992. This compact established a formal process whereby a state could obtain outside assistance from other states if its own resources and capabilities were overwhelmed. In 1995, the compact was expanded so that states outside of the South could join, and it was renamed the Emergency Management Assistance Compact (EMAC). Then, in 1996, the U.S. Congress gave its approval to the interstate mutual aid system and officially endorsed EMAC. Today, all fifty states, Puerto Rico, the U.S. Virgin Islands, Guam, and the District of Columbia are members of EMAC (National Emergency Management Association 2006, 2008).

In order to obtain assistance through this nationwide EMAC system, a governor must declare that an emergency exists and request that personnel, equipment, or supplies from the outside are needed in order to respond to the emergency. EMAC helps disaster-stricken states submit requests for outside aid, it channels these requests to other jurisdictions, and it facilitates the mobilization of personnel and supplies from one state to another. States do not have to rely upon the EMAC system to obtain extra resources. EMAC is a voluntary system of interstate mutual aid; it is not an official component of the intergovernmental response process; and it is administered by the leading professional association for state emergency management directors, not the national government. But EMAC does provide a valuable mechanism for states to obtain outside assistance for their disaster relief operations: it can be used to mobilize, deploy, and coordinate valuable resources across jurisdictions during emergency situations (National Emergency Management Association 2006; Waugh 2007).

The last step in the intergovernmental response process is direct involvement by the national government. The conditions under which the federal government can intervene are specified in federal statutes—particularly, the Disaster Relief Act of 1974 (Public Law 93-288), the Robert T. Stafford Disaster Relief and Emergency Assistance Act of 1988 (Public Law 100-707), the Disaster Mitigation Act of 2000 (Public Law 106-390), the Post-Katrina Emergency Management Reform Act of 2006 (Public Law 109-295), the Pets Evacuation and Transportation Standards Act of 2006 (Public Law 109-380), the Security and Accountability for Every Port Act of 2006 (Public Law 109-347), and the Department of Homeland Security Act of 2007 (Public Law 109-295). These statutes indicate that the national government cannot step in and take charge of every natural disaster situation. For the vast majority of situations, the federal government only becomes directly involved when a state or territorial governor makes a formal request for assistance. When this occurs, all subsequent steps are delineated by the previously mentioned statutes.

A governor's request is first reviewed and evaluated by the Federal Emergency Management Agency (FEMA). Based upon their reading of the situation, FEMA officials prepare a recommendation for the president. The president must officially decide whether the magnitude of a crisis really is beyond the capacity of state and local governments. If so, he issues a formal declaration that a "major disaster" has occurred (Federal Emergency Management Agency 2011e).[1]

A "major disaster" declaration by a president has far-reaching consequences. It indicates that a severe event that exceeds the capabilities of state and local governments has occurred. It also suggests that the disaster may warrant extensive involvement and long-term assistance by the federal government.

The presidential declaration is vitally important to the directly affected population. It legitimizes their situation, and it is a necessary first step for obtaining federal aid. To the general public, that is, those who are not directly affected by the disaster, the president's declaration is also a significant piece of information. At a rather basic level, it signifies that a major event has occurred, requiring the involvement of the federal government. The content of the presidential declaration structures popular perceptions about the nature and scope of the natural disaster.

Beyond its immediate effects, the president's disaster declaration also has a profound impact on the nature of subsequent relief efforts. The declaration of a "major disaster" can open the door to an array of federal assistance and an infusion of federal funds (Federal Emergency Management Agency 2011a; 2011b,). However, not all forms of federal assistance will be forthcoming, even if a "major disaster" is declared. Instead, an assessment is made of each particular situation to determine what type of support is warranted and who will receive it. So the disaster declaration specifies the geographic boundaries of the affected area, thereby delineating exactly who is eligible for relief in the first place. The presidential declaration also contains an initial statement about the types of assistance that will be provided to the stricken populations and communities. This is extremely important because it determines whether disaster victims will receive temporary shelter, emergency medical care, direct cash grants, housing supplements, and so on.

Once a "major disaster" has been declared, the president must appoint a Federal Coordinating Officer (FCO) to serve as the federal government's representative to the stricken area. In general, the FCO is responsible for coordinating all subsequent response/recovery efforts. The FCO's position is delineated in federal statutes and regulations, but the specific responsibilities of the post are not explained in detail. Consequently, this individual has a great deal of discretion over the nature and scope of governmental actions in a particular disaster situation. For example, the FCO can: extend the boundaries of disaster areas beyond those originally defined by the president; alter and/or extend specific assistance requests to meet situations as they arise; and direct resources into particular parts of the disaster area to best meet the needs of the affected population. In sum, the FCO has broad, open-ended, authority.

Of course, the FCO does not act alone in organizing, directing, and implementing relief activities. Instead, he or she provides overall direction to the activities of emergency management officials at the federal, state, and local levels. And the FCO works very closely with other personnel in the Federal Emergency Management Agency, the Department of Homeland Security, and across the entire federal government to mobilize all necessary and available resources. These federal officials start their work by signing an agreement with the governor of the affected state (Giuffrida 1985; McLoughlin 1985; Federal Emergency Management Agency 2011b). This agreement covers several important topics. First, it includes a plan that delineates federal, state, and local responsibilities in the recovery effort. Second, it identifies the exact nature of the federal assistance that will be provided. And third, it specifies various ways that federal resources can be employed.

At this stage of the process, FEMA works directly with the state's emergency management officials. Here, there are two key contacts: the first is the state's emergency management agency. Recall that each state is required by federal guidelines to establish and maintain a single agency for emergency management. This preexisting agency serves as one of the two major focal points for federal relief and assistance. The state's emergency management agency is expected to have the mechanisms in place that will enable it to channel all available resources to the disaster-stricken areas.

The second key state-level contact is the State Coordinating Officer. This position is specified in federal regulations. Once a "major disaster" is declared, the governor of the affected state must appoint a State Coordinating Officer to serve as the state's counterpart to the Federal Coordinating Officer (FCO). This individual is responsible for organizing and mobilizing state and local relief efforts and for coordinating these efforts with those of the federal government. In theory, these two contacts should facilitate communications and interactions between state and federal officials, as well as the overall implementation of disaster relief through the intergovernmental system.

Since 2005, the primary mechanism for ensuring intergovernmental cooperation has been the National Incident Management System (NIMS). NIMS is a comprehensive framework for emergency management that is supposed to be applicable at all jurisdictional levels and across all types of disasters. It establishes a unified command system at the onset of a crisis situation so that the actions of all public and private agencies are coordinated and focused on achieving the same basic objectives. This system has been promoted extensively by the Department of Homeland Security as a way of improving the development and implementation of disaster relief through the intergovernmental framework (Sylves 2008).

In addition to coordinating efforts across governmental levels, FEMA also serves as a clearinghouse for other federal assistance programs. Many ongoing national policies take on special relevance during disaster situations. Therefore, FEMA tries to link disaster victims with federal agencies that may be able to provide them with assistance. For example, it helps local businesses obtain loans from the Small Business Administration so they can repair or replace damaged facilities. Similarly, it helps farmers and ranchers obtain emergency loans from the Farmers Home Administration. And FEMA can encourage the Internal Revenue Service to give disaster victims special consideration in filing their income tax returns. Many other examples of this kind of activity have occurred. In every case, FEMA does not *control* the assistance that other federal agencies provide, but it does serve as a central point of contact. In this way, the disaster relief system tries to make the most efficient use of previously existing governmental institutions and programs.

Along with its responsibilities for coordinating other agencies, FEMA also administers several programs on its own. The agency can make temporary housing available, providing tents, mobile homes, or rent money to people whose homes have been damaged or destroyed. It can distribute cash grants to individuals and families who are in need but ineligible for other types of aid. It can also make funds available to government agencies and private companies in order to restore or replace public facilities and property. Thus, FEMA acts as a direct source for certain kinds of assistance.

Finally, FEMA plays a key role in physically getting federal aid to disaster-stricken areas. One way it does so is by bringing in relief workers. FEMA maintains a nationwide registry of part-time, reserve personnel. When a major disaster occurs, it calls up these reservists and moves them into the affected area. But even with this ongoing part-time pool of reservists, FEMA does not have enough employees on its own. Therefore, it usually asks state and local officials, as well as other federal agencies, for their assistance in carrying out the federal effort. This assistance is assumed to be different from, but complementary to, the efforts that subnational governments make on their own behalf.

FEMA also provides important transportation facilities during the period following a natural disaster. The victimized population is often sorely in need of reconstruction and habitation materials such as plywood, plastic sheeting, safe drinking water, and so on. While these kinds of goods are often available elsewhere, serious problems arise in their delivery to affected areas. FEMA has the major responsibility of securing these resources and transporting them into disaster-stricken communities. But the agency does not possess its own fleet of trucks, railroad cars, and so forth. FEMA is simply too small to justify maintaining such facilities on a day-to-day basis. The vehicles would actually go unused most of the time. So, FEMA calls upon federal and state agencies (such as the U.S. Army, the federal Department of Transportation, and state National Guard units), that do have these resources readily available for other purposes.

Another aspect of FEMA's responsibility involves public relations (Federal Emergency Management Agency 1993). Most victims simply do not know where to turn for help during the confusion that follows a major disaster. So FEMA sets up one or more Disaster Application Centers where the affected public can apply directly for aid. But disaster victims must know that these centers exist before they can use them. Therefore, FEMA uses the mass media: the agency runs commercials on television and radio stations, takes out advertisements in local newspapers, and disseminates informational pamphlets and brochures. Agency officials also try to make face-to-face contact with disaster victims. This is particularly important in rural areas where lines of communication are tenuous even in the best of times. In such cases, media-based efforts would simply miss the neediest victims. So, caseworkers go out into stricken areas to locate and inform people who otherwise would be ignorant of relief procedures and opportunities.

FEMA is also an essential information source for state and local officials who are anxious to make aid applications for their own governmental units. Federal requirements for institutional relief and recovery are very difficult, lengthy, and confusing. Local officials, who are already under a great deal of pressure, are often overwhelmed with the paperwork required for federal assistance. FEMA personnel are specifically designated to assist them with this aspect of the relief effort. A major portion of their responsibilities is to explain the federal requirements and to help state and local officials collect the voluminous amount of documentation—primarily damage assessments—that is a precondition for federal aid. Thus, FEMA provides vital information to governmental officials as well as to the general public.

It is important to point out that the federal government should not step in and take charge during most major disaster situations. Instead, it should stay in the background, providing general guidance, financial support, and technical assistance to lower governmental units. This bottom-up process—starting at the local level, moving up through the states, and ultimately to the national government if necessary—is believed to work best for the vast majority of disasters (S. Schneider 1990, 1992, 2008a; Federal Emergency Management Agency 2011g, 2011h).

However, the federal government does have the ability to assume a more proactive leadership role during natural disasters. The September 11, 2001, terrorist attacks made it clear that some events could immediately overwhelm the capabilities of state and local governments. During such situations, it would be difficult, even impossible, for the traditional "bottom-up" framework to work effectively. Therefore, federal officials should not wait for a response to work its way up through the intergovernmental framework. Instead, the national government becomes involved at an earlier stage so that critical resources can flow more quickly and easily into the stricken area (U.S. Department of Homeland Security 2008b). For most disasters, this means that the federal government can deploy personnel, resources, and equipment into the "emerging" situations to help state and local officials respond. Even though the national government is on the scene to advise and assist, the response still operates according to the standard bottom-up process.

There are times, however, when the federal government should become more actively and directly involved in emergency relief. Following the terrorist attacks of September 11, 2001, these situations were referred to as "incidents of national significance" (White House 2003; U.S. Department of Homeland Security 2004a), and the Secretary of the Department of Homeland Security was placed in charge of the response to these situations. The DHS Secretary would have designated a Principal Federal Official (PFO) as the official representative in such situations. However, if a PFO was not appointed, then the FCO would continue to lead the efforts of the federal government and coordinate activity between federal, state, and local officials (U.S. Department of Homeland Security 2004a). An important element of the PFO's, or FCO's, responsibility involved the immediate creation of a unified command team, bringing together individuals from across all three levels of government as well as the private sector.

Following the governmental response to Hurricane Katrina, the roles of the FCO and PFO were clarified. According to the provisions of the Post-Katrina Emergency Management Reform Act of 2006, the FCO is responsible for coordinating and overseeing the government's response operations, while the PFO's actions are described as subordinate to those of the FCO. But the Post-Katrina Reform Act also reiterates the need for more direct federal-level intervention during unusually severe disasters. Specifically, it states that "accelerated federal assistance and federal support" may be necessary, with or without specific state-level requests for aid in order to facilitate "the rapid deployment, use, and distribution of critical resources to victims of a major disaster" (Federal Emergency Management Agency Law Associates 2006). This provides the rationale for conducting a top-down intergovernmental response. The 2008 National Response Framework clarifies when and how such a response will be conducted. The Framework eliminates the requirement that the Secretary for the Department of Homeland Security officially declares an "incident of national significance" before direct federal action is warranted; instead, catastrophic events are included in the basic intergovernmental response process, albeit requiring more proactive and aggressive federal involvement (U.S. Department of Homeland Security 2008b, 2008d).

Regardless of how the response unfolds, federal officials are still supposed to work directly with state, and local, officials to assess the severity of the situation and determine the type of assistance needed. Here, several state-level contacts are key, including the state's emergency management agency, the State Coordinating Officer, and the Governor's Authorized Representative (GAR). The state emergency management agency serves as a major focal point for federal relief and assistance and will channel all available resources to the affected areas.

To summarize, the current U.S. disaster response system involves three different layers, corresponding to the local, state, and federal governments. Private and non-profit organizations are also very involved in the nation's emergency management system. But the foundation for the system is based on the multi-layered structure of American government. The framework for this process is depicted in Figure 3.1.

For the vast majority of situations, the disaster response process is supposed to work from the bottom-up. Municipal, township, and county governments are to provide the first response to most disasters. If the state and national levels become involved, these local governments continue to identify and communicate the needs of stricken areas. The state supplies some aid in the form of money, manpower, and training, but its most important contribution is the development and execution of a comprehensive preparedness/response plan. This is intended to mobilize and coordinate activities across the entire state. Finally, the federal government is to provide technical assistance and training to augment the operations of state and local governments. It can also make additional funds and other essential resources available during large-scale relief efforts. But federal assistance must still be requested from lower governmental units. And federal engagement rests heavily upon intergovernmental communication and cooperation.[2]

Immediate and direct federal intervention is warranted only when an overwhelming, catastrophic event occurs, or is likely to occur. During such circumstances, the national government has the ability to step in and take action, even before a situation becomes catastrophic. In such instances, however, the national government must continue to rely upon state and local governments to perform a variety of important functions—that is, assessing the extent of the damages, providing advice on how to distribute aid, assisting in the response and relief operations, and so on. The disaster response system still uses the intergovernmental framework with all three levels of government playing critical roles in the implementation of emergency assistance. But the flow of intergovernmental activity is supposed to shift from a bottom-up to more of a top-down pattern during catastrophic situations.

Basic Assumptions of the System

The preceding description shows that the governmental response system for natural disasters involves a widespread and complicated structure. The viability of this structure is based upon several crucial assumptions about the nature of disaster situations and the responsibilities of governmental institutions.

The first and most fundamental assumption is that disaster preparedness and response is best handled at the local level (Drabek 1984; S. Schneider 1990; Sylves 2008; U.S. Department of Homeland Security 2008b; Federal Emergency Management Agency 2011a, 2011b). Officials in city and county governments are believed to be

Figure 3.1   **Basic Structure of Intergovernmental Response System**

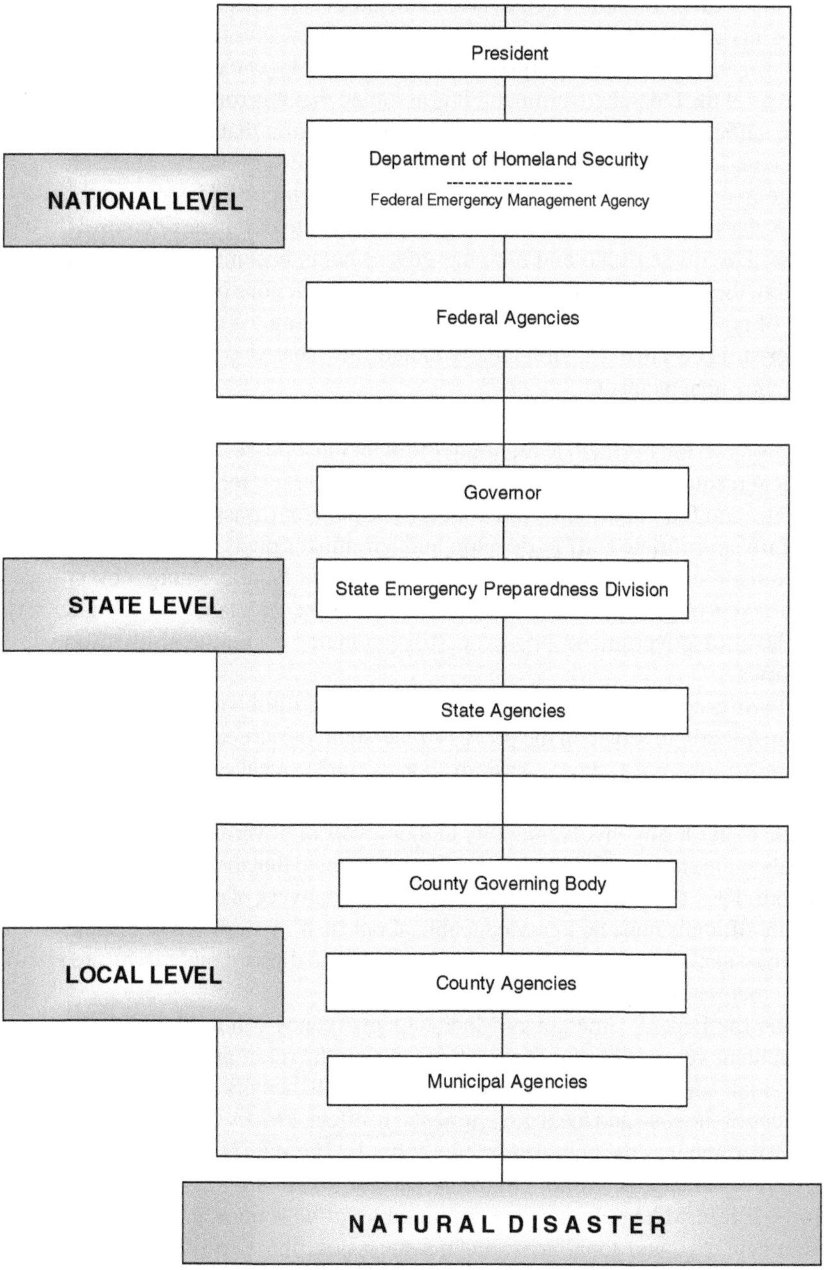

```
                        ┌─────────────────────────────────────┐
                        │             President                │
                        └─────────────────────────────────────┘

  ┌──────────────────┐  ┌─────────────────────────────────────┐
  │  NATIONAL LEVEL  │  │   Department of Homeland Security    │
  └──────────────────┘  │   ---------------------              │
                        │   Federal Emergency Management Agency│
                        └─────────────────────────────────────┘

                        ┌─────────────────────────────────────┐
                        │           Federal Agencies           │
                        └─────────────────────────────────────┘

                        ┌─────────────────────────────────────┐
                        │              Governor                │
                        └─────────────────────────────────────┘

  ┌──────────────────┐  ┌─────────────────────────────────────┐
  │   STATE LEVEL    │  │ State Emergency Preparedness Division │
  └──────────────────┘  └─────────────────────────────────────┘

                        ┌─────────────────────────────────────┐
                        │           State Agencies             │
                        └─────────────────────────────────────┘

                        ┌─────────────────────────────────────┐
                        │        County Governing Body         │
                        └─────────────────────────────────────┘

  ┌──────────────────┐  ┌─────────────────────────────────────┐
  │   LOCAL LEVEL    │  │           County Agencies            │
  └──────────────────┘  └─────────────────────────────────────┘

                        ┌─────────────────────────────────────┐
                        │          Municipal Agencies          │
                        └─────────────────────────────────────┘

        ┌─────────────────────────────────────────────────────┐
        │               NATURAL DISASTER                      │
        └─────────────────────────────────────────────────────┘
```

Note: This figure shows the major lines of communication. Others may develop in a disaster. The sizes of the boxes do not represent the sizes of the agencies.

most capable of anticipating and meeting the particular needs of their constituents; they only look elsewhere when disaster-related events exceed their capabilities. Of course, it is anticipated that a few situations will require involvement by state governments. An even smaller proportion will exceed state-level capacities and require the resources of the federal government. It is assumed that this rolling, bottom-up process will be sufficient to handle any kind of disaster situation that arises.

Second, local, state, and national governments are supposed to share emergency management responsibilities (Mushkatel and Weschler 1985; May and Williams 1986; Sylves 2008). No single level of government is to dominate or control the entire process. Even when state and national governments become involved in a disaster situation, they are not to supersede or overpower the actions of lower levels. All three levels of government are supposed to continue working together to provide relief to disaster-stricken citizens. This idea is called the "shared governance" approach to emergency management.

Third, it is assumed that all governmental units take their emergency management obligations seriously. Each level of government must possess the administrative and technical resources necessary to perform its own disaster relief responsibilities. Local, state, and federal officials must set aside funds for disaster relief purposes, they must hire appropriate staff to develop and administer plans, and they must possess the requisite equipment and technical expertise to handle emergency situations. Lower levels of government can usually obtain some assistance from higher levels. Each level of government, however, still maintains a great deal of responsibility on its own.

A fourth crucial assumption—closely related to the third—is that the public officials who are directly involved in the process understand the structure and operation of the entire governmental response system. For example, local emergency management officials must know that they are to provide the first response to a disaster, and that they are to guide any involvement by higher levels of government. At the same time, officials at the state and federal levels must understand that their role is supplementary in nature. They are to mobilize and coordinate the delivery of extra resources. In short, all relief officials must be knowledgeable about their own roles and responsibilities. They must also be aware of how their actions relate to those of others who are involved in the emergency management process.

Fifth, the Federal Emergency Management Agency can hold the state and local governments responsible for their actions during the relief process. FEMA is a relatively small administrative unit so it is forced to rely heavily upon the personnel and resources of the state and local governments. In effect, FEMA views a disaster-stricken state government as the grantee for federal funds. The state is actually responsible for determining emergency relief eligibility and for distributing resources to those who qualify. But FEMA holds the state accountable for its actions, and it also determines how much state and local governments must contribute to offset the non-federal share. For these reasons, FEMA must try to obtain the cooperation and participation of relevant state and local governments (S. Schneider 1990).

Sixth, unusually severe, catastrophic events—incidents of national significance—require the immediate attention and resources of the national government. Local communities and state governments are simply not equipped to handle these situations. And it is not appropriate for the response to "bubble up" through the intergovernmental framework when extraordinarily severe circumstances occur. Hence, the national government should become more quickly and more directly involved during these disaster situations. Even here, however, the federal government is to work closely with state and local governments, as well as private organizations, to mobilize, coordinate, and implement an effective response to an incident of national significance.

Finally, it is assumed that people outside of the immediate relief system—political leaders, private individuals, and other governmental officials—understand how the disaster response system operates. Emergency management officials are primarily responsible for organizing, coordinating, and mobilizing the governmental response. But they cannot possibly perform all disaster relief activities themselves. Other governmental agencies, private organizations, and individual citizens, therefore, must be involved in the process. Problems invariably arise when non-emergency management personnel do not understand how the system is supposed to work, when they consciously ignore it, or when they deliberately take steps to circumvent standard operating procedures. Similarly, serious breakdowns can occur when confusion exists about the severity of the disaster situation and/or the type of response that should unfold. In particular, uncertainty over whether the standard bottom-up process should be used versus top-down procedures for incidents of national significance can create delays and confusion. An effective response can only be mounted when everyone involved understands how the emergency preparedness system is supposed to operate for the situation at hand (McLoughlin 1985; Sylves 2008).

How the System Really Works: The Reality of the Governmental Response System

The previously described system depicts how the governmental response is *supposed* to work. Ideally, there exists a well-coordinated, integrated management system that will automatically handle each and every emergency, no matter when or where it occurs. In reality, however, the process operates quite differently. Overall, the existing governmental response system is more accurately described as disconnected, uncoordinated, underfunded, and discredited. There are several reasons for this negative characterization.

First, different perspectives often develop across different governmental levels. Local, state, and national officials tend to view the process strictly from their own vantage points in the system. Local and state officials feel that their responsibilities have ended once they pass the response up to the federal government (Riley 1989; S. Schneider 2008a). But federal officials view the system as a team effort where the three units of government have separate, but clearly interdependent and continuous, obligations (Hall 1989; Federal Emergency Management Agency 2011b). The differing perceptions of these roles affect the way that the entire governmental response process operates. When all three governments share the same view of the process, the whole response system operates smoothly and effectively. When perceptions differ across governmental levels, however, complications, confusion, and even breakdowns in the disaster response effort are likely.

Second, emergency management officials are often unable to coordinate the actions of other participants in the process (U.S. General Accounting Office 1991; U.S. House of Representatives 2006). Theoretically, they are supposed to mobilize and organize available resources within their respective jurisdictions. However, they simply cannot control the actions of other public officials, political leaders, and private citizens. For example, a county civil defense director has little influence over the chief of the local police force. Similarly, the head of the state emergency preparedness agency cannot make the director of the state social service agency respond to the health and welfare needs of disaster victims. And the Secretary of the Department of Homeland Security or the Director of FEMA cannot actually take over the operations of other federal agencies, such as the Department of Agriculture or the Department of Transportation. There are simply too many agencies and officials involved in disaster relief operations. Each has its own set of rules, regulations, and policies, with different leadership, personnel, and organizational structures. As a result, emergency management officials find it difficult, and sometimes even impossible, to coordinate the overall response process.

Third, disaster relief operations are severely underfunded throughout the entire intergovernmental system (Mushkatel and Weschler 1985; Cigler 1988; Rubin and Popkin 1990; Waugh 1990; National Emergency Management Association 2004, 2006). At the local level, many emergency management agencies operate on limited budgets, with part-time personnel. The situation is not much better at higher governmental levels. In most states, the emergency preparedness division is usually the last agency to receive any kind of funding or resources. Similarly, FEMA—the lead federal agency in most major disasters—has a staff of only several thousand trained reservists who can be deployed to any given disaster situation, and a relatively small operating budget to cover all of its day-to-day, natural disaster-related activities (Federal Emergency Management Agency 1993; U.S. General Accounting Office 1993b; Waugh 2006; Sylves 2008; Federal Emergency Management Agency 2011a). Moreover, the funds available to FEMA for major emergencies—contained in the Disaster Relief Fund—are usually kept so low that Congress must appropriate additional, supplemental money before FEMA can mobilize an adequate response (Federal Emergency Management Agency 1993; National Emergency Management Association 2004; Bea 2006; Sylves 2008). Funding to prepare for, and respond to, natural disasters is simply not considered a top priority at any level of government.[3]

Finally, emergency management operations have not always had much respect or credibility within the overall governmental system. The general impression is that the officials who work in this area are untrained and unprepared for their duties (Cook 1989). There have been repeated complaints that emergency management agencies are nothing more than the dumping grounds for old military personnel or for political hacks who cannot find other employment (Bandy 1989a; Jeff Miller 1992; Wamsley 1993; Kettl 2006). Instead of recruiting individuals who could provide leadership and direction during times of crises, emergency management agencies seem to attract personnel who are incompetent, untrained, and unqualified (Democratic Study Group 1989). This leads to the overall impression of an inept, ineffective emergency management system (Sylves 2008).

The situation is one in which intentions are very different from reality. A well-organized, efficient system to guide governmental activity during any type of natural disaster exists on paper. In reality, however, this system is not well understood, not completely supported, nor fully developed (U.S. House of Representatives 2006). This creates problems for those involved in the response process even before a disaster occurs. These problems are exacerbated by the pressures and strains that always arise as a natural disaster unfolds. And they become especially difficult and trying when confronting extremely severe, catastrophic events. The causes and consequences of these tensions are examined in the next chapter.

Notes

1. The president could issue an "emergency declaration," instead of a "major disaster declaration." Emergency declarations are made when situations are beyond the scope of local authorities, but they are believed to be more limited in nature. Hence, they should require short-term federal assistance, instead of long-term recovery aid and funding.

2. No single statute, regulation, or document describes the structure of the entire inter-governmental disaster response system. Instead, each level of government has policies and procedures that identify its roles and responsibilities in the process as well its relationships with other governmental entities. The bottom-up and top-down frameworks presented in this analysis were constructed by the author to show how all three levels of government are supposed to interact with one another during the vast majority of major disasters, as well as during the more severe, but rare, incidents of national significance. These structural arrangements match the representations found in the academic literature (May and Williams 1986; Stratton 1989; Popkin 1990; Sylves 2007, 2008), and they coincide with the descriptions provided by emergency management personnel themselves (Bourgin 1983; McAda 1989; Peterson 1992; U.S. House of Representatives 2006; Sullivan and Kallestad 2009; Federal Emergency Management Agency 2011a).

3. Federal funding for disasters has been criticized on other grounds. Supplemental emergency appropriations bills are often laden with "riders" which confer benefits for special legislative interests unrelated to disasters (Sylves 2008). In addition, there have also been charges that FEMA and other federal agencies have mismanaged these funds, improperly dispensing money to cover potentially fraudulent claims (Arnone 2006; U.S. Government Accountability Agency 2006d) or providing benefits in an uneven and inequitable fashion (Fletcher 2010).

4

Human Behavior and Governmental Activity in Disasters

Two Sets of Norms

This chapter examines the various norms, expectations, and values that guide human behavior during disaster situations. In everyday life, people rely heavily upon norms to help determine their own activities and their interactions with others. Norms delineate a set of stable and comprehensive expectations for human behavior. They help individuals differentiate between acceptable and unacceptable conduct on a regular, day-to-day basis.

Norms also serve as fundamental building blocks or frameworks for organizational and institutional life (Simon 1976). They give meaning, direction, and significance to individual participation in group activities. They also shape how individuals operate within organizations, as well as their external relationships with others. As a result, norms are key mechanisms for societal integration and organizational cohesion. By delineating the guiding principles for both individual and group behavior, norms provide continuity, order, and stability within a society (Durkheim 1895, 1915; Sherif 1936; Smelser 1964).

But during natural disasters, the regular, routine modes of human behavior are severely disrupted. In such situations, people often question the legitimacy and viability of established principles, and they may develop new norms and behavior patterns to guide their actions. The problem is that these newly emergent norms may conflict with existing governmental policies and procedures. When this kind of conflict arises it has a direct impact on the disaster response process. Let us look more closely at the two dominant sets of norms that exist—and often collide—in natural disasters.

Bureaucratic Norms: The Governmental Response Process

As we have seen, the governmental response system is an amalgam of various organizations, plans, regulations, and individuals. Taken together, the components of the system define the role of public institutions in natural disaster situations. More specifically, the system identifies the nature and scope of governmental intervention; it delineates a basic framework for intergovernmental and intragovernmental cooperation; and it provides direction for all subsequent governmental activity. If we look at this system as a whole, it clearly possesses the same basic characteristics as most other governmental institutions and organizations. Stated simply, the disaster response system is a bureaucracy, and it is dominated by the same norms commonly found in that type of structure.

Characteristics of Bureaucracy

The term "bureaucracy" is often used in a derogatory, negative manner. To many Americans, it represents a complicated maze of rules, procedures, and organizations that are unnecessary, duplicative, and wasteful (Niskanen 1971; Goodsell 2004). Bureaucracy is synonymous with rigidity, red tape, confusion, and indifference (Wilson 1989). It is often publicly identified as a main cause of governmental inefficiency, waste, and unresponsiveness (Kaufman 1981; Hill 1992; Meier and O'Toole 2006).

But the term "bureaucracy" also has a more technical meaning. It represents a general way of organizing human activity so that complex tasks can be carried out in a coordinated, routine, and efficient manner (Weber 1958; Downs 1967; Wilson 1989). Bureaucracy enables people to combine their efforts and achieve social objectives that would be otherwise unattainable. Consequently, bureaucratic organizations exist in all contemporary societies, and they are integral components of all modern governmental systems (Meier and O'Toole 2006; Gormley and Balla 2008; Peters 2009b).

In order to be considered a bureaucracy, an administrative structure must exhibit several basic characteristics.[1] The exact description of these characteristics varies from one analyst to the next (Weber 1958; Downs 1967; Simon 1976; Rourke 1984; Wilson 1989; Goodsell 2003; Meier and Bohte 2006; and Peters 2009b). However, five of the most commonly identified bureaucratic properties are: (1) clearly defined objectives; (2) a division of labor; (3) a formal structure underlying the process and tying together the various component organizations; (4) a set of policies and procedures guiding organizational activity; and (5) specialized training, expertise, and experience. These characteristics are the fundamental hallmarks of contemporary bureaucratic organizations, and they affect the ability of any particular bureaucracy to carry out its assigned tasks and responsibilities (Goodsell 2004). Let us briefly consider each of these characteristics in turn.

First, bureaucratic organizations are established to address specific problems and achieve clearly articulated goals (Wilson 1989). Of course, all organizations, regardless of size or substantive focus, have similar general purposes: they are created to reach collective objectives that cannot be attained through the actions of individuals working on their own (Hill 1992). A bureaucracy, however, is different in that it represents a highly rationalized organizational form (Weber 1958). There must be a clear justification for the existence of a bureaucracy, and there must be explicitly stated purposes to guide bureaucratic operations. In short, the goals of bureaucratic activity—that lead to the creation and continuation of bureaucratic operations—must be known and clearly defined.

Second, bureaucratic organizations possess a straightforward division of labor. A bureaucracy brings together a large number of individuals in order to accomplish its pre-specified goals and objectives. But each person who works in the bureaucracy cannot possibly perform all of the organization's tasks. If they attempted to do so, the result would be wasteful and redundant allocations of resources. Instead, each bureaucratic employee is assigned to a particular operation or function. This enables individuals to concentrate their efforts and develop high levels of expertise in their respective spheres of activity. This, in turn, allows the bureaucracy to carry out relatively complex tasks in a rational, efficient manner.

A bureaucracy must, however, find some way of coordinating its activities. If it fails to do so, the bureaucracy cannot achieve its organizational mission. This potential problem is addressed by the third characteristic—a formal structure that guides bureaucratic activity. Several different types of bureaucratic structures have been identified.

At the one extreme, there is the centralized, hierarchical pattern that Weber (1958) and others (Taylor 1911; Gulick and Urwick 1937) identify as the hallmark of the classical bureaucracy. Here, a definite chain of command exists throughout the entire organization: decisions are made at the top, and they are implemented by lower-level officials. This results in a rigid, vertical bureaucratic structure.

At the other extreme, there are bureaucracies that possess a decentralized structural form. Power, control, and responsibility are dispersed and spread throughout the organizational framework. Top-level officials are still leaders, but they coordinate rather than direct organizational activity. Lower-level bureaucrats do not simply follow orders; instead they are directly involved in agency decision making (Kaufman 1969; Wilson 1989; Barzelay 1992). This creates a relatively flexible, horizontal bureaucratic structure.

Of course, an infinite variety of structures fall somewhere between these two extremes.[2] Even though many different kinds of bureaucratic structures exist, they all possess a common characteristic: an identifiable framework that links together all of the specialized units and operations within the organization.

Fourth, a bureaucracy operates on the basis of established policies and clearly designated procedures (Rourke 1984). The rules and guidelines necessary for achieving bureaucratic objectives are codified into a set of standard operating procedures. This expedites bureaucratic activities by reducing uncertainty about what is to be done in any given situation. Standard operating procedures also enhance communication within the organization. Bureaucratic employees can identify their respective superiors and subordinates; they know exactly to whom they report and to whom they give instructions.

Standard operating procedures also facilitate the coordination of tasks. By clearly assigning responsibilities to administrative units and personnel, they reduce redundancy and minimize the duplication of efforts. Standard operating procedures allow organizations to treat similar cases in a uniform, expedient manner. This enhances bureaucratic effectiveness by reducing favoritism and inequitable treatment across different situations. Bureaucratic employees are expected to be familiar with the standard operating procedures relevant for their respective positions. When a situation arises they are expected to use the rules, find the appropriate procedure, and apply it in a relatively straightforward, unambiguous fashion: improvisation is strongly discouraged. In summary, the formalization and institutionalization of rules is a critical bureaucratic attribute (Rourke 1984; Meier and O'Toole 2006). It is intended to provide consistent, speedy, and effective policy implementation.[3]

Finally, specialization, expertise, and experience are key components of modern bureaucratic organizations (Rourke 1984; Wilson 1989). It is assumed that all those involved in bureaucratic activity take their duties and responsibilities seriously. By devoting continuous attention to particular situations, bureaucratic agencies acquire a level of organizational knowledge that enables them to address situations in a relatively effective and efficient fashion. Hence, bureaucratic expertise stems from the concentrated attention that organizations give to particular problems and circumstances. Bureaucratic expertise also flows from the training, experiences, and skills of those who work in the organization. Each unit should be staffed by personnel with the requisite backgrounds and capabilities to perform their pre-assigned tasks.

The preceding five characteristics define an ideal bureaucracy. In reality, no organization fully conforms to this description (Goodsell 2004). Instead, Anthony Downs (1967) describes "bureaucratization" as a continuum. The larger the number of bureaucratic traits manifested by an organization, the more closely it comes to becoming a complete bureaucracy. Many organizational structures possess most or all of these characteristics, and they clearly do adhere to a common set of norms. These norms provide guidance for individual and organizational activity. Moreover, they produce a certain style of administrative behavior that is quite distinctive. For obvious reasons this style is called bureaucratic behavior. It is really this behavior or conduct that sets bureaucratic institutions and systems apart from all others.

Bureaucratic Norms in the Governmental Disaster Response System

At least on paper, the governmental system for responding to natural disasters conforms precisely to the formal characteristics of a bureaucratic organization. First, the U.S. government's current disaster response process has one primary mission: "to protect the nation from all hazards, including natural disasters, acts of terrorism, and other man-made disasters" (Federal Emergency Management Agency 2009a). In order to accomplish this task, emergency management organizations are supposed to focus on four explicit objectives: (1) mitigating or preventing a disaster from occurring in the first place; (2) preparing areas for potential emergency situations; (3) providing immediate relief after a disaster strikes; and (4) helping individuals and communities recover from the effects of natural disasters (McLoughlin 1985; S. Schneider 1992; Waugh 2000; Sylves 2008).

These objectives were first advocated by the National Governor's Association in the late 1970s. Since that time, the federal government has become the strongest proponent of these principles (Giuffrida 1983; May 1985a; May and Williams 1986; Waugh 2000). It has encouraged all those involved in the process—particularly state and local governmental institutions—to adopt these objectives. As a result, most public agencies engaged in disaster management espouse these principles and they use them to develop comprehensive programs that are designed to handle any and all types of emergency situations. This is referred to as the "all-hazards" approach to emergency management (Waugh 2000; Harrald 2006, 2007; Sylves 2008).

Second, a division of labor within the disaster response system is easily discernable. Each level of government has specific roles and responsibilities. As explained in the previous chapter, the basic framework is designed to work from the bottom up" (S. Schneider 1990, 2008a; U.S. Senate 2006c; Scavo, Kearney, and Kilroy 2007). Local governments are the first point of mobilization: they initiate governmental activity, and they provide a critical, ongoing link between private citizens and governmental resources (Rossi, Wright, and Weber-Burdin 1982; Rubin, Saperstein, and Barbee 1985; Col 2007; Scavo, Kearney, and Kilroy 2007; Federal Emergency Management Agency 2011hg, 2011h). State governments are supposed to coordinate and support all emergency relief activities within their respective states. They also act as the primary intermediaries between local governments and federal agencies (Mushkatel and Weschler 1985; National Emergency Management Association 2004, 2006, 2008; Landy 2008). Finally, the federal government's primary role is to provide technical and financial aid to lower governmental units. In most disasters, federal agencies are *not* supposed to step in and take over a situation. Instead, they should stay in the background, providing general guidance, financial support, supplemental assistance, and coordinative abilities to facilitate emergency response activities within and across governmental units (White House 2003; U.S. Department of Homeland Security 2004a, 2008b, 2008c, 2008d; U.S. Senate 2006c; Federal Emergency Management Agency 2011a, 2011g, 2011h, 2011i).

This division of labor between the local, state, and national governments is intended to provide the most efficient utilization of public resources (Landy 2008; Federal Emergency Management Agency 2011g; U.S. Department of Homeland Security 2008b). Each level of government makes its own unique contribution. Local governments have the best knowledge of immediate conditions and situations; state governments can provide additional equipment and personnel; and the national government has the resources to supplement subnational efforts. Each governmental jurisdiction must be able to perform its functions in order to make the entire system work effectively.

Third, the disaster response system definitely possesses a formal structure, composed of a number of recognizable organizational units located throughout the intergovernmental framework (Comfort 1988; Waugh 2000; Haddow and Bullock 2006; Sylves 2008). These emergency management agencies tie the entire response system together, providing structure and stability to governmental emergency relief operations.

All local communities must establish basic emergency management procedures and they must identify the organizations that will be responsible for them. But it is up to each local community to determine how these operations will be organized and how they will coordinate their efforts with other organizations. Thus, local emergency preparedness and response activities may fall under the jurisdiction of a single organization, they may be divided between several agencies, or they may even be spread across multiple local units and geographic areas (Drabek and Hoetmer 1991; Waugh 2000). Regardless of the specific administrative configuration, local emergency management agencies are to serve as the primary "first responders" when a natural disaster strikes (Federal Emergency Management Agency 2011g; U.S. Department of Homeland Security 2008b, 2008d).

The structure is a bit easier to pinpoint at the state level. Each state is responsible for developing its own emergency management operations. But as mentioned in the previous chapter, a single agency must be placed in charge of emergency prepared-ness and relief within each state (National Emergency Management Association 2004, 2006). The exact names and organizational placements of these agencies do vary. In some states, emergency management functions are housed in separate divisions or offices, while others have located these operations within larger departments of pub-lic safety or homeland security. Although the vast majority of states call these units "emergency management" or "emergency services" organizations, other states refer to them as "civil defense units" (Hawaii), "disaster services" (Idaho), or "homeland security" (Wyoming). Regardless of the trappings, these state agencies play a critical role in the response process. They are responsible for coordinating state-level activi-ties, and they serve as liaisons between local and federal relief organizations (National Emergency Management Association 2008).

The Department of Homeland Security (DHS), a cabinet-level unit within the fed-eral government, is currently positioned at the top of the nation's intergovernmental disaster response system (Kettl 2006; Harrald 2007). DHS is responsible for developing and "coordinating federal operations within the United States in order to prepare for, respond to, and recover from terrorist attacks, major disasters, and other emergencies" (White House 2003; U.S. Department of Homeland Security 2008b). Within the De-partment of Homeland Security, the Federal Emergency Management Agency (FEMA) is the lead agency for coordinating, mobilizing, and directing the vast majority of the nation's hazard mitigation efforts (U.S. Congress 1974, 1988, 2007).

Fourth, the disaster response activities of public organizations are based upon a set of formal policies and procedures. Some of these are derived from legislative statutes. For example, state and federal laws identify the conditions that must exist in order for a response to move upward from the local level to the state and finally to the national level. During most major disaster situations, officials from the lower levels of gov-ernment must formally request assistance from the next higher level (U.S. Congress 1974, 1988, 2007). State and federal laws also specify that the scope of the disaster should exceed the capacities of lower governmental units before requests for additional assistance can be made (Federal Emergency Management Agency 2011g).

Other operating procedures have been developed by the disaster relief organiza-tions themselves. For example, the Department of Homeland Security established guidelines to clarify the overall intergovernmental framework of emergency relief, as well as the roles and responsibilities of various federal-level organizations and individuals involved in the process. The most recent set of guidelines is contained in the *2008 National Response Framework* (U.S. Department of Homeland Security 2008b). Such guidelines are extremely important because they delineate the basis for direct federal involvement in an emergency situation, as well as how assistance will flow through the entire intergovernmental structure (U.S. Department of Homeland Security 2008c).

The practice of combining statutory and administrative regulations is typical of all governmental operations in the United States. Legislative bodies set the broad parameters of public policies, while the public organizations involved in the actual implementation of services specify more precise guidelines (Lowi 1979; Rourke 1984; Meier 2000; Meier and Bohte 2006). Of course, a degree of flexibility is built into the process: administrators do have some discretion in how they carry out their responsibilities. If they stray too far from their designated tasks, however, the institutionalized response process breaks down. As a result, they experience considerable pressure to abide by standard routines (Wilson 1989; Gormley and Balla 2008).

Finally, the governmental disaster response system relies heavily upon bureaucratic expertise. At the state and local levels, emergency management agencies are supposed to possess the administrative and technical skills necessary to perform their pre-assigned disaster relief tasks (Waugh 2000; Comfort 2007). Hence, local and state officials should set aside funds for disaster relief purposes; they must hire appropriate staff to develop and administer plans; they must possess requisite equipment and technical competency to handle emergency situations; and they must be able to direct their resources so that they can respond to different types of disasters.

Many local jurisdictions cannot afford to have a permanent emergency management staff (Mushkatel and Weschler 1985; Cigler 1988; Waugh 1988, 2000; Drabek and Hoetmer 1991; Col 2007). So they use officials who are already serving in other capacities (for example, firefighters and emergency rescue squads) or they temporarily activate private citizens as their emergency management personnel. At the state level, most emergency management agencies have relatively small staffs: they often "borrow" employees from other state agencies (such as highway construction personnel, social service workers, and so on) to perform important activities (National Emergency Management Association 2008). Regardless of the specific composition of their staffs, these state and local organizations coordinate relief efforts within their respective jurisdictions and they link the activities of one government level to those of the others. Essentially, these agencies—and the personnel who work within them—tie the entire response system together, providing structure, stability, and continuity to emergency relief operations.

At the national level, bureaucratic expertise should be most evident within those agencies that possess the primary responsibility for disaster relief. The Federal Emergency Management Agency (FEMA), the key agency within the Department of Homeland Security for most of the national government's activities, uses a core of full-time professionals on an everyday basis. Specifically, as of 2011, it has between 3,000 and 4,000 permanent employees, most of whom are located in regional officials around the country (Federal Emergency Management Agency 2011a). During actual disaster situations, FEMA calls upon a larger group of "reservists" to help deliver emergency assistance. FEMA provides the funding to train these reservists, and it sets the qualifications for their participation in relief efforts. In addition, FEMA can look to other units within the Department of Homeland Security (for example, the U.S. Coast Guard and the Office of Health Affairs) and to other agencies across the national government (for example, the Small Business Administration, the Army Corps of Engineers, the Department of Transportation) to draw upon the expertise and skills of personnel from the entire federal bureaucracy (U.S. Department of Homeland Security 2008b).

Thus, the governmental disaster response system possesses the basic properties of a bureaucracy. It has a set of clearly defined objectives and principles. It has a division of labor between national, state, and local governmental actors. It has a formal structure that organizes organizational activity. It uses a set of formal rules, procedures, and policies to guide its actions. And it relies heavily upon a well-equipped, well-qualified workforce to carry out its activities. These properties give order, stability, and predictability to the governmental response process. They allow emergency response organizations at the local, state, and national levels to address different types of disasters in a relatively uniform and consistent manner, no matter when or where they occur (Goodsell 2004).[4]

Why, then, are emergency relief agencies unable to unable to respond quickly, effectively, or efficiently to some disasters? Before we can answer this question, we must first examine several important aspects of disaster situations themselves. Natural catastrophes often create problems that are extremely difficult to handle. Any type of administrative system would have trouble responding to such events. But bureaucratic institutions face a special challenge. Natural disasters can produce behavior patterns within the affected population that are almost directly antithetical to those found in bureaucratic systems.

Emergent Norms: Human Behavior in Natural Disaster Situations

On a day-to-day basis, people naturally develop beliefs and expectations about their own lives and about their interactions with others. These expectations help guide and coordinate patterns of activity during normal, routine situations (Merton 1957). For example, a person goes to the end of the grocery store checkout line to purchase food, drinks, and other items. This behavior facilitates service and provides coordination to an activity that invariably involves several people pursuing individual goals. Similarly, drivers learn to comply with traffic signals because they impose order on vehicular activity, they lead to reliable predictions about other drivers' behaviors, and they are legal requirements.

The mere existence of a dominant set of social norms does not imply that individuals always agree with their merit and usefulness. Nor does it mean that people will always obey the accepted rules (Turner and Killian 1972, 1987). There may be times when individuals cut into a checkout line ahead of others because they are in a particular hurry or because they simply believe that no serious sanctions will result in doing so. Similarly, there may be occasions when a driver runs through a stop light. Other traffic may be nonexistent, rendering the stop unnecessary in the first place, or there may not be a police officer in the vicinity to observe the violation. But these are easily recognizable exceptions to more general patterns of behavior. Most people abide by traditional norms and values because they accept them as beneficial and useful for facilitating interactions with others. Thus traditional norms, values, and expectations generate a sense of continuity and regularity for members of society. They also provide stability and order for the larger social and political systems.

Effects of Unanticipated Events

Human interactions are usually guided by the existing social norms. Standard forms of interaction, however, are upset when an unanticipated event occurs. Many different types of situations and conditions technically can qualify as unanticipated events. The sudden death of a relative, for example, can transform a family's everyday world into one of shock, confusion, and pain. Similarly, a dramatic change in a colleague's personality might leave a co-worker confused or unsure about how to react to this person. What is important is that the people who are immediately affected by such events did not expect them to occur; they have no standardized way of dealing with them. But events like those just mentioned are relatively limited in scope. They do not lead to fundamental transformations in ongoing social norms. Such personal disruptions are usually handled by individuals or small groups who maintain, as much as possible, their adherence to traditional norms in their interactions with others, such as non-family members or other co-workers in the two examples mentioned here.

Other unanticipated events are so severe that universally understood and accepted values no longer appear to be relevant. The people most directly affected are confronted with previously unimaginable and often incomprehensible conditions. The natural response is for people to try to figure out what has happened to them. Some individuals may wander around aimlessly in search of explanation and guidance. Others may resort to unusual behavior, such as screaming or hysterical crying. And a few people may engage in extremely unconventional, or even illegal, acts like looting and rioting, because they feel it is no longer necessary or useful to conform to traditional behavioral standards. Human behavior during such severe situations may appear to be abnormal and chaotic. It is not, however, completely random. To predict *precisely* how individuals will react to unanticipated events is impossible. But there does appear to be a relatively invariant sequence of behaviors that occurs in nearly every such disruptive situation. This phenomenon is known as *collective behavior*.

Collective behavior is defined as non-institutionalized interactions and behavior patterns (Blumer 1957; Lang and Lang 1961; Smelser 1963, 1964; Turner and Killian 1972, 1987; Weller and Quarantelli 1973; Lofland 1981).[5] It can occur anytime a disruption in everyday, ordinary life occurs. Collective behavior, however, is most likely to arise when the disruptions are large enough to intrude upon interpersonal interactions and broader social activities. In such cases the irrelevance of traditional social guidelines easily facilitates the emergence of new norms and values—that is, the collective behavior itself (McPhail 1991).

Natural disasters are certainly some of the most obvious, sudden, and significant environmental disruptions that can occur (Fritz 1961; Barton 1969; Drabek 1986; Kreps 1989; Mileti 1999; Tierney, Lindell, and Perry 2001). They differ from some other unexpected events, such as automobile accidents, in that they can affect large numbers of people in a relatively short period of time. Natural disasters also do not allow participants a choice about their involvement, unlike some situations, such as a riot, that give rise to collective behavior. Disasters cause large-scale disruptions to everyday activities and social life, forcing many people to deal with them. Thus natural disasters are exactly the type of events that make people question the relevance of existing norms and values. This, in turn, facilitates the emergence of collective behavior.

According to some of the prominent analysts in the field (Turner and Killian 1972, 1987; Quarantelli and Dynes 1977; Harvey and Bahr 1980; Perry and Mushkatel 1984; Stallings and Quarantelli 1985; McPhail 1991), there are four basic components to human interaction during a collective behavior situation: milling, rumor circulation, keynoting, and emergent norms.[6] These four components tend to occur sequentially, in the previously mentioned order. But during some disaster situations, these activities can overlap with each other to some extent, or they may even occur almost simultaneously. Each of these activities plays a distinct and extremely important role in the development of collective behavior. Therefore, it is useful to consider each of the four components separately.

Milling

As the immediate disaster recedes, people are confronted with situations and problems that lie outside the bounds of normal, everyday existence. Damaged houses, blocked roads, contaminated water supplies, and power outages all contribute to this unprecedented environment. The natural and immediate reaction that most individuals experience is: "How do we deal with this?" This leads to the first stage of collective behavior, called the "the milling process" (Turner and Killian 1972, 1987).

Milling is defined as the widespread search for meaning and appropriate standards of behavior among the affected population. Of course, the individuals who actually engage in this activity probably do not recognize that they are doing so. However, numerous case studies of collective behavior situations demonstrate that the milling process definitely occurs (Fritz 1957; Drabek 1968; Dynes and Quarantelli 1968; Perry and Mushkatel 1984).

Milling is most pronounced when existing organizations and institutional procedures are inadequate or inappropriate for the situation at hand. It is further exacerbated by breakdowns in communication and transportation systems. These breakdowns prevent authorities from establishing and maintaining social order and from reaffirming the relevance of traditional, that is, pre-disaster, behavioral norms. As McEntire (2007) writes, "individuals see needs that are not being met and therefore attempt to address them in an informal manner" (p. 175). In summary, the milling process represents a situation where people search for direction because their usual sources of guidance are unavailable or irrelevant to current conditions (Tierney, Lindell, and Perry 2001).

Rumors

During the milling process, new forms of interaction and communication develop among the population affected by the disaster (Quarantelli 1983). People emerge from their homes and shelters, and begin talking to one another. They want some kind of explanation for their situation. If they do not receive an appropriate or believable account from traditional authorities, they look elsewhere (Phillips 1993; Similie 1995). They place more reliance on informal and unconventional channels of communication. For example, they may pay greater attention to stories relayed by the media, family members, neighbors, or even strangers. This facilitates the development of rumors.

Rumors may appear to be random and sometimes malicious accounts of ongoing situations. They may focus on certain individuals or organizations in order to shift blame from existing social units (Drabek 1968; Wenger 1987; Quarantelli 1988; Neal 1997). They do serve, however, an extremely important function. Rumors are a means of transmitting critical information about the nature, causes, or impacts of a disaster situation within the affected population. This information may be simplistic, incomplete, and even incorrect (T. Lee 2010). Nevertheless, it gives disaster victims some guidance and structure in a highly unusual, uncertain situation (Ripley 2008).

Keynoting

At any given point in the milling process, many rumors will likely be in circulation. As the situation evolves, some rumors are discarded, that is, people stop reporting them, while others become distorted and change into new rumors. Over time, certain ideas and features come to be repeated more frequently and hence emphasized by the participants in the rumor process. The selection of specific ideas, and the concurrent elimination of others, is called "keynoting" (Smelser 1963; Turner and Killian 1972, 1987; S. Wright 1978). In some situations, keynoting occurs rather quickly. The nature of the event and/or the pre-existing attitudes of the affected population give some images a definite advantage. For example, the observable occurrence of looting, even though it may be quite isolated and infrequent, would help legitimize rumors about the breakdown of public authority (R. S. Olson and Drury 1997; Tierney, Bevc, and Kuligowski 2006); obviously, such rumors would also negate rumors about the reestablishment of the existing social order. Similarly, isolated rural residents could easily interpret the slow pace of response efforts as evidence of society's indifference and hostility to their plight.

In other situations, the keynoted image develops more slowly, as it takes people more time to sort through all possible explanations for their current predicaments.

Ironically, this tends to occur in areas where some communications are available or in areas where citizens have at least partially prepared for the disaster. In such cases, people simply have more information, knowledge, and understanding of what has happened. However, it is still difficult for the affected population to settle upon a single, consensual explanation of the situation. The severity and complexities of disaster situations mitigate against shared perceptions or beliefs. For example, consider the attitudes and reactions of people who live along an unstable geological fault line. Such individuals are generally aware of their precarious situation, and they are usually at least somewhat prepared for the occurrence of seismic events. Yet, their lives are still severely disrupted and unhinged when an earthquake actually occurs. At the same time, it is also easy to imagine that many previously unanticipated problems would slow down and inhibit the effectiveness of relief efforts. For example, victims might find that evacuation routes are blocked, or that emergency supplies have been rendered unusable. In cases like these, general, comprehensive explanations of the disaster situation would not be clear or immediately forthcoming.

Regardless of the speed with which it occurs, keynoting is extremely important. The keynoting information identifies the specific themes and symbols that will eventually give meaning to the disruptive situation. Keynoting provides potential direction for individual and group activity. In time, it is the keynoted, or shared, image of the situation that enables the affected population to end the milling process.[7]

Emergent Norms

The dominant symbols and ideas that emerge from keynoting activity serve as a new set of norms for guiding behavior. These emergent norms help disaster-stricken individuals understand what has happened to them. Newly developed norms give people the reassurance they need to cope with their conditions and circumstances, and they indicate the appropriate courses of action for disaster victims to pursue. As the situation stabilizes, and pre-disaster conditions are restored, traditional norms come back into play and the emergent norms themselves are discarded. In summary, they function as acceptable, albeit fairly temporary, guides for human interaction during a disaster situation (Quarantelli 1966; Dynes and Quarantelli 1968; Drabek 1970, 1984; Dynes 1970).

Collective behavior and the attendant development of emergent norms is a perfectly natural phenomenon. As Quarantelli (1983) and others (Dynes 1970; Drabek 1984; Sugiman and Misumi 1988; National Research Council 2006) have written, it reflects an innate human desire to understand and "resolve" disruptive, disorienting conditions. Essentially, people want to comprehend their own environment. So they search for explanations that give "meaning" to their current situations (Stallings and Quarantelli 1985). Furthermore, individuals engage in forms of activity and behavior that will facilitate the development of reasonable explanations for their predicaments. When these innovative behavior patterns stabilize, they tend to crystallize as emergent norms, which facilitate a return to normal life.

The human response to disasters centers on the development of emergent group norms. These norms are the direct consequence of the larger, ongoing collective behavior process. Natural disasters are triggering events: they set the entire process into motion. Milling usually begins immediately after a disaster strikes—as soon as it is clear that traditional norms and institutions are irrelevant to the current situation. The duration of the milling process varies, depending upon several factors, such as the scope of the disaster, the degree of interpersonal interaction among the affected population, and the specific content of rumor communication (Aguirre, Wenger, and Vigo 1998). Within the constraints imposed by the disaster, the milling process is completed as quickly as possible. People engage in rumor collection and keynoting, and the net result is the development of emergent norms and emergent group behavior (Gillespie, Mileti, and Perry 1976; Tierney, Lindell, and Perry 2001).

The exact content of emergent norms is situation specific and highly variable, so it cannot usually be predicted on a priori grounds (Drabek 1986). In most disasters, the norms and cues that develop among the affected populations are close to those that guide everyday activities. Here the emergent norms coincide with accepted behavior patterns, such as orderly evacuations and voluntary relief efforts (Tierney, Lindall, and Perry 2001). In such situations, emergent group activity is quite positive and therapeutic: it enables the affected community to deal with the disruptive conditions in a constructive manner (Wilmer 1958; Fritz 1961; Barton 1969; Kartez and Lindell 1990). However, in a fairly small number of disaster situations, emergent norms are at odds with traditional modes of activity and behavior (Neal and Phillips 1995). This conflict may take many different forms, from vocal public dissatisfaction to more extreme acts of social unrest or violence (Dynes and Quarantelli 1968; Quarantelli and Dynes 1972). What is predictable, however, is that emergent norms will develop as natural, automatic by-products of disaster situations (Parr 1970).

Notes

1. There is an enormous literature on bureaucracy, and it would be impossible to provide references for all of the studies that have focused on some aspect of bureaucratic organizations. Hill (1992) provides an excellent account of the major studies in this area from the 1940s through the 1980s. Also, see Merton (1940), Selznick (1943), von Mises (1944), Bendix (1947), Hyneman (1950), Marvick (1954), Blau (1955), V. Thompson (1961), Woll (1963), Crozier (1964), Alford (1969), Gawthrop (1969), Bennis (1970), Niskanen (1971), Warwick (1973), Suleiman (1974), Benveniste (1977), Aberbach, Putnam, and Rockman (1981), Yates (1982), Burke (1986), Stillman (1987), Gormley (1989), and Wilson (1989). For more recent research, see Meier (2000), Goodsell (2004), Gormley and Balla (2008), and Peters (2009b).

2. The structure of organizational activity is, perhaps, one of the most frequently examined topics in the field of public administration. There is a wealth of literature that focuses on the best way to organize the internal operations of individual agencies, as well as on how to arrange entire administrative systems across governmental jurisdictions. See, for example, Gulick and Urwick (1937), V. Thompson (1961), Waldo (1961), Crozier (1964), Katz and Kahn (1978), and March and Olsen (1989).

3. For an excellent account of the advantages and disadvantages of standard operating procedures in administrative policymaking, see Lowi (1979), Rourke (1984), Goodsell (2004), and Peters (2009a).

4. It is important to note that the governmental response system also relies heavily on networks of actors that operate within and across levels of government. These networks comprise of a variety of public, private, and non-profit organizations. And tremendous differences exist across the country in the composition and activities of these networks. Hence, generalizing about their operations is extremely difficult. But regardless of the differences, public institutions at the local, state, and national levels are the linchpins in this process: they hold the networks together and they have primary responsibility for emergency management and disaster response.

5. I do not attempt to present a comprehensive account of collective behavior in this study. Instead, I only touch upon those aspects of the phenomenon that are the most relevant for the discussion. For a comprehensive account of the origins, development, and current controversies surrounding the general concept of collective behavior, see Turner and Killian (1972), McPhail (1991), Aguirre (1994), Dynes and Tierney (1994), Stallings (1998), and Rodriguez, Quarantelli, and Dynes (2006).

6. These four components compose what some scholars refer to simply as the "emergent norm perspective of collective phenomena" (McPhail 1991). As in any field of inquiry, there have been fairly heated discussions about the viability and usefulness of this interpretation of the collective behavior process. For alternative views, see Couch (1968, 1970), Berk (1974), Miller, Hintz, and Cough (1975), Tilly (1978), Tierney (1980), and Lofland (1981, 1985). However, the emergent norm perspective is used in this analysis because it provides the most appropriate explanation for the type of collective action that occurs following a disaster situation. As McPhail writes, the emergent norm perspective does fit those situations where people confront a mutual problem, "engage in some temporary gatherings," and then construct "an ad hoc solution to the problem" through their "interactions with one another" (1991, p. 103).

7. For a slightly different account of keynoting, see Mead (1936), Lofland (1981), Bruner (1983), Reicher (1984), and McPhail (1991).

5

The Gap Between Bureaucratic Norms and Emergent Norms

As discussed in the last chapter, two distinct sets of norms operate together during a disaster situation. On the one hand, bureaucratic norms provide the foundation for the governmental response system. These norms facilitate the mobilization, organization, and implementation of disaster relief by public institutions. On the other hand, emergent norms serve to structure human behavior within the affected population. These norms provide guidance and meaning to the victims of natural catastrophes so that they can cope with the disorientation, disruption, and chaos that surround them. Both sets of norms perform extremely important functions during natural disasters. Without them, governmental institutions and the affected public would be unable to handle disaster situations. The problem, however, is that these two sets of norms might not be consistent with one another. If they are not, serious consequences for the entire relief effort can result.

Nature and Significance of the Gap

The sources of bureaucratic and emergent norms are largely independent of each other. The two sets of norms emanate for different reasons, within different groups of people, and even at different points in time. Bureaucratic norms develop slowly and methodically inside public organizations; they set the parameters for acceptable governmental activity. Emergent norms originate instantaneously and spontaneously within a disaster-stricken population, providing a framework for individual and social behavior. Given the contrast in their sources and nature, there will inevitably be some discord or disagreement between bureaucratic and emergent norms.

Each type of norm will naturally change or evolve over time. Organizations can become more or less bureaucratic in their orientation. Some agencies develop a strict, unshakable adherence to established rules and procedures, and they tend to frown on any deviations from standard operating policies. Other organizations acquire a more flexible, fluid approach to their operations; they rely less on routinized procedures and more on creative, problem-solving behavior and adaptable organizational solutions (Downs 1967). Similarly, emergent norms can also develop in a variety of ways. In some rare situations, the values and expectations guiding human behavior in disasters take a dramatic turn: individuals become so frustrated and confused that they engage in unconventional, previously incomprehensible behavior—such as looting and rioting.

In other disasters, people are momentarily disoriented and confused, but they quickly regain their composure and their footing. They revert back to more traditional and acceptable behavior guidelines (Turner and Killian 1972, 1987; McPhail 1991). So the evolution of norms is not, by itself, a cause for concern.

The problem, however, is that the two sets of norms may evolve in very different directions. When this occurs, a noticeable difference, or gap,[1] develops between governmental plans and the needs of the affected population. Some discrepancy of this type evolves in every natural disaster situation. So the mere existence of a gap between emergent and bureaucratic norms is not surprising. However, the size of the gap is important: it has significant consequences for the quality and effectiveness of the relief effort.

In some situations, the gap remains relatively small: governmental operations coincide fairly well with the needs of disaster-stricken victims. In other instances, the gap is extremely wide: governmental plans and procedures are completely at odds with the expectations and behavior of the affected population. So the size of the gap captures the degree of harmony or discord that exists between bureaucratic and emergent norms in any given disaster situation. As such, it gives us a useful indicator of the match, or mismatch, between governmental activity and citizen's expectations. More important, however, the size of the gap can be used to explain the variability of relief efforts across several different disasters. It accounts for the overall performance of the governmental emergency management process.

Factors Affecting the Size of the Gap

Five variables affect the size of the gap: (1) the magnitude of the disaster; (2) the degree of administrative preparedness; (3) the level of communication and coordination that exists; (4) the goals of the governmental response system; and (5) the prevailing orientations and behavior patterns of the affected population. Each of these factors influences the degree of congruence between the behavior of the disaster-stricken population and the activities of the public emergency management agencies. This congruence is important because it is the major determinant of the success or failure of overall governmental disaster response effort.

Magnitude of the Disaster

The severity of the disaster is clearly a major contributing factor to the size of the gap. Obviously, large-scale, catastrophic events are more difficult to handle than smaller, less disruptive disasters (Barton 1969; Drabek 1986; Porfiriev 1998; Platt 1999). Neither the public nor government officials like to think or talk about the possibility of a major natural catastrophe occurring (Donahue and O'Keefe 2007). Such events are simply unpleasant to contemplate. They are also extremely difficult to predict. They can occur suddenly and unpredictably, even in locales that are considered to be hazard-prone, high-risk areas. Moreover, they can produce large-scale disruptions in the physical environment, leading to major changes in the accompanying social structure (Kreps 1998; National Research Council 2006). This, in turn, can set off a wide variety of collective behavior within the affected population.

In such cases, human activities are very likely to take on a number of different forms and patterns. The only commonality among these activities is that they are unanticipated in pre-existing emergency preparedness plans. For example, people who are impatient with delays in governmental distribution procedures may simply break into stores and businesses to obtain food, tools, and reconstruction supplies. At the same time, outsiders may view disasters as economic opportunities. They bring in desperately needed supplies and then gouge the disaster victims by selling these materials at highly inflated prices. These kinds of activities are perhaps understandable, but they are certainly not consistent with the normal patterns of citizen behavior that are assumed in emergency preparedness plans. Therefore, public officials must deal with this kind of conduct by diverting resources that could be channeled into other, presumably more constructive aspects of the response process.

Major cataclysmic events can also create severe problems for governmental agencies no matter how well-prepared or well-equipped they are to handle more routine natural disasters (Petak 1985; Platt 1999). In theory, the disaster response system in the United States is designed to handle any kind of emergency that may occur, in any area of the country. But in reality, emergency response personnel focus much more heavily on the kinds of events that are likely to arise in their own regions. As a result, they are simply less capable of dealing with the kinds of disasters that occur more infrequently in their locales, such as an earthquake that hits in a hurricane-prone area of the east coast or a freak snowstorm that paralyzes communities in the South, which are more accustomed to severe heat and drought.

At the same time, catastrophic disasters almost inevitably place extremely heavy demands on emergency management agencies. Under such conditions, response organizations will naturally have greater difficulty putting pre-existing plans and contingencies into effect. Their task becomes almost impossible if they lack the proper personnel and resources. Unfortunately, this is often the case with the perennially understaffed, underfunded emergency response organizations.

In summary, very large-scale natural disasters produce exactly the kinds of situations where emergent norms are likely to be completely at odds with the prevailing bureaucratic norms. Highly unusual events lead people to behave in ways that deviate markedly from their normal, everyday routines. Similarly, extreme situations cause governmental agencies to depart from their standard operating procedures. Both of these tendencies magnify the disparity between the behavior of the affected population and that of emergency response personnel.

Nature of Governmental Preparedness

Second, the size of the gap is affected by the degree of prior governmental preparation and administrative training. The entire disaster response system in the United States rests on the premise that the government can and should plan for natural disasters (McLoughlin 1985; Petak 1985; Waugh 2007; Sylves 2008). This belief assumes that public officials have anticipated and prepared for all possible contingencies. Accordingly, they have developed standard operating procedures to deal with a variety of events, and they have integrated these procedures into the basic activities of emergency relief agencies. It is also assumed that the participants who are directly involved in emergency relief know and understand their respective roles; they must be willing to carry out their responsibilities; and they must possess the necessary skills and resources to perform their pre-assigned tasks (Rubin and Barbee 1985). In sum, government agencies and the personnel who work within them are prepared to handle natural disasters.

The problem is that these assumptions frequently do not conform to the realities of the nation's emergency management system. Actual governmental capacities for handling natural disasters are highly variable and inconsistent. For one thing, state and local governments differ widely in their degrees of disaster planning, coordination, and readiness (Mushkatel and Weschler 1985; Quarantelli 1988; Waugh 1988, 1990, 1994, 2000; Kreps 1991; Tierney, Lindell, and Perry 2001). Some subnational governments take disaster relief very seriously. They have developed comprehensive emergency management plans, and they have devoted many resources and a great deal of time to hazard mitigation activities. For example, some coastal communities establish and publicize evacuation routes, to be used when hurricanes threaten. Similarly, communities located along geological fault lines conduct earthquake simulations, training exercises, and drills. In such cases, local officials are relatively well prepared to deal with the kinds of emergencies that they can be expected to face. Accordingly, disaster relief efforts tend to operate smoothly in these communities.

In contrast, other state and local governments have shown far less interest in many aspects of disaster planning. Their emergency management plans are incomplete and/or too limited in scope. They do not carefully prepare or train their officials in disaster response procedures, and they make little effort to inform the general public about the dangers and hazards of emergency situations. This orientation to emergency management is understandable, given all the other functions that state and local officials are now expected to perform, often in the face of dwindling resources levels (National Emergency Management Association 2004). In fact, most local emergency preparedness units are housed within larger law enforcement or fire prevention agencies (Quarantelli 1988; Waugh 1990, 1994). Similarly, some state emergency preparedness agencies are located within broader public safety, homeland security, or military departments, while others are a part of the governor's office (National Emergency Management Association 2006). And the personnel who are responsible for addressing natural disasters have other, ongoing responsibilities that they must deal with on a day-to-day basis. This situation enables state and local governments to retain emergency response personnel, but it also makes it far less likely that these personnel will be able to focus sufficient attention on natural disasters when they occur, versus all of the other problems that they must confront.

At the national level, the issues are somewhat different but just as severe. Critics have charged that many of the top officials who occupy key positions at the federal level are not qualified to handle major natural disasters ("Advance Men in Charge" 2005; Bumiller 2005). In addition, many senior positions in the federal government have often been filled only on an acting, temporary basis, and a number of long-time experienced emergency management employees have left the federal government entirely (Lozana 2005). This has led to persistent questions about the qualifications and capabilities of the people leading the federal government's emergency management efforts.

Level of Communication and Coordination

The third factor affecting the size of the gap is the level of communication and coordination that exists within the response system. The government's bureaucratically derived emergency management system is predicated on the assumption that the different actors and components of the system will be able to communicate with each other. Furthermore, it assumes that relevant public officials, such as law enforcement officers, national guard unit commanders, and so on, and private organizations, such as the American Red Cross and the Salvation Army, are all on the scene, capable of directing their respective responsibilities, and able to coordinate their actions with others.

Things often do not work out this way. Communication channels almost always break down, at least temporarily, in natural disasters (Perry and Nigg 1985; Lindell and Perry 1996; Comfort 2007). Communication difficulties are exacerbated by the fact that activities usually have to be coordinated across a variety of distinct organizational units and geographic areas (U.S. House of Representatives 2006) under extremely chaotic and highly stressful situations.

When communication networks break down, public officials cannot receive and follow directions from their superiors or give instructions to their subordinates. As a result, the disaster relief system experiences division-of-labor problems because those who are involved in the process do not know exactly what their responsibilities are supposed to be. Moreover, they do not have a clear picture of how their actions fit into the entire process (Rubin, Saperstein, and Barbee 1985; U.S. General Accounting Office 1991; U.S. House of Representatives 2006). Hence, they are unable to integrate their actions with those of others who are also involved in the response operations (Landy 2008).

This situation is compounded if the roles and responsibilities of various actors are supposed to change, depending upon the nature of the disaster situation. As explained earlier, there are really two different intergovernmental response processes: one for more normal types of disasters, and the other for extreme, catastrophic events. During the vast majority of emergencies, the process is to start at the local level, moving up to the state and national levels as extra resources are required (S. Schneider 1992, 2008a). A fairly long-standing, well-established process has been put in place to guide governmental activity during such situations. But for unusually severe circumstances, the federal government is to assume a direct, proactive role.

Although general protocols and guidelines have been presented to guide governmental action in these extreme situations, they have not been fully developed, practiced, or implemented (S. Schneider 2008a). There are several reasons for this. First, the process to guide intergovernmental activity during catastrophic circumstances is relatively new, especially compared to the longer-standing bottom-up, rolling process that is used for the vast majority of major disasters. Second, extremely disruptive events occur quite infrequently, compared to other types of emergencies; hence, emergency management officials naturally spend most of their time anticipating and planning for other situations that confront them on a more regular basis. Finally, disaster relief personnel may not know exactly when or how they should deal with extreme, catastrophic situations, even if they had the time and resources to focus on them. As the national government itself admits, it is not always obvious when a situation will, or has, become an incident requiring greater federal involvement (U.S. Department of Homeland Security 2006, 2007). Moreover, federal officials may also be reluctant to take this step: they may simply be afraid of overstepping their pre-assigned tasks or straying from institutionalized norms and behavior patterns (Peterson 1989; U.S. House of Representatives 2006). Other federal personnel may be willing, but generally unprepared to take on added responsibilities. After all, they are not trained in many areas of local administration; they do not have the legal authority to take over state and local responsibilities; and they are often unfamiliar with the details of local conditions (Zensinger 1992; U.S. Senate 2006c).

The net result is that coordination across levels of government simply breaks down. Instead of a smooth and efficient allocation of resources, governmental activity is disjointed, disorganized, and chaotic. This clearly reduces the effectiveness and responsiveness of the overall relief effort. Unfortunately, it also has a negative impact on the attitudes and expectations of those who are directly affected by the disaster. It magnifies feelings of uneasiness, uncertainty, and hopelessness within the disaster-stricken population.

Goals of the Governmental Response System

Over the years, the focus of the nation's emergency response system has shifted, making it extremely difficult to pinpoint the government's objectives and priorities in the area of disaster response. These fluctuations are, perhaps, most evident in the approach and actions of the Federal Emergency Management Agency (FEMA), one of the key units in the governmental response system. FEMA was originally established to deal with all kinds of catastrophic situations. Consequently, both nuclear attack and natural disaster-related activities were specifically placed under FEMA's jurisdiction because this seemed to be the most practical and efficient way of combining similar emergency-type operations (May and Williams 1986).

During the 1980s, however, FEMA began to pay much more attention to preparing and defending the civilian population against a nuclear war (National Academy of Public Administration 1993). This shift reflected the policy and funding priorities of the national leadership during that time. Unfortunately, it produced an emergency management system that was overly focused on preparations for nuclear attack, even though the need for such activities was apparently waning. As a result, the nation's disaster relief system was unable to mobilize effective responses to several large-scale natural disasters during the late 1980s and early 1990s. This, in turn, led to intense demands to reform the entire governmental response system. Since FEMA occupied the central position in the nation's emergency management system, it was the target for many of these reform efforts.

In response to these concerns, a number of changes were made in the leadership, focus, organization, and operations of the Federal Emergency Management Agency during the early 1990s. An experienced emergency manager, James Lee Witt, was appointed as the director of FEMA by President Bill Clinton in 1993. Immediately upon assuming his post, Witt had FEMA articulate its general, overriding mission: to provide "leadership and support for all-hazards, comprehensive emergency management" (Witt 1993, p. 1). Then Witt initiated a number of organizational and structural reforms designed to improve FEMA's own operations, as well as those of other agencies within the entire disaster response framework. Witt created three directorates within the agency with jurisdiction over the agency's major activities: mitigation; preparedness training/exercises; and response and recovery. A major part of these changes involved an effort to refocus emergency management operations more clearly and directly on natural disasters and less on civil defense (S. Schneider 1998; Sylves 2008). Witt served as FEMA's director during Bill Clinton's two terms in office; he was replaced by Joe Allbaugh when George W. Bush assumed the presidency.

Then, following the events of September 11, 2001, the main orientation of the nation's emergency management system shifted once again, away from natural disasters toward antiterrorism activities. Perhaps the most obvious manifestation of this change occurred when FEMA was moved, along with twenty-one other agencies, into the newly created Department of Homeland Security (DHS) in 2003. As a consequence of this move, FEMA lost its status as an independent, cabinet-level agency. It became a small unit of a large department with a number of other, sometimes competing, program responsibilities—for example, protecting the American people from terrorist attacks, monitoring the nation's borders for illegal activity, maintaining the safety and security of public transportation systems, and so forth (U.S. Department of Homeland Security 2004a, 2007). Although FEMA once had a clear mission and fairly specific focus, it now had to operate within an organization which had a more diverse set of policy objectives and program responsibilities (Kettl 2006; Harrald 2007; Sylves 2008). FEMA also lost its control over important areas of hazard mitigation and disaster response, and it had to compete with other units, both within DHS and in other federal departments, for critical resources and influence (Harrald 2007).

Hurricane Katrina forced the nation to re-think, once again, how it was responding to natural disaster situations. As a result, changes were made in the organizational framework of the nation's emergency response system. In the Post-Katrina Emergency Management Reform Act of 2006, FEMA was given more autonomy and organizationally positioned as a distinct unit within the Department of Homeland Security (Suburban Emergency Management Project 2008). The core functions of comprehensive emergency management—preparedness, response, recovery, and mitigation—were moved back under FEMA's jurisdiction (Gall and Cutter 2007; Suburban Emergency Management Report 2008). And the term "incident of national significance" was eliminated in the 2009 National Response Framework because it had become "an arbitrary and confusing trigger point for various levels of response activities" (U.S. Department of Homeland Security 2008c). With these changes, FEMA once again became identified as the leader of the nation's emergency response efforts for all types of hazards (Sylves 2008).

But the post-Katrina policy changes do not clarify the responsibilities of various federal agencies and officials in the disaster response operations. FEMA's director must still notify the secretary of the Department of Homeland Security of any emergency-related recommendations or actions that FEMA takes. And the secretary of the Department of Homeland Security remains the "principal federal official responsible for domestic incident management," while the FEMA director is described as the "principal advisor" for federal emergency management activities (U.S. Department of Homeland Security 2008b, 2008d; Sylves 2008). Consequently, confusion still exists about FEMA's role vis-à-vis that of its parent Department of Homeland Security.

This makes it extremely difficult for those who are involved in emergency management across all three levels of government to know what they are to do, who they are to follow, and how they are to respond during a major disaster situation (Kettl 2006; Sylves 2008).

Orientations of Disaster Victims

Finally, the orientations of disaster victims affect the size of the gap that develops between bureaucratic and emergent norms. The prevailing values and previous experiences of the affected population play an important role in this respect (Perry and Greene 1983; Quarantelli 1983; Drabek 1986; Wenger 1987; Aguirre, Wenger, and Vigo 1998). Close-knit communities with long traditions of cooperative interaction are more likely to provide mutual support and reinforcement for their members when a disaster strikes. This helps maintain social order during the disruptive situation, and it facilitates a relatively prompt return to "normal," pre-disaster lifestyles. For example, the Cajun communities in rural Louisiana usually experience very little disaster-related disruption, even during the kinds of major floods and hurricanes that would incapacitate most other areas. Similarly, the close interpersonal ties that exist in many midwestern agricultural communities help farmers cope with adverse conditions such as droughts and crop failures. In contrast, other communities have little internal cohesion. The population may be composed of temporary residents or there may be an extremely high level of mobility among the inhabitants. For example, many hurricane-ravaged communities in Florida are populated by resettled northerners. Similarly, an earthquake that strikes an urban area in California may affect thousands of commuters; these people generally live elsewhere, and they have no immediate connection with one another. In either case, social norms may not be well known or clearly articulated. At the same time, people in these latter situations are less likely to turn to those around them for support during disruptive situations. This clearly encourages the breakdown of any pre-established norms that may have existed before a disruptive event. It also leaves an "empty slate" for the establishment of new forms of interaction, thereby facilitating the onset of collective behavior and the widening of the deviation from governmental disaster relief policy.

Another factor affecting the population's orientation is its experience with previous disasters (Drabek 1986; Mileti, Sorenson, and O'Brien 1992; Tierney, Lindell, and Perry 2001). Floods, tornadoes, hurricanes, and blizzards occur frequently in some communities. The people who live in these areas learn how to cope with the kinds of disasters that occur on a somewhat regular basis. They use their past experiences to guide their reactions to subsequent disruptive events. Victims have a basic under-standing of what has happened to them, and they have a general sense of what actions they should take to alleviate their situation (Barton 1969; Dynes 1970; Lindell and Perry 1992; Riad, Norris, and Ruback 1999). Thus, people in riverfront towns begin their clean-up efforts immediately after floodwaters recede. The residents of "tornado alley"—an area in the Midwest frequently hit by tornadoes—start repairing damaged buildings as soon as they know a storm system has passed. And citizens in northern regions quickly clear roadways and re-establish transportation facilitates after major blizzards subside.

In stark contrast, consider a situation where the victims of a disaster have never be-fore experienced, or perhaps even considered, their current predicament. For example, imagine the reactions of people whose town has just been unexpectedly ravaged by a tornado or those of inland residents who have just gone through a major hurricane for the first time. In such instances, the affected population has trouble comprehend-ing what has happened. They also have a great deal of difficulty trying to determine exactly how they can or should respond to the situation. They have no precedents upon which to base their behavior. The nature of the public response is quite uncertain and volatile. In fact, research on this topic indicates that the prior disaster experience is quite variable. For example, citizens who have experience with one type of disaster may not be able to apply that experience to another type of situation, or they may use their prior experiences in appropriate or unhelpful ways (Drabek 1986; Palm, Hodg-son, Blanchard, and Lyons 1990). Thus, it is extremely difficult to assess the impact of citizens' prior experiences on response behavior. This, in turn, can produce very different patterns of interaction, which are almost impossible to anticipate or predict. Consequently, public officials have no established procedures or specific contingen-cies for dealing with these new and different forms of citizen conduct. When this kind of inconsistency occurs, a discrepancy grows between governmental planning and human behavior.

To summarize, the five factors mentioned above—the magnitude of the disaster, the degree of governmental preparedness, the level of communication and coordination, the goals of the governmental response system, and the orientations of disaster victims—influence the way governmental institutions and the affected population respond to a particular disaster situation. Any one of these agents, by itself, can increase the gap between governmental activity and human behavior. However, the larger the number of these factors that exist in any given situation, the greater the probability of a mismatch between governmental plans and public expectations. And the gap between bureaucratic and emergent norms is likely to be extremely wide when large-scale, catastrophic events occur in completely unanticipated circumstances: for example, communities that have not previously experienced such disasters or contexts where governmental preparation is inadequate or inappropriate.

Immediate Consequences and the Inevitability of the Gap

Discrepancies between emergent norms and bureaucratic norms have a direct impact on the operations of the public institutions involved in emergency relief. The gap affects local governments' efforts to mobilize a first response, identify the most critical problems of disaster-stricken areas, and communicate these needs to higher authorities. As we have already seen, local emergency relief agencies are usually understaffed, underfunded, and overburdened (Cigler 1988; Gillespie 1991; Tierney, Lindell, and Perry 2001). Therefore, in order to operate effectively, they must depend on the immediate compliance and orderly behavior of the disaster-stricken population. But this is exactly what breaks down in the presence of emergent norms. The resultant collective behavior, in turn, has a negative impact on the effectiveness of local relief operations. For example, it is impossible to make accurate property damage and personal injury assessments if public officials are busy preventing looting and restoring order within the community.

The gap also affects the actions of state governments in several ways. First, local-level problems have immediate consequences for the state's ability to coordinate and channel additional resources to the affected areas. State officials simply cannot perform this function if they fail to receive the necessary first-hand information from local authorities. Second, local governments themselves often deviate from pre-existing plans, thereby creating further problems for state governments. For one thing, local communities often believe that they are in competition with one another for state emergency relief resources, so they tend to exaggerate the severity of their problems. At the same time, local officials sometimes bypass state governments and appeal directly to federal authorities in the hope that this will expedite relief efforts. And third, state emergency preparedness agencies, like their local counterparts, are often unprepared for realistic disaster conditions. They do not have sufficient resources and personnel to implement their emergency management plans, especially when they are confronted with major catastrophic events. Consequently, they are also incapable of adjusting their operations to meet the new demands that arise from unanticipated forms of human behavior—emergent norms. Thus, several factors related to the gap have a detrimental impact on state governments.

Finally, the gap compromises the effectiveness of the federal government's disaster relief efforts. A great deal of the problem stems from the breakdowns that have already occurred at the lower levels. When the local and state governments fail to carry out their responsibilities, it is impossible to conceive of national authorities "supplementing" their efforts. Instead, federal officials often have to step in and perform "first-response" operations. But once again, this is not supposed to be the national government's primary responsibility within the current and ongoing disaster response system. When federal officials are forced to carry out first-response activities, their attention is deflected away from their own pre-assigned duties. This, in turn, decreases the effectiveness of the overall relief effort.

In summary, the nature and size of the gap between emergent norms and bureaucratic norms has profound consequences for the implementation of disaster assistance efforts. This being the case, it might seem reasonable to assert that everyone involved should try to prevent the gap from developing in the first place. But this is usually impossible to do. The emergence of the gap is an inevitable consequence of a natural disaster situation. Discrepancies between prior planning and existing conditions—that is, the gap—are not particularly surprising given the general difficulties of public policy development in an intergovernmental framework, along with the unusual dilemmas that arise for bureaucratic agencies and affected populations during natural disasters.

The previous literature on intergovernmental relations and policy implementation shows that problems are inevitable when all three levels of government are simultaneously involved in policy development (Pressman and Wildavsky 1973, 1984; Bardach 1977; Edwards 1980; Anton 1989; Palumbo and Calista 1990; Matland 1995; deLeon and deLeon 2002; O'Toole 2006; Agranoff 2007; Mischen 2007; Mischen and Sinclair 2009; Robichau and Lynn 2009).[2] The federal, state, and local governments have widely varying resources, capabilities, and support systems. In addition, each layer of government has its own perspective on policy implementation.

These differences across the three levels of government have created serious difficulties and controversies in a number of important substantive policy areas. For example, consider the problems that have surfaced in American social policy development. All levels of government have important responsibilities in the process: the national government sets the general parameters for many social programs; state governments determine specific program requirements; and local governments direct the actual day-to-day administration of the programs. Although there may appear to be a clear division of labor on paper, it does not work out that way in practice. Over the years there have been continuous struggles across the three levels of government. Disagreements have occurred over who actually determines the funding of, and makes decisions within, social programs. The net result is a very fragmented, disjointed social welfare system with benefits and services varying widely across the nation (Skocpol and Amenta 1986; Cottingham and Ellwood 1989; M. Katz 1989; Winston 2002; Riccucci 2005; Grogger and Karoly 2006; Rodgers 2006). Nobody seems to be in charge of providing services, and nobody seems to have the primary responsibility of controlling the system's development. Intergovernmental relations issues are widely believed to be the root cause of many of the most serious problems in American social welfare programs (Browning 1986; Peterson and Rom 1990; Brown 2006).

These same problems are found in a multitude of policy areas (for example, education, environmental regulation, health care, infrastructure development) that depend upon the intergovernmental framework for program implementation. Therefore, it is not surprising that they exist in the area of disaster response. On paper there is a fully articulated, well-integrated structure to guide the implementation of disaster relief policies across and within governmental levels. In practice, however, the lines of authority and responsibility are unclear, the channels of communication are garbled, and the means for cooperation are blocked. This, in turn, creates serious problems for specific disaster relief efforts.

The previous research on disaster relief emphasizes that disasters, by their very nature, comprise unpredictable, difficult, and diverse events. They can create situations and conditions that are impossible to anticipate. Moreover, they occur in a variety of different forms—hail storms, volcanic eruptions, tidal waves, and so on. Even if a community is prepared for one kind of event, it may not be expecting another type of disaster. Natural disasters also strike in widely varying locations, thereby involving many different and highly diverse public and private institutions. Some of these organizations are reasonably well-equipped to handle natural disasters; others are totally unprepared. In addition, the size and magnitude of disasters are quite variable. Some incidents are relatively small and quite limited in scope, while others may affect large geographic areas and extensive populations. Thus, the sheer uniqueness of each crisis situation contributes to even greater uncertainty about the consistency of the governmental response. It makes it even more likely that disaster relief will not be implemented exactly the same way in all disaster situations.

Three Implementation Patterns for Disaster Relief

Understanding the gap between emergent and bureaucratic norms is critical to understanding the governmental response to natural disasters. The gap influences how disaster assistance will be implemented. Since the size of the gap differs from one disaster situation to the next, we would expect this to create different patterns of policy implementation. Specifically, we can identify three general implementation patterns for disaster assistance in the United States: the "bottom-up," "confusion," and "top-down" approaches.[3] It is important to note that these patterns do not represent pre-established or pre-planned systems of intergovernmental activity. Instead, they characterize the actual behavior of emergency response personnel during natural disaster situations. The three patterns highlight quite different intergovernmental dynamics and tensions within emergency management and recovery efforts. But which pattern accurately describes the relief effort in any given disaster situation? The answer to this question depends upon the degree of agreement or disagreement between the beliefs and expectations of disaster-stricken populations on the one hand and the actions of governmental officials on the other. In short, it is the size of the gap between emergent and bureaucratic norms that determines the nature of policy implementation in governmental disaster relief efforts.

Bottom-Up Approach

The first implementation pattern for disaster relief that we will consider here is one in which the intergovernmental process operates from the bottom up (Lipsky 1978; Elmore 1979; Sabatier 1986; Goggin, Bowman, Lester, and O'Toole 1990). The relief effort begins at the local level. City and county officials provide direct emergency services and assess the scope of damages. If the magnitude of the disaster extends across several local jurisdictions, then the state government becomes involved to mobilize and coordinate activities. It also provides additional resources for local governments to deal with disruptive conditions and the problems of the affected populations. When a disaster is large enough to exceed the state's relief capabilities, then the state officials can appeal to the federal government for further assistance. The federal government supplies a vast array of additional resources that simply do not exist at the state level. Similarly, it can provide financial assistance on a scale that would be impossible if state treasuries were the only sources of funding.

The bottom-up process conforms precisely to the basic governmental response system (described in Chapter Three), which has been designed for the vast majority of disaster situations. For present purposes, it is merely important to emphasize that the different levels of government initiate response activities sequentially rather than simultaneously. As higher levels of government become involved, they work *through* the lower levels; they do not *take over* the entire response and recovery operation.

Some analysts (e.g., May and Williams 1986; Hy and Waugh 1990) have called this system the "shared governance approach" to policy implementation. This seems to imply that the three levels of government have overlapping responsibilities and that they tend to concentrate on the same functions. The term "bottom-up," however, provides a more accurate and graphic description for this pattern of policy implementation. Instead of sharing responsibilities, a clear division of labor exists, with each level of government focusing on distinct duties and activities. Furthermore, the officials who are actually involved in disaster relief use the terms "up" and "down" to describe their own perceptions about the intergovernmental structure of policy implementation (McAda 1989). They clearly believe that, when the system works as it is intended, the needs of the affected population will be communicated upward and appropriate assistance will be channeled back down. Of course, the terms "up" and "down" refer to a path that leads from the local governments through the states and ultimately to the federal government and vice versa. This system makes the most effective use of public officials' expertise and knowledge of local conditions. It also provides the most efficient allocation of intergovernmental resources.

The bottom-up implementation pattern can only occur when the gap between bureaucratic norms and the emergent norms that follows a natural disaster is quite small. This small gap develops when two conditions are met simultaneously. First, public officials must carry out their duties in a manner that is consistent with pre-existing emergency management plans. They are attentive to their own duties and do not encroach on the responsibilities of other officials and agencies. This first condition is contingent upon a second provision: the behavior of the affected population conforms to prior expectations. In other words, emergent norms do not deviate very sharply from those anticipated in the standard, pre-disaster guidelines (formal and informal) developed by the affected communities.

This kind of outcome characterizes the majority of disaster situations that arise in the United States. Midwestern tornadoes can cause serious disruptions in the social systems of that region. Both the government and the public, however, usually react to these situations in a relatively routine manner. Consequently, these major disasters can be handled and resolved with very little public attention beyond that of those citizens and public agencies immediately involved. The rest of the country may not even be aware that a natural catastrophe has occurred. This lack of widespread popular concern is one of the key elements of a successful relief effort.

Confusion Pattern

As its very name implies, the confusion pattern of policy implementation is difficult to describe succinctly. Many different kinds of disaster-related situations fall under this general heading. For example, the confusion can arise very quickly. This occurs when public officials fail to mobilize a response in the immediate aftermath of a natural disaster. Local governments may be unprepared either because the disaster itself was unexpected or because officials have received inadequate training. Alternatively, they may be unwilling or incapable of acting because local capacities are overwhelmed by the magnitude or severity of the disaster. Similarly, the state and national governments may hesitate because they are waiting for the lower levels to take the first initiative. Regardless of the exact reason, the confusion pattern can develop quickly, when government fails to establish a clear presence in the affected area, and does not make itself visible to the stricken population.

The confusion implementation pattern can also develop more slowly. This occurs when governments initiate responses, but fail to monitor their own activities very closely. Public officials may take the initiative, and, in so doing, depart from their assigned tasks. For example, a local leader may request federal assistance without going through appropriate channels at the state or national levels. At the same time, state personnel may try to handle a situation on their own, thereby delaying the delivery of critical resources and supplies from *other* states and the federal government. When these conditions exist, the public may be aware of a great deal of governmental activity. However, there is no overall framework or general order to guide the emergency response effort. As a result, specific response activities may be isolated and ineffective, or redundant and wasteful. The only appropriate term to describe such conditions is "confusion."

The confusion implementation pattern is likely to occur when a moderately sized gap develops between bureaucratic and emergent norms. In most cases, relief efforts are already underway and disaster victims are trying to deal with their own problems. However, the process develops in such a way that the two sets of actors tend to "work past each other" rather than in coordinated ways that effectively resolve the disaster conditions.

The confusion pattern can stem from the actions of emergency management officials, the behavior of disaster victims, or both. Public officials may act, but they fail to abide by standard operating procedures. At the same time, disaster victims may behave in ways that may be rational, reasonable responses to existing conditions; but they are simply unanticipated in the government's emergency response plans. For example, citizens may refuse to evacuate a threatened area or they may insist on returning to their communities before the latter are deemed safe. Similarly, people may rebuff governmental offers of assistance, such as tents and mobile homes, or they may demand forms of relief that not readily available, such as restoration of utility services, reconstruction supplies, and so on.

In any case, the confusion pattern does not signal a *complete* breakdown of the social order or of the governmental response system. Instead, everyone involved is taking steps that they themselves perceive to be reasonable reactions to the existing situation (Anton 1989; O'Toole 2000). These actions simply do not conform to prior expectations or plans. And as a result, they have an unintentionally detrimental affect on the governmental relief effort. The confusion pattern impairs efficiency and it slows down the response effort.

As an example of this confusion implementation pattern, consider a major volcano that becomes active in a region that has little recent history of geological activity—Mount St. Helens. Emergency preparedness officials in the United States have little previous experience with volcanoes, so they are very uncertain about what needs to be done. They try to respond to the situation, but only do so in a confused, makeshift manner. Similarly, the public has had no prior contact with volcanic activity; hence, people do not know what to do to prepare for, or protect themselves from, a major eruption. In this kind of situation, little ties together bureaucratic procedures and patterns of human behavior. So the gap between the two widens. The response appears slow, misguided, and confused, and frequent charges of governmental non-responsiveness and ineffectiveness are made. In the end, the government receives mixed reviews for its relief and assistance efforts (May 1985b). Its motives are not really at issue, but its specific actions, operations, and its ability to deliver needed services are seriously questioned.

Top-Down Approach

Finally, disaster relief could be implemented from the top down (Mazmanian and Sabatier 1983; Sabatier 1986; Goggin, Bowman, Lester, and O'Toole 1990; Weible,

Sabatier, and Lubell 2004). This pattern can be described very simply: the federal government steps in and takes control of emergency management activities. U.S. military personnel are sent to stabilize the situation, restore order within affected communities, and open up lines of transportation and communication to the external environment. At the same time, federal officials assume responsibility for mobilizing and coordinating critical resources, equipment, and personnel: they do not wait for state and local personnel to ask for help or until their resources and capabilities are overwhelmed. The national government becomes the focal point of the relief effort.

The top-down implementation pattern differs markedly from the standard governmental response system that has been designed to handle the vast majority of disasters. In the top-down pattern there is no rolling or "bubbling up" process of intergovernmental activity, starting at the local level, moving up through the states and beyond. Instead, the federal government assumes a proactive, leadership role in the process, in order to coordinate and mobilize essential resources. Local and state authorities are still required to provide assistance, help assess damages, and distribute aid to disaster-stricken populations. But their participation is much more limited and subordinate in nature. Essentially, the national government bears most of the responsibility for the emergency relief and recovery activities.

The top-down pattern is likely to occur when an extremely wide gap between bureaucratic procedures and the behavior of disaster victims develops. Radical inconsistencies of this type develop when two conditions arise simultaneously. First, subnational governments cease to exist as meaningful entities. Public officials may be disaster victims themselves; as such, they are incapable of addressing other people's problems no matter how serious they may be. Or local and state governmental authorities may be incapable of contacting their constituents. When communication channels breakdown, it is difficult for public officials to be able to direct emergency response or relief efforts.

The second condition that causes an extremely wide gap is closely related to the lack of governmental authority. Emergent norms may encourage forms of human behavior that would be considered unusual, unconventional, or even illegal under normal circumstances. People may resort to hostile or aggressive acts against others in order to protect their own lives or personal property. They may also engage in activities to obtain critical supplies for themselves and their families. Or people may simply refuse to obey instructions from authorities if they perceive the latter to be ineffective or inappropriate for the given situation. In any case, the demands of the disaster situation completely outstrip the capacities of local and state governmental institutions. The federal government has no choice but to step in and take charge of the response effort.

Superficially, the top-down implementation pattern may seem like the most effective way of dealing with natural disasters, particularly catastrophic events.[4] This is precisely why the federal government presented a variant of the top-down process to handle what it initially referred to as "incidents of national significance." According to this process, the national government should assume a proactive, leadership role during extraordinarily severe circumstances; it should not wait for requests to work their way up through the system. Such action is deemed necessary in order to ensure that all available resources are quickly and efficiently mobilized. In essence, the response should be initiated and coordinated from the top down. Thus, recent policy changes have given legitimacy to the top-down implementation pattern of emergency relief, recognizing that it is the only feasible strategy for addressing large-scale disaster situations.

However, it is important to note that this top-down process for dealing with unusually severe events has never been fully developed. It was first presented in 2003 as a way of dealing with incidents of national significance But it was not clear what types of events qualified as incidents of national significance, what the national government should do if such circumstances developed, or how other assistance would flow through the intergovernmental framework. These problems contributed to the breakdown of governmental relief efforts in 2005 during the response to Hurricane Katrina. As a result, the national government has tried to refine the process, clarifying the roles and responsibilities of various governmental officials. Current policy identifies a proactive leadership role for the national government during unusually severe, difficult situations. But it also emphasizes that the national government should *not* take control of the entire relief effort. Instead, federal officials should continue working closely with state, local, and private organizations. In essence, this means that the national government can "jump start" the response, but it must still use the standard, bottom-up intergovernmental framework to mobilize, coordinate, and deliver emergency assistance.

In practice, top-down responses have not operated very smoothly or effectively. For one thing, the nation's emergency management system has not developed clear policies or protocols to guide top-down responses. It has, however, established fairly extensive standard operating procedures to handle less severe types of events that occur more frequently. As a result, emergency management personnel are simply much more familiar with the bottom-up approach for handling major natural disasters.

In addition, federal personnel do not have the ability to mobilize an effective top-down governmental response. Federal personnel simply are not equipped to carry out the responsibilities of local officials, such as mayors, county administrators, law enforcement officials, and so on. They do not have the legal authority to step in and take over the operations of lower-level governmental jurisdictions. In addition, they usually are unfamiliar with the details and particulars of local conditions and situations. This situation is exacerbated by the fact that federal administrators often do not want to exercise these functions, and are accordingly very hesitant to do so. They are trained to follow a basic set of policies and guidelines that stress the national government's *supplementary* role in emergency management.

Moreover, it is still not exactly clear who is in charge at the national level and who would lead a top-down response. Prior to 2001, FEMA was the chief federal agency for emergency management. But FEMA did not always perform this role in a consistent manner. At times, FEMA was unable to obtain cooperation from other federal agencies; it was uncertain of its own roles and responsibilities; it lacked the leadership to perform its duties; and it was often severely under-funded and under-staffed. When the Department of Homeland Security was created in 2003, DHS, specifically the secretary of DHS, was given the primary responsibility for leading the federal government's response to major, catastrophic events—initially identified as incidents of national significance. But DHS never developed the necessary protocols or procedures to conduct a top-down response during these situations, and emergency management personnel throughout the system were not prepared to implement such a process. As a result of the Post-Katrina Reform Act, FEMA was once again placed in charge of the federal government's relief efforts. But FEMA remains a unit within the larger Department of Homeland Security; the FEMA Director still reports to the secretary of DHS; and specific protocols to guide a more proactive federal response have not been fully developed or circulated. For all of these reasons, the top-down pattern is still unlikely to result in an effective governmental response to a major natural disaster situation.

In situations like this, the government faces a serious dilemma. No matter what the government tries to do, its actions will probably be intensely criticized. Most private citizens cannot be expected to fully comprehend the difficulties and complexities involved in any recovery effort: they depend upon the government for guidance and assistance. At the same time, disaster-stricken individuals are naturally absorbed with their own personal problems caused by the disaster. So the public is likely to be dissatisfied with anything short of immediate, direct, and comprehensive help. This leads to widespread criticism of governmental activities, and, in the end, it produces the impression that the governmental response is a failure.

Fortunately, the extreme catastrophes that tend to necessitate a top-down response pattern have been relatively rare. One example would be the 1955 flooding that occurred throughout the New England region. Conditions were so severe that local and state authorities were immediately overburdened by the demands placed upon them. In what was a pathbreaking effort at the time, the federal government stepped in to provide flood insurance, loan contracts, and re-insurance for the affected population. These actions set an important precedent that future disaster victims would automatically be eligible for similar kinds of federal assistance (May 1985b). In short, the top-down governmental response seemed to be required by the magnitude of the 1955 disaster. This action, however, did not preclude the development of broader criticisms of the entire governmental effort. There was a widespread belief that the government failed to alleviate the adverse conditions caused by the floods. In the end, the federal government's efforts were still judged to be inadequate; this popular perception caused both short-term problems for flood victims and longer-term problems for public expectations about disaster relief.

As we shall see, more recent instances of the top-down response pattern have not been any more successful.[5] Even when it seems clear that more direct and extensive federal-level intervention is required, the national government has responded slowly, inconsistently, and ineffectively. This, in turn, has created serious problems for the entire governmental relief system. And it has also left a lasting negative impression on the American psyche about the government's ability to handle natural disaster situations.

In summary, the gap between bureaucratic norms and emergent norms is a critical component of the disaster response process. It determines which of three policy implementation patterns will be put into effect in any given disaster situation. This, in turn, has a direct bearing on the nature and effectiveness of the entire governmental response process. It affects the allocation of scarce governmental resources during times when demands for these resources are particularly vocal and strident. It determines the speed and efficiency with which disaster victims are able to obtain needed assistance. It also affects broader perceptions about the government's ability to cope with natural disasters. Stated simply, the size of the gap ultimately determines whether the public perceives the government's disaster relief efforts to be successes or failures.

From a more objective perspective, virtually all governmental relief efforts could be easily labeled "successes." Over the last twenty years, the federal government has assisted hundreds of thousands of citizens across the nation recover from dozens of natural disasters, with costs running in the billions of dollars (Federal Emergency Management Agency 2010v, 2011b). Moreover, the governmental response system has successfully restored many disaster-stricken areas to their earlier, pre-disaster conditions (U.S. General Accounting Office 1989; Rosenbaum 2003). In fact, some analysts have argued that the government's disaster relief funds have enabled some communities to markedly improve their conditions (Wolensky and Wolensky 1991; Platt 1999; Miskel 2008); ironically, they may even end up better off as a result of the natural disaster. For example, disaster assistance funds are used to construct newer, stronger private homes and places of businesses. Similarly, disaster relief is often used to redesign and rebuild public works, such as bridges, dams, and roadways.

But objective indicators of governmental efforts are often outweighed by subjective assessments of disaster situations. Stated simply, the acknowledged success or failure of the governmental response is almost entirely a matter of public perception. And citizens' perceptions about relief activities are often strongly influenced by the media. For a number of reasons, the media tend to focus on the problematic aspects of a response and recovery operation, rather than the smooth, predictable, but less exciting process of implementing emergency aid (Scanlon, Alldred, Farrell, and Prawzick 1985; Masel-Walters, Wilkins, and Walters 1989; Goldman and Reilly 1992; West and Orr 2007). News reports about orderly evacuations and the efficient distribution of supplies can present the picture of a successful response. Unfortunately, however, they cannot compete with other more striking images or portrayals of other aspects of the disaster situation, some of which may not be backed up or supported by more systematic data or verification. Stories about waste, fraud, and mismanagement in the allocation of relief funds are frequently the topic of news reports, and they convey the image of governmental incompetence or dishonesty (Bandy 1989a, 1989b; "After Katrina, A Deadly Nightmare" 2005; Tierney, Bevc, and Kuligowski 2006). Similarly, vivid media reports of looting, martial law, and acute scarcities of vital supplies suggest the complete breakdown of governmental authority and societal order (Wenger and Quarantelli 1989; Quarantelli 1991c; Barsky, Trainor, and Torres 2006; Tierney, Bevc, and Kuligowski 2006; Scanlon 2008). But again all of these circumstances are by-products of the size of the gap. Thus, it is no exaggeration to say that the gap between bureaucratic norms and emergent norms provides an accurate mechanism for identifying and explaining the success or failure of governmental disaster relief efforts.

Notes

1. The term "gap" is used in this analysis because that same term was used spontaneously and independently by several officials who were directly involved in the disaster relief efforts examined for the first edition of this study. And this particular term seems to capture the precise phenomenon of interest—discrepancy between bureaucratic principles and public expectations. Hence, I have continued to use "the gap" to describe the discrepancy that can exist between emergent and bureaucratic norms during natural disaster situations.

2. For more information on the problems of implementing public policies in the American federal system, see Van Meter and Van Horn (1976), Bardach (1977), Lipsky (1978), Nakamura and Smallwood (1980), Williams (1980), Mazmanian and Sabatier (1983), Goggin, Bowman, Lester, and O'Toole (1990), Ripley and Franklin (1991), Scheberle (2004), and Honig (2006).

3. The three implementation patterns described in this study are most similar to the intergovernmental policy models presented by Sabatier (1986) and Anton (1989). They also resemble the two approaches mentioned in Weible, Sabatier, and Lubell (2004). There are, however, some basic differences. For example, Anton calls the confusion model a "diffusion" pattern; Sabatier concentrates almost entirely on the top-down and bottom-up approaches, giving little attention to anything in between the two extremes; and Weible and his co-authors compare the top-down approach to collaborative management, stressing the differences in stakeholders' preferences between these two in scientific decision making. For more on the impact of the intergovernmental framework on policy implementation, see Elazar (1962), Grodzins (1966), Sundquist (1969), Peterson (1981), Chubb (1985), and Wright (1988), Stephens and Wickstrom (2006), O'Toole (2006), and Agranoff (2007).

4. Over the years, there have been a number of recommendations to change the entire governmental response system. Some of these recommendations propose some type of top-down framework of policy implementation; others stress ways of strengthening the basic bottom-up framework by improving communication and collaboration between and among governmental units, as well as with the general public. These suggestions will be discussed in greater detail in the last chapter of the book.

5. Other more recent examples of the top-down pattern are examined in Chapter Seven—governmental response to Hurricane Hugo in the Caribbean Islands—and in Chapter Twelve—the governmental response to Hurricane Katrina in Louisiana.

Part Two

Case Studies of Natural Disasters

6

A General Framework for Examining the Success or Failure of the Governmental Response to Natural Disasters

Up to this point, the discussion has been couched in fairly abstract terms with virtually no coverage given to specific events that have occurred in actual natural disasters. For present purposes, this general orientation is preferable to a more detailed, particularistic approach precisely because it directs our attention toward the common patterns of human behavior that occur during and after natural disasters. Otherwise it is all too easy to think of specific disasters as totally unique events. After all, many different phenomena fall under the general heading of "disaster": severe floods, tropical storms, volcanic eruptions, earthquakes, and so on. Moreover, these cataclysmic events occur in a wide variety of settings: river valleys, ocean coastlines, midwestern plains, mountainous areas, and so on. The apparent uniqueness of these events is further emphasized by the mass media, who link each natural disaster with its own set of potent, nearly unforgettable images: devastated forests marking the destructive swath of a hurricane; homes toppling down cliffs during mudslides; automobiles disappearing into a gap torn into a roadway by an earthquake; and dejected farmers paddling boats through water that covers normally dry fields.

If natural disasters truly are unique events, then it would be impossible to prepare effectively for them or to deal systematically with their destruction and disruption. But across the nation, communities *do* have plans for handling disasters, from the evacuation routes that exist along the southeastern seaboard, through the tornado drills carried out in midwestern schools and businesses, to the earthquake simulations held by officials along the West Coast. At the same time, communities and people *do* recover from disasters. In most cases, the physical destruction caused by hurricanes, tornadoes, and floods is repaired very quickly. In other situations, the physical evidence of the disaster may be longer lasting: collapsed overpasses in the California freeway system following major earthquakes; the deforestation of productive timberlands following east coast hurricanes; and the major beach erosion that results from the pounding of coastal storms. But even in many extreme cases, most people adjust to the situation and get on with their lives (Friesema, Caporaso, Goldstein, Lineberry, and McCleary 1979; Wright, Rossi, Wright, and Weber-Burdin 1979; Wright and Rossi 1981; Petak and Atkisson 1982; May 1985b; U.S. General Accounting Office 1991). The historical record shows that the American public can cope with natural disasters.[1] However, it is far easier to see this if we take a more comprehensive approach, rather than viewing each disaster as an isolated incident. This, in turn, requires a general framework for understanding disaster-related behavior regardless of the specific nature or details of the disaster situations themselves.

In fact, the governmental response system is itself based upon a comprehensive view. Since the 1970s, the federal government has promoted an "all-hazards" approach to emergency management that stresses the common or generic elements of disasters, instead of their unique qualities. This enables emergency management personnel to develop standard operating procedures to cover any type of contingency, no matter when or where it occurs. And it also allows disaster relief organizations to plan and prepare for a wide variety of disasters, whether they are man-made or natural in origin. Such an approach definitely has its advantages: it is certainly more cost-effective to develop a single disaster response plan, rather than a number of different ones for each type of emergency (Sylves 2008).

But this generic approach can also have a detrimental impact on response operations by imposing a rigid, inflexible structure to the process. In some situations, public officials may not be able to adjust their activities to meet the unique needs of a specific disaster situation. And they may simply not have sufficient training, expertise, or resources to handle different types of emergency situations. As a result, the comprehensive, "all-hazards" nature of disaster response planning itself can have a detrimental impact on the response and recovery process. A more effective, flexible framework is needed—one that integrates both the common elements of emergency management and the unique behavioral components of particular disaster situations (Waugh and Streib 2006; Comfort 2007).

The concept of the gap between bureaucratic norms and emergent norms can be used as exactly this kind of framework. It provides a parsimonious means of subsuming many specific activities, carried out by a wide array of different actors—primarily governmental emergency management personnel and disaster victims within the affected population. The notion of the gap serves as a skeletal structure. It can be "fleshed out" with details of the many different natural disasters that have hit the United States in the past. The gap also provides an ongoing mechanism for viewing and understanding future disasters that will inevitably occur. The overall objective in the following chapters is to show how this can be done.

Part Two covers the governmental responses to a series of natural disasters: Hurricane Hugo in the Caribbean, South Carolina, and North Carolina in September 1989; the Loma Prieta Earthquake in California on October 17, 1989; Hurricane Andrew in South Florida and Louisiana in August 1993; the Los Angeles Earthquake of 1994; Hurricane Georges in Puerto Rico, the Florida Keys, and along the Gulf Coast in September 1998; Hurricane Katrina in Louisiana and Mississippi during August 2005; and major flooding that occurred in the states of South Carolina during the fall of 1990 and Tennessee in the spring 2010. Note that for the purposes of this study, several of the hurricanes actually comprise a number of distinct disaster situations: two in the case of Andrew and Katrina; three in the case of Hugo and Georges. Although there was only a single storm in each case, the relief and recovery operations varied across these different political jurisdictions. At the same time, the affected populations within each state, and within U.S. territories in the case of Hugo and Georges, reacted quite differently to the respective hurricanes. For these reasons it is more appropriate to treat the various responses to Hugo, Andrew, and Georges as separate incidents.

These particular events have been selected as case studies for three basic reasons. First, the seven situations share some common characteristics. One obvious similarity is their severity: they all unambiguously qualify as *major* natural disasters, which placed unusually difficult burdens on governmental institutions and processes. In addition, all of these disasters occurred from September 1989 to May 2010. Thus, the events that will be analyzed took place across a relatively long time frame. This is important because it allows us to also look at the changes that have occurred in the governmental response structure over this period. As we will see, the effectiveness of the response process varies widely across these seven major disasters.

The second reason for selecting these disasters is that they clearly illustrate the wide variability in the perceived effectiveness of the governmental response. At one extreme, there is the complete collapse of the governmental response system in the Caribbean Islands following Hurricane Hugo. At the other end of the continuum, there is the calm, successful resolution of problems during the 1990 South Carolina floods and to a lesser extent during the 2010 Tennessee severe rains and floods. The other cases fall at intermediate points along the success/failure dimension. The governmental responses to Hurricane Katrina in Louisiana, Hurricane Andrew in Florida, and Hurricane Hugo in South Carolina are located closer to the failure pole. The relief efforts associated with the Loma Prieta Earthquake, Hurricane Georges in Puerto Rico, and Hurricane Katrina in Mississippi are positioned almost exactly midway between the two extremes. The remaining responses—Hurricane Hugo in North Carolina, Hurricane Andrew in Louisiana, Hurricane Georges along the Gulf Coast and the Florida Keys, and the Los Angeles Earthquake—are much closer to the success side. Thus, the disasters that will be examined here truly illustrate the full range of perceived success and failure in governmental disaster responses. The approximate placement of each of the case studies on the success/failure continuum is shown in Figure 6.1.

Third, these disasters occurred during different time periods, illustrating the evolution of emergency management policy in the United States since the late 1980s. Several of the events, such as Hurricane Hugo, Hurricane Andrew, the Loma Prieta Earthquake, and the South Carolina floods, happened in the late 1980s and early 1990s. Although a national response framework was in place at this time, it was not clearly articulated, well supported, or sufficiently developed (S. Schneider 1992). Hurricane Georges occurred during the "golden" days of emergency management in the United States (S. Schneider 1998). National, state, and local organizations received more resources and were viewed with more credibility, enabling them to strengthen their disaster response management capabilities (Sylves 2008). Hurricane Katrina struck in the summer of 2005. By this point, the nation's disaster response framework had been redirected away from natural disasters toward anti-terrorist–related operations.

Figure 6.1 **Continuum Showing Relative Successes and Failures of Selected Governmental Responses to Natural Disasters**

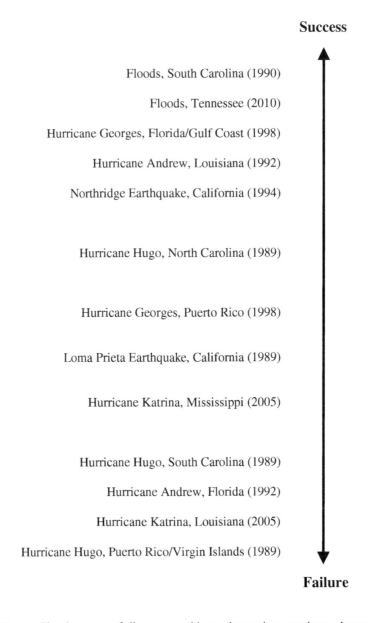

Success

Floods, South Carolina (1990)

Floods, Tennessee (2010)

Hurricane Georges, Florida/Gulf Coast (1998)

Hurricane Andrew, Louisiana (1992)

Northridge Earthquake, California (1994)

Hurricane Hugo, North Carolina (1989)

Hurricane Georges, Puerto Rico (1998)

Loma Prieta Earthquake, California (1989)

Hurricane Katrina, Mississippi (2005)

Hurricane Hugo, South Carolina (1989)

Hurricane Andrew, Florida (1992)

Hurricane Katrina, Louisiana (2005)

Hurricane Hugo, Puerto Rico/Virgin Islands (1989)

Failure

Note: The specific placement of disasters on this continuum is approximate; however, the ordering conforms to the analysis presented in this study.

Although the government advocated comprehensive policies to handle any and all types of disasters, natural disasters were clearly not receiving the same degree of attention as other types of man-made situations (Kettl 2006; Waugh 2006a; Harrald 2007; Sylves 2008). The severe rains and floods that developed in Tennessee during May of 2010 occurred after the governmental response system had been re-focused, once again. Because of the collapse of the system in 2005 during Hurricane Katrina, a number of modifications were made in the response process to improve the capabilities of emergency management personnel, the coordination between agencies, and the overall "chain of command" for emergency responses. As we shall see, changes within the emergency response system have noticeable impacts on the success and/or failure of the governmental relief efforts.

The case studies presented here in Part Two are not intended to provide complete descriptions of the disasters discussed.[2] Instead, the coverage will focus on the factors that contribute most directly to the effectiveness of governmental relief efforts: emergent norms; bureaucratic norms; the size of the gap between the two sets of norms; and the resultant pattern of policy implementation in the response process— top-down, confusion, or bottom-up. Once again, by focusing on the common features of seven events that seem to be vastly different, I hope to demonstrate that a general and discernible structure underlies the ways that private citizens and public officials behave during natural disasters. This immediately contributes to the more general objective of this study: a clearer understanding of why some governmental disaster responses are believed to be successful, while others are deemed to be failures. It also provides insights into how the governmental response process can be strengthened, so that public organizations can address future disasters in a more effective and efficient manner.

Notes

1. It is important to recognize that there are many different types of disaster-related consequences. These include the more obvious physical changes to the natural environment as well as the severe economic losses to families, businesses, and public entities. Disasters can also produce psychological disruptions and changes within individual disaster victims that are less visible, but perhaps more profound. Clearly, some of these problems are more easily handled than others. Moreover, the recovery process may not be the same for all members of the affected population. There is evidence to suggest that low-income individuals do not recover as quickly or as completely from a disaster situation as do victims from middle- or upper-income groups (Cochrane 1975; Rossi, Wright, and Weber-Burdin 1978; Petak and Atkisson 1982; Wright et al. 1983; May 1985b; Cochrane 1990). Further support for the differential impact of disasters across various population groups is also provided in several of the case studies described in this book.

2. The specific events associated with these seven disaster situations have been described in detail in many newspapers and news magazines. For information on many of these disasters, see the *New York Times*, *Washington Post*, *Time*, and *Newsweek*. For specific information about any particular event, see local newspaper archives (that is, the *Miami Herald* for Hurricane Andrew, *Times-Picayune* for Hurricane Katrina in Louisiana, *The State* for Hurricane Hugo in South Carolina, *Los Angeles Times* for the Northridge Earthquake, and so forth).

7

Hurricane Hugo

Hurricane Hugo is the first natural disaster discussed in this book. Hugo was a massive Category Four hurricane that caused extensive damage to U.S. territory in the Caribbean and to the U.S. mainland, particularly in the states of South and North Carolina. According to the Federal Emergency Management Agency (FEMA), Hurricane Hugo ranks as the tenth most costly disaster in the United States, in terms of money distributed through the federal government's disaster relief fund (Federal Emergency Management Agency 2010v).

As we shall see, this event demonstrates the wide variability of the governmental response to disasters. In fact, all three patterns of policy implementation occurred as a result of one hurricane. The normal response process broke down completely in the Caribbean, leading to widespread confusion and discontent among the affected population. This situation, in turn, forced the government to implement relief from the top down. In South Carolina, governmental operations unfolded slowly and sporadically, causing the disaster-stricken population to become very frustrated with, and critical of, the relief efforts. This, in turn, created a very confused pattern of policy implementation. The situation was quite different in North Carolina, where, the government was able to invoke standard operating procedures and policies that facilitated the distribution of emergency assistance to those in need. In the end, the response to Hurricane Hugo in North Carolina proceeded from the bottom up in a fairly smooth and routine manner with minimal fanfare and public discontent. The rest of this chapter examines each of these three disaster situations caused by Hurricane Hugo.

Hurricane Hugo in the Caribbean

Hurricane Hugo began as a band of thunderstorms off the coast of Africa. It was upgraded to a tropical storm on September 11, and then given hurricane status a few days later. It first touched American territory in the Caribbean. On September 18, 1989, Hugo slammed into the U.S. Virgin Islands, including St. Croix, St. John, and St. Thomas. On the following day, it struck Puerto Rico. After assaulting the northeast portion of Puerto Rico with 125 mile per hour winds and ten to twenty inches of rain, the huge storm headed back out into the Atlantic Ocean. But Hurricane Hugo had already transformed the islands of the Caribbean from a tropical paradise into a tropical nightmare.

Parts of buildings, pieces of furniture, and articles of clothing were thrown everywhere. Trees were stripped of their leaves and uprooted. Roofs were torn from homes

Severe housing damage near the airport on Culebra, Puerto Rico, due to Hurricane Hugo, September 1989. *(National Oceanic and Atmospheric Administration photo by Dr. Joseph Golden)*

and businesses. Entire neighborhoods were leveled. Electrical power was knocked out. Water and sewer systems were disrupted. In its wake, Hugo left at least eighteen people dead, thousands more homeless, and over $1 billion in physical destruction. On the island of St. Croix alone, 95 percent of the buildings were damaged and nine out of ten citizens experienced storm-related damages (U.S. General Accounting Office 1991).[1]

The destruction caused by Hugo in the U.S. Virgin Islands and Puerto Rico was so massive that it could not be handled by individual citizens or private organizations. Clearly, governmental resources were needed, yet conditions on the islands made it extremely difficult for any governmental entity to initiate a relief effort. A sizable gap developed between the norms that guided the behavior of disaster-stricken victims and the government's pre-existing plans and policies. Thus, emergency management agencies had to circumvent standard operating procedures and design a top-down method of implementing disaster relief. Eventually, the governmental response system was able to provide critical assistance to disaster-stricken areas. But the public perception was, and is, that the government's response to Hurricane Hugo in the Caribbean "failed."

Development of Emergent Norms: Deviant Behavior

In the Caribbean, the milling process began immediately after the hurricane. Hugo destroyed virtually all transportation and communication systems on the islands.

This made it difficult for individuals to contact others who were also affected by the storm. "Thousands of . . . citizens wandered dazed through the streets . . . amid almost unbelievable wreckage" (Harrison 1989). Moreover, the damages were so severe that local inhabitants could not communicate with the outside world. In the words of one disaster victim, "As far as we knew, the rest of the world had disappeared" (Branigin 1989b).

Reports from survivors indicated a general feeling of helplessness and alienation. An officer in the Virgin Islands National Guard remarked: "In all my military experience, I had never seen anything like it" (Branigin 1989b, p. A1). But the severity of the situation is perhaps best summed up in the statement of one local resident: "It looked and felt like the day after a nuclear holocaust" (Branigin, 1989b, p. A1)

Local and territorial leaders were similarly disoriented and paralyzed. They, themselves, were unprepared and ill-equipped to provide guidance or assistance to their own citizens, particularly in the face of such a cataclysmic event. During the first twenty-four hours of the crisis, most local police and territorial emergency management personnel could not even be located by their superiors, let alone be called upon to respond to the situation (Branigin 1989b). Consequently, island authorities were unable to alleviate the most pressing conditions and to maintain social order within the disaster-stricken areas. This created a truly non-institutionalized situation where traditional norms and values did not apply at all.

Local residents engaged in activities that they would not even consider during more normal circumstances. Widespread looting and domestic violence erupted on the islands of St. Thomas, San Juan, Guadeloupe, and St. Croix (York 1989). In the words of an American tourist who was vacationing on the island of St. Croix, "There was no control. There was anarchy in town" (Harrison 1989). Others described the situation as carnival-like, punctuated by periods of rampant hysteria and looting frenzies (Branigin 1989b). There were reports that gangs of citizens roamed the streets of Christiansted in St. Croix with rifles, ransacking local stores and businesses. Virtually everything worth taking was stolen. These chaotic, near-anarchic conditions existed for several days in some of the disaster-stricken areas that were hardest hit.

Keynoting behavior took place when acts of social deviance went unpunished. Territorial leaders were unable to stop the looting and pilfering; consequently, they implicitly encouraged more such acts. In addition, local officials may have even played a more direct role in this process: there were numerous reports that some local police, national guardsmen, and political leaders were actual participants, not just innocent bystanders, in the looting frenzy (Branigin 1989b; Christian 1992). Thus, deviant behavior emerged as a new norm. It is important to emphasize that this deviant behavior was not the result of criminal activity within one segment of society. Instead, it represented the actions of a broad cross-section of normal citizens. Literally thousands of island residents from all age groups and from all social strata engaged in looting activity. Small children and old women alike were spotted among the mobs, grabbing merchandise from local stores (Harrison 1989); poor residents from public housing projects, as well as some of the most prominent island citizens, were charged with offenses ranging from grand larceny to possession of stolen goods (Branigin 1989b). Amazingly, however, very few incidents of personal violence or malicious acts occurred. Most participants simply got "caught up" in undisciplined, unsupervised conduct. According to one analyst, "They had the opportunity and they took it" (York 1989). Most of the looting and pilfering appeared to be primarily motivated by panic and hysteria. The vast majority of residents who engaged in unorthodox activities were simply trying to obtain the basic necessities of life, which were in extremely short supply. Their actions quickly developed into normal behavior.

Bureaucratic Norms and the Governmental Response

All of these conditions made it extremely difficult for the government to administer disaster assistance using routine procedures and processes. To start, territorial officials on the islands could not even ask for help from the national government. By law, only the governor of a territory or state can request federal assistance, and the federal government has been unwilling to bend this rule no matter how severe the situation.

Yet, the governor of the Virgin Islands, Alexander Farrelly, could not be contacted. He was on the island of St. Thomas, and he had no means of communicating with officials on the other side of the island, let alone with the U.S. mainland. Fortunately, he had access to a ham radio. When federal officials discovered this, they set up a special high-frequency radio communication channel. This makeshift device enabled Governor Farrelly to submit a verbal request for federal aid. Two hours later, President George H.W. Bush declared the Virgin Islands a "major disaster." Almost immediately after this, the federal government received another verbal request for federal assistance—this time from Governor Rafael Hernandez Colon of Puerto Rico. Within a matter of hours, President Bush declared another emergency, this time in Puerto Rico (G. Peterson 1989). Now, the federal government could officially initiate a full-scale response to both disaster situations.

The national government had to deal with three immediate problems in the Caribbean (G. Peterson 1989). First, it had to address the general breakdown in civil order. Public officials had to stop the looting and vandalism, and counter the development of additional chaotic acts. Second, the government had to resolve life-threatening issues. Island water supplies had been contaminated, food reserves destroyed, and shelters demolished. The third problem was air traffic control. Even in normal times, the islands depend entirely on outside resources and support for subsistence. However, all U.S. air traffic in the Caribbean is controlled from Puerto Rico, and Hugo had knocked out those facilities. Thus, there were severe difficulties in reaching the islands.

Agencies from the government, particularly at the federal level, worked fairly quickly to address these problems (McAda 1989). The Federal Emergency Management Agency established a temporary mechanism for directing air traffic in the U.S. territory of the Caribbean. Then the agency authorized an airlift of millions of pounds of water, food, and plastic sheeting, to be used as makeshift covers, for the islands.

FEMA also had electrical generators, utility equipment, and medical supplies flown in from the mainland to restore essential services as quickly as possible. Finally, President Bush dispatched federal law enforcement officials and military police to the islands in order to restore social stability and public order.

Once the most immediate problems had been alleviated, national governmental organizations could begin to administer the basic package of disaster assistance programs. FEMA was the main coordinating force, overseeing the delivery of supplies and equipment to the Virgin Islands and Puerto Rico. First, the agency established field headquarters on the islands as well as a number of Disaster Assistance Centers (DACs) in several locations in islands. Then it began the process of accepting claims, verifying their content, and dispensing funds to the needy. FEMA also constructed thousands of makeshift housing facilities and airlifted tons of debris off the islands.[2]

Emergency relief was not, however, dispensed quickly or efficiently throughout all the disaster-stricken areas. On the island of Puerto Rico, several thousand displaced residents were still living in makeshift shelters six weeks after the storm (Branigin 1989a). And it took several months for some hurricane victims in the Virgin Islands to receive safe drinking water and appropriate medical supplies (Christian 1992). Electrical power and communication systems were not repaired in some areas for almost a year (U.S. General Accounting Office 1991).

In the end, FEMA did play a critical role in facilitating recovery efforts in the Virgin Islands and Puerto Rico. It distributed massive amounts of financial aid to private businesses and governmental institutions. And the agency helped over 200,000 victims obtain essential disaster assistance (McAda 1989).

Extreme Gap Between Emergent Norms and Bureaucratic Norms

The Caribbean illustrates an extremely wide gap between emergent norms and bureaucratic norms. The norms that developed following Hurricane Hugo centered on acts that would be considered socially deviant by normal standards. At the same time, the government was virtually powerless to do anything about the situation. Although the Caribbean is a frequent target of tropical storms and hurricanes, the local response bureaucracy never anticipated a situation of this nature and magnitude. The system was designed to deal with normal disasters in which communication and transportation networks could be easily restored and where local officials would provide an effective first response. By almost any standard, Hurricane Hugo's devastation of the Caribbean was not a normal disaster; consequently, existing bureaucratic institutions were incapable of dealing with the situation. From this perspective, it is hardly surprising that the institutionalized governmental response process broke down entirely.

Top-Down Implementation Pattern

The experience in the Caribbean clearly illustrates an approach to policy implementation that is almost the exact opposite of the intended bottom-up pattern. In this situation, the federal government stepped in as soon as possible and took control over virtually the entire effort. Disaster relief was initiated, directed, and actually implemented from the top down.

There are three main reasons why this top-down pattern occurred. First, the scope and severity of the disaster was itself a factor. Even before Hurricane Hugo struck the Caribbean, it was clear that this was an abnormally massive, extremely violent storm and that a *major* natural disaster situation requiring the resources of the federal government was highly likely. Normally, it takes almost two weeks after an event occurs for a governor to request federal aid, and then another ten days for the president of the United States to reach a decision (U.S. General Accounting Office 1991). In the case of the Virgin Islands and Puerto Rico, standard procedures were accelerated greatly. Federal officials played a critical role in expediting this process. They located and established contact with appropriate territorial authorities, instructed them on how to ask for federal assistance, obtained their requests over makeshift telephone devices, and then hand-carried each request to the White House.

Second, local and territorial governments were unprepared and ill-equipped to handle the massive destruction. They had not developed adequate emergency alert, recovery, and response plans. And they were unable to perform even the basic functions of government, such as maintaining law and order. Local situations deteriorated to such an extent that the federal government could not wait to supplement local and territorial efforts (U.S. General Accounting Office 1991). Consequently, the federal government stepped in and took control of virtually all activities. U.S. troops were sent in to stop the looting and pilfering. This was an extremely unusual scenario. It marked the first time since the 1960s that federal law enforcement officials had been used to curtail an outbreak of domestic unrest on U.S. soil (Christian 1992). The ineffectiveness of local and territorial organizations prompted this action. More specifically, the collapse of subnational institutions made it necessary for the governmental response to begin at the federal level.

Third, pre-existing economic and demographic factors also created difficulties. Hurricane Hugo hit some of the most densely populated, economically depressed, geographically dispersed, and racially tense areas of the Caribbean (York 1989). For example, St. Croix in the U.S. Virgin Islands has a higher population density than any of the fifty states. Similarly, almost one third of the residents of Puerto Rico live below the federal poverty level. Even under the best scenario, it would be difficult to provide relief to disaster-stricken locales like these. In the wake of one of the most violent hurricanes of the century, the utter absence of local and territorial support made it impossible to administer government assistance to these areas using the normal implementation procedures.

Perception of the Governmental Response: Failure

By almost all accounts, the government's response to Hurricane Hugo in the Caribbean was extraordinary. Standard operating procedures and processes quickly proved to be unworkable in the face of complete confusion and chaos. So the federal government stepped in and took charge of the situation. The top-down implementation pattern allowed the government to address some of the most pressing concerns on the islands. Order was restored, water and food were distributed to those in need, temporary housing was provided to thousands of victims, debris was cleared and removed, electrical systems were reconnected, and communication and transportation systems were rebuilt. Hurricane Hugo caused about $3 billion in damages in U.S. territory in the Caribbean. The federal government provided most of the resources, supplies, and money that enabled individuals, families, and businesses recover from this disaster ("Billion Dollar Disasters" 2008).

But these efforts are overshadowed by other images. Most reports focused on the outbreaks of civil disobedience, such as the looting and domestic violence, the total failures of communication linkages with the U.S. mainland, and the massive breakdown in electrical power systems on the islands. In addition, serious issues surround the government's handling of this crisis (Branigin 1989b; Piacente 1989; York 1989). Why were local and territorial governments so ineffective? Why was the federal government caught off guard? Why did it take so long to provide assistance to some disaster-stricken citizens? And why was it necessary to bypass normal policies and procedures and create a top-down implementation pattern for emergency relief? In sum, the government seemed to be almost totally unprepared for this disaster situation (U.S. General Accounting Office 1991). Thus, the public perception of the governmental response to Hurricane Hugo in the Caribbean Islands is clearly one of failure.

Hurricane Hugo in South Carolina

Hurricane Hugo's path of destruction did not end in the Caribbean. Shortly after midnight on September 22, 1989, Hugo struck the U.S. mainland approximately forty miles northeast of Charleston, South Carolina. Although most hurricanes weaken when they reach land, this one did not. Instead, it pounded the coastal areas for several hours, and then it moved quickly and violently in a northwesterly direction up through the center of the state.

By sunrise the next morning, the storm was far to the north. However, Hurricane Hugo had left an indelible mark on South Carolina. Power was out in approximately half of the state; houses were torn apart, moved, or destroyed. Personal belongings were scattered everywhere. Roads, bridges, and fishing piers were demolished. Trees were twisted, toppled, and uprooted. Thousands of people were left without shelter, food, water, electricity, and sewer facilities. Overall, much of the state of South Carolina looked like a "war zone" (S. Schneider 1989).

Once again, it was clear that governmental resources would be needed to address this disaster situation. Emergency management personnel at all governmental levels took steps to activate the response process even before the storm hit the coast of South Carolina. But the government was simply unable to administer disaster relief using the standard bottom-up process. Problems at the local, state, and federal levels produced a

Ben Sawyer Bridge to Sullivan's Island, Charleston, South Carolina, after Hurricane Hugo struck the state in September 1989. *(National Oceanic and Atmospheric Administration, National Hurricane Center photo)*

confusion pattern of policy implementation. This affected the speed and efficiency of the governmental response and influenced the public's perceptions of the governmental effort. Similarly, it led to sharp criticisms of the actions, and inactions, of the federal government, particularly those of the Federal Emergency Management Agency. In the end, it fostered a lasting impression of governmental non-responsiveness.

Milling Process Begins Early

The milling process began almost immediately in South Carolina. Hugo had altered, and in some cases completely changed, the entire landscape. Buildings were flattened, and automobiles were crushed beyond recognition. Sidewalks were pulled up from the ground, and bridges were twisted apart. Boats were resting on top of garages and lawns, having been picked up out of the water and placed ashore miles from their original locations. In addition, the storm had disrupted almost all transportation and communication systems in the affected areas. Streets and roads were impassable because of waist-deep water and mounds of debris. Airports were inoperable due to the storm's damage to planes, runways, and hangars. Telephone and television service was almost nonexistent.[3]

These conditions made it extremely difficult for the affected population to comprehend exactly what had happened to them. Many victims were now faced with problems that

Large oak trees over 100 years old came down all over Charleston, South Carolina, after Hurricane Hugo made landfall in September 1989. *(National Oceanic and Atmospheric Administration, National Hurricane Center photo)*

they had never before even contemplated, let alone experienced. They were stunned, almost shell-shocked. They felt that their world had been turned upside down. One resident described his family's reactions as they emerged from their house immediately after the storm: "At first when we walked outside, we couldn't figure out where we were. . . . It was desolate." Another victim remarked: "I was just numb with feelings . . . It seemed like the day after the end of the world" (*And Hugo Was His Name* 1989, p. 14).

Unlike events in the Caribbean, however, no instances of social unrest or disorder in South Carolina occurred. Disaster victims were disoriented and confused, but they did not engage in extreme forms of unconventional conduct or behavior, such as looting or rioting. This was partly due to the actions taken by public officials before the storm moved onto the U.S. mainland.

Governmental Response Is Activated, Then Stalls

The governmental response process was already well underway before Hurricane Hugo hit the South Carolina coastline. At the local level, steps were taken to prepare coastal communities for a major storm. Disaster relief agencies alerted residents in the storm's path to take precautionary measures, and they began to activate their own emergency response plans. Mayor Joseph P. Riley of Charleston, South Carolina, used a series of radio and television announcements to urge people, especially those in low-lying areas, to move immediately to higher ground. Mayor Riley used the strongest terms to convince people that the storm was extremely dangerous and that they had to evacuate (Riley 1989).

The state's response system had also been activated. The South Carolina Emergency Preparedness Division had been tracking the storm for several days and had already alerted local disaster agencies, as well as other state officials, of the impending emergency. Based upon these warnings, South Carolina Governor Carroll Campbell officially declared a "state of emergency" and recommended that residents leave coastal areas. The governor also sent the National Guard to the coast to help state and local law enforcement officials evacuate the areas and maintain order. The governor issued a stark warning that the state would not tolerate any looting or disorder after the storm (Beckham 1989). In addition, the governor established his own communication and command center, separate from the existing state apparatus. This was done so that the governor could receive information directly from the counties and deploy the state's resources more "swiftly and effectively" (L. Carter 1989). On September 21, 1989, Governor Campbell took the extreme step of ordering a mandatory evacuation of the coastal areas around Charleston (L. Carter 1989; Sponhour 1989a).

The federal government was also involved by this time. In fact, FEMA had already sent personnel, on September 20, to the three areas on the U.S. mainland most likely to be hit by Hugo—Georgia, South Carolina, and North Carolina. When it became clear that South Carolina was to bear the brunt of the storm, FEMA was able to concentrate its efforts and go to work quickly (Mosco 1989; G. Peterson 1989). The night before Hugo struck, top-level FEMA personnel met with Governor Campbell and his staff in Columbia, the state capital. They began to prepare the materials necessary to document a gubernatorial request for federal aid to South Carolina (L. Carter 1989).

Around 8 o'clock the next morning, on September 22, 1989, FEMA headquarters in Washington, D.C., received Governor Campbell's official request for federal assistance. Approximately two and a half hours later, President Bush declared an emergency and initiated the federal response. Thus, the South Carolina gubernatorial request and the presidential declaration both occurred less than six hours after Hugo's departure from the state (G. Peterson 1989). Again, the response moved quickly through local and state governments up to the federal government. Almost immediately, the federal government became the focal point for disaster assistance, and once again, FEMA was in charge of the relief efforts.

To the greatest extent possible, FEMA tried to create order out of chaos (P. Hall 1989). FEMA determined that one of its first priorities was to restore electrical power. Electricity was needed in order to provide many other essential services. So the agency focused much of its early efforts on locating and transporting emergency generators and on repairing power lines in disaster-stricken areas. Along with this, FEMA concentrated on clearing roads, clearing debris, and re-opening bridges and ferry services so that life-sustaining supplies, such as food, water, and medicine, could get to affected areas. The agency also quickly authorized and financed a number of important construction and clean-up activities—such as repairs to roadways and bridges, extensive debris

An old brick building destroyed in downtown Charleston, South Carolina, by Hurricane Hugo, September 1989. *(National Oceanic and Atmospheric Administration, National Hurricane Center photo)*

removal activities, public health and safety precaution measures, and the construction of an emergency sand dune in the Myrtle Beach area (G. Peterson 1989).

Once these basic steps had been taken, FEMA tried to take an active role in directing federal assistance to severely damaged areas. The agency's actions added more counties to the list of federal disaster areas, beyond those originally specified in the presidential declaration. After FEMA's extensions, more than half of the state—twenty-six of the forty-six counties—qualified for federal aid (P. Hall 1989). FEMA eventually set up more than thirty Disaster Application Centers in these counties in order to help people obtain public and private relief.[4]

As a result of these massive efforts, most of South Carolina recovered fairly quickly from the disaster. Food, water, and medical supplies were distributed to those in need. Temporary housing facilities were transported into the state, providing immediate shelter to individuals and families who had lost their own homes. In many of the affected areas, power was restored, bridges and roads were repaired, and tons of debris were removed within several weeks. However, this was not the situation everywhere.

Milling Process Accelerates

Many small coastal towns and cities were largely cut off from the rest of the state, and they received little outside assistance and relief. Even more severe isolation occurred among rural families located in the swampy, low-lying areas of eastern South Carolina. Many of these people had experienced the full force of the hurricane, and their needs were particularly acute. Yet the government was unable to provide relief to these victims in a timely or effective fashion. Consequently, some families lived for months without electricity, telephones, or any real contact with the outside world (M. Lewis 1989).

The sense of helplessness and anomie intensified among disaster victims as the recovery effort progressed in South Carolina. Many disaster victims were told that it would be weeks, even months, before they would receive emergency relief. Others still had not been informed that they could obtain assistance. When one victim was asked if he would apply to FEMA for help, he replied, "I haven't heard of them" (Lancaster 1989). The impression developed across the state that no one seemed to be helping those truly in need and that no one really appeared to be in charge of the response or recovery efforts.

Because of these conditions and sentiments, the milling process continued in South Carolina for several months. During this time, the most prominent keynoting behavior was exhibited by Charleston Mayor Joseph Riley and U.S. Senator Ernest Hollings. Both of these officials were highly critical of the federal government. Mayor Riley (1989) initially complained that the federal response had been slow and inadequate. He later stated that "the *national* government should assume *full* responsibility for a *national* disaster like Hugo" (Riley 1989). Senator Ernest Hollings was even more critical of the federal government's efforts, particularly the actions of FEMA. Senator Hollings called the Federal Emergency Management Agency a "bunch of bureaucratic jackasses," and he claimed that it was more concerned with regulations, forms, assessments, and inspections than with helping those in need (Bandy 1989b).

The media provided support for these charges. There were numerous reports that FEMA's obsession with paperwork and documentation was preventing the release of critical emergency assistance to disaster victims (Lancaster 1989; Livingston 1989; J. Miller 1989b; Sponhour 1989b; Bandy 1990). This led to the widespread perception that FEMA was ineffective, inefficient, and unresponsive (Bandy 1989a; Cook 1989; Parker 1989). Beliefs about FEMA's incompetence became the emergent norm during the recovery process in South Carolina.

On the other side, the government departed from its standard operating procedures in several ways. First, local-level emergency management officials were largely ineffective because they were untrained and unprepared: they simply did not know what procedures to follow or how to work within the existing response system (Rubin and Popkin 1990). Consequently, they often failed to submit requests to proper authorities, or they used bureaucratic end-runs to obtain relief through unofficial means (Lancaster 1989; M. Lewis 1989).

There was also a serious problem at the state level. Instead of one central disaster response unit in South Carolina, there were two. The first was the South Carolina Emergency Preparedness Division, a permanent unit within the state government. The second was hastily created in the governor's office, during the night before the storm hit. The result was a dual system that added to the already chaotic situation created by the hurricane itself (Eichel 1989; S. Schneider 1990; U.S. General Accounting Office 1991). This adversely affected standard operating procedures and generated confusion within the entire intergovernmental response system.

The federal response effort—particularly FEMA—had severe problems of its own. FEMA's organizational resources were simply inadequate. Immediately after Hugo, hundreds of FEMA workers were activated from around the country and sent to South Carolina (McAda 1989). Nevertheless, this large contingent was quickly overwhelmed by the demands placed upon it. Furthermore, FEMA's reporting, assessment, and inspection procedures were inappropriate for the severity of the disaster and much of the extreme isolation of the affected population. FEMA officials expected Hugo's victims to come to them. There was, at least initially, no provision for the people who were out of contact with government and the rest of society (Fretwell 1989a, 1989b). Hence, they were largely forgotten during the weeks immediately following the hurricane (Applebome 1989; Tuten 1989).

Large Gap Between Emergent Norms and Bureaucratic Procedures

In South Carolina, the gap between the public's expectations and the government's efforts was quite large. This occurred because the predominant emergent norm was overtly hostile to the governmental response process itself: the public thought the *federal* government was primarily responsible for the relief effort, even though the response system depends upon *state* and *local* guidance. The gap also developed because the government's response process did not conform to prevailing conditions within the affected areas of South Carolina. Even when governmental officials followed standard operating procedures, their actions often appeared to be inappropriate for the situation at hand.

Confusion Implementation Pattern

As explained above, FEMA officials as well as state and local governments anticipated the hurricane before it hit the coast of South Carolina. But there was no clear-cut line of communication from counties and municipalities through the state and then up to the national government. Thus, South Carolina is a perfect example of the "confusion" pattern of intergovernmental policymaking. The response process was initiated simultaneously at the federal, state, and local levels, but there was little coordination or integration between and across different governmental units. For example, Governor Campbell and Mayor Riley worked independently of each other to bring relief to the Charleston area. And South Carolina Senator Ernest F. Hollings tried to channel needed relief into the state apart from the ongoing, institutionalized efforts (S. Schneider 1990).

Many of the problems experienced in South Carolina stem directly from the existence of the confusion pattern. This affected the response effort in at least five different ways. First, the scope of the disaster was itself a problem. Most normal disasters, such as floods and tornadoes occur in fairly limited geographic areas. In such situations, the federal response is less urgent because state and local officials can usually handle the most pressing concerns. Even most hurricanes do not require an immediate federal presence. State and local officials usually have time to alert the population and to prepare their own response (G. Peterson 1989). However, Hugo caused massive destruction across hundreds of square miles. Many of those who were hit the hardest lived in isolated, economically depressed, rural communities throughout the eastern portion of the state. It would be difficult to reach these individuals even under the best of circumstances (Sponhour 1989c). Given the scope and severity of the situation, however, it was virtually impossible to provide relief to these victims quickly or effectively. The normal response and recovery system was ill-equipped to handle a catastrophe of this magnitude.

Second, the confusion pattern revealed several basic weaknesses in the local response system. The entire intergovernmental process is based on the assumption that federal aid will supplement state and local efforts. In order for this to work, local governments must be able to identify the needs of disaster-stricken areas and communicate them through the proper state channels to the federal government. However, Hugo made it clear that many local officials in South Carolina were not fully aware of their own responsibilities in a crisis or how the response system worked (Mittler 1988). They did not know that they had to determine local needs and then process them through the governor's office before the federal government could respond. Even those who understood the system were not prepared or equipped to cope with a disaster of Hugo's magnitude. They simply did not have the experience, expertise, or resources to handle such a massive emergency. They thought the federal government would step in and take charge of the situation (S. Schneider 1990). Stated simply, they developed unrealistic expectations about the federal government's capabilities and obligations. Hence, they became extremely frustrated with, and critical of, the agency leading the federal effort—FEMA.

Third, the existence of two emergency management units at the state level added to the already confused state of affairs in South Carolina. A basic assumption of the intergovernmental response system is that each state has a well-developed coordinated disaster response mechanism and that a single state agency is in charge of this process. This is absolutely essential so that requests for assistance can be channeled quickly and efficiently to appropriate sources of relief. On paper at least, South Carolina has such a system. According to state statutes and regulations, the Emergency Preparedness Division is the primary state agency responsible for disaster relief. It serves as the designated, coordinating point of contact between the state and local governments during an emergency situation (South Carolina Emergency Preparedness Division 1985).

But the night before Hugo hit the South Carolina coast, the governor used his emergency powers to create a second emergency management command post. This allowed the governor to communicate more directly with local communities and to mobilize additional state resources; for instance, agents from the South Carolina Law

Enforcement Division were utilized in relief operations. The creation of a second command post also allowed the governor to circumvent the existing state emergency management system. Perhaps there were doubts about the state's ability to handle a crisis like Hugo using standard organizational mechanisms. After all, the South Carolina Emergency Preparedness Division had a long history of being underfunded and understaffed (Eichel 1989; U.S. General Accounting Office 1991). Moreover, the agency reportedly had internal management and leadership problems, which had led to seriously sagging morale within the agency (J. Miller 1992).

Although it may have seemed like a sound decision at the time, the creation of a second state emergency management system weakened the pre-existing intergovernmental response framework. More specifically, it undermined state government's ability to serve as a clearinghouse for the overall relief effort. This, in turn, severely hampered efforts to deploy critical resources, even though plenty were available for distribution. There is some evidence that local requests for supplies, electrical generators in particular, were directed to the wrong source or completely lost in the system (Thrift 1989). As a result, the proper authorities never received some of the requests, and appropriate relief was not provided to some needy victims.

Finally, FEMA's own policies were another obstacle. FEMA, like all bureaucratic organizations, has developed a set of policies and standard operating procedures. Many of these procedures facilitate the response process; they enable the agency to implement assistance almost automatically when a disaster strikes. However, other procedures are designed to prevent unnecessary or inappropriate government spending. Taken together, these measures try to reconcile routine agency decision making with guarantees to ensure that only those who fit pre-established criteria and follow specific guidelines will obtain federal assistance (Hall 1989). However, such regulations may also impede the responsiveness and adaptivity of an agency like FEMA. The resultant questions raised by disaster victims and their advocates are easily understandable: How can FEMA expect people who have lost everything to produce evidence documenting their losses? Why does FEMA have to assess and inspect damages before it distributes aid? And why does FEMA have to be asked, by the governor, before it responds? Bureaucratic procedures and regulations may be necessary to prevent fraud, but they are of little consolation to those with urgent disaster-related problems (Miller 1989b).

In addition, FEMA's own resources were literally stretched to the limit. In the fall of 1989, the agency had an annual operating budget of about $450–500 million, a staff of about 2,400 full-time employees located in offices throughout the country, and only a handful of supplies and equipment at its immediate disposal (McAda 1989). Moreover, FEMA's position within the federal government at this point in time was considered to be somewhat ambiguous. Like many other small federal agencies, FEMA suffered from internal management problems (Ingraham 1987). It had eight political appointees within its leadership ranks, and had gone without a permanent director since June 1989 (Democratic Study Group 1989).

Furthermore, natural disasters were not considered to be FEMA's primary responsibility. Instead, most of the agency's planning, resources, and activities had focused more heavily on dealing with nuclear strikes against the United States (National Academy of Public Administration 1993; Wamsley 1993). Thus, the agency had to scramble to cope with even one major natural disaster. But South Carolina was FEMA's third major disaster in less than a week, following closely on the heels of the Virgin Islands and Puerto Rico. Because of this, FEMA personnel from across the country were called to South Carolina. Full-time employees from as far away as Seattle and Denver were reassigned. On-call reservists and volunteers were activated, state employees were recruited, and additional personnel, such as school teachers not currently employed, were hired to work in local areas. Eventually, FEMA was able to get over 3,000 people into the field in South Carolina, but doing so took several weeks (P. Hall 1989).

Public Perception of Governmental Response: Failure

The relief effort in South Carolina following Hurricane Hugo represents a classic example of intergovernmental confusion. Local, state, and national governments all tried to respond to the disaster, but their efforts were not integrated or linked together. Moreover, the government's own policies and procedures were simply inappropriate for the severity of the disaster and the extreme isolation of the affected population.[5] As a result, disaster assistance was implemented sluggishly and ineffectively.

These problems facilitated intense criticisms of the entire governmental response. Overall, there was a nationwide perception that the government's disaster relief efforts—particularly those of the federal authorities—were a failure in South Carolina. But FEMA, the federal agency in charge of the response process, received most of the blame: FEMA, not Hurricane Hugo seemed to be the real disaster (Cook 1989).

Hurricane Hugo in North Carolina

Hurricane Hugo moved out of South Carolina and into North Carolina shortly after 6:00 A.M. on September 22, 1989. At this point, nobody expected the hurricane to have much power or strength. After all, it had just barreled its way across an entire state and was now 200 miles from the Atlantic coast. But Hugo was still able to deliver one last devastating blow.

The storm was in North Carolina for only a relatively brief period of time, but its impact was still extremely violent. One-fifth of the state suffered serious damages from heavy winds and flooding. Thousands of North Carolinians, especially residents in the Charlotte metropolitan area, lost electrical power. Overall, Hugo caused seven deaths and several billion dollars in damages to homes, businesses, and natural resources in North Carolina. And of course, these losses came on top of the damages previously produced by the devastating storm.[6]

North Carolina's experience with Hugo was severe; however, this disaster seemed to place few additional strains on governmental resources. Emergency management personnel stayed within their standard operating procedures, and the public seemed to work with, and not against, these officials. The gap between emergent norms and bureaucratic procedures was virtually nonexistent. So the response process actually flowed from the bottom up, exactly as it was supposed to: local governments responded first, then the state, and finally the federal government stepped in to help. This, of course, was a much more conducive environment for governmental operations. There was little confusion, hesitation, or fanfare concerning the governmental efforts in North Carolina. As a result, the North Carolina situation represents a much more successful response to a major natural disaster than those considered previously in this chapter.

Milling Process Begins Immediately, but Ends Quickly

Unlike the situations in the Caribbean and South Carolina, the milling process was short-lived during North Carolina's response to Hurricane Hugo. Everyday activities and routines were still disrupted. Immediately after the storm, "dazed residents scrambled for food, ice, flashlights, and candles and exchanged stories of destruction" (*And Hugo Was His Name* 1989, p. 49). Some residents in the Charlotte area went without electrical power for several weeks. Despite these conditions, however, there was no extended period during which normal institutions were unable to provide guidance and direction. As Gerald Fox, the Manager of Mecklenberg County, testified: "Clearing of streets to provide emergency and normal access; property security and functioning without electrical power; damage assessment; and public information were the early orders of the day" (U.S. House of Representatives 1990). Hence, there was no need for the affected population to engage in an ongoing search for meaning.

Instead, the public seemed to focus immediately on getting conditions back to normal. With the help of emergency management officials, disaster victims themselves originated a "Hugo Citizens Task Force" to help individuals and families who were "falling through the cracks" of the relief effort (Fox 1990). Public and private agencies worked together and demonstrated that the situation was manageable by restoring transportation, power, and communication systems within a very short period of time. Stated simply, life went on after a brief, albeit serious, disruption (McAda 1989).

The brevity of the milling process meant that keynoting behavior was relatively unimportant. Telephone and radio communications were available and accessible to most of the population. As a result, people looked to the usual authorities—law enforcement officials, emergency management personnel, and private insurance carriers—for assistance (Faust 1989).

Bureaucratic Response Runs Smoothly

For its part, the government had already taken important precautionary steps before the storm hit. Anticipating the hurricane's onslaught, state and federal officials met in Raleigh, North Carolina, on September 20, 1989—two days before Hugo moved onto the U.S. mainland. They monitored the path of the storm, and they determined that Hugo would likely strike a major blow to the state of North Carolina. So person-nel from the Federal Emergency Management Agency worked with state officials to prepare a request for federal assistance.

Immediately after Hugo left the state on the morning of September 22, state and local officials began assessing the storm's damage. Then on September 24, North Carolina Governor James Martin officially asked President Bush for federal assistance. Within twenty-four hours, the president declared four North Carolina counties to be "federal disaster areas" (G. Peterson 1989). Once again, the federal government was almost immediately involved in another major relief effort. This time, however, the system actually operated quite smoothly—unlike the earlier situations involving Hugo.

The governmental response in North Carolina functioned in a fairly routine, straight-forward fashion (U.S. General Accounting Office 1991). State and local emergency management personnel stayed within their standard operating procedures. Overall, they seemed to have a better understanding of their own responsibilities—perhaps because they had been involved in several other disaster situations over the previous year. And public officials seemed to work *with*, and not *against*, these emergency management personnel.[7]

Virtually No Gap Between Emergent Norms and Bureaucratic Procedures

The emergent norms in this situation were entirely consistent with the ongoing social structure: no looting or rioting occurred as happened in the Caribbean. And unlike the situation in South Carolina, little dissatisfaction with governmental efforts was voiced. Prominent political leaders in North Carolina did not try to interfere in the process. For example, Senator Terry Sanford visited the disaster-stricken areas in North Carolina shortly after Hugo's departure. He tried to reassure North Carolinians that assistance would be forthcoming, and he explicitly refused to criticize the relief effort (Faust 1989).

Of course, problems did develop during the process. There was some confusion about getting material assistance to the areas of the state that most needed it. For ex-ample, local representatives in a heavily damaged county did not understand the proper procedures for debris removal, which unnecessarily delaying the clean-up efforts (U.S. General Accounting Office 1991). However, these difficulties were resolved fairly quickly, and there was no serious effort to work outside the basic structure.

Bottom-Up Implementation Pattern

In North Carolina, the governmental response conformed to prior expectations and planning. Local governments responded first, then the state, and finally the federal government was called in to help. Moreover, when higher levels of government became involved, they did not take over the relief effort. Instead, they worked with and through lower levels. All three levels of government continued to function closely with one another throughout the entire relief and recovery effort. Consistent with the structure of the ongoing disaster response system, governmental activities "bubbled up" from the local level through the state and ultimately to the national government.

Several factors contributed to this bottom-up implementation pattern. First, there were better disaster preparedness plans at both the state and local levels (Mosca 1989). Moreover, the state conducted an average of four training sessions every year to ensure that all relevant parties knew how to implement these plans in an actual emergency situation (U.S. General Accounting Office 1991). This provided North Carolina officials with very effective, tested guidelines for carrying out their responsibilities. More importantly, perhaps, it enabled state and local personnel to acquire first-hand experience with the actual implementation of hazard mitigation policies (Mittler 1988).

Second, state and local personnel had more resources and manpower available to handle the recovery effort. North Carolina spends more money than South Carolina on disaster relief activities. The state uses some of these funds to support a fairly large staff of full-time emergency management personnel. It funnels the remainder of its money to local governments so the latter can enhance their own capabilities. In turn, this allows the state to *coordinate* rather than actively *direct* a recovery effort (U.S. General Accounting Office 1991).

Third, North Carolina used its pre-existing emergency management system to coordinate disaster relief. Unlike the situation in South Carolina, there was no bifurcated communication or command structure at the state level. Consequently, all information and assistance flowed through the appropriate channels (McAda 1990).

Because of these factors, FEMA was able to maintain its designated role. It supplemented the state's resources and channeled federal assistance into the areas where North Carolina officials said it was needed. FEMA became involved in the relief effort almost immediately after the hurricane (Morrill, Williams, and York 1989). The agency quickly opened a disaster field office in North Carolina, and it began accepting applications for assistance within seven days (U.S. General Accounting Office 1991). FEMA officials eventually added twenty-five more North Carolina counties to the list of federal disaster areas. Over the next three months, FEMA processed more than 30,000 claims and provided $37 million in relief (McAda 1990). In this state, the recovery effort wound down very quickly. FEMA closed its disaster application centers by December 1, 1989, precisely at the end of the normal sixty-day application period.

Public Perception of the Governmental Response: Effective

North Carolina's experience with Hurricane Hugo represented a response pattern that was close to optimal. The process unfolded more slowly, giving officials time to organize and coordinate their efforts. In addition, the norms that developed within the affected population were supportive of existing policies and procedures. Thus, virtually no gap between emergent norms and bureaucratic procedures existed. As a result, the process flowed exactly as it was intended to flow, from the bottom up.

This episode shows how effective the system can be when all relevant governments work together. If public agencies perform their previously defined disaster responsibilities, no need to depart from standard operating procedures exists. This, in turn, reduces the level of confusion, and it produces an environment conducive to governmental operations. The government can step in, provide relief, and terminate its efforts within its pre-established time frames. Overall, there is very little fanfare, no widespread criticism of any kind, and indeed, little public notice outside of the immediately affected areas.[8] In the end, the image is one of a successful governmental response to a major natural disaster. North Carolina's experience with Hurricane Hugo fits this scenario almost perfectly.

Notes

1. Much of the information for this case study was collected directly from the *Briefing Books* and *Mission Assignment Statements*, maintained by the Federal Emergency Management Agency in Washington, D.C.

2. For additional information on the governmental response to Hurricane Hugo in the Caribbean, see the *Interagency Hazard Mitigation Team Reports*, prepared by the Region II Interagency Hazard Mitigation Team, Federal Emergency Management Agency. For more recent accounts and updates, see the National Research Council report, *Hurricane Hugo* (1994) and the report by the National Weather Service Forecast Office, "Hurricane Hugo: 20th Anniversary" (U.S. Department of Commerce 2010b).

3. For more graphic accounts and illustrations of Hurricane Hugo's destruction in South Carolina, see *And Hugo Was His Name* (1989), *Hugo* (1990), and *Hurricane Hugo: Storm of the Century* (1990).

4. Much of the information on the governmental response to Hugo in South Carolina comes directly from the "Mission Assignments" issued by the Federal Coordinating Officer and obtained from the Federal Emergency Management Agency Disaster Field Offices in North Charleston, South Carolina, from September through December 1989.

5. FEMA accepted applications from disaster victims in South Carolina for six months following Hurricane Hugo, representing the longest application period for any major disaster situation up to that time point (Heflin 1990).

6. For more detailed information on Hugo's impact in North Carolina, see the *Charlotte Observer*, particularly the daily issues from September 22 through October 8, 1989, and the Special Supplement to the October 11, 1989, edition that was devoted entirely to "The Wrath of Hugo."

7. The information on the governmental response to Hurricane Hugo in North Carolina was obtained from a variety of sources, including the Federal Emergency Management Agency's Office of Public and Intergovernmental Affairs in Washington, D.C., and the *Interagency Hazard Mitigation Team Report* prepared by Region IV of the Federal Emergency Management Agency, headquartered in Atlanta, Georgia.

8. In fact, the lack of media and public attention given to this disaster situation is probably one of the main reasons why the relief effort proceeded smoothly and routinely.

8

The Loma Prieta Earthquake in California

Shortly after 5:00 P.M. on October 17, 1989, an earthquake shook the San Francisco Bay area. The quake, later called "Loma Prieta" by geologists, rocked the region for about ten seconds with a force measuring 7.1 on the Richter scale (U.S. Geological Survey 1990). Severe damage was reported within a hundred-mile radius around the quake's epicenter, located eight miles northeast of Santa Cruz; tremors were felt for several hundred miles in all directions. The quake destroyed or damaged thousands of buildings. Roads were cracked open and bridges crumbled. Natural gas and power lines snapped apart, water pipes exploded, and structural fires erupted everywhere. In all, there were more than sixty deaths, thousands of injuries, and an estimated $6.8 billion in direct damages (*The October 17, 1989 Loma Prieta Earthquake 1989*),[1] resulting in over $10 billion in total costs (National Research Council 1994).

Smoldering remains of the apartment complex at the corner of Beach and Divisadero Streets, Marina District, San Francisco, California, following the Loma Prieta Earthquake, September 1989. *(U.S. Geological Survey photograph by J.K. Nakara)*

A worker surveys the damage caused by the fire in San Francisco's Marina District after the Loma Prieta Earthquake struck, September 1989. *(Federal Emergency Management Agency: FEMA News photo)*

Another major disaster had occurred while the nation was still reeling from Hugo's destructive rampage through the Virgin Islands, Puerto Rico, and the Carolinas. And to make matters worse, the earthquake was actually seen on television by millions of Americans who were preparing to watch the third game of the 1989 World Series, being held in San Francisco's Candlestick Park. Yet, the governmental response system was put into effect once again. This time, private citizens and public institutions reacted calmly and quickly. Consequently, the gap between emergent norms and bureaucratic procedures was initially quite small. Over time, however, the gap increased in size. This was due to both a growing sense of frustration and the local governments' departure from their pre-established roles in the recovery process. The size of the gap had a direct impact on the implementation of disaster assistance. More specifically, it produced another example of the confusion pattern, or the breakdown in orderly cooperation and coordination between levels of government. Therefore, the government's disaster response efforts received mixed reviews.

Initial Public Reaction to the Disaster Is Calm and Orderly

The Loma Prieta Earthquake certainly disrupted normal routines and behavior patterns. Yet the public's immediate reaction was largely calm and directed toward the alleviation of the most pressing problems (Archea 1990). Numerous reports of normal citizens engaging in heroic efforts were made. Rescue workers and volunteers took extraordinary steps to locate survivors and pull them out of dangerous situations (Magnuson 1989). For example, a construction worker spent two hours extracting a man trapped in his crushed car on Interstate 880, and a firefighter spent over three hours freeing a woman who had been pinned between the beams of her crushed apartment complex (*The State*, 1989). Attention was given to rescuing those who were in life-threatening situations, preparing for the aftershocks of the quake, and surveying the extent of the damages. Overall, the public's initial response was remarkably composed and orderly.

Initial Governmental Response Is Calm and Routine

The government also seemed to respond quickly and effectively to the situation in California (Piacente 1989). Early on October 18—the morning following the earthquake—local, state, and federal officials surveyed the damages in stricken areas. It was abundantly clear to all observers that the resources and assistance of the federal government were needed. State and federal officials worked closely together to activate the emergency response process. Within hours, President Bush declared San Francisco and surrounding communities a "major disaster area" and authorized the Federal Emergency Management Agency (FEMA) to mobilize and coordinate the relief effort (Hamner 1990; Bolin 1990). Search and rescue operations began almost immediately.

The government's response to the San Francisco earthquake was different from its response to Hurricane Hugo in at least five important ways. First, it is crucial to recognize that there are fundamental differences between earthquakes and hurricanes after which, in turn, affect the nature of the governmental response (J. Miller 1989a; P. Hall 1989). Earthquakes cannot be predicted, and there is no time to evacuate or even alert the population prior to the event. So the focus must be on immediate rescue efforts (National Research Council 1991; Quarantelli 1991a, 1991b). This is in direct contrast to the hurricane relief efforts in the Carolinas, where there was ample warning, which allowed South Carolina's governor and other public officials to urge the evacuation of coastal areas long before the hurricane struck. This precautionary step clearly saved many lives (Wagar 1990).

Second, the federal government is especially prepared for earthquakes in the areas of the West Coast where they are likely to occur. Several years ago, Congress mandated the development of a Comprehensive Earthquake Hazards Reduction Program. This plan identifies key emergency support responsibilities and describes how federal agencies will work together to provide assistance to quake-stricken areas (Piacente 1989). A central facet of the plan is the assignment of one federal agency to take the lead in coordinating each of the pre-specified emergency support functions.[2] As an extension of this program, FEMA has spent a great deal of time and money developing its earthquake response capabilities. It has worked closely with states on the West Coast in order to establish more efficient and faster emergency procedures for earthquakes. In August 1989, just two months before the Loma Prieta Earthquake,

Search and rescue crews looking for victims at a collapsed department store in the Pacific Garden Mall, around Santa Cruz, California, following the Loma Prieta Earthquake, September 1989. *(U.S. Geological Survey photograph)*

FEMA had conducted a major earthquake training exercise in California. Federal and state officials simulated their response to a major earthquake. This gave them a dress rehearsal to test the implementation of their plans (Piacente 1989). It also helped to delineate the responsibilities assigned to the respective governmental officials and institutions (Hamner 1990). Thus, governmental officials at all levels not only knew what their responsibilities were, they actually had some timely practice in carrying them out.

Third, the White House seemed to respond with greater urgency to the earthquake than to Hugo. The day after the quake, Vice President J. Danforth Quayle arrived at the scene to survey the damages and explain proper procedures to state and local officials. Three days after the quake, on October 20, President George H.W. Bush flew to the Bay area to assess the situation firsthand. Other top-level officials were also sent immediately to California to guide the federal effort. For example, Transportation Secretary Samuel K. Skinner inspected the damages caused by the collapse of Interstate 880 less than twenty-four hours after the quake. In its actions, the White House was sending a clear message: the federal government would respond quickly to the Loma Prieta disaster (Hamner 1990). This was a sharp contrast to the low presidential visibility and lack of concern during the situation in the Caribbean and the Carolinas. The president never visited the areas affected by Hugo in Puerto Rico or the Virgin Islands. And he did not survey the situation in the Carolinas until ten days after the hurricane. Moreover, no cabinet secretaries were sent to any Hugo-related disasters. In the period immediately following Hugo, Marilyn Quayle, the wife of the vice president, was the most visible representative of the White House (S. Schneider 1989, 1990). The sluggish, lackadaisical response of the federal government during Hurricane Hugo did not sit well with state and local officials in the Caribbean or the Carolinas. Some political leaders complained vociferously about the incompetence of FEMA and the uncaring attitude of the Bush administration (Riley 1989; Thrift 1989). These criticisms contributed to a widespread perception—correct or incorrect—that the federal government was indifferent to the suffering of Hurricane Hugo's victims.

Fourth, FEMA acted quickly to inform Californians about its services, procedures, and responsibilities during the earthquake disaster. A toll-free hotline was immediately put into operation; in fact, this was a part of the initial presidential declaration. Within fifteen hours after the quake, top-level FEMA personnel held a nationally broadcast news conference. This was the first of many public information campaigns to explain what the agency could and could not do (Hamner 1990). On October 22, FEMA opened its first disaster application center in California. Shortly thereafter FEMA established three other major centers. FEMA also used a number of mobile units, making it easier and more convenient for people to apply for assistance (McAda 1990). FEMA even tried a unique "mass registration" technique. Instead of taking applications one at a time, several hundred people were brought into a facility where an overhead projector was used to explain the application forms to everyone at once. FEMA also took steps to streamline other facets of the process: The agency issued temporary housing checks immediately to all those whose homes had been completely destroyed; their inspectors delivered checks at the same time that they assessed the extent of other damages. FEMA seemed to be doing everything it could to get the San Francisco Bay area back on its feet (Hamner 1990). By February 1990, it had processed over 77,000 applications for assistance and distributed more than $31 million to individuals and families (Federal Emergency Management Agency 1990b). By that date, it had also funded almost $600 million in repairs to roads, bridges, buildings, and other facilities. In California, FEMA's actions often appeared to be more decisive and oriented toward expediting widespread assistance to the public than they were in the east coast disasters. There seemed to be much less emphasis on standard operating procedures and bureaucratic red tape than there had been before (Hamner 1990). Overall, this looked like a "new" FEMA.

Fifth, state and local governments also seemed to be better prepared to respond to the Loma Prieta Earthquake. Local disaster preparedness plans went into place almost automatically: emergency personnel knew what to do, and they took action without state or federal prompting or supervision. State officials played a major role in the emergency response operations. They were able to coordinate local efforts and serve as intermediaries between local and federal officials (U.S. General Accounting Office 1991). They possessed the resources—expertise and personnel—and the ability—preparation and organization—to perform this function. In addition, having just gone through the training exercise in August they were more knowledgeable about their

Aerial view of collapsed sections of the Cypress viaduct of Interstate Highway 880 follow-ing the Loma Prieta Earthquake, September 1989. *(U.S. Geological Survey photograph)*

responsibilities and the capabilities of other governmental units. Overall, the govern-ment's initial efforts—particularly those of state and federal officials—proceeded relatively smoothly. However, problems soon developed.

Milling Process Begins During Recovery and Intensifies

The milling process actually began in California during the recovery phase, as the population began to realize that life would not immediately return to normal. Col-lapsed highways and badly disrupted traffic patterns in the Bay area, damaged houses in the outlying regions, and problematic aspects of processing insurance claims led to a mounting sense of public frustration (Piacente 1989).

There were few life-threatening, dangerous situations remaining by this time. However, there was definitely a popular belief that public institutions were not solving problems and operating the way they should (Fitzpatrick and Mileti 1990; Wagar 1990). This triggered the ongoing search for meaning, which, itself, involves the milling process.

Keynoting behavior in California was carried out largely by the mass media (Magnuson 1989, p. 40; Rogers, Berndt, Harris, and Minzer 1990). The dominant message, drawn in part from previous experiences in South Carolina, was that FEMA was incapable of providing disaster assistance to earthquake victims. The agency had lost a great deal of respect and credibility with the public. Many Californians had heard the stories about the federal government's non-responsiveness and inefficiency in dealing with Hurricane Hugo. They became afraid that their concerns and problems would also get lost in the government's bureaucratic jungle. As a result, thousands of Californians called the agency and hundreds more lined up at the doors before FEMA even opened the first application centers. When the agency officially began to process applications, it was immediately faced with a backlog of 10,000 requests for assistance. The impression developed that the government was not doing all it could to help disaster victims (Wagar 1990).

Gap Between Emergent Norms and Bureaucratic Norms Is Initially Quite Small, but Grows Larger Over Time

The emergent norm in this context was an extreme sense of disillusionment. California citizens responded to the disaster itself, and in the initial phase the government operated effectively—maintaining order, dealing with life-threatening situations, and restoring essential services. However, citizens felt abandoned during the later recovery period. People tended to believe that they would have to help themselves: they did not think they could depend on the government for assistance.

The sense of anomie and frustration was probably greatest within low-income population groups in and around the city of San Francisco. The governmental response system was unable to provide adequate shelter or emergency services for quake victims living in the most depressed, economically disadvantaged areas. Poverty and housing shortages made it difficult for the government to relocate people displaced by the disaster (Gross 1990). Moreover, there were also serious language barriers to overcome: many government assistance workers only spoke English, and they were unable to communicate with the Spanish-speaking segments of the affected population (Panetta 1990). Consequently, some quake victims took matters into their own hands. In the city of Watsonville about 1,200 displaced people who had lost their homes during the quake constructed a tent city to protect themselves and their families from the elements. Basically, these victims formed their own independent community because they lacked confidence in the governmental relief system.

Confusion Implementation Pattern

Although local officials did deal with the immediate dangers of the earthquake, they were less successful in addressing longer-term aspects of the relief effort—for example, helping residents file insurance claims, providing adequate housing, and directing supplies to appropriate areas.[3] Despite greater general preparedness, some local officials still had difficulty dealing with the disaster. Like the situation in South Carolina, local officials were often not familiar with their own responsibilities or with the role of other governmental agencies. Some disseminated inaccurate information. For example, officials in Watsonville did not realize the severity of the situation in their area, and they did not request help for several days (Wagar 1990). A few localities did not understand that they had to assess their own damages and ask for appropriate assistance. They simply expected the federal government to step in and do everything. And a very common breach of procedures occurred when local officials bypassed county personnel and tried to get help directly from state and federal agencies. Undoubtedly, such actions seemed appropriate and necessary at the time. But they disrupted the functioning of the entire intergovernmental response process (U.S. General Accounting Office 1991).

The net impact of these problems was more pronounced because local governments always serve as the main interface between the government and the affected population. As Thomas Hamner (1990), FEMA's federal coordinating officer for Loma Prieta, remarked, "Local interface was a problem." He said that local officials should have been included in the government's disaster preparedness and training exercises. This would have given them a better understanding of how the entire system works.

In addition, FEMA itself was working under several tremendous handicaps. The agency was now seriously understaffed and ill-equipped to handle its fourth major disaster in the span of a month. And in addition to the three Hugo-related situations, several others had developed during the same time period, primarily another hurricane in Texas and floods in the upper southern states. This placed even more severe strains on the agency's resources. In order to respond to California, all available FEMA personnel across the country were activated; staff members no longer needed in the Caribbean and the Carolinas were relocated to the area. Employees from other federal agencies, such as the Army Corps of Engineers, and from state government were also used to supplement FEMA's personnel (Peterson 1989).

In California, the state and federal governments did work fairly well together. But the intergovernmental partnership did not extend to the localities. As a result, their role in the recovery process was never defined very clearly. This ambiguity had a direct effect on the entire governmental response system. Although the recovery efforts in California differed from those in South Carolina following Hurricane Hugo, both situations conform to the confusion pattern of intergovernmental activity. The hallmark of this pattern is the breakdown of orderly cooperation between levels of government. As we have seen, this problem can occur in a variety of different ways, across all three levels of government or concentrated within a single layer. But clearly this breakdown in cooperation occurred in California, just as it did in South Carolina.

Perception of Governmental Effort: Partial Success/Partial Failure

In California, the gap between emergent norms and bureaucratic norms was initially quite small. It increased in size due to the growing sense of public frustration over the slow progress and ineffective nature of the recovery efforts (Bolton 1993). Another contributing factor was the local governments' departures from their pre-established role in the recovery process, which produced serious "kinks" in the response process. Thus, California represents another example of the confusion pattern of intergovernmental policy implementation.[4]

Yet even at its most severe point, the gap between emergent norms and bureaucratic procedures remained quite narrow, especially when compared to the previous hurricane recovery situations in the Caribbean and South Carolina. The government was effective in restoring normal social conditions immediately following the quake (Nigg 1998). However, its efforts did not proceed smoothly or effectively during the longer-term recovery phase. Consequently, the governmental response to the Loma Prieta Earthquake can accurately be placed about midway between the success and failure poles.

Notes

1. Total damage estimates for the Loma Prieta Earthquake have varied from $6 billion (U.S. Geological Survey 1990) to $10 billion (Fairweather 1990). Part of the variability stems from how "social costs" are determined—that is, the costs of replacing low-income houses or relocating lower-income populations (Bolin 1990; Tubbesing 1994; Page, Stauffer, and Hendley 1999).

2. For a more detailed and comprehensive account of the governmental approach to earthquakes during this period, see the *Federal Catastrophic Earthquake Response Plan* (Federal Emergency Management Agency 1988).

3. Fitzpatrick and Mileti (1990) argue that some local officials failed to heed and respond to aftershock warnings. This suggests that local governments involved in the Loma Prieta disaster also had problems carrying out their immediate emergency response functions, as well as their long-term recovery and relief responsibilities.

4. For additional information about the 1989 Loma Prieta Earthquake, see *The October 17, 1989 Loma Prieta Earthquake* 1989; U.S. House of Representatives 1989; Bolin 1990; U.S. Geological Society 1990; Bolton 1993; Tubessing 1994; Nigg 1998; Makata et al. 1999; and Page, Stauffer, and Hendley 1999.

9

Hurricane Andrew

In August 1992, a Category Five hurricane named Andrew hit south Florida and coastal Louisiana. Andrew was an extremely powerful and destructive storm. It destroyed over 125,000 homes, and it was responsible for sixty-one deaths (U.S. Department of Commerce 2011). Andrew also caused $27 billion in property damages (Woolsey 2007): the Federal Emergency Management Agency (FEMA), alone, distributed over $1.8 billion from the President's Disaster Relief Fund to help individuals, families, and businesses affected by the hurricane (Federal Emergency Management Agency 2010p).[1] Andrew ranks as one of the most expensive natural disasters to ever hit the United States (Strategic Risk 2009).

There was little doubt that governmental resources were needed to address the problems created by Andrew. Unfortunately, however, the response process did not operate consistently across the disaster-stricken communities that were affected by the storm. Local and state emergency relief personnel were unable to deal with the problems in south Florida, and the national government did not act quickly to supplement their efforts. Consequently, emergency relief was administered in a sporadic, inconsistent manner, and a sizable gap developed between citizens' expectations and governmental abilities. The governmental response to Hurricane Andrew in south Florida is widely perceived to be a failure.

In contrast, the response to Andrew in Louisiana progressed quite well. The process began at the local level and worked its way up through the intergovernmental system, exactly as it was supposed to operate. There was little confusion or criticism of the relief operations. Virtually no gap existed between the behavior of the disaster response agencies and the expectations of disaster victims. Overall, the lasting impression of governmental efforts to Hurricane Andrew in Louisiana is quite positive. Similar to the situation following Hugo, Hurricane Andrew provides more evidence for the variability of the governmental response to the same natural disaster in different locations.

Hurricane Andrew in South Florida

On August 14, 1992, a low-pressure weather system materialized off the coast of Africa. At first, nothing distinguished this atmospheric ripple from the dozens of others that formed every summer in this region of the world. However, this one turned out differently: instead of dying out, this weather system slowly gained strength. By August 16, 1992, it had grown into a tropical depression. And the following day, it was upgraded to a tropical storm and given the name "Andrew."

Over the next week, Andrew meandered nonchalantly across the South Atlantic. Then it suddenly picked up strength, gathered momentum, and developed into a Category Four hurricane. Hurricane Andrew struck its first blow late on August 23. It hit the Bahamas with 120 mile-per-hour winds, leaving at least four people dead and thousands more homeless. Then, the huge storm moved back out into the Atlantic Ocean, where it rapidly intensified in strength and proceeded to move quickly in a northwesterly direction.[2]

Early on August 24, Hurricane Andrew smacked into the U.S. coastline just thirty-five miles south of Miami, Florida. For several hours, Andrew pummeled the areas of Homestead, Cutler Ridge, and South Dade with 145–160 mile-per-hour winds and torrential rains. After ravaging this area, Andrew moved across the tip of south Florida. Everything in the storm's path was either leveled or severely disrupted. Gradually the storm moved back over open water in the Gulf of Mexico.

Andrew had changed the face of south Florida, perhaps forever (*The Big One: Hurricane Andrew* 1992). At least thirty people died, over 175,000 were left homeless, and about one and a half million residents lost electrical power. Several communities were severely damaged: for example, 65 to 75 percent of all the buildings in Homestead were completely obliterated. In total, the storm caused $20 billion in property damage in south Florida, making it the one of the most costly natural disasters to ever hit the United States (EQE International 1992).

The government's responsibility in the recovery process seemed perfectly clear: it was expected to mobilize, organize, and channel all available resources in order to address the conditions in south Florida. Once again, however, the system was ill-equipped to handle a disaster of this magnitude. Many public organizations were simply unable to respond, or they reacted slowly and ineffectively. And to make matters worse, there seemed to be little, or no, coordination across the relief efforts initiated by different governmental units.

Almost immediately, disaster victims began to feel that they were on their own: Floridians did not think that they could count on the government for assistance. As a result, a sizable gap developed between the attitudes of disaster victims and the policies of the government's emergency response organizations. In an attempt to deal with this situation, the government tried to alter many of its standard operating procedures. Unfortunately, these changes did more harm than good. They produced a disorderly, confusing system of policy implementation, which led to even greater criticism of the government's efforts. As a result, the governmental response to Hurricane Andrew in south Florida is widely regarded as an abysmal failure.

Milling Process Begins Immediately and Lasts Several Weeks

Hurricane Andrew left south Florida in a "collective mess" (*Andrew: Savagery from the Sea* 1992, p. 14). The storm caused extensive property damage across a 1,100-square-mile area. Entire electrical systems were knocked out of commission, because everything, from wooden utility poles to oil-powered transformers, was destroyed. Roads,

Dadeland Mobile Home Park after Hurricane Andrew struck the area in August 1992.
(National Oceanic and Atmospheric Administration, National Weather Service photo)

highways, and airports were blocked by so much debris that normal transportation systems were virtually paralyzed. "A drive that would normally take less than an hour was a daylong obstacle course of downed trees, limp power lines, wrecked vehicles" (Manegold 1992a, p. A1). In addition, communication channels were disrupted, and in some cases totally destroyed, making it extremely difficult to place telephone calls into or out of the area (Federal Emergency Management Agency 1992a). All of these factors created an eerie, desolate situation. Many disaster-stricken communities were isolated, their residents' fates unknown (Manegold 1992a).

Because of these conditions, the milling process began almost immediately. Hurricane victims stumbled around the rubble looking for food, water, and shelter in an environment that was entirely transformed (Booth 1992a). Everyday surroundings appeared strange and unfamiliar. Nothing looked the same; nothing sounded the same; nothing smelled the same; nothing *was* the same (*Andrew: Savagery from the Sea* 1992).

First, people asked: why? Then they wondered: where do we go from here, and how? The situation was simply too severe for individuals and families to handle on their own. One factor that made matters worse was that many of the disaster victims were relatively new to Florida, and they had never before experienced a serious hurricane, certainly not one the magnitude of Andrew. Some residents had been attracted to south Florida because of the climate. Others had moved into the area because of the Homestead military base or because of employment opportunities (Manegold 1992d, p. A9). As a result, they probably had greater difficulty grasping the scope

"Andrew Was Here." A local resident expresses an opinion about the impact of Hurricane Andrew in Florida, August 1992. *(National Oceanic and Atmospheric Administration, National Weather Service photo)*

and severity of their predicament. So their natural reaction was to begin searching for some direction and assistance.

Local officials tried to help. But they themselves were disaster victims (*Andrew: Savagery from the Sea* 1992, p. 24). Their own homes had been damaged or destroyed. And their families, friends, and neighbors were experiencing the same problems as everyone else. Therefore, local officials were only able to respond to the most serious requests. It was simply impossible for them to address the vast majority of emergency calls (G. Peterson 1992). This, in turn, led to massive chaos and confusion. Or, as one bystander described the situation: "One zone of society came unglued" (Treaster 1992b).

Law and order became a major problem. Frightened and frustrated disaster victims stole supplies from neighborhood stores where they had once shopped. People simply took whatever food, water, and clothing they could find (Booth 1992a). Normal citizens became thieves and looters. "In malls, record shops, liquor stores, groceries, and electrical stores from Coral Gables to Florida City, it was like an insane party as laughing thieves helped themselves" (*Andrew: Savagery from the Sea* 1992, p. 40). Then, to make matters worse, greedy storeowners sold those supplies that were available at outrageous prices. Such gouging was widespread throughout the affected areas (Booth and Jordan 1992; Jordan 1992a; Treaster 1992a).

Local police and Florida national guardsmen were dispatched in order to stabilize the situation. But these forces were relatively small in numbers, and dispersed throughout

A victim of Hurricane Andrew in Dade County, Florida, issues a warning to looters following Hurricane Andrew, August 1992. *(Federal Emergency Management Agency/ Bob Epstein: FEMA News Photo)*

the disaster-stricken areas. So they were no match for the mini armies of looters and price-gouging citizens. Law enforcement officials were unable to stop the disorderly and unlawful behavior (Gore 1993). So local residents felt they had to take matters into their own hands. Homeowners walked the streets with pistols, rifles, and shotguns to protect what little remained of their dwellings and possessions. Business owners hired private security guards to prevent further looting and theft (Jordan 1992a).

Disaster victims were engaged in behavior that previously, before Andrew, was universally deemed unacceptable. Now, however, they believed that such actions were necessary for their own survival. Erratic, deviant behavior became the norm. One storm victim was caught taking food from a convenience store and rationalized the deviant behavior by explaining: "I need food. I need milk for my cousin's baby. We have nothing. You don't understand. What can I do?" (*Andrew: Savagery from the Sea* 1992, pp. 40, 42). This truly chaotic situation continued for several days following the hurricane.

Governmental Response Is Slow and Misguided

For many years, experts had been issuing warnings about exactly this kind of disaster: a monster storm hitting a major urban area. And Andrew was also the type of event that the government, itself, had been expecting. Several months earlier, in April of 1992, the federal government presented a set of policies and procedures to guide public and private actions during a major disaster situation (Federal Emergency Management Agency 1992b; Lippman 1992a). The fundamental assumptions, structure, and workings of this system were outlined in a document called the Federal Response Plan. This plan was to provide the basic "architecture for a systematic, coordinated, and effective federal response" (Federal Emergency Management Agency 1992b, p. 1). Signed by twenty-seven federal agencies, the plan had already been "field proven" for implementation during a large-scale natural disaster (G. Peterson 1992). This was the basic plan that was supposed to guide governmental activity before, during, and after Hurricane Andrew.

Several days before Andrew hit the U.S. mainland, hurricane watches were issued for south Florida from Titusville to the Keys. And the entire intergovernmental emergency response system was activated (Rohter 1992b). Local emergency preparedness personnel were put on alert. City and county officials issued warnings to citizens who lived in low-lying, coastal communities. Florida's emergency management and civil defense personnel were placed on standby status. The Federal Emergency Management Agency alerted its own personnel and sent an advance team into Florida to assist state and local operations (G. Peterson 1992).

Then, on Sunday, August 23, the National Weather Service issued a hurricane warning for south Florida. It was now clear that Andrew would strike somewhere between Vera Beach and the Florida Keys. Florida's Governor Lawton Chiles declared a "state of emergency." He ordered the mandatory evacuation of about a million people who lived on the barrier islands, and he strongly encouraged other residents living along the coast to leave their homes. The governor opened emergency shelters for those who could not or would not leave the area. By mid-afternoon, the evacuation was in full swing, and the highways heading out of south Florida were almost completely jammed with evacuees. Later that evening, just about the time that Andrew reached the Bahamas, major airports in the area were shut down and Miami Beach was closed. FEMA personnel, who were already pre-positioned in the area, set up their own Emergency Operations Center and convened a Catastrophic Disaster Response Group with other federal agencies. The FEMA officials who were working in Governor Chiles's office in Tallahassee immediately began preparing the necessary paperwork for a presidential declaration of a "major disaster" (Federal Emergency Management Agency 1992a).

Within hours of Andrew's onslaught, emergency management personnel began assessing the damages in south Florida, and it was quite obvious that extraordinary measures were needed. Governor Chiles called in the National Guard to help local law enforcement officials, and he formally requested that President George H.W. Bush declare south Florida a "federal disaster area." Within hours, the president approved Governor Chiles's request, thereby authorizing the federal government's intervention in the disaster. Later that same day, Bush flew to the area to inspect the damages firsthand (Federal Emergency Management Agency 1992a). It appeared as though the government would mobilize all its powers and resources to address the catastrophe. And it would use the new Federal Response Plan to coordinate and guide the entire effort. However, it would take time to "prime the pump" of the giant governmental response system to

President Bush is given a tour of a disaster site by FEMA officials following Hurricane Andrew, August 1992. *(Federal Emergency Management Agency/Bob Epstein: FEMA News Photo)*

get the necessary resources of the system into position (G. Peterson 1992). Until that occurred, the disaster-stricken communities in south Florida would be on their own.

For the first few days after Andrew, local emergency management personnel tried to respond to the disaster. County officials opened shelters for citizens who had lost their homes, and they provided free public transportation for local residents. However, these measures were woefully inadequate for the situation at hand (*Governor's Disaster Planning and Response Review Committee* 1993). For example, in Dade County, the police force, a team of 1,500 officers, only responded to "life-threatening emergencies and crimes actually in progress." They simply could not answer or handle any other call or request for assistance. Dade County's emergency officials were like "children battling a forest fire with squirt guns" (*The Big One: Hurricane Andrew* 1992, p. 17).

State officials tried to supplement local-level actions. Florida's emergency operations center was activated for twenty-four–hour operations, and all available personnel were sent to the disaster-stricken areas to augment local efforts. Governor Chiles had already called up five battalions of National Guard troops to augment local efforts. These troops were primarily used to maintain law and order. They patrolled devastated neighborhoods and business areas with rifles in order to stop the stealing and looting. And they set up checkpoints and roadblocks along major thoroughfares in order to turn back sightseers and those who were trying to take advantage of the situation.

When conditions in the disaster-stricken areas did not improve, the governor sent in additional National Guard troops (*Governor's Disaster Planning and Response Review Committee* 1993).

Meanwhile, the Federal Emergency Management Agency concentrated on implementing the Federal Response Plan. It deployed a mobile Emergency Response Support unit to Orlando, sent additional personnel into the disaster areas, and established a disaster field office at the Miami International Airport. Basically, FEMA focused its initial efforts on getting itself into position, so that it would be ready to respond (Federal Emergency Management Agency 1992a). It was waiting for the state of Florida to submit specific requests for aid. This was precisely what FEMA was supposed to do, according to the policies and procedures of the intergovernmental response system.

Unfortunately, this did not bring relief to the disaster-stricken victims of south Florida. In fact, it actually exacerbated their problems. Local officials were completely overwhelmed and unable to respond. The state of Florida erroneously believed that it could handle the situation without direct federal intervention (Zensinger 1992). And FEMA would not circumvent standard operating policies to initiate actions on its own. The entire intergovernmental response system was paralyzed.

Emergent Norms Develop: "Where the Hell Is the Cavalry?"

Private donations poured into south Florida from all over the country, and volunteers flocked to the area to provide assistance. But many roads and highways remained blocked because of hurricane-related debris and traffic jams. As a result, it was virtually impossible to get supplies and equipment to those in need (Hamilton and Johnson 1992). Four days after the hurricane, a quarter of a million people lacked food and water and about 50,000 were homeless. Over a million residents were still without electrical service (Federal Emergency Management Agency 1992a).

Theft, looting, and price gouging continued to be major problems. "Many residents struggled with deep fear for their own safety" (Treaster 1992b, p. A8). In general, people were becoming more frustrated, more impatient, and more irritable. Disaster victims had to stand in long lines to obtain even basic necessities, such as food and water (Barron 1992b). The relief effort seemed to be almost totally uncoordinated. No one appeared to be in charge.

The milling process continued as stories and rumors proliferated (Booth 1992b). There were accusations that the government agencies responsible for the relief effort were actually conducting a massive cover-up. Some residents believed that the government was not reporting the real death toll. Others even claimed that public authorities were, themselves, removing dead bodies and burying them in secret mass gravesites (Rohter 1992d). Most public attention, however, focused directly on the federal government's emergency response activities. The day after Andrew hit, President Bush had promised storm victims that "help was on the way." But local and state officials claimed that the federal government was not responding (Rohter 1992a). Governor Chiles complained that urgent requests for federal assistance had been delayed or

Victims of Hurricane Andrew wait in long lines for ice rations, August 1992. *(National Oceanic and Atmospheric Administration, National Weather Service photo)*

hopelessly lost because of bureaucratic red tape and confusion (Jordan 1992b). Kate Hale, the Director of Dade County's Emergency Office stated: "We have appealed through the state to the federal government. We've had a lot of people down here for press conferences. But (in the end) it is Dade County on its own. . . . Where the hell is the cavalry on this one?" (*Andrew: Savagery from the Sea* 1992). This question captured the overall sense of frustration and helplessness that disaster victims felt. Moreover, it characterized the public's general impression of the government's efforts—particularly those at the federal level. The emergent norm in south Florida was the image of an uncaring, unresponsive, and inept federal government.

In order to change this image, the government tried to modify its own policies and procedures (U.S. General Accounting Office 1993b; Federal Emergency Management Agency 1992a, 1993). Two days after the storm, President Bush appointed Andrew Card, the secretary of transportation, to lead a Task Force on Hurricane Andrew Recovery (G. Peterson 1992). Secretary Card went to south Florida as the president's personal representative. His major objective was to "cut through the bureaucratic mess" (Mathews et al. 1992, p. 27). Secretary Card monitored the entire relief effort, and he became involved in the actual implementation of disaster assistance. For example, he encouraged FEMA personnel to distribute money directly to storm victims without going through the lengthy assessment and verification processes. Basically, he wanted relief workers to provide assistance quickly and expeditiously, regardless of standard operating procedures (Federal Emergency Management Agency 1992b). Unfortunately, this only created more problems

An aerial view showing the temporary housing for storm victims in Dade County, Florida, following Hurricane Andrew, August 1992. *(Federal Emergency Management Agency/ Bob Epstein: FEMA News Photo)*

and delays for the governmental response system. Normal procedures were circumvented, but there were no new policies or measures to replace them. Thousands of disaster victims were still without food, water, electricity, and shelter (Treaster 1992b).

In order to address this situation, President Bush decided to take additional steps. He ordered federal troops to south Florida. The first U.S. Army and Marine forces arrived on Saturday, August 29—five days after the storm. Almost immediately, they airlifted in supplies and began distributing food, water, and generators (G. Peterson 1992). They set up field kitchens to feed storm victims and relief workers. They also constructed tent cities to shelter the homeless, and they started clearing roads and airport runways of debris so that transportation systems could reopen (Rohter 1992b, p. A1). In addition, military forces were sent to stabilize conditions in the most devastated areas: their mission was to help state and local law enforcement officials stop the looting, pilfering, and price gouging (Treaster 1992b).[3]

The federal government now seemed to be aware of the problems in south Florida, and it was pouring personnel, materials, and supplies into the storm-hit area (Wines 1992). In fact, federal agencies were channeling an extraordinary array of resources to the affected areas. In order to view the relief effort firsthand, President Bush flew back to south Florida. During this second visit, the president expanded the scope of federal disaster assistance even further. He promised that Homestead Air Force Base would be completely rebuilt and that the federal government would shoulder the entire financial burden for such clean-up projects as debris removal, sewer maintenance, and school reconstruction (Rohter 1992c). At this time, estimating the cost of all this federal aid was impossible. Yet, President Bush indicated that such actions were necessary because of the extraordinary magnitude of the disaster.

Clearly, however, strong political pressures were also involved in the decision to bring additional federal resources to bear on this situation. Hurricane Andrew struck Florida in the summer of a presidential election year. And Florida was considered by many analysts to be a vital state in determining the outcome of the election (Davis 1992b; Rohter 1992e). As one campaign official remarked, "It wouldn't be so bad if Andrew blew on up to Kentucky and the rust-belt states" where Bush was behind in the polls (Mathews et al. 1992, p. 27). Overall, the politics of disaster relief are easy to follow: "Show up, express concern, promise money—and you will be rewarded with votes" (Mathews et al. 1992, p. 27).

Large Gap Between Emergent Norms and Bureaucratic Procedures

In south Florida, a wide gap developed between the public's expectations and the government's actions. The general public felt that the federal government should be responsible for a disaster of this magnitude. Clearly, the situation in south Florida was beyond the capability of state and local authorities. But the federal government did not step in and take charge of the relief effort. Instead, it dealt with this situation like it had hundreds of other disasters by trying to get itself into a position from which it could supplement state and local actions. During the interim, however, conditions in south Florida deteriorated even further. Thousands of storm victims still lacked even the most basic life-support services—food, water, ice, electricity, and shelter. So frustrated, irritable, and disenchanted citizens took matters into their own hands in order to obtain essential supplies for themselves and their families. Looting and security were major problems (G. Peterson 1992).

The federal government did modify its standard operating policies and procedures to address these unusually severe conditions. Unfortunately this did not change the way people viewed the relief effort. In fact, it actually raised more questions and concerns about the federal government's role in the catastrophe.[4] After all, why did disaster-stricken communities have to ask for federal assistance? Why did the federal government respond so slowly? Why wasn't the military called in sooner? Why was it necessary to appoint a presidential representative to lead the relief effort? And where was FEMA? To paraphrase the quote from Dade County's Emergency Management Director, Kate Hale, "Who the hell was the cavalry, and why didn't they charge in and address the problems?"

Mass Confusion Implementation Pattern

The governmental response to Hurricane Andrew in south Florida conforms, once again, to the confusion pattern of policy implementation. Clearly, the process did *not* move smoothly and methodically from the local level to the state and ultimately to the national government—as it should have, according to the bottom-up pattern. Nor did it resemble a top-down approach in which the national government stepped in and took over the process. Instead, different actors at each level of government tried to respond to the situation, without any real coordination or synchronization to guide these efforts. As a result, there was both intergovernmental and intragovernmental confusion in the implementation of emergency relief.

First, there was almost complete chaos at the local level. As previously mentioned, local emergency management officials were, themselves, victims of the storm. Their concerns, naturally, were about their own situations. This made it extremely difficult for local relief workers to focus on all of the other problems that existed in what was left of their communities. Even if this had not been the case, local officials still would not have been able to mobilize an effective first response to an event like Andrew. They simply did not have the resources, manpower, or the authority to handle a disaster of this magnitude. In addition, they were ill-equipped to perform their pre-assigned responsibilities once the relief effort was initiated (*Governor's Disaster Planning and Response Review Committee* 1993). Exactly *what* should they request from higher levels of government? It seemed as though everything was in short supply. *Who* should they ask for help? Several federal agencies were on the scene, but none of them seemed to be in charge. *How* should they request assistance? They were unable to communicate with their own personnel, let alone with higher governmental units. In sum, local officials were completely overwhelmed by the severity of this disaster.

Problems at the state level were also serious. In the intergovernmental response system, state governments play an important, intermediary role. They are to direct all their resources to situations that are clearly beyond the scope of local authorities. And they must request and then coordinate the federal government's intervention during major disasters. If these functions are not performed, the intergovernmental process collapses. Unfortunately, this is exactly what happened in south Florida following Hurricane Andrew.

The state of Florida appeared to be totally unprepared for this kind of emergency. A major hurricane had not hit Florida in a number of years. And some state officials may simply have believed that they did not really need to worry about disaster preparedness or response. This attitude seems to have been prevalent even within the state's emergency management system. Officials from the Florida Department of Community Affairs had not attended regional meetings on disaster preparedness for quite some time. In sum, they seemed to have adopted a "don't bother us" approach (McKay 1992). Clearly, emergency preparedness was not a high priority in the everyday agenda of Florida state government.

Florida officials also may have seriously underestimated the severity of this particular situation (*Governor's Disaster Planning and Response Review Committee* 1993). Governor Chiles did submit a request to President Bush for federal aid almost immediately following the hurricane. But state officials did not have any clear idea about the extent of the damages in south Florida (Mathews et al. 1992). As a result, they did not ask for certain critical resources. For example, the governor apparently thought that the Florida National Guard could handle the situation. So he did not initially request federal military support (G. Peterson 1992). However, state and local enforcement officials were quickly overwhelmed. They were unable to deal with the problems—looting, pilfering, price gouging, and so forth—that emerged almost immediately within the disaster-stricken areas. Eventually, federal military troops were called in to stabilize conditions. However, serious questions have been raised about why the state did not request federal law enforcement assistance earlier.

Overall, Florida did not perform its intermediary role in the emergency response process (Zensinger 1992). The state did not effectively channel local requests upward to the federal government, nor did it direct federal assistance back downward to the areas most in need. As a result, Florida was a "non-player" in the intergovernmental response system. At times, it almost disappeared from the scene altogether.

Unquestionably, however, the largest degree of confusion occurred at the national level. The federal government did not respond quickly to the situation in south Florida. And when it did respond, it did not act in a unified or coordinated fashion. Instead of one focus, or one central organization, for the federal effort, there were actually three: FEMA, Transportation Secretary Card, and the U.S. military. All three of these "leaders" played an important role in channeling federal assistance to the storm-damaged areas of south Florida. Unfortunately, each one usually acted independently of the other two. This led to miscommunication and duplication among federal agencies, and it created massive confusion within the entire intergovernmental response system.

The Federal Emergency Management Agency was supposed to be the official leader of the national-level governmental response. The agency did try to mobilize and coordinate the relief effort. Before Hurricane Andrew struck the U.S. mainland, FEMA officials were in south Florida helping the state prepare the necessary paperwork required to request federal assistance. Immediately after President Bush declared the area a "major disaster," FEMA sent in additional personnel and established field operations in the storm-damaged communities; it distributed water, food, and supplies to thousands of storm victims. FEMA set up disaster assistance centers (DACs) within the affected areas so that storm victims could apply for emergency relief. It also used a national tele-registration system, actually located in Denton, Texas, which enabled the agency to double its processing capacity for disaster assistance requests. By the end of 1992, three and one-half months after Andrew, FEMA had approved approximately 44,000 applications for temporary housing and over 48,000 requests for individual and family grants. It had already distributed hundreds of millions of dollars in aid, and it was projecting total expenditures to run in the billions (Federal Emergency Management Agency 1993). Thus, FEMA played a major role in helping the south Florida disaster victims recover from Hurricane Andrew.

Despite these accomplishments, however, FEMA did not react to this disaster in a timely or efficient manner. The agency did not step in immediately with sufficient resources to provide emergency assistance to storm victims, and it did not coordinate

FEMA workers providing food, water, and supplies to people affected by Hurricane Andrew in Dade County, Florida, August 1992. *(Federal Emergency Management Agency/ Bob Epstein: FEMA News Photo)*

the actions of other public or private disaster assistance organizations. In sum, it did not mobilize, coordinate, or lead the governmental response.

The second leader for the federal government's operations was Transportation Secretary Andrew Card. Card was put in charge of the Hurricane Andrew Relief Effort, the impromptu task force which was hastily created by President Bush in order to cut through the bureaucratic red tape and "to make the response happen" (Matthew et al. 1992, p. 26). Secretary Card took charge of the federal command system, and he issued a series of directives to jump-start the entire response process. For example, he ordered relief workers to make immediate eligibility determinations for individual assistance, without waiting for the normal inspection of damages. And he doubled the maximum amount of money that storm victims could receive for making repairs to their homes. Although these measures helped expedite the delivery of governmental assistance, they also bypassed existing policies and processes. In the end, they were quite disruptive, confusing, and expensive.

The federal government placed a third leader on the scene when the military was sent in to bring order to the affected areas. The Department of Defense effectively used Army and Marine troops to assess the seriousness of the situation and to develop appropriate strategies for dealing with the most pressing problems. The military established order, transported goods, dispersed supplies, and provided medical care. The presence of Army and Marine troops also helped to reassure citizens that relief was on its way and to remind them to refrain from unorthodox behavior.

The military played a critical role in the government's relief efforts; however, it often acted independently of other organizations and agencies. It followed an internally focused command structure, which provided guidance and direction for military personnel; but this structure did not enable military personnel to work well with government officials or civilian institutions. As a result, military activities often bypassed the official disaster response structure as well as the "unofficial" presidential emergency operation (U.S. General Accounting Office 1993a).

Thus, there were three parallel relief systems all trying to administer disaster assistance. Consequently, the delays, disorder, and at times even complete chaos at the federal level were not surprising. Moreover, this "three-headed" leadership of the federal government's operations undoubtedly created more confusion throughout the entire intergovernmental response system: state and local governments may simply not have known who to contact to receive appropriate assistance. Once again, no one appeared to be in charge of the relief effort. In the end, the government reacted in a sluggish, haphazard, and disjointed fashion.

Public Perception: Abysmal Failure

The government was eventually able to mobilize a massive relief operation to help the storm victims in south Florida. In so doing, the federal government provided an unprecedented amount of assistance to the Hurricane Andrew victims. Despite these efforts, however, the public's perception of the governmental effort is primarily negative (Walden 1992). The government did not react quickly, and it did not respond immediately to this disaster situation, even though thousands of storm victims lacked critical life-sustaining supplies. Local citizens were forced to take matters into their own hands because the government did not provide effective guidance or support. Even when the government did respond, it did not act in a coordinated or unified manner. This created further delays in the administration of disaster assistance.

The national government is widely believed to be primarily responsible for the apparently poor performance of the disaster relief system. Local and state governments were completely overwhelmed; only the federal government had the resources and the authority to handle a disaster of this magnitude. But where was FEMA? Unfortunately, FEMA was both unable and unwilling to respond quickly and effectively to this disaster. Just like the situation in South Carolina following Hugo, FEMA, not the hurricane, was considered to be the real disaster (Lippman 1992b).[5] As a result, the entire governmental response was regarded as a complete failure.

Hurricane Andrew in Louisiana

Hurricane Andrew moved off into the Gulf of Mexico after its assault on south Florida. First, the huge storm swirled in a westward direction. Then it turned toward the northwest and moved at a steady pace across the Gulf waters. Early on the morn-

A victim of Hurricane Andrew expresses an opinion about the long wait to receive disaster assistance: "Where's the Check?" *(Federal Emergency Management Agency/ Bob Epstein: FEMA News Photo)*

ing of August 26, 1992, Andrew hit the coast of Louisiana, about twenty-five miles southwest of Morgan City. The storm ripped its way up through the south-central portion of the state. It destroyed between thirty and forty thousand homes and left over 50,000 residents homeless. Andrew was responsible for nine more deaths and an additional $300 million in damages in Louisiana beyond those losses already incurred in the Bahamas and Florida. As Andrew moved on to the north, it was downgraded from a hurricane to a tropical storm and then to a tropical depression. By Thursday, August 27, the storm had finally exerted its last punch; it was now classified as just "severe weather" (U.S. Department of Commerce 1998, 2006a).

It was clear that governmental resources would once again be needed to help citizens deal with and recover from this disaster. Unlike what happened in south Florida, however, the government seemed willing and able to handle the problems caused by Hurricane Andrew in Louisiana. Emergency management officials responded quickly and appropriately. Moreover, the entire process worked exactly as it was supposed to with the response moving from the bottom up.

There was also little, if any, conflict between the public's expectations and the government's pre-existing plans. For its part, the affected population reacted calmly and quietly; they focused their efforts on getting their lives back to normal, not on disruptive, deviant behavior. As a result, disaster assistance was implemented smoothly, quietly, and effectively. Louisiana's experience with Hurricane Andrew is an example of a more optimal and successful governmental response to a major natural disaster.

Milling Process Begins Early, Ends Quickly

Hurricane Andrew caused extreme havoc and destruction in southern Louisiana. The powerful storm blasted its way through the state unleashing 140–mile-per-hour winds, heavy rain, and tornadoes. It smashed homes, toppled trees, and leveled neighborhoods. The storm knocked out electrical service to over 150,000 residents, and it left many communities without basic necessities, such as safe drinking water and food supplies. In addition, travel into and within the affected areas was a severe problem. State and local highways were washed out, and the Intracoastal Waterway was closed from the Texas-Louisiana border to Morgan City (Federal Emergency Management Agency 1992a).

The milling process began almost immediately in south Louisiana. Local residents were naturally confused and disoriented by the severity of the situation. Their normal surroundings had been transformed. Everything seemed to be disheveled and out of place. In order to deal with this situation, some citizens resorted to unusual behavior and actions. Looting occurred in several of the most devastated communities, and there were reports of price gouging across the entire hurricane-ravaged area (Sanchez 1992). However, these instances of unconventional behavior were fairly isolated in Louisiana, especially when compared to the situation in Florida.

The entire milling process did not last long in south Louisiana. Instead, a sense of calm and order quickly returned to the hurricane-stricken areas. There are several reasons why the milling process ended so abruptly in this particular situation (Zensinger 1992). First, Hurricane Andrew did not cause a complete breakdown of communication and transportation systems in south Louisiana. Several major highways, railroad lines, and airports were initially closed; however, they were reopened within a matter of days. So travel in the disaster-stricken communities was only temporarily disrupted. Telephone service in the area was congested immediately following the hurricane, but it never completely broke down (Federal Emergency Management Agency 1992a). As a result, disaster victims in south Louisiana were able to talk with one another about their situation. And they were also able to communicate with people outside of the disaster-stricken areas. In sum, they were never really cut off from their neighbors, friends, and relatives, or from the rest of society.

Second, the local population may have been better equipped to handle a major hurricane. Louisianians saw the reports from south Florida, and they knew that Andrew was a fierce, deadly storm. Accordingly, they took the warnings for their areas very seriously and began to make the necessary emergency preparations before the hurricane arrived (Marcus 1992). Since many of the local residents had lived in low-lying areas all their lives, most had already experienced other large storms and floods. So they knew how to plan for and respond to such events. As one local resident remarked: "We've been running from hurricanes for years . . . it is just part of living in the bayou" (Covington 1992, p. 8).

In addition, many residents in this part of Louisiana have Cajun ethnic backgrounds. This is relevant because Cajuns have strong attachments to their families, their community, and their heritage. They also have a fairly positive outlook, no matter how severe their predicament (Sanchez 1992). As one victim remarked: "It's just us poor crawfish Cajuns here. If we don't get city water, well we're just going to go get clean in the bayou. That's what our people have always done" (Suro 1992a, A11). In times of trouble, Cajuns tend to "stick together" and help one another. Basically, the victims of Hurricane Andrew in southern Louisiana possessed exactly the kind of values and attitudes that are antithetical to milling.

Finally, the government played an important role in ending the "search for meaning," or milling, in south Louisiana. As we shall see, the government's standard operating procedures seemed to fit this particular disaster situation very closely. Existing policies were appropriate and believable guides for citizen behavior. Under such circumstances, there was really no reason for the affected population to search for *other* standards to guide their actions. Consequently, the milling process ended abruptly, almost as soon as it began. The affected population focused its efforts on getting life back to the way it was before the storm.

Governmental Response Is Orderly and Routine

The government took steps to prepare the Gulf Coast region for Hurricane Andrew immediately after the storm swept across the tip of southern Florida. The National Weather Service posted hurricane warnings from Port Arthur, Texas, to Pascagoula, Mississippi. Emergency management officials in states all along the Gulf Coast were closely monitoring the movement of the storm. Residents from Texas to Alabama were warned to take precautionary measures (Federal Emergency Management Agency 1992a; Maraniss 1992a).

The exact path the storm would take was unknown. But forecasters predicted that Andrew would probably hit land again around the mouth of the Mississippi River, just west of New Orleans. Local and state officials in Louisiana accelerated their efforts to prepare for the storm. The mayor of Grand Isle, Louisiana's only inhabited barrier island, issued a mandatory evacuation order for all island residents and visitors. The New Orleans Levee Board closed the floodgates surrounding the city of New Orleans to prevent widespread flooding throughout the area. Mayor Sidney Barthelemy encouraged all people living in low-lying areas around New Orleans to evacuate. Louisiana's Governor Edwin Edwards declared a "state of emergency," and urged all coastal residents to leave their homes before the hurricane struck (Mariniss 1992a).

The national government was also monitoring the situation in Louisiana. The Federal Emergency Management Agency activated its regional office in Denton, Texas, and it placed other regional offices on alert. FEMA deployed a package of critical resources to the area, and it sent in an advance team of emergency personnel to help state and local officials prepare for the storm (Federal Emergency Management Agency 1992a).

Almost immediately after Hurricane Andrew moved out of the state, Louisiana Governor Edwin Edwards submitted a request to designate the storm-damaged areas between Baton Rouge and New Orleans "major disaster areas." Several hours later, President Bush declared a "major disaster" for Louisiana, making eight parishes eligible for federal disaster assistance. Once again, the national government was involved in another major disaster situation. This time, however, the federal officials did not try to take control of the entire relief effort. Instead, they worked closely with state and local governments to coordinate their activities in a very effective manner (G. Peterson 1992).

Local parish officials assessed the extent of the storm's damages and identified their most urgent problems. Recognizing that they could not handle the situation on their own, they immediately called on the state for assistance. State officials quickly stepped in to alleviate some of the most pressing problems that existed at the local level. For example, the Louisiana National Guard was extensively involved in maintaining law and order throughout the hurricane-ravaged parishes; they also took an active role in distributing emergency supplies. But state officials had no illusions about their own capabilities in this disaster. They were more than willing to pass local requests that they could not handle up to the federal government.

For its part, the federal government acted quickly to get supplies and personnel into Louisiana. The Federal Emergency Management Agency immediately sent 100,000 military field rations, 8,000 cots, and 1,000 rolls of plastic sheeting. It deployed a Mobile Emergency Response Support unit to Alexandria to facilitate a range of emergency operations. And FEMA called up personnel from across the country to supplement its efforts. Within the first twenty-four hours, the agency had set up a temporary field office at Camp Beauregard, Louisiana, and it had identified several possible locations for disaster assistance centers (Federal Emergency Management Agency 1992a).

By the following day, August 28, FEMA established a permanent Disaster Field Office in Baton Rouge, Louisiana. Agency officials focused their efforts on making sure that water was available to the affected population. So the agency ordered thousands of gallons of water delivered into the area, and it sent for generators to restore electrical power to water treatment facilities. FEMA also issued contracts for the removal of hurricane-related debris, and it worked with private relief agencies to get truckloads of food, supplies, and clothing to storm victims. The agency opened four disaster assistance centers (DACs) and added seven more parishes to the list of those eligible for federal assistance (Federal Emergency Management Agency 1992a). All of this was accomplished within the first forty-eight to seventy-two hours after the storm struck Louisiana.[6]

Virtually No Gap Between Emergent Norms and Governmental Actions

Unlike what happened in south Florida, virtually no gap between emergent norms and bureaucratic actions developed in southern Louisiana. Clearly, the hurricane's impact was less severe. Hence, the situation was inherently more manageable. Yet the attitudes of the affected population were extremely important.

Basically, the victims of Hurricane Andrew in Louisiana understood what had happened to them, and they knew what actions to take in order to overcome their situation (Maraniss 1992b). They did not panic. They did not behave irrationally or erratically. They did not blame others for their predicament. Instead, they concentrated on helping one another in order to get conditions back to normal. They focused their efforts on "pulling themselves up" (Suro 1992a, p. A8) and rebuilding their homes, their communities, and their lives.

Governmental actions complemented those of private citizens. Emergency management personnel across all three levels of government seemed to be fairly well prepared for the disaster. Local and state officials in Louisiana had been emphasizing hazard mitigation and disaster planning, so they were able to perform their pre-assigned emergency response operations (G. Peterson 1992). This, in turn, allowed the federal government to supplement, not supplant, their efforts. Basically, emergency officials relied on existing procedures and policies, and they worked with, not against, each other to address the most pressing problems. As a result, they were able to provide credible and consistent guidance to the affected population.

Rolling, Bottom-Up Implementation Pattern

In Louisiana, local governments were the first point of mobilization. Parish officials identified the needs and problems of disaster-stricken areas. They recognized immediately that they could not address this situation on their own. So they quickly requested assistance from higher authorities. Local officials did not, however, disappear from the recovery effort. They continued to work closely with state and federal authorities to get aid into the hurricane-ravaged communities. They were the clearinghouse for local needs throughout the entire relief effort.

The state of Louisiana served primarily as the intermediary between local communities and the federal government; of course, this is precisely its mandated role in the general response system. State personnel mobilized available resources to support local efforts. And they channeled requests beyond their means up to the national government. These officials knew that the state simply could not handle the situation: federal assistance was essential. So state officials were willing and eager to do everything that they could to facilitate federal involvement. They took their intermediary role within the intergovernmental response system quite seriously (Federal Emergency Management Agency 1992a).

The efforts of state and local governments made it easier for the federal government to respond. Federal authorities did not have to take over the entire governmental effort: they could actually supplement the actions of the lower units of government. This enabled the federal authorities to mobilize their own resources more quickly and coordinate the entire intergovernmental relief system more effectively.

In sum, the response to Hurricane Andrew in Louisiana closely paralleled the ideal intergovernmental pattern. Local, state, and national governments were involved in the implementation of disaster relief, and each level of government performed its pre-assigned duties and responsibilities. As in any disaster situation, instances when local-level requests were "lost" or misdirected did occur. But overall, the governmental effort unfolded quite routinely. The entire process operated almost exactly as it was supposed to: from the bottom up.

Perception of Governmental Response: Success

In Louisiana, public expectations coincided with governmental actions. The affected population had fairly realistic notions about the government's role in a disaster situation. They did not expect the government to step in immediately and solve all of their problems. Instead, they were willing to work with governmental authorities to alleviate storm-related conditions. This, in turn, allowed the government to address the situation more slowly and carefully. Public organizations at the local, state, and national levels relied more directly on standard operating procedures, and the relief effort proceeded according to pre-existing plans and processes.[7]

In the end, there was very little criticism of the governmental response to the disaster. Perhaps, most of the attention and publicity remained focused on south Florida, which may have enabled Louisiana to recover from the disaster more quietly and with less fanfare. Nevertheless, the general impression developed that the governmental response to Hurricane Andrew in Louisiana was a successful effort.

Notes

1. This figure does not include money provided by other federal agencies, such as the Small Business Administration or the Farm Service Agency in the Department of Agriculture.

2. Most of the material on the origin and movement of Hurricane Andrew was obtained from the National Weather Service in the National Oceanic and Atmospheric Administration (U.S. Department of Commerce 1998, 2006a).

3. For a more complete description of the military's role during the Hurricane Andrew relief efforts in south Florida, see U.S. General Accounting Office Report (1993d) entitled *Disaster Assistance: DOD's Support for Hurricanes Andrew and Iniki and Typhoon Omar.* As the title implies, this report also contains information on the military's efforts in other disaster situations.

4. There are several excellent newspaper articles on the inability of the federal government's relief agencies, particularly FEMA, to respond quickly and effectively to the situation in south Florida. See, for example, Davis (1992a, 1992b), Lippman (1992a, 1992b), Kilborn (1992), and Claiborne (1992a, 1992b).

5. Criticism of the government's actions during this disaster led to a series of investigations into and analyses of the federal response system. See, for example, the following sources: U.S. House of Representatives (1993), U.S. Senate (1993a, 1993b), U.S. General Accounting Office (1993b), Federal Emergency Management Agency (1993), and the National Academy of Public Administration (1993).

6. Much of the information on the governmental response to Hurricane Andrew in Louisiana was collected directly by the author from the *Briefing Books* at the Federal Emergency Management Agency, Washington, D.C., in December 1992. This information was then supplemented with material from additional governmental reports, that is, the *Interagency Hazard Mitigation Team Report, Prepared by the Region VI Interagency Hazard Mitigation Team in Response to*

the August 26, 1992, Disaster Declaration, as well as by phone and personal interviews with federal, state, and local public officials involved in the relief effort.

7. It is important to note that several other disasters occurred as the relief effort was underway in Louisiana. First, there was the situation in south Florida, also created by Hurricane Andrew. In addition, however, the territory of Guam was declared a "major disaster area" on August 29 as a consequence of Typhoon Omar, and a major recovery effort was initiated and mobilized by the federal government to deal with that situation. Then on September 12, a "major disaster" was declared in Hawaii when Hurricane Iniki struck the islands; once again, federal resources were channeled into still another hurricane-stricken area.

10

The Northridge Earthquake in Southern California

Early in the morning on January 17, 1994, an earthquake struck about twenty miles northwest of the city of Los Angeles, California. The quake erupted along a little-known, blind thrust line close to the San Andreas Fault (Southern California Earthquake Data Center n.d.). It was centered in Northridge, a suburb of Los Angeles; hence, it became known as the Northridge Earthquake.

The main jolt of the Northridge Earthquake reached a magnitude of 6.7 on the Richter scale, and it lasted between ten and twenty seconds (U.S. Geological Survey 2009b; Bolt 1999). During the next several weeks, over 14,000 aftershocks occurred, registering from 4.0 to 5.0 in terms of impact (Petak and Elahi 2000). Rumblings were felt across an extremely wide area of land, spanning 214,000 square kilometers. Buildings shook in San Diego and Las Vegas, several hundred miles away from the epicenter of the quake. Electrical power was disrupted as far away as Oregon, Wyoming, and Canada (Lancaster 1994).

But the most severe impacts of the Northridge Earthquake occurred in the suburban communities of the San Fernando Valley and in the city of Los Angeles—areas located relatively close to the quake's center (Pacific Earthquake Engineering Research Center 2005). In this region, the quake caused extensive structural damages. Thousands of buildings crumbled, major roads buckled, gas lines ruptured, and water lines broke apart (Petak and Elahi 2000). Perhaps the most publicized "victim" of the quake was the area's massive freeway system. A number of major interstates and other highways collapsed, including the Santa Monica Freeway, the nation's busiest urban thoroughfare.

Early estimates indicated that economic losses from the quake would reach between $13 and $15 billion (U.S. General Accounting Office 1994). But these figures have been continuously revised upward: according to more recent reports, the quake caused over $41 billion in damages (Petak and Elahi 2000). In terms of financial losses, the Northridge Earthquake ranks as the most expensive earthquake in American history (Woolsey 2007). And it is one of the worst natural disasters ever to hit the United States (Federal Emergency Management Agency 2010v).[1]

The government responded to the Northridge Earthquake fairly quickly. Emergency management personnel conducted search and rescue missions, inspected homes and buildings to insure that they were structurally sound, and directed local residents to safe locations. Despite these efforts, however, relief workers were unable to address some of the most critical problems caused by the quake. Consequently, a gap developed between the expectations of the affected population and the actions of the response

Extensive damage to an elevated highway following the Northridge Earthquake, Los Angeles, California, January 1994. *(Federal Emergency Management Agency: FEMA News photo)*

organizations. But the gap closed fairly quickly when emergency management personnel altered their standard operating procedures and routines. This enabled them to expedite the distribution of aid and reassure quake victims that emergency assistance would be provided. As a result, the general impression of governmental efforts during the Northridge Earthquake is quite positive, placing the response to the disaster closer to the success end of the continuum.

Public Reactions: Initially Confused, but a Sense of Normalcy Quickly Returns

The impact of the tremors on the local population was severe, but surprisingly minimal considering the quake's magnitude and the density of the population in this region (*Earthquake Museum* 2009). About 95,000 residents lost electrical power, over 100,000 people had no water, and more than 20,000 people were displaced from their homes. The Northridge Earthquake was responsible for sixty deaths and over 7, 000 injuries (U.S. Geological Survey 2009b).

   Local citizens were naturally dazed and disoriented by the quake. One resident of an apartment building that took a direct hit described the scene as follows: "People were screaming . . . they were crawling all over each other. People came down in front and between your legs" (Cannon and Crosby 1994, A8). Throughout the quake-stricken region, many residents remained outdoors, unwilling to go back inside their homes because they were afraid that more buildings would collapse. Thousands of people stood shivering in their driveways or in parking lots, wearing their sleeping clothes from the night before (Adler 1994). Others got in their cars and drove around aimlessly in the dark on barely usable roads (Cannon and Crosby 1994, A8). Overall, quake victims were in a state of collective shock (Adler 1994; *Boston Globe* 1994).

As the aftershocks continued to rumble through the area, people became even more anxious and uncertain about what to do. The situation was exacerbated by the dramatic changes that had occurred. Many residents had no electricity or water, and they were unable to travel on many of the area's roads and highways. Quake victims were confronted with a "changed world" (J. Anderson 1994, 7a). So it is not surprising that some instances of unconventional behavior occurred. Store windows along Hollywood Boulevard were smashed, clothing and electronic equipment were stolen (Leff 1994), and about seventy-five people were arrested for disorderly behavior (J. Anderson 1994). There were also several reports of price gouging by a number of stores and businesses throughout the area (Adler 1994).

Overall, however, the victims of the Northridge quake initially responded fairly calmly, in an orderly manner to their predicament. "Whatever their doubts and fears, local residents found themselves focusing once again on the ordinary concerns of life" (Mydans 1994c, A16). As a result, the milling process ended fairly quickly following the Northridge Earthquake.

Several factors contributed to the rapid stabilization of conditions. First, many local residents had experienced *other* disruptive events—the Los Angeles riots two years before, as well as fires, floods, drought, and previous earthquakes. Hence, they had a better idea of what to expect when a disaster strikes and how they should react. As one local resident expressed it: "Californians are a resilient bunch. By tomorrow, they'll pick up the pieces and move on again" (Crosby 1994, A9). In addition, the population of southern California is well-informed about earthquake preparedness. Local residents receive a great deal of information about what they should do before, during, and after an earthquake. Such warnings and preparation clearly helped people respond more calmly to the quake, particularly during the first few days after it struck.

Governmental Response Process Is Quickly Activated

Governmental actions also helped to calm local citizens and provide order to affected communities. Immediately following the quake, Mayor Richard J. Riordan of the city of Los Angeles called for cooperation and asked local residents to "stick together" (Mydans 1994c, A16). Los Angeles police chief Willie L. Williams issued a "dusk to dawn" curfew to prevent looting and other unwanted behavior, and he dispatched law enforcement personnel into the area to enforce the curfew. City officials urged people to stay home in order to forestall massive traffic jams on those highways that remained open, and they warned residents to boil their drinking water in order to remove possible contaminants (J. Anderson 1994).

A disaster worker makes his way through the rubble in Northridge, California, following the Northridge Earthquake, January 1994. *(Federal Emergency Management Agency: FEMA News photo)*

State officials acted quickly to supplement local efforts. The California Office of Emergency Services sent in about 300 search and rescue teams to go through collapsed buildings and find any stranded quake victims. Governor Pete Wilson mobilized the National Guard and dispensed troops into the most severely damaged areas to maintain law and order (Anderson 1994; Mydans 1994c).

Almost immediately after the quake hit, the federal government was also involved in the response operations. President Bill Clinton declared Southern California a "major disaster area" on the evening of January 17, authorizing the release of federal funds and assistance into the area. Federal Emergency Management Agency Director James Witt and Department of Transportation Secretary Anthony Cisneros began mobilizing federal resources and they made arrangements to travel immediately to Los Angeles. In addition, FEMA activated its own search and rescue teams to augment local recovery efforts, and it sent medical teams, communication units, generators, and emergency water supplies into the quake-stricken region (Cannon and Crosby 1994; Claiborne 1994d).

Federal officials focused their activities on ensuring that the remaining structures were sound and assuring citizens that governmental assistance would be available to them. FEMA Director Witt promised that his agency would stay in the Los Angeles area until all needs were met (W. Hamilton and Spolar 1994). Vice President Al Gore and Transportation Secretary Cisneros visited the damaged areas; they stressed that federal assistance was on the way and encouraged local residents to go to local shelters and apply for federal disaster assistance (Claiborne 1994a, A4).

President Clinton visited the area on January 19, just a day and a half after the earthquake hit. He toured some of the most damaged communities and experienced some of the strongest aftershocks of the quake. President Clinton promised that the federal government would take "unusual and unprecedented" steps to help the region recover: he authorized the Small Business Administration to release immediately about $240 million in low-interest loans, and he had the Department of Transportation make $45 billion available for debris removal and structural repairs (Mydans 1994b, A19). Within several days following the quake, FEMA opened its first disaster assistance centers and began accepting applications for individual aid—several days sooner than the centers were opened after the Loma Prieta Earthquake in 1989.

Milling Process Begins

Unfortunately, the needs and expectations of the affected population exceeded the capacities of the relief organizations (Rivera 1994a). Roads and highways remained closed; homes and businesses were in shambles; water and power services were still unavailable in many areas; thousands of people were displaced and homeless. Emergency response agencies could not distribute aid quickly enough to the large

Vice President Al Gore tours damaged neighborhoods and talks to residents and volunteers following the Northridge Earthquake, January 1994. *(Federal Emergency Management Agency/Andrea Booher: FEMA News Photo)*

FEMA Director James Witt talks to residents and volunteers following the Northridge Earth-quake, January 1994. *(Federal Emergency Management Agency: FEMA News photo)*

numbers of people in need. Consequently, people waited in long lines to apply for disaster assistance. Angry crowds formed outside several of the emergency relief centers (Mydans 1994a).

Quake victims became extremely frustrated with the slow pace and arduous require-ments of the governmental aid process. As one quake victim asked: "Nobody is helping us. How are we going to support ourselves? How are we going to get food, pay the rent?" (Jones 1994, A19). Disaster victims were unable to make sense of what was happening to them. They had no safe place to go and no assurances that they would receive help. They felt helpless, lost, and deserted (Spolar and Duke 1994). This situation triggered the onset of the milling process among the quake-stricken population.

Emergency relief officials and political leaders tried to provide leadership and guidance. But they were unable to assuage the immediate concerns of the disaster's victims. Some people were afraid to go back to their own homes because they thought they were unsafe and dangerous. Others were so rattled by the initial earthquake and its subsequent aftershocks that they were reluctant to go inside any building or facility—including Red Cross shelters. Instead, they preferred to stay and sleep in open areas, like parks and parking lots. This made it difficult for relief organizations to administer aid to people throughout the affected area.

The situation was compounded by poor planning and preparation. The government had underestimated the extent of the damages and the subsequent needs of the affected population (Mydans, 1994a). The Northridge Earthquake left far more people without water, food, power, and shelter than had been anticipated. Consequently, government agencies were unable to dispense critical supplies and arrange adequate shelter to all those who were affected by the quake.

The government's own policies slowed down the process. Federal agencies used new procedures to distribute vouchers to quake victims so that they could receive housing assistance for longer periods of time, up to eighteen months. But these new procedures required government officials to perform extensive verifications of claims in order to prove that homes were truly uninhabitable (Mydans 1994a; U.S. General Accounting Office 1994).

Tensions decreased when the government adjusted key elements of the relief process in order to expedite the delivery of aid. FEMA opened more disaster assistance offices and it sent more personnel into the area to help process applications (Spolar and Claiborne 1994). FEMA also created a "fast track" process, designed to issue checks and vouchers to quake victims in need of housing assistance. These efforts did help to alleviate some of the anxieties and frustrations of the quake-stricken population. However, the shortage of adequate shelter continued to be a major problem (Mydans 1994a; Claiborne 1994c).

After several days of negotiations between federal and state officials, the California National Guard was given the go-ahead to erect large tents, provided by FEMA, throughout the hardest-hit areas (Fritsch 1994). State and local officials had initially expressed concern that the erection of large tent cities would create additional problems: it would encourage even more people to leave their own homes for the "safety" of the tents and lead to the establishment of permanent tent city communities that would be difficult to dismantle (Claiborne 1994c). But the tents helped meet the temporary housing demands of quake victims. Once this situation was addressed, the ongoing search for meaning that characterizes the milling process ended.

Gap Between Emergent and Bureaucratic Norms Is Very Small, Widens, and Then Closes

Initially, the gap between emergent norms and bureaucratic behavior was small. People were shocked and stunned by their circumstances, but they seemed to cope with their conditions fairly well. Emergency personnel stepped in quickly to make sure that people were safe and to stabilize local conditions.

As relief operations got underway, the gap between the needs of the affected population and the behavior of governmental agencies widened. Quake victims thought that aid should be dispensed quickly, with minimal hassles. But emergency relief agencies tried to follow their standard operating procedures in dispensing aid, which required fairly detailed damage assessments. This created a mismatch, or noticeable gap, between public expectations and bureaucratic capabilities.

The situation was alleviated when the government altered its standard operating procedures and relaxed its policies. This enabled the government to distribute aid more quickly to the victims of the Northridge Earthquake (Bolin and Stanford 1998). And it also quieted public complaints about the governmental response process. The

FEMA sets up tents to house the victims of the Northridge Earthquake, January 1994.
(Federal Emergency Management Agency/Andrea Booher: FEMA News Photo)

gap between emergent and bureaucratic norms closed and the relief effort proceeded quite smoothly.

Overall, a Relatively Smooth Implementation Pattern

Once adjustments were made to the response process, the government was able to provide emergency assistance much more quickly and effectively. By the end of the Northridge relief effort's first week, FEMA had opened eighteen disaster centers and fourteen mobile centers in the greater Los Angeles area, accepted 160,000 damage claims, and distributed over $27 million in federal aid (Suburban Emergency Management Project 2009).

FEMA establishes Disaster Field Offices like the one shown here to assist the victims of the Northridge Earthquake, January 1994. *(Federal Emergency Management Agency/ Andrea Booher: FEMA News Photo)*

Within two months after the quake hit, FEMA set a national record for disaster assistance: it had received more than 450,000 disaster aid applications and it issued checks totaling more than $870 million (Ayres 1994). The federal government extended the deadline to receive applications several times, eventually ending the application process for most types of assistance on January 20, 1995. Even after that point, FEMA continued to accept applications from those with "extenuating circumstances" well into the following year (Bolin and Stanford 1998). Over 600,000 applications for aid were received across the full period (California Governor's Office of Emergency Services 1997).[2]

But one of the most amazing accomplishments of the recovery effort involved the reconstruction of the Santa Monica Freeway, one of the nation's busiest highways. It was severely damaged during the quake. But less than three months after its collapse, the Santa Monica Freeway was reopened to traffic (Balz 1994). The federal government provided all of the funds for this operation (Spolar 1994).

By the time of the quake's one-year anniversary, FEMA had issued checks to over 500,000 individuals and businesses and it had paid out more than $5 billion in federal assistance (Simon and Levin 1995). Federal officials had already labeled the relief effort "the largest mass assistance to people in an urban setting in the history of the United States" (*The State* 1994, p. 3A). And the federal government was providing the vast majority—90 percent—of the funds to pay for the recovery efforts.[3]

A FEMA community relations worker explains disaster aid to a displaced resident of the Northridge Earthquake, January 1994. *(Federal Emergency Management Agency/Andrea Booher: FEMA News Photo)*

Lasting Impression of the Governmental Response: Successful

As we have seen, public expectations and bureaucratic behavior were in conflict during the response to the Northridge Earthquake. But many of these conflicts were resolved, and the relief efforts proceeded fairly quickly and smoothly. As Bolin and Stanford conclude: "By most measures, Northridge was dealt with effectively, given its scale, and the short-term needs of vulnerable groups were at least recognized and resources made available by federal and state agencies" (1998, p. 223).[4]

For their part, public officials were aware of the missteps and confusion of previous governmental response efforts: in particular, they did not want to see a repeat performance of the breakdowns that had occurred during the governmental response to the Loma Prieta quake in 1989 (see Chapter Eight). As a result, emergency personnel adjusted their routines and operations so that they could better address the needs of disaster-stricken communities (Spolar 1994).

Local residents were also better prepared to handle the conditions that developed during and after the Northridge quake. Naturally, they were very frustrated when they were unable to receive critical supplies and safe shelter immediately after the earthquake. But these negative feelings didn't last very long, and didn't have long-range consequences. Quake victims adapted their lifestyles relatively quickly to deal with the conditions that confronted them (Gross 1994); they focused their efforts on getting their lives back to normal. In fact, the affected areas rebounded so well that some observers reported that stricken communities were better-off after the recovery than they had been before the quake occurred (Schaff 2004).

The gap between bureaucratic procedures and emergent norms closed, the governmental response process unfolded fairly well, and the general picture that emerged was one of a successful governmental response to a major natural disaster. As U.S. Representative Julian Dixon said in a Congressional hearing to review the government's response to the disaster, "I would like to say that, as we talk about the overview of how FEMA performed in the last disaster, the earthquake, I am very pleased to say that from my observation, their performance was excellent" (U.S. House of Representatives 1996). Such remarks stand in marked contrast to those that were made about FEMA as well as other agencies involved in the intergovernmental response process during previous disaster situations.

Notes

1. The San Francisco Earthquake of 1906 tops the list as the deadliest earthquake to ever strike the United States. The impact of the quake, itself, was severe—with a magnitude of between 7.7 and 8.3. But the quake also set off numerous fires, which in turn caused extensive damage and destruction (Fleury 2009). The quake, and the resultant fires, killed 3,000 people and left over half of the total population of the area—225,000 out of 500,000 people—homeless (Hansen and Condon 1989; U.S. Geological Survey 2009b). In 1906 dollars, the quake caused property damages of about $400,000,000 million (U.S. Department of Commerce, National Oceanic and Atmospheric Administration 1972, p. 20).

2. In fact, one of the concerns that later surfaced about governmental relief efforts during the Northridge quake involved the distribution of government assistance. The Government Accounting Office found that FEMA issued checks so quickly that they ended up giving aid to people who had not even asked for it (Rivera 1994c). FEMA discovered the problem and discontinued the practice within a week, but not before they had already processed a number of these "unwanted" aid applications (Rivera 1994b).

3. For more detailed information about the governmental response to the Northridge Earthquake, see the reports by Federal Emergency Management Agency (1996), the California Governor's Office of Emergency Services (1995, 1997), and the U.S. House of Representatives (1994, 1996). There are also several excellent accounts of the geological aspects (for example, EQE 1994; U.S. Geological Survey 2009b) and the societal dimensions (Bolin and Stanford 1998; Cowin, Mahoney, and Mahin 2000; and Petak and Elahi 2000) of the Northridge Earthquake.

4. Not all communities recovered quickly or effectively from the Northridge quake. These discrepancies are described in Bolin and Stanford (1998).

11

Hurricane Georges

Hurricane Georges struck United States territory in three locations during September 1998—in Puerto Rico, in the Florida Keys, and along the northern Gulf Coast. The impact of the storm varied significantly across these three areas—it was much more severe in Puerto Rico than it was by the time it hit the U.S. mainland.[1] In addition, the capabilities of territorial and local and state emergency management personnel were also quite different: Puerto Rican officials were certainly less prepared for, and capable of dealing with, the situation they confronted than were their counterparts in the Florida Keys and along the Gulf Coast. Consequently, the government used different implementation processes to address the problems that surfaced in different locations.

Despite these differences, all of the governmental responses to Hurricane Georges in the U.S. functioned fairly smoothly. Emergency assistance was provided quickly and the affected populations almost immediately focused on getting their lives back to normal. Overall, there was little, if any, discrepancy between the expectations of disaster victims and the bureaucratic procedures used by public emergency management organizations. Clearly, this made it much easier for the government to administer aid to those in need. Within a month following the storm, the Federal Emergency Management Agency (FEMA) had registered more disaster assistance applications in response to Hurricane Georges than it had for any other hurricane in its history (Federal Emergency Management Agency 1998g). By early 1999, FEMA had distributed more than $400 million in disaster housing assistance to the victims of this storm, making Hurricane Georges one of the most costly natural disasters in terms of housing damages (Federal Emergency Management Agency 1999). In the end, FEMA relief costs for Hurricane Georges reached $2.245 billion, giving it the dubious distinction of being the fifth most expensive natural disaster in U.S. history, behind Hurricane Katrina, the 1994 Northridge California Earthquake, Hurricane Rita in 2005, and Hurricane Ivan in 2004 (Federal Emergency Management Agency 2010p). Despite the magnitude of the problems caused by Hurricane Georges, emergency management personnel handled the situations that arose quite well. This, in turn, produced images of successful disaster response activities and positive impressions of overall governmental performance.

Hurricane Georges in Puerto Rico

On September 16, 1998, a tropical storm named Georges developed off the coast of Africa. The storm intensified in strength as it moved westward across the warm waters of the

A young boy views the soaked remains of his family's possessions piled outside their home following Hurricane Georges in Puerto Rico, September 1998. *(Federal Emergency Management Agency/Dave Gatley: FEMA News Photo)*

Atlantic Ocean. By the next day, Georges was upgraded to a hurricane (U.S. Army Corps of Engineers 1998). Then, within twenty-four hours, it grew even stronger, attaining the status of a dangerous Category Four hurricane with maximum sustained winds of 150 miles per hour ("Georges Becomes Category 4 Hurricane" 1998). The storm lost some of its punch and was downgraded to a Category Two hurricane as it passed over several of the islands located in the northeastern section of the Caribbean. Then, late in the evening on September 21, Georges re-intensified again to a Category Three hurricane and slammed directly into Puerto Rico. It continued to track westward across the Dominican Republic, Haiti, and Cuba. During its four-day rampage across the Caribbean, Hurricane Georges caused billions of dollars in property damage (Rohter 1998a) and it left over 300,000 people homeless (Kovaleski 1998b). More than 600 people died or were reported missing as a result of the storm (U.S. Department of Commerce 1999).

Hurricane Georges caused extensive damage to several islands in the Caribbean, particularly to the U.S. territory of Puerto Rico. Here, the powerful storm ripped down telephone lines, knocked out satellite communications, washed out roads, and toppled trees (Kovaleski 1998a). Nearly all major roads on the islands were impassable and 80,000 of the island's homes were destroyed or damaged (Kovaleski 1998b). In Puerto Rico alone, 13 people died, 1 million citizens lost electricity, 700,000 had no drinkable water, and 28,000 residents had to seek refuge in temporary emergency shelters. Damage estimates for Hurricane Georges in Puerto Rico exceeded $2 billion (Rohter 1998a).

As a result of these conditions, everyday activities on the island were disrupted; it was extremely difficult, and in some cases impossible, for residents to follow their normal routines and daily patterns of behavior. Immediately after the storm, the residents of Puerto Rico were naturally terrified, nervous, and uncertain. Dazed citizens ventured outside of their homes to survey the extent of the destruction. Widespread power, communication, and transportation problems existed across the islands, making it difficult for local citizens to obtain accurate or complete information.

But despite these conditions, disaster victims seemed to comprehend what had happened to them. As one islander put it, "What can you do? This is life on the islands. You take the good with the bad" (Kovaleski 1998b, p. A1). In addition, many local residents were able to cope with the conditions that developed. They had taken precautionary steps to prepare for the storm by seeking refuge in emergency shelters or stockpiling supplies in their own homes. Hence, they already understood what happened to them and how to deal with it. This made it less necessary for the affected population to engage in a search for new meaning or guidance to help them handle the situation. As a result, the milling process was short-lived in Puerto Rico after Hurricane Georges.

Governmental Response Is Quickly Activated

For its part, the government had already taken important precautionary steps before the storm hit. Anticipating the hurricane's onslaught, Governor Pedro Rosello of Puerto Rico declared a state of emergency and he submitted a request to receive federal assistance and funds. Governor Rosello strongly encouraged local residents to make emergency storm preparations, to remain indoors, or to take refuge in temporary shelters (Rohter 1998d) and activated the National Guard to ensure the safety of the island's residents (British Broadcasting Company 1998).

The federal government had been monitoring the path of the storm closely. The National Hurricane Center warned the island residents to "prepare for the worst" (British Broadcasting Company 1998). FEMA alerted local officials in Puerto Rico to activate their emergency preparedness measures, and it sent an advance Emergency Response Team to the Caribbean in order to lay the necessary groundwork for relief activities two days before Georges moved into U.S. territory. Emergency agencies began transporting personnel, equipment, and supplies into the area so that they would be available to respond to any critical problems ("Georges Becomes Category 4 Hurricane" 1998). Then on September 20, FEMA established a twenty-four–hour Emergency Support Operations Unit and placed it in charge of any possible full-scale response effort. Federal officials were clearly *present* in Puerto Rico in advance of the storm (Federal Emergency Management Agency 1998a).

Immediately after Georges left the area, Governor Rosello sent an expedited request for relief to the federal government. Within a matter of hours, President Bill Clinton declared Puerto Rico to be a major disaster area, ordering the immediate release of

A family in the *barriada* of the Villas del Sol in Toa Baja, Puerto Rico, surveys the damage to their home along with FEMA officials following Hurricane Georges in Puerto Rico, September 1998. *(Federal Emergency Management Agency/Dave Gatley: FEMA News Photo)*

federal emergency resources to the area (Federal Emergency Management Agency 1998a). The disaster proclamation authorized the use of federal personnel, equipment, and lifesaving systems for the recovery efforts, and it also released federal funds to finance the delivery of power generators, plastic sheeting, food, medical supplies, and other essential emergency materials.

Over the next several days, FEMA coordinated and mobilized the response of a number of critical federal agencies, including the U.S. Army Corps of Engineers, the U.S. Forest Service, and the U.S. Department of Transportation. FEMA also worked closely with territorial and local officials to identify the most pressing needs of disaster victims and to marshal essential resources into the affected areas. In addition, FEMA sent in teams of its own agency experts to restore electrical power, provide temporary housing and shelter to disaster victims, and inform residents about the availability of disaster assistance (Federal Emergency Management Agency 1998a).

Emergent Norms Are Consistent with Governmental Plans

As in any disaster situation, keynoting behavior did take place. However, it was carried out by those officials who are *supposed* to provide guidance and direction—local agencies, private relief organizations, and federal emergency response units. The

FEMA Director James Lee Witt with Angel Morey, chief of staff to the governor of
Puerto Rico, Resident Commissioner Carlos Romero Barcelo, and Small Business
Administration Administrator Aida Alvarez at a news conference held at the governor's
mansion in Old San Juan, Puerto Rico, following Hurricane Georges, September 1998.
(Federal Emergency Management Agency: FEMA News photo)

particular nature of the milling process and keynoting activity meant that emergent
norms, which deviated from traditional, legally sanctioned norms and standards of
behavior, did not develop. According to all indications, disaster victims did not feel
that existing institutions were inappropriate or incapable of dealing with the damages
caused by the severe storm. Most residents appeared to view the situation as a disruptive, but manageable, condition in their lives (Centers for Disease Control 1998). As
one disaster victim put it, "This was just an expected part of living on the islands"
(Klein 1998, 23A).

Governmental Response Unfolds Fairly Smoothly, but from the Top Down

Public officials involved in the disaster concentrated on getting assistance to those in
need as quickly as possible. For the most part, emergency personnel seemed to understand what needed to be done, and they seemed willing and able to work with others
to attain their objectives. As a result, the response moved along quite smoothly.

This does not mean that every governmental activity worked exactly as it was supposed to. Local and territorial officials were unable to deal with the magnitude of the situation on their own. Consequently, the national government assumed a more proactive role in the response process than is normally the case. Hundreds of federal workers were immediately deployed to the island to help organize the response activities and to ensure that relief was provided to those in need. But the infusion of personnel and resources from the federal government into Puerto Rico was delayed for several days because the runways of the island's international airport were so cluttered with debris that flights could not land or take off (Rohter 1998a). The federal government also experienced problems processing disaster assistance applications, providing temporary shelter to storm victims, and distributing food, water, and emergency supplies (Federal Emergency Management Agency 1998e; "Georges Plows Into Puerto Rico" 1998; Klein 1998; Robles 1998a).

Fortunately, however, these problems were resolved fairly quickly. Three months after Hurricane Georges struck Puerto Rico, the national government had issued more than 137,000 low-interest loans to help individual families and businesses rebuild on the island. It had also distributed more than $400 million in disaster housing assistance (Federal Emergency Management Agency 1999).

Size of the Gap Is Small

The size of the gap between emergent norms and bureaucratic behavior was quite small during the response to Hurricane Georges in the Caribbean. The post-disaster emergent norms of the affected population in Puerto Rico complemented the actions of the response agencies. Disaster victims acted calmly, and they behaved quite rationally throughout the entire process. This, in turn, made it easier for governmental agencies to administer emergency assistance in a timely manner.

Hurricane Georges in the Florida Keys

After causing massive destruction in the Caribbean, Hurricane Georges moved back into open waters. At first, it seemed that Georges might be losing its punch. But the storm strengthened once again and it started moving directly toward the southern tip of Florida. At this point, Georges was not nearly as powerful as it had once been. But it was still an extremely dangerous Category Two hurricane.

On Friday, September 25, Hurricane Georges struck the Florida Keys just before midday. It slammed into the area with 105 mile-per-hour winds and storm surges of over seven feet. Georges produced widespread flooding throughout the low-lying areas of the Florida Keys. It knocked out electrical power to thousands of residents (Jervis 1998). In its path, Georges destroyed homes, businesses, roads, and bridges (Rohter 1998c).

Governmental Response Is Activated, Precautionary Steps Are Taken

Emergency response personnel were carefully monitoring Georges long before it struck the Florida Keys. The National Hurricane Center had issued hurricane watches from Deerfield

FEMA and state civil defense officials meet with residents to discuss the flood damages following Hurricane Georges, Arecibo, Puerto Rico, September 1998. *(Federal Emergency Management Agency/Dave Gatley: FEMA News Photo)*

Beach south along the west coast of Florida and Bonita Beach south along Florida's east coast (Federal Emergency Management Agency 1998c), and it told residents that if they were "anywhere in the warning area . . . to prepare for the worst" (British Broadcasting Company 1998). City and county officials issued public announcements asking visitors and nonresidents in the watch areas to leave as soon as possible (Kovaleski 1998b; Rohter 1998e). State emergency management personnel began developing pre-landfall mandatory evacuation procedures (Booth 1998); FEMA officials were dispatched to the Florida Emergency Operations Center in Tallahassee to mobilize federal relief efforts.

On September 23, two days before Georges hit the U.S. coast, Florida Governor Lawton Chiles declared a state of emergency. Local officials in the southernmost counties ordered mandatory evacuations of the Florida Keys. A total of 1.4 million people, nearly a tenth of the state's total population, were asked to leave low-lying areas (Rohter 1998c). State and local officials identified places out of the hurricane's path for evacuees to stay, and they began to identify temporary housing and shelters for residents who did not evacuate (Booth 1998; *Miami Herald* 1998b). Government offices in the central and southern counties were closed, as were all southbound roads from Florida City to the Keys; services were suspended at local airports and railroad stations (Rohter 1998c). Governor Chiles sent National Guard Troops to the Homestead Air Force base armory (Rohter 1998c). FEMA assembled a National Emergency Response Team, it placed an Emergency Support Team on alert, and it also deployed

Mobile Emergency Response Support technicians from surrounding states to Talla-hassee. Over 1,000 federal personnel were already pre-positioned in Florida ready to deal with the impending storm (Federal Emergency Management Agency 1998d). On September 25, 2009, the day that Georges struck the Keys, President Clinton signed an emergency declaration, which authorized the release of federal funds for emergency protective measures and debris removal for the Keys (Federal Emergency Manage-ment Agency 1998h). FEMA Director James Lee Witt designated seventeen counties eligible for emergency aid, which authorized the release of federal aid, personnel, equipment, lifesaving systems, and emergency materials. President Clinton remarked: "We are as ready as we can be, and we pray that the human and material cost will be limited" (Rohter 1998c, p. A).

Milling Process Begins, but Ends Quickly

Hurricane Georges inflicted severe damage to the coastal communities in the Florida Keys. Georges uprooted trees, knocked down power lines, washed out roads, and damaged hundreds of homes. Over a hundred thousand people were left without power, some of them stranded in local shelters and evacuation centers (Rohter 1998c). Conditions along the Gulf Coast were severe enough to cause major disruptions in everyday routines and behavior patterns. This, in turn, triggered the immediate onset of the milling process.

Milling was most pronounced in areas where the local population was caught off guard. In some communities, the flooding occurred so quickly that residents did not know what they should do to protect their families, their belongings, and their homes from the rising floodwaters. They were confused and disoriented. As one survivor in the Florida Keys remarked, "People are all stressed out. The generators run all night. You can't get a good night's sleep. You're still dreaming about the storm coming back. . . . You're kind of terrorized" (Morgan and Long 1998, p. 9A). These feelings led to the usual search for meaning that defines the milling process.

However, the situation in the Keys stabilized fairly quickly. Affected citizens regained their composure and began dealing more calmly with their problems. The short duration of the milling process was due to several factors. First, compared to the devastation caused by Hurricane Georges in the Caribbean, the storm's impact in the Florida Keys was not as severe. By the time it reached the Straits of Florida, Georges had weakened from a Category Three to a Category Two hurricane, its winds had diminished, and it was producing far less rain. Although Georges was still a major storm when it struck the Florida Keys, it was not the "killer" storm that had hit the Caribbean (U.S. Department of Commerce 1999). This certainly made it easier for local residents to deal with the hurricane-related problems that did develop.

Second, foresight and preparation played a major role in way that local residents approached the storm. More than 75 percent of the residents in the Keys heeded the evacuation warnings and left the area before Georges even hit (Washburn and Bridges 1998). This was the largest evacuation in Florida history, involving about

10 percent of the entire state's population (Washburn and Haj 1998). The federal government referred to this evacuation as a "textbook operation," which allowed many residents to get out of the way of the impending storm. But the success of the evacuation stemmed from the degree to which local residents heeded the warnings to leave their homes and move out of the path of the hurricane (Zaneski 1998). Moreover, those who stayed took the necessary precautions; for example, they boarded up their homes, stocked up on food and water, and so forth. One local resident expressed it quite succinctly: "We did good, we were prepared" (*Miami Herald* 1998a, 25A).

Third, many Floridians had vivid memories of another hurricane—Andrew. As a result, they were more knowledgeable about what they should do before the storm hit (Etheart 1998). As one local resident put it, "Andrew made us want to be prepared" (*Miami Herald* 1998d, p. 1B). Andrew also made Floridians more aware of how they should respond to the storm after it struck, as well as the possible consequences of not reacting appropriately. They concentrated on helping one another and working with public officials to expedite the relief effort. According to one observer, "You see people after the hurricane. They're in a daze. They see a friend; they tell their story. It's a great catharsis. It gets them out of denial into acceptance so they can make decisions. I think we'll recover here very quickly" (Cocking 1998, p. 5B). As another disaster victim expressed it, "There's a lot of people pulling together" (Fountain and Saulny 1998, p. A18).

Governmental Response Is Implemented from the Bottom Up

Public officials at all three levels of government dealt with the situation in the Florida Keys using standard operating procedures and protocols. Local emergency management personnel provided an effective first response to the situation: they focused on the most critical needs—restoring power and water supplies in the affected areas (McNair 1998). And they took the necessary steps to mobilize and organize the response. For example, Miami-Dade Mayor Alex Peneles, became the area's self-appointed spokesperson and mobilizer for the local response effort: he held a series of conferences to coordinate the actions of local emergency management organizations; he dispatched search and rescue teams into storm-damaged areas; and he sent crews of workers to clean up and remove storm debris.

Such actions were extremely important. They enabled local relief workers to provide an effective first response to the situation. As a result, little disruption or confusion in the delivery of emergency assistance occurred. And there was no need for officials at higher levels to step in and take over. In addition, the efforts of local-level agencies also played a significant role in helping to calm and reassure the population. Their actions demonstrated to storm victims that government assistance was on the way (Branch 1998).

State officials worked quickly to bolster local-level actions. Florida Governor Chiles asked President Clinton to declare the Florida Keys a major disaster area. He sent about 600 members of the Florida National Guard to help stabilize the affected communities, and mobilized state personnel and resources for emergency response operations. Governor Chiles also established priorities for the response effort: reestablishing communications systems; dispatching search and rescue teams; dispensing critical supplies, such as water, food, and shelter; and removing storm debris (Driscoll, Long, and Merzer 1998). Such actions helped activate and organize the operations of emergency personnel across the entire intergovernmental system.

The federal government responded to the disaster in the Keys fairly quickly and effectively. President Clinton declared the area a major disaster area on Monday, September 29, four days after the storm hit the area, authorizing the mobilization of greater federal support and the release of additional federal funds into the area. FEMA sent medical teams, search and rescue units, and mobile transportation and telecommunication equipment into Florida Keys; the U.S. Army Corps of Engineers deployed response teams to help distribute ice and water and to restore power; the U.S. Coast Guard established a crisis action center to coordinate disaster response operations; and the U.S. Department of Agriculture sent supplies from nearby food stores (Federal Emergency Management Agency 1998d). FEMA Director Witt indicated that the federal government was willing and able to assist in the recovery operations: "FEMA is prepared to handle Hurricane Georges, even if we must operate in several theaters of operation" (Federal Emergency Management Agency 1998e).

The actions of local and state officials made it possible for the federal government to assume its traditional role. Unlike what happened in Puerto Rico a few days earlier, the federal government did not have to step in and assume control over the relief effort. Instead, federal-level actions supported and supplemented those of state and local emergency management organizations. This allowed disaster assistance to be implemented using the more standard bottom-up process during the response to Hurricane Georges in the Florida Keys.

Size of the Gap Is Small

The gap during Hurricane Georges in the Florida Keys was quite small. The postdisaster emergent norms in the population were almost fully consistent with the bureaucratic norms of the response agencies. Citizens usually reacted calmly and behaved quite rationally throughout the entire process (Booth 1998). People waited patiently in long lines to get food, ice, and medical supplies. In areas where National Guard troops were directing traffic and guarding against possible looters, people even applauded. Overall, there was a "good feeling" that the people would "be back on their feet again" fairly quickly (Silva, Bousquet, and Bridges 1998, 8A).

This created exactly the kind of situation that facilitated the smooth implementation of disaster assistance. Emergency response agencies were able to use standard procedures and protocols to mobilize necessary resources and distribute them to the affected populations.

Hurricane Georges Along the U.S. Gulf Coast

Hurricane Georges was still not finished, however. Three days after plowing its way through the tip of Florida, Georges hit the U.S. mainland once again. On September 28, Georges came ashore near Biloxi, Mississippi. It was still a strong Category Two hurricane with winds of 100 miles per hour. Here, it produced torrential rain and tidal surges of 8.5 to 9 feet (U.S. Army Corps of Engineers 1998).

Then Georges moved gradually in an east-northeasterly direction into the coastal areas of southern Alabama and the panhandle region of Florida. Georges dumped up to twenty to thirty inches of rain, caused extreme flooding, and created serious storm surges. As it drifted farther and farther inland, Georges was downgraded from a hurricane to a tropical storm and then to a tropical depression. But it continued to produce large amounts of rain, high winds, flooding, and isolated tornadoes (National Oceanic and Atmospheric Administration 1998). Finally, the huge, slow-moving storm lost its punch. Georges eventually died out near the Alabama-Georgia border.

Another Governmental Response Is Activated

Once again, the governmental response system was activated *before* Hurricane Georges hit the northern sections of the Gulf Coast. Even as the storm was battering the Florida Keys, local authorities in Louisiana, Mississippi, and along the Florida panhandle urged people to evacuate low-lying areas, to seek refuge in temporary shelters, and to take all necessary steps to fortify their homes (Ayres 1998b). State emergency Operations Centers were set up in Mississippi and Alabama, non-essential state offices were closed, and state agencies began collecting emergency supplies and equipment. For its part, the federal government expanded its response operations to include Georges's potential landfall sites along the northern Gulf Coast: Emergency Operations Centers were established in Mississippi and Alabama, and FEMA personnel were sent to these locations to facilitate a more coordinated relief effort (Federal Emergency Management Agency 1998c).

As the storm moved closer and closer to the northern Gulf Coast, the governmental response accelerated. Local authorities issued mandatory evacuation orders and established curfews in order to ensure the safety and security of those who stayed behind (Ayres 1998b). The governors of Mississippi, Alabama, and Florida ordered mandatory evacuation orders of residents along the coast, they closed non-essential state services and offices, and they took steps to stockpile emergency supplies and equipment (Ayres 1998b; *New York Times* 1998). States of emergency were declared in Mississippi and Alabama, and Emergency Operations Centers became fully operational (Federal Emergency Management Agency 1998e). FEMA put the National Emergency Response Team on "standby" notice in order to jump-start an interagency response to another series of major disasters, and it set up a federal Disaster Field Office in Baton Rouge in anticipation of another federal disaster declaration (Federal Emergency Management Agency 1998f). Other federal agencies were also already on the scene: the Department of Veterans Affairs had deployed doctors and nurses; the Army Corps of Engineers had procured sandbags and generators; the U.S. Department of Agriculture authorized the release of food supplies for use in emergency shelters; and the U.S. Coast Guard reported that it its units were in position and prepared for the hurricane's arrival (Federal Emergency Management Agency 1998f). FEMA Director James Lee Witt announced: "FEMA is prepared to move into affected areas as soon as it is safe" (Federal Emergency Management Agency 1998d).

Milling Process Is Short-Lived

Hurricane Georges' impact along the northern sections of the Gulf Coast was severe. The storm damaged hundreds of homes and businesses; it uprooted trees and washed out roads throughout the area; it caused massive power outages; and it created serious shortages in the supply of suitable drinking water (Bousquet, Silva, and Merzer 1998). Here, Georges was responsible for three more deaths (Fountain 1998).

Such conditions triggered the milling process in communities along the Gulf Coast. A number of local communities resembled ghost towns: streets were deserted, signs were thrown everywhere, trees littered the roads, and traffic lights were inoperable or nonexistent (Fountain 1998). Quite naturally, local residents were anxious about what had happened to them. They searched for explanations and guidance to help them cope with the situation.

But the milling process did not last long. Affected citizens regained their composure and began dealing with their problems. Most disaster victims felt equipped to handle the situation and they reacted in a calm and orderly manner. This truncated the ongoing search for meaning among the affected population. And it allowed disaster-stricken communities to focus on those activities that would facilitate recovery efforts (Fountain and Saulny 1998).

There were at least two reasons for the short duration of the milling process in this area. First, the storm's impact was less severe. By the time Georges hit this part of the U.S. mainland, it had lost some of its punch. Compared to the situations elsewhere, flooding was relatively minor, and many buildings escaped major damages (Ayres 1998a). Clearly, this made it much easier for residents to deal with the conditions that confronted them.

Second, citizens along the northern Gulf Coast were prepared for Georges. They had been given plenty of warning about the storm's destruction in the Caribbean, as well as the damages it had inflicted in the Florida Keys. And most Gulf Coast residents had heeded these warnings, taking the necessary precautionary to protect themselves from the impending storm. Stated simply, residents were better equipped to handle the storm (Ayres 1998a; Sattler and Kaiser 2000).

Bottom-Up Implementation Pattern

The governmental response to Hurricane Georges along the northern Gulf Coast worked from the bottom up, exactly as it was designed. Before the storm hit, local officials

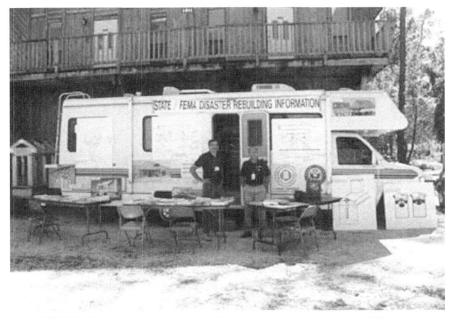

One of FEMA's disaster rebuilding information vans used to assist storm victims in Alabama following Hurricane Georges, September 1998. *(Federal Emergency Management Agency/John Pilger: FEMA News Photo)*

concentrated their efforts on evacuating residents, establishing temporary shelters for stranded citizens, and creating emergency operation centers to coordinate the relief efforts (Ayres 1998b). The respective state governments were also involved before the storm struck the Gulf Coast area—issuing evacuation warnings and mobilizing law enforcement agencies (Ayres 1998b). For its part, the federal government had already deployed hundreds of federal officials from various agencies into areas likely to be hit by the hurricane. These officials were immediately on hand to assess the storm's preliminary damages, to assist state officials in preparing requests for federal disaster aid, and to help coordinate the response efforts. In addition, federal personnel had been dispatched to the Gulf Coast to help evacuate citizens, assist in search and rescue operations, and re-establish communication systems (Federal Emergency Management Agency 1998c).

Following the storm, local officials focused on helping the affected populations, and they handled immediate problems. They organized search and rescue operations, clean-up activities, and power restoration efforts. Some communities issued curfews while others mobilized additional law enforcement units to ensure the safety of residents (Ayres 1998a). In short, local emergency management personnel provided an effective first response.

At the next level, state personnel coordinated activities across local jurisdictions and they channeled state resources, such as social service personnel and road mainte- nance crews, into the affected areas. State emergency management officials acted as coordinators and facilitators; they effectively served as intermediaries between local and federal organizations.

The national government provided critical support and assistance to state and local authorities. Within twenty-four hours, President Clinton authorized the release of federal emergency resources and funds to support the Hurricane Georges relief efforts in the ravaged states along the Gulf Coast. Soon thereafter, federal aid was expanded to cover the long-term recovery of families and communities affected by the hurricane (Federal Emergency Management Agency 1998g, 1998i). This enabled citizens in affected communities to receive additional assistance so that they could repair or rebuild their homes and businesses. FEMA also sent in damage assessment teams and inspectors who evaluated the ongoing integrity of buildings, roads, dams, bridges, and other public facilities. Finally, FEMA officials oversaw a comprehensive review and evaluation of the emergency management systems in place across the disaster-stricken areas.

Throughout the response to Hurricane Georges in the Gulf Coast, the national government acted in a *supportive* capacity. Officials from FEMA and other federal entities never took over the process or supplanted the activities of lower-level governmental personnel. Instead, they provided the necessary resources and additional support that was needed in order to get emergency assistance into the storm-damaged communities.

Virtually No Gap Between Emergent Norms and Bureaucratic Norms

In this situation, the post-disaster norms of the affected population were quite consistent with the bureaucratic norms of the emergency response agencies. Most people reacted calmly, and they behaved quite rationally. They did not panic or act erratically, and did not blame others for their predicament. Instead, they concentrated on helping one another in order to get conditions back to normal. According to one report, "In the coastal cities of Mississippi and Alabama, even before the drizzly remains of Georges were fully departed, a chain-saw cavalry of tree cutters arrived to help drenched residents dig out" (Silva, Bousquet, and Bridges 1998, p. 8A).

A sense of camaraderie developed among those who experienced the storm. In the words of one local resident, "There's a lot of people pulling together, a lot of people that are trying to help each other" (Fountain 1998, p. A3). Disaster victims focused their efforts on "pulling themselves up" and rebuilding their homes, their communities, and their lives (Suro 1992a, p. A8).

Governmental actions complemented those of private citizens. Emergency management personnel across all three levels of government seemed to be fairly well prepared for the disaster. Local and state officials had been emphasizing hazard mitigation and disaster planning, so they were able to perform their pre-assigned emergency response operations.

This, in turn, allowed the federal government to supplement, not replace, their efforts. Emergency officials relied upon existing procedures and policies, and they worked with, not against, each other to address the most pressing problems. As a

A victim of Hurricane Georges in Alabama expresses an opinion about the impact of the storm, September 1998. *(Federal Emergency Management Agency/John Pilger: FEMA News Photo)*

result, they were able to provide credible and consistent guidance to the affected population.

Thus, the gap during Hurricane Georges along the Gulf Coast was quite small. The post-disaster emergent norms in the population were fully consistent with the bureaucratic norms of the response agencies. Citizens reacted calmly and behaved quite rationally throughout the entire process. Emergency relief personnel were prepared for the situation, and they followed basic procedures and protocols. Hence, little conflict between what citizens expected and what governmental agencies provided existed.

Overall Perception of the Governmental Responses to Hurricane Georges: Positive and Successful

The governmental responses to Hurricane Georges in Puerto Rico, the Florida Keys, and the Gulf Coast demonstrate what happens when the gap between emergent norms and bureaucratic procedures is fairly small: public expectations coincide closely with governmental actions. The populations affected by Hurricane Georges had fairly realistic notions about the government's role during disasters. They did not expect governmental agencies to immediately solve all of their problems. Instead, they were willing to work with other storm victims and public authorities to alleviate conditions. This, in turn, facilitated the actions of emergency management personnel.

For their part, public officials seemed to be directly focused on the impending danger. They provided the appropriate guidance to help disaster victims prepare for and respond to the hurricane. And they worked fairly closely with one another to identify the needs of the affected populations and to distribute aid to them. They were also willing to adjust their actions in order to accommodate the problems and circumstances that developed in specific areas.

It is important to note that the governmental response did not work the same way in all three of these situations. As stated earlier in this chapter, the national government assumed a more commanding role in the Caribbean than it did in the Florida Keys or along the Gulf Coast. Indeed, the governmental response to Georges in Puerto Rico more closely resembled a top-down implementation pattern, while the latter responses conformed more closely to the traditional bottom-up process. Clearly, the magnitude of the storm's impact, as well as the inability of territorial personnel to handle the situation, altered the flow of assistance through the intergovernmental framework in Puerto Rico.

In the end, however, there was very little criticism of the governmental responses to Hurricane Georges in any of these locations. Perhaps some of this was due to the fact that more attention was focused on *other* areas, that is, those outside of U.S. jurisdiction, including the Dominican Republic, Haiti, Antigua, St. Kitts, Nevis, and Cuba, which were hit more severely by the storm. For example, in the Dominican Republic, Hurricane Georges killed over 200 people, left 100,000 homeless, and caused more than $1 billion in damages. And in the small neighboring country of Haiti, the storm destroyed many dozens of homes, left hundreds of residents homeless, and was responsible for another 167 deaths (U.S. Department of Commerce 1999). Many residents on these islands seemed to be unprepared for the hurricane or unwilling to take precautionary steps (*Miami Herald* 1998c; Robles 1998b; Pierre-Pierre 1998). Government officials waited too long to issue evacuation orders, and they failed to activate emergency response measures in an expeditious manner (Robles 1998b). As a result, relief efforts in these areas proceeded very slowly and chaotically. And there was intense criticism of the responses to Hurricane Georges in these situations (Colon 1998; Klein 1998; Robles 1998a; Treaster 1998).

Ironically, the attention that was focused on these other responses to Hurricane Georges may have enabled the relief efforts in the United States to proceed more quietly and smoothly. Overall, the behavior of emergency response personnel in U.S. territory seemed to match the expectations of the disaster-stricken populations. The gap between emergent and bureaucratic norms was quite small in all U.S. areas hit by the hurricane. As a result, the general impression is that the governmental responses to Hurricane Georges in Puerto Rico, the Florida Keys, and the Gulf Coast were largely successful.

Note

1. For more information about Hurricane Georges and the governmental response to it, see media reports by *Miami Herald, Washington Post,* and *New York Times,* particularly from September 20 through September 30, 1998 (for example Silva, Bousquet, and Bridges 1998; Kovaleski 1998a–c; and Fountain 1998). The Federal Emergency Management Agency also provided day-by-day updates during this period through their Office of Media Affairs (Federal Emergency Management Agency 1998a–1998i, 1999). And several useful accounts of specific aspects of the hurricane were prepared by the Centers for Disease Control (1998) and the National Climatic Data Center of the National Oceanic and Atmospheric Administration (U.S. Department of Commerce 1999).

12

Hurricane Katrina

Hurricane Katrina struck the Gulf Coast region of the United States in August 2005. This intensely powerful storm transformed 90,000 square miles of land across 138 parishes and counties in four states. Katrina was directly responsible for more than 1,800 deaths, and led to the relocation of more than 800,000 residents (Federal Emergency Management Agency 2006b). Although estimates vary, total economic losses due to Hurricane Katrina (including the loss of revenue and jobs during rebuilding, as well as the loss of property) could exceed $100 billion (Hamman 2005; U.S. Department of Commerce 2006). This hurricane, by itself, represents one of the most destructive, deadliest, and costly storms to ever hit the United States (Blake, Rappaport, and Landsea 2007).[1]

Over five years later, major rebuilding efforts are still underway in many of the storm-damaged areas. And, the federal government has promised that it would help defray much of the public expense in order to restore the disaster-stricken areas of the Gulf Coast (VandeHei and Baker 2005; Federal Emergency Management Agency 2005z, 2005aa, 2006a, 2009b; Cooper and Block 2006). Hurricane Katrina was one of the worst natural disasters in our nation's history, and it triggered an unprecedented level of governmental assistance (Federal Emergency Management Agency 2010m).

Given the scope and severity of the storm's impact, it is not surprising that the government assumed a major role in the nation's response to Hurricane Katrina. The magnitude of this disaster left little doubt: governmental involvement was absolutely necessary. What is surprising, however, is that the governmental response to Katrina was so abysmal. After all, the nation's entire emergency management system was re-organized in 2003, following the September 11, 2001, terrorist attacks. A new cabinet-level department was established, emergency relief operations were consolidated, and separate procedures were created in order to handle extreme catastrophic events. Hence, the government should have been better equipped to handle a major disaster like Katrina.

The victims of Katrina needed immediate assistance. But the government was unable to respond to their needs in a quick or effective manner. Initially, there were numerous reports of communication breakdowns, extremely slow rescue operations, the misguided use of available resources, and the lackadaisical actions of public officials (S. Schneider 2005). Subsequently, a steady barrage of reports revealed the inappropriateness of governmental planning, partisan bickering between political leaders, and the misdirection of public funds.[2] All of this has created the general, lasting impression that the governmental response to Katrina was a complete, indeed an unparalleled, failure.[3]

As we shall see in this chapter, a noticeable gap between public expectations and bureaucratic behavior in the response to Hurricane Katrina existed. But the size of the gap varied across different areas of the disaster-stricken region. Specifically, it was much larger in Louisiana than it was in the neighboring state of Mississippi. Katrina caused severe devastation throughout the entire area, but the disaster that occurred in Louisiana was quite different from the one that developed in Mississippi. Also there were noticeable differences across the two states in the operations of emergency response agencies, the degree of media attention devoted to the two disaster situations, the implementation patterns for emergency relief, and the level of dissatisfaction expressed by disaster victims themselves. These factors affected the size of the gap that developed in each case. And once again, the size of the gap determined the overall perception of the effectiveness and responsiveness of governmental efforts.

Hurricane Katrina in Louisiana

On August 23, 2005, a tropical depression formed off the southeastern coast of the Bahamas. Over the next couple of days, the storm intensified and strengthened into a Category One hurricane, and it acquired the name Katrina. Hurricane Katrina first made landfall off the tip of the Florida peninsula near Hallandale Beach on the Dade-Broward county line. The storm immediately made a hard left, skirting along the densely populated coastline near metropolitan Miami. Then it moved in a southwesterly direction through the unpopulated Everglades National Park and exited the state near the southern tip of mainland Florida. Here, the storm was responsible for fourteen deaths, and it caused serious damages in coastal communities. As significant as these impacts were, Florida was spared from the most severe consequences of the storm. Luckily, Katrina hit some of the most sparsely populated areas along the Florida coast.

For the next couple of days, Katrina remained in the warm waters of the Gulf of Mexico where it grew into a Category Five hurricane. The monstrous storm moved northward toward the Louisiana coast. Then, at 6:10 A.M. on Monday, August 29, Katrina made a second landfall in Plaquemines Parish in southeastern Louisiana. Although the storm had just weakened to a Category Four level, it still produced sustained winds of 125 miles per hour and wind gusts over 150 miles per hour. Katrina continued to move northward. About four hours later, it made its third and final landfall along the Mississippi-Louisiana border. Then it plowed upward through the southern tip of Louisiana, into central Mississippi, and on to portions of Alabama and Tennessee before finally weakening.

Louisiana experienced some of the most severe consequences of Katrina. Powerful winds and exceptionally high storm surges flattened communities and infrastructure for hundreds of miles. Homes were destroyed, trees uprooted, vessels beached, and storm debris scattered throughout the affected area. In New Orleans, the city's flood walls and

Cars are scattered throughout flood waters and mud following the breaking of the levees surrounding the city as a result of Hurricane Katrina, New Orleans, Louisiana, August 2005. *(Federal Emergency Management Agency/Jocelyn Augustino: FEMA News Photo)*

levees were breached, producing catastrophic flooding across portions of the city. At its height, approximately 80 percent of the city of New Orleans was filled with water up to twenty feet deep (U.S. Department of Commerce 2005b).

Here, Hurricane Katrina was responsible for 1,400 deaths and the displacement of over 1 million people. The huge storm caused over $100 billion in damages to public and private property across Louisiana (U.S. Department of Commerce 2006b). Katrina also triggered an unprecedented governmental relief effort, aimed at rebuilding the city of New Orleans and its surrounding communities (Federal Emergency Management Agency 2006a).

Traditional Governmental Response Is Activated

The governmental response process was already underway before Hurricane Katrina hit the Gulf Coast region of Louisiana. Local officials advised residents to evacuate and they set up shelters to facilitate the orderly movement of citizens out of low-lying areas. At the next governmental level, Governor Kathleen Babineaux Blanco declared a "state of emergency" and mobilized relevant assets. Responding to state needs, the federal government was also involved before the storm hit. The Federal Emergency Management Agency (FEMA) moved supplies and personnel into the region so that they could be more quickly dispatched into areas affected by the storm

(Federal Emergency Management Agency 2005i). At the request of Governor Blanco, President George W. Bush issued an emergency declaration on August 27 (Federal Emergency Management Agency 2005l) and then declared Louisiana to be a "major disaster" early on August 29, the day the storm hit the Louisiana coast (Federal Emergency Management Agency 2005bb). At this stage, government officials at the local, state, and national levels all seemed to understand their own emergency management responsibilities, and they were working with one another to get assistance to affected areas. But this situation did not last for very long.

Milling Process Begins Quickly, Continues for Several Days

The milling process in Louisiana began almost immediately after Hurricane Katrina moved through the region, particularly in the hardest-hit areas. When the levees surrounding the city of New Orleans failed, water began draining into the streets. Local residents were told to get out of the city immediately.

Those who were unable to leave on their own were instructed to go to the New Orleans Convention Center and the Louisiana Superdome to get transportation out of the flooded areas. However, these makeshift facilities were quickly overwhelmed with people seeking water, food, and shelter: the temporary evacuation centers were simply not equipped to handle the volume of people in need.

Buses were commissioned to transport people out of these facilities, but they were left stranded outside of the city because there were no drivers to operate them ("After Katrina" 2005). As a result, thousands of Katrina's victims endured several more agonizing, nightmarish days and nights after the storm without supplies and assistance. "There was no security, no water, no medical help . . . no sign of any organized relief . . . Just people crying 'Help us!' " ("After Katrina" 2005, p. 49).

The images of this situation are still quite vivid in the minds of most Americans: families stranded on rooftops with floodwaters surrounding them waiting for someone to rescue them; people sleeping side-by-side on makeshift cots in the convention center and Superdome; children roaming around the shelters and evacuation centers in stifling heat looking frantically for friends and relatives; elderly victims lying on chairs and benches as they waited to be transported out of the city; and dead bodies floating in the flooded streets of New Orleans.

As a result of these conditions, disaster victims resorted to different types of behavior. Most of this activity was quite positive and "prosocial": people pitched in and helped one another. Disaster victims initiated their own search missions to locate those who were unable to evacuate; they used their own boats to transport other residents out of flooded areas; and they distributed critical food and medical supplies to fellow disaster victims (Rodriguez, Trainor, and Quarantelli 2006; Tierney, Bevc, and Kuligowski 2006). But some of the behavior was not typical or conventional. There were numerous accounts of looting, stealing, and pilfering in many sections of New Orleans (Gugliotta and Whoriskey 2005; McFadden and Blumenthal 2005; Philbin 2005; Robinson 2005; Treaster and Kleinfield 2005; Treaster and Sontag 2005).

Residents lining up with their belongings to get into the Superdome, which was opened as a shelter for victims of Hurricane Katrina, New Orleans, Louisiana, September 2005. *(Federal Emergency Management Agency/Marty Bahamonde: FEMA News Photo)*

Reports also surfaced that violent crimes were committed against fellow storm victims, as well as against law enforcement officers and other emergency response personnel (McGill 2005; Lee 2010). Scalping and price gouging were reported to be common problems throughout much of the storm-damaged areas. Reports surfaced about inappropriate and illegal behavior on the part of the police officers who were supposed to be maintaining law and order (Baum 2006; Robertson 2009, 2010). Overall, the prevailing picture was that a "state of anarchy" had developed ("After Katrina" 2005; Anderson, Perlstein, and Scott 2005; Dowd 2005; Haygood and Tyson 2005; "System Failure" 2005).

Bottom-Up Governmental Response Collapses

Everyone involved in the response appeared to be paralyzed by the severity of the situation. Local officials were so overwhelmed that they were unable to take quick or

A warning posted by a local resident to those who are thinking about looting following Hurricane Katrina in New Orleans, Louisiana, September 2005. *(Federal Emergency Management Agency/Liz Roll: FEMA News Photo)*

decisive action. New Orleans Mayor Ray Nagin delayed issuing a mandatory evacuation of the city until twenty-four hours before the storm hit, even though it was clear that Katrina was going to be a "once-in-a-lifetime event" which would exceed the city's capabilities (van Heerden and Bryan 2006, p. 59). The mayor encouraged people with special needs to go to the Superdome as a "shelter of last resort" and bring food and water with them, even though the Superdome was ill-suited to serve as such a make-shift shelter for stranded citizens ("System Failure" 2005, 37). The mayor also failed to authorize the use of city buses to evacuate citizens who were unable to leave. As a result, hundreds of buses sat unused and were submerged in water in various lots around the city while thousands of residents were stranded in nursing homes, hospitals, makeshift shelters, and crowded evacuation facilities ("After Katrina" 2005).

In fact, conditions were so severe that many local officials were simply unable to perform their basic role as "first responders." Emergency personnel could not implement some of the most critical elements of their own emergency management plans, such as evacuating the elderly and people with special needs, providing basic services to affected populations, and so on. They were also unable to stabilize local conditions or maintain law and order, particularly in the most devastated areas of the city of New Orleans ("After Katrina" 2005). Some local police officers abandoned their posts in order to protect their own families and belongings (Baum 2006), while others turned in their badges expressing frustration and concern about their own capabilities ("After Katrina" 2005). As a result, some of the most serious breakdowns

School buses are stranded by the floodwaters following Hurricane Katrina, New Orleans, Louisiana, September 2005. *(Federal Emergency Management Agency/Liz Roll: FEMA News Photo)*

in the governmental system occurred at the local level. This made it impossible for the response to work its way upward through the intergovernmental structure as it was supposed to do.

The situation was not any better at the state level. Public officials tried to implement the state's emergency response plan, but they did not take the necessary steps to get essential resources into the most devastated areas. Governor Blanco asked for additional assistance from the federal government, but she did not indicate exactly what type of assistance was needed or where it should be directed ("System Failure" 2005). She also refused to declare martial law or a "state of emergency," and she declined a proposal from the White House to put National Guard troops under the control of the federal government (Luo, 2005; Shane, Lipton, and Drew 2005).

Other state personnel exhibited similar behavior and did not act quickly or forcefully to implement key emergency response and recovery operations (van Heerden and Bryan 2006). For example, the Louisiana National Guard was unable to stabilize local conditions even when they were deployed into the most devastated locations ("Anatomy of a Disaster" 2005). Afraid of the growing numbers of stranded disaster victims, the Louisiana National Guard troops actually retreated from the Convention Center, stating that they were not there to restore "law and order" (Roig-Franzia and Hsu 2005; Brinkley 2006). All in all, Louisiana state officials did not seem to understand their functions and responsibilities in the intergovernmental disaster relief process.

The federal government tried to implement assistance according to pre-established policies and procedures. FEMA dispatched urban search and rescue teams to evacuate stranded storm victims; it called up medical assistance teams from across the country to provide emergency medical aid; it sent convoys of food, water, and ice into the impacted areas; it assisted in transporting and sheltering stranded hurricane victims; and it tried to coordinate the efforts of law enforcement personnel in order to stabilize local conditions (Federal Emergency Management Agency 2005a, 2005b, 2005x).

But federal officials were unwilling to step in and take charge of the response effort (Lipton, Drew, Shane, and Rohde 2005; Steinhauer and Lipton 2005). Michael D. Brown, Undersecretary, Emergency Preparedness and Response, Department of Homeland Security and Director of the Federal Emergency Management Agency urged federal personnel not to respond to the counties and states affected by Hurricane Katrina without first being "requested and lawfully dispatched" by state and local authorities (Federal Emergency Management Agency 2005i). And he "asked for patience from individuals who may be uncomfortable while we conduct search and rescue efforts for those who are stranded and without commodities" (Federal Emergency Management Agency 2005j).

The Department of Homeland Security Secretary Michael Chertoff did declare Katrina an "incident of national significance" the day after the storm made landfall and this should have helped to jump-start federal activity. But by this time, the traditional bottom-up system of intergovernmental relief had already been initiated. As a result, federal personnel assumed that they were to wait for requests—referred to as the "pull"—from lower-level governments before taking action. But as we have seen, lower-level officials were completely overwhelmed in their efforts to address the problems created by Katrina. The normal bottom-up response process was simply not designed to deal with such catastrophic conditions (U.S. House of Representatives 2006). Some federal emergency management officials in the field quickly realized the magnitude of the disaster and the need for more proactive national leadership. So they took it upon themselves to initiate a top-down, or "push," system. But their actions did not coincide with the normal protocols or standard operating procedures for governmental relief (U.S. House of Representatives 2006). Consequently, federal aid was further delayed and less certain because there were more questions about who was supposed to be doing what (Brinkley 2006; Cooper and Block 2006).

Other federal-level decisions were made far too slowly. Secretary Chertoff convened the Interagency Incident Management Group (IIMG)—a group of high-level officials from across the federal government who provide advice and guidance for federal assistance during crisis situations—on Tuesday, August 30, almost thirty-six hours after Katrina hit the Gulf Coast of Louisiana. But according to the 2004 national response plan, the IIMG was supposed to be created at the same time, or even before, an incident of national significance occurs. By waiting more than a day, the national government missed an important chance to pre-deploy emergency response units and mobilize federal support into the disaster-stricken areas. As the *Final Report of the Bipartisan Select Committee to Investigate the Preparation for and Response to*

Hurricane Katrina states, "We will never know what the IIMG would have done" if it had been created early on in the process (U.S. House of Representatives 2006, p. 134). But it seems quite likely that the creation of the IIMG would have accelerated federal involvement and clarified the national government's role in the relief efforts.

To make matters worse, the statements and actions of prominent federal officials involved in the governmental response process did little to convey an air of competency, leadership, or expertise at the national level. FEMA Director Michael D. Brown and Secretary of Homeland Security Michael Chertoff both stated publicly that they were unaware of the terrible conditions in New Orleans even though the mass media had provided graphic and nearly continuous coverage for several days. Brown also remarked that the death toll in New Orleans was attributable to "people who did not heed evacuation warnings." But many of stranded citizens were simply unable to leave the city because they had no money, no transportation, and no place else to go (White and Whoriskey 2005). Similarly, Secretary Chertoff described accounts of the heinous conditions in the New Orleans Convention Center as exaggerated (*System Failure* 2005, p. 40), and he stated that local conditions were "secure" (Treaster and Sontag 2005).

President Bush, himself, did little to alter public perceptions of governmental incompetence. In his initial visit to New Orleans after Hurricane Katrina, President Bush said that FEMA Director Brown was doing a "heck of a job" (Hsu and Glasser 2005), and later pledged the national government's full support for the rebuilding of the city of New Orleans (Bumiller 2005). But, the failure of national government officials to provide clear guidance and firm leadership impeded the response process during its critical, earliest stages (U.S. House of Representatives 2006). This led to greater confusion and more hesitation by government agencies at all levels. It also created more anxiety and frustration within the disaster stricken population.

Milling Process Accelerates, Keynoting Occurs, and an Emergent Norm Develops: "The Bureaucracy Has Killed People in New Orleans"

Three days after the flooding began in New Orleans, Mayor Ray Nagin issued a "desperate SOS to the federal government." President Bush responded by mobilizing additional federal resources and sending more supplies into the affected areas. FEMA dispatched urban search and rescue teams to evacuate stranded storm victims; it dropped sandbags to stop the flow of water from the breeched levees; it facilitated the evacuation of local residents out of flooded neighborhoods; and it distributed over 170,000 meals a day to storm victims.

National Guard troops, border patrol agents, and law enforcement personnel from surrounding states were deployed and sent into the area (Federal Emergency Management Agency 2005b). However, local conditions did not begin to stabilize until five days after the storm (Dao and Kleinfield 2005).

During this period, the media continued to provide ongoing coverage of the situation in Louisiana, particularly in New Orleans. Many of these stories relayed the personal

A Chinook helicopter drops sandbags into a breeched levee that is flooding a residential neighborhood following Hurricane Katrina, New Orleans, Louisiana, September 2005. *(Federal Emergency Management Agency/Jocelyn Augustino: FEMA News Photo)*

turmoil and tragedies of disaster victims—for example, their harrowing rescues from the rooftops of buildings, chaotic evacuations to temporary shelters, desperate searches for friends and family members, and the horrendous experiences of storm victims at the Superdome and Convention Center.

A large number of media accounts focused on the governmental response to the disaster. Almost all of these stories were negative (Alexander 2006; Rodriguez and Dynes 2006). Local officials were depicted as unprepared, inept, and even corrupt (see, for example, "Anatomy of a Disaster" 2005; Connolly 2005; ABC News 2005). State leaders were portrayed as confused and erratic ("After Katrina" 2005). But it was the national government that received most of the attention and criticism (Benac 2005; Grunwald and Glasser 2005; Hsu 2005; Hsu and Glasser 2005; Simao and Christie 2005; Witte and O'Harrow 2005). The federal government was criticized

A national guardsman walks through a residential area in the Lower Ninth Ward that is severely damaged following Hurricane Katrina, New Orleans, Louisiana, September 2005. *(Federal Emergency Management Agency/Andrea Booher: FEMA News Photo)*

for being slow, unprepared, disorganized, and indifferent in its response to Hurricane Katrina in Louisiana. The leaders of the federal response appeared unwilling to take charge of the relief effort, unable to mobilize sufficient resources, ill-equipped to provide aid to those truly in need, and out of touch with the realities of the situation (Fournier 2006; Hsu 2006; Lipton, Drew, Shane, and Rohde 2005; Steinhauer and Lipton 2005; Vedantam and Starkman 2005; White and Whoriskey 2005). An editorial in the *New York Times* on September 9, 2005, expressed the situation this way: "What America needs are federal disaster relief people who actually know something about disaster relief" ("Advance Men in Charge" 2005). The *New Orleans Times-Picayune* (September 4, 2005) provided a harsher assessment of the capabilities of federal disaster relief workers: "Every official at the Federal Emergency Management Agency should be fired, Director Michael Brown especially" (*New Orleans Times-Picayune* 2005, p. 15).

The media were not the only ones to criticize the governmental response efforts. For example, Representative Charles W. Boustany Jr. (R-LA) remarked that Louisianans "needed direct federal assistance, command and control, and security—none of the three were present" (White and Whoriskey 2005). Representative William Jefferson (D-LA) said that the federal government had not stepped up "to do its job" and Senator David Vitter (R-LA) gave the federal government a grade of "F" in its handling of Hurricane Katrina's problems (Alpert 2009). But one of the harshest condemnations of the governmental response to Hurricane Katrina came from Aaron Broussard, the president of Jefferson Parish in Louisiana, who summed up the entire situation this way: "The bureaucracy has murdered people in the greater New Orleans area" (Scallan 2005, p. 5). Indeed, this perception of bureaucratic ineptitude, delay, confusion, apathy, and dereliction of duty became the emergent norm in Louisiana. The bureaucracy—particularly the federal bureaucracy—was responsible for the breakdowns in the governmental response (Roberts 2006; Schneider 2008a). Even President Bush blamed "the bureaucracy" for getting in the way of the recovery efforts (Barr 2005).

In order to rectify this image, the federal government made a number of changes in its administrative organization and operations. Shortly after President Bush described Michael D. Brown as doing a "heck of a job" as FEMA's Director, Brown was asked to step down from this position (Stevenson and Kornblut 2005). David Paulison, an individual who had more experience in emergency management, was appointed as the Acting Director of FEMA, so that the federal government could provide stronger and more effective leadership. Unfortunately, it did little to quell the sharp criticisms that were already made about bureaucratic indifference, incompetence, and bumbling during the governmental response to Katrina in Louisiana.

Profound Gap Between Emergent Norms and Bureaucratic Norms

A wide gap developed between the public's expectations and the government's actions during the response to Hurricane Katrina in Louisiana. The American public believed that the national government should have assumed primary responsibility for the situation. The conditions that developed in Louisiana simply were too severe to be handled by local or state officials. The national government was the only entity with the necessary resources and capability. But the federal government hesitated and delayed: it seemed unwilling to assume a leadership role. Instead, it looked to local and state officials to serve as the primary first responders to the disaster. But state and local authorities were completely overwhelmed. They could not provide basic assistance to the affected populations, and they were unable to stabilize local conditions. Moreover, they were also unable to communicate their needs clearly or effectively to the national government. Hence, they did not request additional assistance, so the national government did not step in and respond.

Unfortunately, this intergovernmental stalemate did little to help the victims of Katrina. Thousands of Louisianians needed medical care, water, food, clothing, and shelter. But critical supplies and assistance did not arrive. Consequently, Katrina's victims were confused, disoriented, disenchanted, and angry. To make matters worse, many people had to be evacuated from New Orleans when the temporary shelters there became unsafe; they were transported to other makeshift, overcrowded facilities like the Houston Astrodome hundreds of miles away.

Katrina's victims simply did not understand what was happening to them, and they were not receiving clear or consistent guidance. The government—particularly the federal government—did not seem to be helping them.

Hurricane Katrina survivors arriving at the Houston Astrodome after being evacuated from New Orleans when the Superdome became unsafe, Houston, Texas, September 2005. *(Federal Emergency Management Agency/Andrea Booher: FEMA News Photo)*

Extremely Disorganized, Confused Implementation Pattern

The governmental response to Katrina in Louisiana definitely did not work from the bottom up: it did not start at the local level, work its way through the state, and then move on to the national government. But it also did not conform to a top-down process. The national government did not assume a proactive leadership role, nor did it step in quickly and mobilize resources into to the affected areas.

Once again, the response to Katrina fits the confusion pattern of intergovernmental relief. Public officials across all levels of government misunderstood key elements of their responsibilities during the response to Hurricane Katrina in Louisiana. Stated simply, they did not seem to know what they were supposed to do or what they could expect from others involved in the process (Glasser and Grunwald 2005; Vedantam and Starkman 2005).

At the local level, many officials assumed that a disaster the magnitude of Hurricane Katrina should be immediately handled by higher-levels of government. In particular, they expected the national government to step in and take charge of the situation almost from the very beginning (Brinkley 2006). Local personnel were unable to serve as first responders. In fact, many were unable to even assist or supplement the efforts of other emergency relief organizations (U.S. House of Representatives 2006).

Moving upward in the response process, Louisiana Governor Kathleen Blanco made general requests to the federal government for additional aid—as the normal response process indicates she should do. But the governor did not seem to know that additional actions were necessary to ensure that the federal government followed through on the state's requests. For example, she asked for federal aid, but she did not identify the specific types of assistance that were needed (Brinkley 2006; "System Failure" 2005). Similarly, the governor identified resources that would be helpful for the relief operations, such as buses and helicopters to transport stranded residents out of the Superdome and other make-shift shelters, but she did not issue explicit orders to locate these resources and move them into the stricken areas ("System Failure" 2005; U.S. House of Representatives 2006).

The most serious problems surfaced at the federal level (Steinhauer and Lipton 2005; Derthick 2007). This was partly due to the new elements of the national response plan, adopted in 2004—just a year earlier. Hurricane Katrina was the first declared "incident of national significance," and the federal government had not yet developed policies and protocols to implement the elements of this process. Consequently, public officials were operating in uncharted territory during Katrina; they simply did not know what they should do. This uncertainty about roles and responsibilities permeated the entire system (U.S. House of Representatives 2006). Adding to the confusion, many national officials continued to act as if the bottom-up process were still in place—even after it had been superseded by the top-down, or push, process which was supposed to characterize an incident of national significance (van Heerden and Bryan 2006). Thus, the national government did not take proactive steps to help resident and communities prepare for the impending storm; it did not act quickly to provide emergency aid to disaster victims; and it did not organize the operations of other public and private disaster assistance organizations involved in the disaster (Lipton, Drew, Shane, and Rohde 2005; Vedantam and Starkman 2005).

Also, a great deal of confusion existed about who was actually in charge of the federal response. Secretary Chertoff appointed FEMA Director Michael D. Brown as the Principal Federal Official (PFO) in charge of the governmental effort. In this position, Brown was to coordinate the overall management of federal activities (U.S. Department of Homeland Security 2004a). But he did not have the legal authority to direct the activities of other federal agencies or commit the expenditure of federal funds for this disaster. Instead, those powers fell to another federal official—William Lokey, who had just been appointed as the Federal Coordinating Official (FCO) for the Louisiana disaster. This meant that during the first critical days of the response, there was no single, unified command structure for governmental efforts (U.S. House of Representatives 2006).

Two weeks later, when Michael Brown was asked to step down from his position as FEMA's Director, Coast Guard Vice Admiral Thad Allen was appointed as both PFO and FCO of the Louisiana recovery operations. This change, along with David Paulison's appointment as FEMA's Acting Director, was made so that the federal government could provide stronger, more effective, and more consolidated leadership. But the de-

Louisiana Governor Blanco speaks at a press briefing at the Louisiana Office of
Emergency Management about Hurricane Katrina. Department of Homeland Security
Undersecretary of Emergency Preparedness and Response Michael Brown looks on.
(Federal Emergency Management Agency/Jocelyn Augustino: FEMA News Photo)

lay in making these personnel changes contributed to an already chaotic situation. As
indicated in the U.S. House of Representatives' 2006 investigation of the governmental
response to Katrina, the confusion and uncertainly in federal leadership "degraded" the
entire relief effort in serious ways (U.S. House of Representatives 2006).

Steps were taken to try to jump-start and re-invigorate the national government's
efforts. President Bush created a White House Task Force on Hurricane Katrina
Response to review governmental actions and to provide immediate recommendations for change. Secretary Chertoff implemented an incident management system
to coordinate public and private relief operations. President Bush made another trip
to New Orleans. Once again he promised that the city would be completely rebuilt
(VandeHei and Baker 2005). And he also indicated that the federal government would
assume most of the financial costs of the rebuilding efforts ("After Katrina" 2005).
This represented an extraordinary commitment of federal resources. The national
government had never before assumed the financial burden of rebuilding a major
metropolitan area after a natural disaster.

The federal government also modified its own policies and operations to expedite the delivery of emergency aid and to facilitate the recovery efforts in Louisiana
(Blumenthal 2006; Eaton 2006a, 2007b). In response to criticisms of excessive red
tape and paperwork in FEMA's assistance policies (Alexander and Henderson 2005;

President George W. Bush reaffirms his commitment to assist those affected by Hurricane Katrina and Rita throughout the Gulf Coast region during a visit to the Joint Field Office in Baton Rouge, Louisiana. Louisiana Governor Kathleen Babineaux Blanco (*center*) and Principal Federal Officer Vice Admiral Thad Allen look on. *(Federal Emergency Management Agency/Win Henderson: FEMA News Photo)*

Eaton 2007a), FEMA bypassed many of its standard operating procedures and began dispensing financial assistance directly to disaster victims (Lipton 2006a). It also changed the application process and extended the deadlines for receiving federal support (Blumenthal 2006; Federal Emergency Management Agency 2006a, 2008, 2009a; Goodnough 2006; Eaton 2007b). The national government conducted extensive evaluations of almost every aspect of the response process in order to prevent bureaucratic breakdowns from occurring during the next disaster (U.S. Department of Homeland Security 2006, 2008a; U.S. Government Accountability Office 2005, 2006a, 2006b, 2006c, 2007a, 2007b, 2007c, 2007d, 2008a; Townsend 2006; U.S. House of Representatives 2006; U.S. Senate 2006c).

However, none of these actions have changed perceptions of the federal government's response to Hurricane Katrina. The public continues to believe that the national government acted too slowly, erratically, and reluctantly to help the citizens of Louisiana recover from this disaster. Perhaps one of the most glaring examples of this situation involves FEMA's efforts to provide housing assistance to the displaced victims of Hurricane Katrina. After much discussion, FEMA did eventually provide money that enabled thousands of families to move into government trailers and apartments as temporary solutions to the housing shortage, and it dispensed loans to help disaster victims rebuild their damaged homes. But FEMA's housing policies were seriously hampered by bureaucratic bumbling, red tape, and delay. In order to obtain assistance, storm victims had to go through a lengthy, cumbersome, and confusing application process (Blumenthal 2006; Eaton 2006a). And even those families who succeeded in obtaining aid could lose their assistance without any real understanding of why or how they could appeal the decision (Nixon 2007; Nixon and Eaton 2007). Federal District Court Judge Richard J. Leon (District of Columbia) found this process to be so convoluted that he likened it to something out of a Kafka novel; he ordered the government to restore housing assistance to those whose benefits it had denied or terminated (Dewan 2006b). As a result, FEMA temporarily suspended its eviction of families living in the trailers that it had provided and it continued the payments for households receiving rental subsidies (Dewan 2006a). However, a federal appeals court reversed parts of the federal district court's decision, enabling FEMA, once again, to suspend payments for housing and rental assistance (Dewan 2006b).

FEMA did heed concerns about the cumbersomeness of the housing process. It took steps to clarify its application procedures, and it extended the time period so that more storm victims could obtain help (Dewan 2007a). It also intensified its efforts to move displaced residents out of temporary housing units, such as trailers and mobile homes, and into more permanent housing. And it offered relocation expenses for those who returned home or found housing elsewhere. On the negative side, however, FEMA continued to give storm victims conflicting signals about what type of assistance would be available to them and for how long (Dewan 2006a, 2006d, 2008). It threatened to cut the rental aid from hurricane victims (Dewan 2006c), and it delayed the movement of families out of temporary units into more permanent types of housing (Dewan 2006b).

Two and half years after Hurricane Katrina hit the Gulf Coast, about 38,000 families were still living in FEMA trailers and mobile homes (Eaton 2007b). After a series of reports indicating that occupants of the trailers were experiencing respiratory and other medical problems, the Centers for Disease Control and Prevention confirmed that many of these FEMA trailers were contaminated with high levels of formaldehyde, a carcinogen that can cause serious health care conditions. FEMA once again pledged to intensify its efforts to move displaced storm victims out of these temporary units into more suitable and safer living arrangements. The federal government's housing assistance policy—and in particular the FEMA trailers—remain a symbol of "government incompetence and inadequacy" (Dewan 2006a, 2008, 2009; Eaton 2007b, 2008; Hsu 2007, 2008; Palank 2007).

Public Perception: Bureaucratic Meltdown, Catastrophic Governmental Failure

The federal government has provided an extraordinary amount of assistance to the victims of Hurricane Katrina. During the first three years of the recovery operations, FEMA dispensed more than $50 billion to the Gulf Coast states. In Louisiana, FEMA

A workman walks across the end of a section of a FEMA trailer park established to house individuals displaced by Hurricane Katrina, in Baker, Louisiana, September 2005. *(Federal Emergency Management Agency/Rachel Rodi: FEMA News Photo)*

paid more than $5.7 billion to individuals, approved financial assistance to over 850,000 households, and made temporary housing units available to 90,000 displaced families (Federal Emergency Management Agency 2008). By August 2010, on the fifth anniversary of the storm, the level of government assistance had climbed even higher: $5.8 billion had been spent to assist individuals with their housing needs and other necessary expenses; $37.8 billion went to help rebuild public facilities; and $1.47 billion was made available to help local communities and Louisiana's state agencies prepare for future disasters (Federal Emergency Management Agency 2010m).

Despite this massive relief effort, the public's perception of the governmental response to Katrina in Louisiana is decidedly, and almost totally, negative (AP/Ipsos 2005a, 2005b, 2006a; CBS News 2005, 2007; Pew Research Center 2005b; Washington Post-ABC News 2005; *New Orleans Five Years After the Storm* 2010). Public officials were not prepared to handle this situation; they reacted too slowly and haphazardly when they did respond; they did not seem to care about helping those who were most in need; and they were not able to deal with disaster-related problems in a efficient or effective manner (AP/Ipsos 2005c; Fletcher and Morin 2005; Jones and Carroll 2005; The Pew Research Center 2005b; Frankovic 2007). Six years after Katrina, some families are still living in temporary housing units and trailers; debris removal is continuing; rebuilding efforts are an ongoing process; and serious social and economic problems persist (Kaiser Family Foundation 2010; Federal Emergency Management Agency 2011c). Overall, the American people think that the governmental response to Hurricane Katrina in Louisiana is a total failure (Schneider 2008b).

Public perceptions about governmental activity during Katrina have had broader consequences for the American political system. They have led to questions about racial and economic inequities in American politics and the impact of these inequalities on governmental operations (Alexander 2006; Strolovitch, Warren, and Frymer 2006;

A banner informs the victims of Hurricane Katrina where they can register for disaster assistance at a Disaster Recovery Center located at 101 France Street in Baton Rouge, Louisiana, September 2005. *(Federal Emergency Management Agency/Win Henderson: FEMA News Photo)*

Tierney, Bevc, and Kuligowski 2006; Miles and Austin 2007; Potter 2007). And they have raised concerns about governmental performance in general (Molotch 2006; Birkland 2007; S. Schneider 2008b). After all, if the government cannot address problems created by a natural disaster like Hurricane Katrina, how can the American public expect it to handle other, even more difficult policy problems and emergency situations?

Hurricane Katrina in Mississippi

Hurricane Katrina first struck in the Gulf region early on August 29, 2005, near Buras, Louisiana. Later that morning, Katrina made landfall once again near the Louisiana-Mississippi border. At this point, the powerful storm qualified as a Category Three hurricane with maximum wind speeds of 120 miles per hour. Then Katrina began moving in a north, northwesterly direction. For the next two days, it proceeded slowly up through the center of the state of Mississippi still packing hurricane-intensity winds, spawning dozens of tornadoes, and creating intense storm surges and flooding across the state. By the time it hit the Tennessee border, Katrina was still quite powerful, but it had been downgraded from a hurricane to a tropical storm.

Hurricane Katrina caused massive destruction across Mississippi. Communication outages were widespread, storm debris prevented residents from traveling on major roads and highways, and 80 percent of the population was left without power (Latham 2005). Thousands of buildings were damaged; many were completely destroyed. Nearly 200,000 residents were displaced from their homes. Katrina was responsible for 231

A sign expresses the feelings of the victims of Hurricane Katrina in Louisiana Southeast Coastal Parish, November 2005. *(National Oceanic and Atmospheric Administration's National Weather Service photo. Collection of Wayne and Nancy Weikel, FEMA Fisheries Coordinators)*

deaths in Mississippi and billions of dollars in property damages (*Sun Herald* 2005; *One Year After Katrina* 2006; U.S. House of Representatives 2006).

Governmental Response Is Activated Before Katrina Hits

The governmental response process was activated before Katrina hit the Gulf Coast communities of Mississippi. Local officials issued emergency proclamations warning residents to take the necessary precautionary steps in preparation for the storm. The Mississippi Emergency Management Agency (MEMA) sent workers into coastal communities to help them manage evacuations, mobilize resources, and set up temporary shelters for any displaced residents (Latham 2005). Mississippi Governor Haley Barbour activated the Mississippi National Guard and sent the Guard's special "hurricane strike" squads into all three coastal counties. The federal government had also deployed personnel and resources into Mississippi prior to Katrina making landfall on the Gulf Coast. FEMA sent a Mobile Emergency Response Support detachment into the area to provide emergency satellite communications capabilities. It had also pre-positioned critical supplies and equipment, as well as search and rescue teams and support staff (Federal Emergency Management Agency 2005l; Latham 2005;). The day before Katrina struck the U.S. Gulf Coast, President Bush issued an emergency declaration for the state of Mississippi. Then the following day, he declared a "major

Aerial view of the destruction caused by Hurricane Katrina in Biloxi, Mississippi, August 2005. *(National Oceanic and Atmospheric Administration's National Weather Service photo collection)*

disaster" in Mississippi, which authorized the release of federal funds to the storm-ravaged areas (Federal Emergency Management Agency 2005dd).

So far, the intergovernmental response process seemed to be operating fairly routinely and smoothly. Local and state emergency management agencies were well prepared for the impending disaster. For several years prior to this event, the Mississippi Emergency Management Agency had been using federal funds to strengthen the capabilities of local response agencies. As a result, many county officials had received training in the National Incident Management System and they were well versed on how to prepare for and respond to a major disaster (U.S. House of Representatives 2006). Unfortunately, the scope and severity of the storm's impact in Mississippi far exceeded the capabilities of governmental relief agencies.

Milling Process Begins Almost Immediately

Katrina caused substantial damage to communities in Mississippi. Power outages occurred across the state; transportation systems were shut down because of the excessive amount of storm debris; and thousands of people were displaced from their homes (U.S. House of Representatives 2006). Local residents were naturally disoriented and confused by the conditions that confronted them. They were unable to resume normal, everyday routines and activities. And they needed guidance and help. But the extent of the damages overwhelmed local authorities. There were reports of looting and other acts of unconventional behavior (Bickerstaff 2005). State officials tried to step in and provide assistance, but even the Mississippi National Guard had difficulty stabilizing local conditions. Disaster victims felt a sense of urgency and were concerned that they would have to take care of themselves (*Sun Herald* 2005). This led to the search for meaning which characterizes the milling process.

Similar to the circumstances that developed in Louisiana, in Mississippi the government's actions, and inactions, became the focus of public attention. As an editorial in the Biloxi newspaper described the situation: "The essentials—ice, gasoline, medicine—simply are not getting here fast enough. . . . [We] have yet to find evidence of a coordinated approach to relieve pain and hunger or to secure property and maintain order" (*Sun Herald* 2005). Local residents were frustrated with the inability of government agencies—at all levels—to meet the needs of disaster-stricken communities.

But unlike what happened in Louisiana, particularly in the city of New Orleans, the milling process ended fairly quickly in Mississippi. There were several reasons for this. First, Katrina created a different type of disaster in Mississippi than in Louisiana. As the U.S. House of Representatives report described it, "Mississippi experienced . . . in essence, a massive, blender-like storm surge versus the New Orleans flooding caused by breached and overtopped levees" (U.S. House of Representatives 2006, p. 7). Although both circumstances produced major disasters, they also required different types of responses. The conditions that occurred in Mississippi were more typical of what happens during a major hurricane. Thus, there was a better sense of what had happened, as well as what needed to be done to address the problems.

Second, emergency management officials in Mississippi were better equipped to handle a major natural disaster. The state's emergency management agency had taken advantage of federal emergency preparedness grant funds in order to strengthen the capabilities of county programs. Federal funds were used to train first responders on the role of unified command systems in large-scale emergency relief operations. Such preparations helped county and state personnel understand the challenges that they would face when a disaster such as Katrina struck.

State Leadership Bolsters the Implementation Response

State governments play a pivotal role in the intergovernmental emergency management system: they are responsible for supplementing local-level efforts, mobilizing additional resources, and channeling federal resources into disaster-stricken areas. As the situation unfolded in Mississippi following Hurricane Katrina, the important role of the state government in the nation's disaster response process became abundantly clear.

On August 23, four days before Katrina made landfall in Mississippi, the Mississippi Emergency Management Agency issued its first situation report, which warned residents of the impeding storm and provided guidance on how to evacuate the area in an orderly manner (Latham 2005). The next day, Mississippi's Governor Barbour declared a "state of emergency" and authorized the use of National Guard troops to assist in the relief effort. He also briefed the heads of all of the state agencies about the potential dangers of the storm and reminded them of their roles and responsibilities. Then on August 27, the State Emergency Operations Center was activated and a unified command system was created (Barbour 2005; Latham 2005). Over the next several days, MEMA officials and National Guard liaison officers were dispatched to coastal communities to facilitate the distribution of water, food, ice, and supplies. State personnel were establishing the mechanisms to mobilize additional resources and implement emergency aid.

Problems developed, however, because the federal government was unable to supplement state-level efforts. When President Bush declared a "major disaster" in Mississippi on August 29, 2005, residents of fifteen counties were immediately eligible to receive assistance for temporary housing, home repairs, and low-interest loans (Federal Emergency Management Agency 2005dd). Several days later, FEMA opened up two disaster recovery centers in Ocean Springs and Pascagoula, Mississippi, to accept registrations for emergency aid, and it extended federal assistance to cover residents in thirty-two additional Mississippi counties (Federal Emergency Management Agency 2005o; 2005v).

Despite these actions, FEMA was unable to send trained personnel to Mississippi, it could not mobilize sufficient emergency supplies, and it did not have an efficient system for distributing aid to those in need. In essence, federal-level operations were dysfunctional and counterproductive (Davis 2005; Warr 2005). Part of the problem was that federal officials were trying to deal simultaneously with major disasters across three states; consequently, it was not surprising that they were overwhelmed and unable to send qualified personnel and adequate resources into all of the affected areas. To make matters worse, the federal government's own centralized procurement and distribution systems prevented FEMA and other agencies from purchasing critical supplies and sending them into affected areas on an expedited basis. This led to further delays in the delivery of essential commodities (U.S. House of Representatives 2006).

In order to jump-start the relief effort, state personnel initiated several important measures. They contracted with private companies to purchase and distribute critical supplies. And they activated the Emergency Management Assistance Compact (EMAC). As a result, Mississippi received invaluable resources and assistance from emergency preparedness personnel in states across the entire country (Barbour 2005). These state-level actions were extremely important: they helped facilitate the distribution of emergency assistance to disaster-stricken communities in Mississippi (Davis 2005), and they provided the impetus to get the intergovernmental response process moving along.

The federal government initiated a number of measures to distribute assistance more quickly and broadly. FEMA launched an expedited assistance process so that disaster victims could access funds directly using their debit cards or through elec-

Mississippi Governor Haley Barbour meets with FEMA Acting Under Secretary R. David Paulson and Principle Federal Officer Administrator Thad Allen to discuss the recovery efforts for Hurricanes Katrina and Rita, Jackson, Louisiana, September 2005. *(Federal Emergency Management Agency/Dave Seville: FEMA News Photo)*

tronic transfers into their bank accounts (Federal Emergency Management Agency 2005h); it created hotlines to coordinate contributions of money and supplies (Federal Emergency Management Agency 2005n); it expanded its public assistance program to cover the cost of restoring roads, bridges, and other infrastructure (Federal Emergency Management Agency 2005h); and it extended the application deadline several times to give Mississippians more time to apply for federal aid (Federal Emergency Management Agency 2005c, 2005k, 2005m).

By September 10, 2005, FEMA had already distributed more than $173 million in assistance to slightly more than 182,000 Mississippians. A month later, more than $2 billion in federal money had been approved and over 400,000 victims had applied for assistance in the state. On the one-year anniversary of Katrina, FEMA had allocated $8.9 billion in Mississippi. And by the four-year anniversary, FEMA had spent $9.5 billion on assistance to over 500,000 people across forty-nine counties in Mississippi (Federal Emergency Management Agency 2009a).

Gap Develops Between Emergent Norms and Bureaucratic Behavior

The gap between emergent norms and bureaucratic behavior was noticeable during the response to Hurricane Katrina in Mississippi. Critical supplies were simply not

Long lines of residents seeking help at the Disaster Recovery Center in Ocean Spring, Mississippi, following Hurricane Katrina. *(Federal Emergency Management Agency/ Mark Wolfe: FEMA News Photo)*

distributed quickly. People waited too long to receive water, food, and medicine. Disaster victims, as well as state and local officials, became extremely frustrated with the slow pace of the relief effort. The federal government's policies and procedures were at least partially responsible for these delays. Initially, FEMA and other federal agencies tried to implement assistance using standard operating procedures. But these procedures required federal agencies to use centralized processing systems and to perform time-consuming assessments that slowed down the distribution of aid. Thus, bureaucratic behavior was at odds with the expectations of storm victims. This is precisely the type of situation that leads to the development of the gap.

The gap remained in existence even after adjustments were made in the governmental response system. Once again, the federal government's policies contributed to this situation. Many disaster victims had difficulty obtaining grants and low-interest loans in order to repair their homes. Storm-damaged communities were unable to get federal funds for emergency services, debris removal, and infrastructure repairs (Burton 2007, 2009a, 2009b; Gulf Coast News 2007a, 2007b, 2008a, 2008b, 2009a, 2009b).

But the most serious and persistent problems surfaced in the government's efforts to provide adequate housing to displaced Katrina residents (Gulf Coast News 2009a). In order to address this critical problem, FEMA moved people into travel trailers, mobile homes, and manufactured housing units (Federal Emergency Management Agency 2005r, 2005x).

It also helped families relocate to locations outside of the storm-damaged areas, and it even commissioned a cruise ship to provide temporary housing for other residents (Federal Emergency Management Agency 2005l). Such efforts eased the housing problem temporarily, but they did not solve the dilemma of finding more permanent housing for those Mississippians who had lost their homes during the storm (Gulf Coast News 2009a). As a result, they did not help to close the gap between public expectations and governmental operations.

Public Perception of the Governmental Response to Katrina in Mississippi: More Failure Than Success

Despite the massive amounts of aid that have poured into the state, serious questions remain about the recovery effort in Mississippi. On the one hand, there is a sense that progress has been made. According to FEMA, federal, state, and local governments have helped Mississippi "rebuild stronger than it was before the 2005 storm" (Federal Emergency Management Agency 2009d). Governor Barbour stated in his 2009 annual progress report that "We have seen phenomenal progress on the Gulf Coast as families, businesses, and communities continue to rebuild" ("Katrina: Four Years After" 2009).

A temporary emergency housing site under construction to help residents displaced by Hurricane Katrina, Long Beach, Mississippi, October 2005. *(Federal Emergency Management Agency/Mark Wolfe: FEMA News Photo)*

The Carnival cruise ship *Holiday* is used to temporarily house Mississippi residents displaced by Hurricane Katrina, Pascagoula, Mississippi. *(Federal Emergency Management Agency/Mark Wolfe: FEMA News Photo)*

On the other hand, concerns and complaints linger about governmental performance, particularly the efforts of the federal government. When Mississippians needed immediate emergency assistance, the federal government acted slowly and reluctantly. It did not respond quickly to supplement the actions of state and local officials, and it was unwilling to adjust its policies in order to better meet the needs of disaster victims.

Once the immediate problems subsided, governmental performance did not significantly improve. There are still complaints that excessive paperwork and strict administrative requirements continue to hinder the recovery efforts (*Gulf Coast News* 2008a, 2008b, 2009a). Also, a question persists about where all of the federal money is going (Burton 2007, 2009a 2009b). To many people, tangible results from all of the money, activity, and effort are difficult to see. The rebuilding process along the Mississippi coast has been excruciatingly slow and cumbersome. This, in turn, has produced an enduring image of an overly bureaucratic emergency management system that is unresponsive, inefficient, and uncertain about its operations (*Gulf Coast News* 2009a). As a result, the overall impression of the governmental response to Hurricane Katrina in Mississippi falls closer to the failure end of the continuum.

The total destruction of a home due to Hurricane Katrina. The owners have posted their names and addresses in order to indicate the location of their home for insurance and assistance purposes, Waveland, Mississippi, January 2006. *(Federal Emergency Management Agency/Leif Skoogfors: FEMA News Photo)*

Notes

1. Less than a month after Hurricane Katrina hit the Gulf Coast, another major storm struck the U.S. mainland. Hurricane Rita made landfall as a Category Three Hurricane on September 24, 2005, near the Texas-Louisiana borders. Rita caused extensive damage from Texas to Alabama; the coastal areas in eastern Texas and southwestern Louisiana were particularly hard hit. Rita was responsible for 119 deaths and approximately $16 billion in property damage (U.S. Department of Commerce 2007). Rita ranks as the third most expensive natural disaster to hit the United States (Woolsey 2008). Once again, the nation's emergency response system was activated to help communities along the Gulf Coast affected by the storm. Since Rita did not strike in exactly the same areas as Katrina, different combinations of public and private organizations were involved in this relief effort. But the Rita and Katrina responses overlapped to a degree because some of the same agencies involved in the Hurricane Katrina efforts, such as FEMA and the state of Louisiana's Office of Emergency Preparedness, also had to respond to the problems created by Rita. Consequently, Hurricane Rita added to the complications of, and demands on, an already taxed emergency response system. For more information about Hurricane Rita, the government's efforts to respond to it, and Rita's impact on the governmental response to Hurricane Katrina, see U.S. Department of Commerce (2005b), U.S. Government Accountability Office (2006a, 2006d), and the Federal Emergency Management Agency's Press Releases on Rita (2005–2010).

Then, another month later, on October 23, 2005, another major storm—Hurricane Wilma—made landfall near the southwestern region of Florida. Before it struck land, Hurricane Wilma was the strongest storm on record to form in the Atlantic Ocean (U.S. Department of Commerce

2007). Although it had diminished to a Category Three hurricane by the time it hit Florida, Wilma was still an extremely powerful and destructive storm (Kasper 2006), causing massive disruptions, power outages, and over two billion dollars in property damages (Woolsey 2008). Once again, the nation's emergency response system was called upon to handle the problems created by Wilma. Governmental resources had to be mobilized and directed toward another major disaster, in addition to those created by Hurricanes Katrina and Rita. For more complete information about Hurricane Wilma, see the reports by the U.S. Department of Commerce (2007), press releases by the Federal Emergency Management Agency (2005–2010), and news reports by the *Sun Sentinel* (2005–2010), National Geographic Society (2005), and the *Miami Herald* (2005–2010).

2. Hurricane Katrina was the focus of a massive number of media stories, documentaries, personal accounts, government investigations, and academic analyses. Indeed, the plethora of reports and discussions of the Katrina disaster makes it impossible to list all of them. Some of the most informative news stories can be found in the *New York Times, Washington Post, Time,* and *New Orleans Times-Picayune* in their reporting from August 2005 to the present (all available online), and in the analyses by National Geographic Society (2005) and the Public Broadcasting Service (2005). For more personal accounts and documentaries of the storm, see Forman (2007), Horne (2006), Brinkley (2006), van Heerden and Bryan (2006), Cooper and Block (2006), and Lee (2006). Perhaps, the most well known executive and legislative reports of what happened before, during, and after Hurricane Katrina are Townsend (2006), U.S. House of Representatives (2006), and U.S. Senate (2006c). But there are a number of other government documents that provide useful insights into various aspects of the relief effort; for example, see the U.S. Government Accountability Office Reports on Katrina from 2005 onward. And for more scholarly analysis of Katrina, see *Shelter from the Storm: Repairing the National Emergency Management System After Hurricane Katrina* (Waugh 2006b) and *Public Administration Review*'s "Special Supplementary Issue on Administrative Failure in the Wake of Hurricane Katrina" (Jurkiewicz 2007).

3. A few months before the fifth anniversary of Hurricane Katrina, the Gulf Coast experienced still another major disaster. On April 20, 2010, an oil rig exploded in the Gulf of Mexico about forty miles from the Louisiana Coast. The explosion killed seventeen workers, injured eleven others, disrupted the fishing and tourism industries, and caused extensive environmental/ecological damage along hundreds of miles of coastline. Although it is not specifically discussed in this research, the Deepwater Horizon disaster, also referred to as the BP Oil Spill, did have negative consequences on recovery efforts in the region to recover from Hurricane Katrina. For more information about the Deepwater Horizon disaster, see the National Oceanic and Atmospheric Administration updates (www.http://response.restoration.noaa.gov) and media coverage, including, for example, the *Wall Street Journal* (http://topics.wsj.com/subject/D/deepwater-horizon-oil-spill/6051).

13

"Normal" Disasters

1990 Floods in South Carolina and 2010 Floods in Tennessee

So far, this study has examined the components of the gap between bureaucratic procedures and emergent norms during *major* disasters. Hurricane Hugo, the Loma Prieta Earthquake, Hurricane Andrew, the Northridge Earthquake, Hurricane Georges, and Hurricane Katrina were extreme events that placed unusually severe strains on the governmental response process. But it is also important to consider what happens during a more typical disaster situation. Of course, to the people who are affected, no disaster is ever really normal. However, certain types of events like floods, tornadoes, blizzards, droughts, and minor hurricanes do occur with some regularity. Emergency management agencies usually respond to these situations in a straightforward, almost automatic manner. As a result, the governmental responses to these kinds of situations are usually quite successful. There are several reasons for the general effectiveness of governmental activities during the kinds of events that might be called "normal" disasters.

First, the sheer magnitude of the situation is a factor (Fritz 1957, 1961; Barton 1969). Normal disasters do not usually produce severe or prolonged disruptions in the social or physical environments. As a result, public organizations can respond to these situations more cautiously and slowly. Such a response is more in line with the customary patterns and routines of public sector activity.

A second consideration is the frequency and regularity of the event (Dynes 1970). Hundreds of natural disasters occur in this country every year. Fortunately, very few of these develop into major catastrophes;[1] most are fairly typical geological episodes or weather patterns. Thus, the American public is relatively familiar with normal disasters because they experience them more frequently and on a fairly regular basis (Perry and Mushkatel 1984). Similarly, governmental institutions are more attuned to these phenomena, and they have designed a response system with exactly these situations in mind.

Third, the degree of attention given to a disaster is also important. A drought in the Southeast, a blizzard in the Northeast, or a mudslide along the West Coast, may not seem unusual or extraordinary to people who are not directly affected. So these events do not receive a great deal of public or media attention.[2] Without such scrutiny, far less vocal criticism of the governmental efforts develops. This gives response agencies greater latitude to work at their own pace, using standard operating procedures. But as we shall see, the lack of publicity can also lead to concerns that disaster victims are being ignored or neglected, especially if other situations are receiving more attention.

Fourth, it is also necessary to consider how the emergency response system itself is prepared to handle different types of disaster situations. When the system is squarely focused on natural disasters, it is more likely to respond more effectively to them. And organizing the system so that it can react quickly and appropriately clearly facilitates a more successful governmental response.

These normal disasters fit perfectly within the theoretical framework presented in this study. Stated simply, they represent situations where we would expect the gap between bureaucratic and emergent norms to be quite small, especially when compared to many of the more disruptive situations previously discussed. This scenario applies to the vast majority of all governmental responses to natural disasters that occur in the United States every year. In this chapter, two of these normal disaster events will be described: the first occurred in South Carolina in the fall of 1990, while the second happened in Tennessee almost twenty years later, during the spring of 2010. Both of these situations involved severe flooding—the most frequent type of natural disaster to occur in the United States. So we would expect the governmental response to unfold fairly smoothly. Yet, as we will see, even normal relief efforts are affected by the scope of the disaster, the level of attention focused on the event, and the extent of governmental preparation.

Severe Floods in South Carolina[3]

During the first week of October 1990, two tropical storms converged off the South Atlantic coast of the United States. These storms sent a continuous band of heavy showers and thunderstorms across the state of South Carolina. In some locations, between twelve and fifteen inches of rain fell in a twenty-four hour period (C. Bennett 1990). The heavy rains caused the water in many creeks and rivers to rise substantially above normal levels. Record flooding was reported in the central portions of the state; several areas reported water levels that exceeded the expected 100-year flood marks (C. Bennett 1990). A number of earthen dams failed, roads washed away, farmland and homes were destroyed, and bridges collapsed. Hundreds of people were evacuated, and nine people died as a result of the floods (Federal Emergency Management Agency 1990a).

Milling Process Begins Immediately, but Is Short-Lived

The flooding in South Carolina was serious enough to be characterized as a natural disaster: it was clearly more than just "severe weather conditions." Twelve of the state's forty-six counties experienced heavy storm-related damages (Federal Emergency Management Agency 1990a). In these counties, the floods disrupted everyday routines and behavior patterns, and they triggered the immediate onset of the milling process.

Milling was most pronounced in areas where the local population was caught off guard. In some communities, the flooding occurred so quickly that residents did not know what they should do to protect their families, their belongings, and their homes from the rising waters. They were confused and disoriented. This led to the usual search for meaning that defines the milling process. However, the situation stabilized very quickly, usually within a matter of hours and never longer than a day. Affected citizens regained their composure and began dealing more calmly with their problems and conditions.

There are several reasons for the short duration of the milling process during the South Carolina floods. First, some people simply did not accept the seriousness of the situation. They insisted on traveling into flood-prone areas and generally refused to admit that anything out of the ordinary had occurred (S. Smith 1990). When individuals believe that life is proceeding normally, the milling process is irrelevant; they feel no need to conduct a search for meaning.

Second, the floods covered a wide area, but their direct impact on people was relatively sporadic and temporary. Some communities escaped the floods entirely, although they experienced the heavy rains that led to them. In other areas, the rivers crested and floodwaters receded quickly. Thus, even when serious social disruptions did occur, they did not last for a long period of time. Accordingly, the relevance of traditional norms and behavioral standards was reestablished quickly.

Third, communication and transportation systems did not break down, even in the areas hit hardest by the storm. Although some roads and railroad lines were blocked, alternate transportation routes were almost always available for people to use. Most residents did not lose electrical power or telephone service. Therefore, channels of mass communication, including radio and television, and interpersonal communication networks remained open throughout the entire period of the disaster (Federal Emergency Management Agency 1990a). With standard information sources available to flood victims, no need to search for further meaning or explanation existed, once again rendering the milling process moot.

Emergent Norms Are Consistent with Governmental Plans

As in any milling situation, keynoting behavior did take place. However, it was carried out by those officials who are *supposed* to provide guidance—law enforcement agencies, fire departments, county rescue squads, and emergency preparedness units. The particular nature of the milling process and keynoting activity guaranteed that emergent norms were virtually nonexistent, at least insofar as they deviated from traditional, legally sanctioned norms and standards of behavior. There was never any perception that the existing institutions were incapable of dealing with the situation caused by the severe weather. Most residents viewed the floods as a temporary and annoying, but manageable, interruption to their everyday lives (S. Schneider 1992).

Government Responds Using Standard Operating Procedures

The floods in South Carolina represent exactly the kind of disaster that is anticipated by the standard response system. Appropriate governmental agencies at all three levels had time to assess the severity of the conditions, to identify appropriate response mechanisms, and to deploy available resources in an organized fashion. Public officials concentrated on working within, not outside, the pre-established structure (S. Schneider 1992). Most emergency personnel seemed to understand their roles and responsibilities in the governmental response process, and they were willing and able to implement disaster assistance according to the pre-specified format. As a result, the process unfolded quite smoothly and methodically.

This does not mean that the entire process worked perfectly. There were problems and breakdowns in the system, most noticeably during the early stages of the disaster. The flooding occurred so quickly, that local emergency management personnel in a few areas were not able to predict or adequately alert their constituent communities (Tuten 1990). Consequently, some citizens were not made aware of the dangerous conditions, and several drowning deaths occurred when people drove into suddenly flooded areas or washed out roads (Federal Emergency Management Agency 1990a).

There were also several instances of miscommunication among governmental officials involved in the response and recovery efforts. For example, some local administrators did not coordinate the release of excess storm water at levees and dams, and from reservoirs with local personnel in neighboring areas, thereby exacerbating the flooding in these other communities (Tuten 1990). Fortunately, however, these kinds of problems were relatively rare, and they were quickly resolved. Overall, the government responded to this disaster in an orderly and routine manner. Here, the procedures of the bureaucratic system worked nearly automatically and quite well.

Size of the Gap Is Very Small

The gap was virtually nonexistent following the 1990 floods in South Carolina. The post-disaster emergent norms in the population were fully consistent with the bureaucratic norms in the response agencies. Citizens generally reacted calmly and behaved rationally throughout the process. This created exactly the kind of situation that had been anticipated in the disaster preparedness plans. As a result, the government followed its basic operating procedures in order to help the affected population recover from the floods.

Bottom-Up Implementation Pattern

The governmental response process worked from the bottom up, exactly as it is supposed to. Local officials dealt with the affected population, and they handled immediate problems. The fact that communication and transportation systems were not completely disrupted facilitated their access to threatened areas and people. Generally, emergency management workers concentrated their efforts on evacuating residents, restricting access to flooded areas, and preventing dam failures before they occurred (Federal Emergency Management Agency 1990a). In short, local emergency management personnel mobilized an effective first response.

Although the state government was peripherally involved during the early stages—issuing evacuation warnings and mobilizing the state police—it became directly involved only when the storm and flood damages spanned several local jurisdictions. At that point, state personnel coordinated activities across local boundaries—for example, warning county governments of water releases that originated in other counties and directing dam maintenance in the most serious trouble spots—and they channeled state resources, such as social services personnel and road maintenance crews, into the affected areas. State emergency management officials initially acted as coordinators and facilitators. Once the national government became involved in the response effort, state personnel served very effectively as intermediaries between local and federal organizations.

Officials from the national government were on hand from the very beginning to provide technical assistance. For example, the Army Corps of Engineers made recommendations regarding water management and flood control. But the federal government did not officially step in until a request was filed through the proper channels. Ten days after the initial flooding, President George H. W. Bush declared the floods to be a "major disaster." At that point, it was clear that the recovery process would require resources beyond those available in South Carolina. But it is important to emphasize the time span between the initial disaster and the presidential declaration. This apparent delay is actually typical of most disaster situations that occur in the United States. In fact, there is no real "delay" at all. Local and state officials—the first two levels of the standard governmental response system—require a certain amount of time to carry out their responsibilities.

After the presidential disaster declaration, federal involvement in the response process took several forms. The initial declaration only covered nine counties, and Federal Emergency Management Agency (FEMA) officials quickly extended coverage to three more (Federal Emergency Management Agency 1990a). This enabled individuals in those counties to receive critical assistance grants for repairing and rebuilding their homes and property. FEMA also sent in damage assessment teams and inspectors who evaluated the ongoing integrity of dams, levees, and other public facilities. Finally, FEMA officials oversaw a comprehensive review and evaluation of South Carolina's emergency management system. It is important to emphasize that, throughout the response process, the national government acted in a *supportive* capacity. Officials from FEMA and other federal entities never tried to take over the process or supplant the activities of lower-level governmental personnel. This is exactly the way the process is supposed to work.

Over the next few months, the government implemented disaster assistance in an orderly and methodical fashion. Federal and state officials worked closely with local emergency management personnel to assess the extent of the damage and to channel resources into affected areas. In addition, representatives from a wide variety of different agencies, at all three levels of government, used this opportunity to make recommendations about future hazard mitigation efforts in South Carolina. Overall, governmental efforts proceeded smoothly, closely following the policies and procedures laid out in the State Emergency Preparedness Plan and in the relevant federal statutes and regulations.

Perception of Governmental Response: Complete Success

The bottom-up implementation pattern has definite advantages. When all involved personnel adhere to designated plans and procedures, governmental efforts proceed with little conflict or controversy. The entire governmental response system operates very effectively. The experience in South Carolina during the 1990 floods demonstrates what happens when the system works as designed. By the standards of both the disaster-stricken population and the governmental officials involved, the recovery effort was highly successful.

One of the interesting aspects of the South Carolina floods was the fact that they attracted very little attention outside of the immediately affected areas. In fact, most South Carolinians were unaware that their neighbors were undergoing the disruptions caused by a major natural disaster. This apparent inattentiveness almost certainly contributed to the success of the recovery effort, because it eliminated the critical and distracting public scrutiny that often accompanies governmental relief operations. The response to the South Carolina floods unfolded quietly and with little fanfare. This enabled public institutions at all levels of government to dispense critical emergency assistance without having to channel resources into the more "cosmetic" components of public relations.[4]

Thus, a great deal of the perception that the governmental response to the South Carolina floods was successful is due to the fact that few public perceptions of the disaster crystallized in the first place. This is the case in the vast majority of the natural disasters that occur in the United States. When a governmental response is successful, it attracts little public attention. And this tends to occur when the disaster conforms to the assumptions underlying the ongoing governmental response system and its bottom-up implementation process.

Severe Storms and Flooding in Tennessee

During the first week of May in 2010, a warm air mass moved up from the Gulf of Mexico into the central portion of the United States. When it got to the Cumberland River Basin in Tennessee, the warm air collided with a slow moving front that set off a series of torrential rains, heavy storms, and deadly tornados. Over the weekend of May 1–2, rainfall amounts reached ten to fifteen inches across western and middle Tennessee. The southern and western sections of the city of Nashville were hit particularly hard, receiving between eighteen to twenty inches of rain. This represented "the highest amount in over 140 years of record and [was] estimated to be well above a 1,000-year rainfall event" (Peabody 2010).

The strong storm system produced significant amounts of lightning, strong straight-line winds, and at least twelve tornadoes. It also caused large-scale, unprecedented flooding along nearly all of the rivers and streams in the region. The situation was particularly severe along the Cumberland River, which runs through metropolitan Nashville. On May 3, the Cumberland River exceeded its "flood stage" by over ten feet and its "major flood stage" by over six feet (G. Carter 2010). Sections of Nashville were almost completely submerged in water, including some of the city's main tourist attractions—such as the Ryman Auditorium, formerly home of the Grand Ole Opry, and the Country Music Hall of Fame (De Nies and Siegel 2010; Hall and Burke 2010). In the Nashville area alone, the storms damaged thousands of homes and buildings, left 45,000 people without power, and caused $2 billion dollars in property damages (K. Hall 2010a). Overall, the intense rains, straight-line winds, tornadoes, and record-breaking floods damaged several hundred thousand homes and killed thirty people in three states (Burke and Loller 2010; De Nies and Siegel 2010; *New Orleans Times-Picayune* 2010a).

Milling Process Begins, Even Before the Storms Are Over

Most of the people living in this region of the country are accustomed to strong spring rains. But they were not prepared for this type of situation, which was very unusual and clearly unprecedented (Harless 2010). The situation was especially severe for residents living along the Cumberland River in Tennessee. Here, the storms were so intense and the flooding so quick that many people were simply caught off guard. They were surprised and overwhelmed. This is exactly the type of situation that leads people to search for meaning in their circumstances. Hence, it is not surprising that it set off the milling process among the affected population in Tennessee.

Contributing to this, local residents also didn't know how to respond to the conditions that confronted them. As one reporter described the situation, "They didn't know if they should flee or stick it out . . ." (Hall and Burke 2010). And unfortunately, they received conflicting signals about what they should do. Initially, local officials thought that it would be safer for people to remain at home than to travel away from the area because the rising floodwaters would make driving too dangerous (Reuters 2010). So they instructed residents to "stay put."

Then, when the floodwaters rose even higher, local officials changed course and encouraged residents to evacuate the affected areas. But by this time, many people were unable to leave. According to one report, " Fast-moving waters flooded homes and roads so quickly that in many cases, there was no time to prepare or escape" (K. Hall 2010b). Buildings were flooded, power was out, communication systems were down, and roadways were impassable (Reuters 2010). Unfortunately, several people died in their own homes trapped by the rising floodwaters; others drowned in their cars as they tried to evacuate (K. Hall and Burke 2010). As one storm victim described the situation, "I did what they said and stayed put. I didn't get out. I didn't drive. Then it just all happened so fast" (Loller and Hall 2010).

The milling process ended fairly quickly—a few days after the storms went through the area. As the floodwaters started to recede, local residents acquired a better un-

An aerial shot of flooded homes in Nashville, Tennessee, May 2010. *(Federal Emergency Management Agency/Dave Fine: FEMA News Photo)*

derstanding of how to deal with the conditions surrounding them. They focused their efforts on ensuring the safety and well-being of themselves and their neighbors. There were numerous reports of citizen volunteerism and collaboration with emergency response workers aimed at rescuing stranded flood victims (CBS News 2010; K. Hall 2010; Morrison 2010), cleaning up debris (De Nies and Siegel 2010; *New Orleans Times-Picauyne* 2010b), and helping to maintain a sense of calm in the storm-stricken communities (Blackburn 2010).

Local residents also continued to work with government authorities as the immediate response operations transitioned to longer-term recovery efforts (Bassham 2010a). Throughout this process, few, if any, instances of unconventional activity occurred. Representative Jim Cooper described the reaction of citizens as follows: "In my district, people are still volunteering, and donating, and wearing proudly the 'We are Nashville' t-shirts in order to help everyone bounce back from the flood" (J. Cooper 2010c, p. 1). Although it would be some time before residents would be able to resume their normal routines, they were no longer confused about what had happened or what steps they should take to respond. And they were beginning to see tangible signs that assistance was being provided (Reuters 2010). As Nashville Mayor Karl Dean expressed it: "We are coming out of this thing. This has been devastating, but right now we're going to be focused on getting our city back up and running" (CNN 2010).

Governmental Response Is Activated and Operates from the Bottom Up

Government officials tried to address the situation in a relatively routine manner, using standard operating procedures. As the first series of storms moved into the area on May 1, local emergency management personnel and political leaders had already been following the situation very closely. They issued warnings to residents that they should "stay put" and not travel unless absolutely necessary (Reuters 2010). Then, on Sunday May 2, they started to encourage residents to evacuate and they launched search and rescue operations to locate people who had remained in their homes because of the rising floodwaters. Later that same day, Nashville's Mayor Dean declared a major disaster for the Nashville area and requested additional governmental assistance. Public officials filled sandbags to prevent more neighborhoods from flooding; they instructed local residents to take additional precautionary measures, such as conserving water, staying out of flooded areas, and the like; and they began hauling away storm debris and flood-damaged possessions in order to re-open roads and businesses (Loller and Hall 2010; *New Orleans Times-Picayune* 2010b).

For their part, state officials were also involved in key aspects of the response. The Tennessee Emergency Management Agency (TEMA) issued warnings to counties before the storm even hit the state. Then, as the first wave of storms moved through the region, TEMA activated the Tennessee Emergency Management Plan, which officially identified a state of emergency in Tennessee due to the storms. TEMA established the State Emergency Operations Center (SEOC) in order to mobilize state-level resources and to direct them into areas where they were needed. As a result, TEMA undertook a number of critical flood response activities, including sending swift-water boats to rescue stranded residents (Cousins 2010) and distributing millions of gallons of drinking water into storm-damaged areas (Bassham 2010a). Other state agencies were also directly involved in emergency operations. For example, the Tennessee Highway Patrol responded to dozens of requests for assistance by stranded motorists, closed several interstate highways that were flooded in order to prevent residents from trying to use them, and worked to reopen roads and highways as quickly as possible (Cousins 2010; Nicely 2010).

Tennessee Governor Phil Bresden assessed the severity of the situation fairly quickly, and requested help from the federal government on May 3, 2010, just a day after the storms swept through the state. Governor Bresden also activated the Tennessee National Guard and sent them into the damage-stricken areas to assist with the relief efforts (Bassham 2010b). The Guard helped with search and rescue operations (*FOX News* 2010; Reuters 2010) and distributed bottled water to residents in communities where water supplies were contaminated (Bassham 2010a). Over the next week, the governor issued several executive orders suspending state regulations and laws that would prevent or delay the implementation of emergency relief to victims of the Tennessee floods (State of Tennessee 2010a, 2010b, 2010c).

Even before the state officially requested the assistance of the national government, federal officials were already involved in the disaster response effort. Forecasters from the National Weather Service identified the threat of heavy rain in the area on April 27, 2010, four days before the storms hit, and they issued a Flood Potential Outlook on April 29, which emphasized the likelihood of heavy rain for the upcoming May 1–2 weekend. On April 30, flash flood watches were issued for the Nashville vicinity and for surrounding areas. On May 1, the National Weather Service issued flood advisories for a large area of middle Tennessee, which were changed to flood warnings on May 2. The National Weather Service continued to provide updated river level forecasts and flood warnings throughout the weekend of May 1–2 (G. Carter 2010). When the water levels of the Cumberland River kept rising, the U.S. Army Corps of Engineers Army Corps released water from the Old Hickory Dam in order to prevent the failure of the area's flood storage capacity (Peabody 2010).

Other federal officials were sent to Tennessee to report back to President Barack Obama and the Homeland Security Secretary Janet Napolitano. FEMA Administrator W. Craig Fugate was dispatched to obtain a "firsthand look at the flooding" (*Telegraph* 2010). A FEMA Liaison Office was also already on-site, working with state officials in the Tennessee Emergency Operations Center to determine the extent of the storm's impact and the type of federal assistance that might be needed (Gibbs 2010; Free Republic 2010).

On May 4, 2010, President Obama declared a major disaster for the state of Tennessee—just two days after the storms had gone through the region (White House 2010a). In the initial presidential declaration, federal assistance was made available to individuals and organizations in four Tennessee counties to cover grants for temporary housing and home repairs, and low-cost loans to compensate for uninsured property losses; the federal assistance was also intended for debris removal programs and emergency protective measures (Federal Emergency Management Agency 2010d,

FEMA Administrator W. Craig Fugate at a press conference in a National Guard hanger, Nashville, Tennessee, May 2010. *(Federal Emergency Management Agency/Andrew McMutrie/Tennessee General Services: FEMA News Photo)*

Department of Homeland Security Janet Napolitano addressing residents and volunteers in Nashville, Tennessee following the severe storms and floods, May 2010. She is holding up the contact information for FEMA assistance. *(Federal Emergency Management Agency/Dave Fine: FEMA News Photo)*

2010g, 2010q; White House 2010a). FEMA Administrator W. Craig Fugate was sent back to Tennessee to assess the situation firsthand (White House 2010b). Homeland Security Secretary Napolitano also visited the damaged areas and promised that "DHS and the entire federal government will do everything possible to support the people of Tennessee and across the Southeast in getting back on their feet quickly—coordinated every step of the way with our state and local partners" (U.S. Department of Homeland Security 2010).

Rumors Surface, Keynoting Occurs, but Emergent Norms Are Still Largely Consistent with Bureaucratic Norms

Overall, the governmental response process seemed to be operating in a fairly smooth and routine manner. But several issues did emerge during the relief effort that led to rumors, keynoting behavior, and general criticisms about governmental performance. The most serious problem revolved around the decision by the Army Corps of Engineers to release water in the Old Hickory Dam several times during the weekend of May 1–2 (Farmer 2010). The Corps contends that their actions prevented water from exceeding lake levels and flooding the Nashville area with an additional four feet of water (Hall 2010a; Peabody 2010). The problem was that the Corps did not inform the National Weather Service about these actions in a timely manner (Finley 2010a; Paine 2010a). As a result, the National Weather Service did not tell emergency officials, city leaders, or the general public that billions of gallons of water were being released: "No one downstream had any idea that the dam was open" (Finley 2010b). So they were caught completely off guard by the extensive flooding: they were "unable to comprehend the potential severity of the event" (G. Carter 2010).

Tennessee Senator Lamar Alexander requested an inquiry into the Corps's actions to determine "whether the public was adequately warned about rising waters downstream" (WSMV 2010). U.S. Representative Jim Cooper also requested a congressional investigation into the Corps's actions (Cooper 2010b), and was even more critical when the Corps initially refused to provide a post-flood report because of budget constraints. Representative Cooper released the following statement in response: "This is completely unacceptable. I am stunned the Corps doesn't feel it is necessary to investigate their response to a multi-billion dollar disaster. The people of Middle Tennessee deserve answers. This shows a serious lack of accountability and leadership at the Corps" (Cooper 2010a).

The Corps defended its actions during the floods, but admitted that mistakes had been made. It produced a preliminary draft describing its operations in July 2010, and it released a final "lessons-learned" report in November 2010. In these reports, the Corps acknowledged that communication breakdowns had occurred between the Corps and the National Weather Service, which left local residents, public officials, and emergency management officials in the dark and confused about how high the floodwaters would rise and when. Although it claimed that it was following standard protocols at the time (Finley 2010b), the Corps promised to make adjustments in how it communicated information to others in order to prevent this kind of situation from happening again (Paine 2010b).

Other keynoting behavior revolved around the question of whether the Tennessee floods were receiving sufficient media attention. Some complained about the lack of national coverage devoted to the conditions in Nashville, especially compared to the coverage during other recent disaster situations (Kurtz 2010; Sheppard 2010). As one reporter put it, "The 'narrative' simply wasn't as strong. The problem for Nashville was that both the Gulf Oil Spill and the Times Square terror attempt are like the Russian novels of this twenty-four/seven media culture, with all the plot twists and larger themes (energy, environment, terrorism, etc.) required to fuel the blogs and cable shows for weeks on end" (Romano 2010). Local residents expressed similar concerns that their problems had been overshadowed because of other disasters (Barnett 2010), or because their behavior during the storms was not "newsworthy." As one Nashvillian blogged, "It [the Tennessee disaster] was not a PR nightmare. It was handled with relative calm, an organized response and a lack of sensationalism." Another Nashville resident expressed it this way: "A large part of the reason that we are being ignored is because of who we are. Think about that for just a second. Did you hear about looting? Did you hear about crime sprees? No . . . you didn't. You heard about people pulling their neighbors off of rooftops" (National Hazards Center 2010). As one clergyman in the Nashville area put it, "It's becoming out of sight, out of mind" (Barnett 2010). There were also complaints that the federal government was not doing enough to help the citizens of Tennessee because of politics. FOX news commentator Sean Hannity stated that President Obama was not concerned about the massive flooding in Tennessee and had "yet to comment on it" (Hannity 2010). CNN contributor Erick Erickson expressed the same sentiment and provided a political reason for this neglect on his blog: Tennessee is a "red state," and the citizens of Tennessee did not vote for Obama in 2008 and were not likely to do so in 2012 (Erickson 2010). On his daily radio show, Rush Limbaugh echoed a similar charge, saying that President Obama was ignoring storm victims in Tennessee because he didn't "have any constituents there to speak of, well seriously. I don't want to poison the well here . . . It's true though you still will not find a donation link at a White House website for Tennessee. You will find it for Haiti, and you will find it for people in the Gulf because of the oil slick" (Limbaugh 2010).

Relatively Small Gap Between Emergent and Bureaucratic Norms; Smooth, Bottom-Up Implementation Pattern

Despite criticisms of the governmental relief efforts, the behavior of storm victims was largely consistent with the expectations and behavior of bureaucratic agencies during the 2010 Tennessee floods. The gap between emergent norms and bureaucratic behavior was relatively small during the 2010 Tennessee floods. The mayor of Nashville described the situation quite succinctly: the area "was overwhelmed. Then people just put their heads down and rolled up their sleeves and went about restoring the city" (Kerr 2010).

As a result, relief organizations were able to administer relief in a fairly routine, coordinated, and timely manner. Local officials acted quickly to address emergency situations, "pulling people from flood waters, cars, and the ruin of their homes" (Blackburn 2010). They continued to be directly involved in response and recovery operations: they helped with search and rescue missions; they provided information to local residents about how to respond to the situation; they played a key role in assessing the extent of the damages; and they communicated the needs of their citizens and communities to higher-level authorities (Friedmann 2010).

The process also operated quite smoothly at the state level. Tennessee government officials quickly activated the state's emergency operations, mobilized the resources of a broad array of state agencies, provided guidance and assistance for local governments, and served as the intermediary between local and federal efforts. During the first weeks after the disaster the Tennessee Emergency Management Agency coordinated the response efforts of 3,000 personnel from twenty-five state departments. These efforts involved providing assistance to local officials in their search and rescue operations, distributing water and supplies to affected communities and clearing storm debris from roadways and other transportation systems (Cousins 2010). Tennessee

General James Bassham, Tennessee Emergency Management Agency Director, and FEMA Administrator W. Craig Fugate speaking to the TEMA emergency operation center responders following the Tennessee storms and floods, May 2010. *(Federal Emergency Management Agency/Dave Fine: FEMA News Photo)*

officials also played a key role in communicating the needs of local communities to the federal government and guiding federal resources back into flood-damaged areas (Friedmann 2010).

This, in turn, allowed the federal government to play a strong supportive role in the disaster response process. FEMA quickly established procedures to allow affected residents to apply for disaster assistance online, and it received more than 7,000 registrations for aid within the first forty-eight hours following the issuance of the disaster declaration in Tennessee. FEMA opened its first disaster recovery center in Tennessee on May 9, 2010, and by the end of May, it eventually had sixty-six disaster recovery centers operating in the major areas affected by the Tennessee storms (Federal Emergency Management Agency 2010a, 2010k, 2010s). FEMA also used mobile disaster recovery units and a social network page on the Internet in order to reach more victims of the floods (Federal Emergency Management Agency 2010e, 2010o).

In addition, FEMA worked closely with local and state officials to get more counties designated for disaster assistance. Eventually, forty-nine of Tennessee's ninety-five counties were included in the federal disaster declarations, thereby allowing individuals and public organizations in these areas to apply for temporary housing benefits, debris removal assistance, emergency protective measures, and loans (Federal Emergency Management Agency 2010a, 2010s). FEMA also worked with its counterpart at the state level (TEMA) to shift the focus from providing im-

Doug Bodem, FEMA community relations unit leader for middle Tennessee, speaks with a resident affected by the Tennessee floods, May 2010. *(Federal Emergency Management Agency/Shannon Arledge: FEMA News Photo)*

mediate assistance to meeting the affected population's longer-term needs (Federal Emergency Management Agency 2010w). Disaster recovery centers were transitioned to disaster loan outreach centers in order to expedite the application process so that residents and businesses could receive funds to rebuild damaged structures (Federal Emergency Management Agency 2010r).

FEMA also established programs to get Tennesseans more involved in the assistance process and to help them prepare for any future disaster situations: FEMA partnered with the United Methodists Committee on Relief to provide caseworker training to local citizens so that they could help disaster victims obtain necessary resources and it promoted the use of "points of distribution" centers where local residents could go to obtain emergency supplies more quickly and efficiently (Federal Emergency Management Agency 2010m, 2010r, 2010t, 2010u). By the end of 2010, FEMA had distributed about a quarter of a billion dollars in assistance to help families and communities in Tennessee recover from the disaster (Federal Emergency Management Agency 2010y).

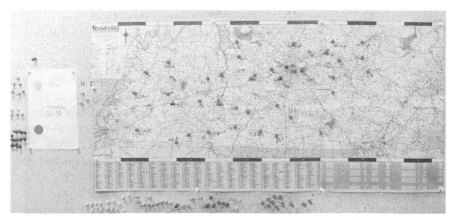

A FEMA map used to create a visual reference for the location of disaster recovery centers following the Tennessee floods, May 2010. *(Federal Emergency Management Agency/Dave Fine: FEMA News Photo)*

General Impression: A Fairly Successful Response

The Tennessee floods are an interesting case study. Some politicians and commentators complained, as mentioned above, that the disaster did not receive enough media and governmental attention. But the lack of media attention may have actually benefited the response effort: it allowed emergency management officials at all levels to carry out their pre-established roles and responsibilities in a more orderly and routine manner, with minimal fanfare or intense scrutiny. This, in turn, probably contributed to the smooth implementation of disaster assistance across and within levels of government.

Miscommunications between federal agencies during the early days of the storm did produce delays in the government's emergency response operations, confusion within the affected population, and quite possibly greater storm-related damages. These breakdowns contributed to the immediate onset of the milling process among the affected population. They were also used by political leaders and the media in their efforts to direct more attention to the Tennessee floods and to raise general concerns about governmental incompetence and/or indifference.

But the breakdowns that occurred in standard operating procedures—particularly by the federal government—figured into a relatively small portion of the government's activities. Overall, most aspects of the intergovernmental response process seemed to work fairly well. The White House posted an Internet blog with the title "On the Ground Before the Raindrops Started Falling." In this blog, the president's press secretary Robert Gibbs indicated that "despite simultaneous response efforts in the wake of the BP Oil Spill in the Gulf Coast, FEMA representatives are on the ground working directly with state and local officials" (White House Blog 2010). Tennessee Governor Phil Bredesen was even more laudatory: "I've never seen this kind of response . . . and we've had our share of tornadoes and so forth . . . FEMA and the White House could not have been more helpful in this thing" (White House Blog 2010).

Many local residents also praised the efforts of state and local public officials. As one Nashville citizen wrote on her blog: "Much of the credit goes to Nashville Mayor Karl Dean and all of the heads of Nashville's public agencies for being organized and acting quickly" (Morrison 2010). Members of the state's congressional delegation applauded the actions of state officials in their letter supporting the governor's request for federal aid: "Tennessee Emergency Management Agency (TEMA) officials have worked diligently to coordinate the state's response to this tragedy," employing resources from a number of state departments (Sullivan 2010). A media commentator described the relief effort as follows: "President Barack Obama and his administration have responded in 'enormously effective ways' to one of the largest non-hurricane disasters in American history. This is according to the majority of residents throughout the state who have expressed a large degree of satisfaction with the way the administration has responded to the catastrophe" (Church 2010).

Federal agencies did make mistakes during the early phases of the disaster. These mistakes created a gap between citizens' expectations and bureaucratic operations, which in turn contributed to rumors and keynoting behavior about governmental indifference and incompetency. But the gap between emergent and bureaucratic norms quickly closed when emergency relief agencies started working together to respond to the needs of the disaster-stricken population in a coordinated, synchronized manner. This, in turn, facilitated the government's emergency response and recovery efforts.

Normal Disasters and the Governmental Response

It is important to reiterate that the 1990 South Carolina and 2010 Tennessee cases involve typical types of disaster situations. Indeed, severe storms and flooding are the most common natural disasters to occur in the United States. Of the 1,102 events that were declared major disasters in the United States from 1990 to 2010, over 60 percent of them were caused by severe rains and flooding (Federal Emergency Management Agency 2011g).[5] Hence, we would expect governmental operations during such situations to operate more effectively. And compared to the governmental responses to other, more severe situations, such as Hurricanes Hugo, Andrew, and Katrina, the relief efforts in these two normal disaster situations did proceed much more smoothly, with less media attention and according to standard operating procedures. In both the South Carolina and Tennessee cases, the behavior of governmental organizations coincided fairly closely with the expectations of the affected population; hence, there was virtually no mismatch or gap between the emergent norms of disaster victims and the bureaucratic norms guiding governmental activity. This enabled emergency relief agencies to implement assistance more quickly and effectively. And in the end, it contributed to more positive impressions of governmental performance during natural disasters.

Notes

1. Since 1937, presidents have declared an average of thirty-three "major disaster" situations every year in the United States (Federal Emergency Management Agency 2011b). Technically, this means that these events were severe enough to warrant the resources and assistance of the national government. It does not mean, however, that all of these events were catastrophic phenomena. Only a handful of all the presidentially declared situations would actually qualify as true catastrophes (G. Peterson 1992; National Academy of Public Administration 1993; U.S. General Accounting Office 1993b; S. Schneider 1995; Sylves 2006, 2007, 2008).

2. For additional information on the role of the media in disaster situations, see Quarantelli and Dynes (1972), Waxman (1973), Scanlon (1977), Scanlon et al. (1985), Quarantelli (1988), Gitlin (1989), Guider (1989), Medsger (1989), Rogers et al. (1990), National Academy of Public Administration (1993), Birkland (1997, 2007), Platt (1999), Kasperson and Kasperson (2005), Tierney, Bevc, and Kuligowski (2006), Dynes and Quarantelli (2007), Ward and Wamsley (2007), and Scanlon (2008).

3. Much of the information for this section was collected directly by the author, who was a member of the hazard mitigation team that assessed the flood damage, monitored the relief effort, and presented recommendations to improve governmental efforts.

4. Public relations is not the same as public information. Public information—issuing evacuation warnings, providing information about the availability of emergency shelter and food, publicizing how and where disaster victims can apply for disaster assistance, and so forth—is a critical responsibility of emergency management agencies. Public relations activities refer to the steps taken by agencies to justify their own actions or to change the public's perceptions of their roles and responsibilities.

5. A number of other storms and floods were identified as emergency situations, not major disasters, and the governmental response process was involved during these situations. The data reported in this chapter cover only those storms and floods that were severe enough to be declared major disasters. The data also do not include major disasters that were primarily identified as the result of hurricanes or typhoons, although such events could certainly have spawned severe rains, tornadoes, and flooding. Hence, the numbers reported here undercount the frequency of this type of disaster occurring in the United States.

Part Three

Summary, Implications, and Conclusions

14

The Paradox of Governmental Performance

The cases described in the previous section fill out the framework presented in Part One of this book. The overall objective of this study has been to explain why variability in public perceptions of governmental performance during natural disaster situations exists. The answer that has been proposed focuses on the size of the gap that develops between bureaucratic norms and emergent norms. The former comprises the rules, regulations, and standard operating procedures that characterize official behavior in virtually all modern large organizations. They guide governmental activity during natural disasters and the period immediately following. In contrast, emergent norms consist of the largely informal behavioral standards that develop during the uncertainty of the post-disaster period. They provide direction and meaning to the stricken population.

When the two sets of norms converge, the size of the gap is relatively small and the disaster response process works well. For example, Hurricane Georges in the Florida Keys and along northern Gulf Coast of the U.S. caused major disruptions in the social system. However, both the government and the public reacted to these conditions in a calm, orderly manner. The situation was handled in a fairly routine way, using standard operating procedures. As a result, the relief effort was largely regarded as a success. Similar processes have developed in most of the presidentially-declared natural disasters that have occurred in the United States over the years. As the 1990 floods in South Carolina demonstrate, when bureaucratic behavior matches public expectations, the response process unfolds fairly smoothly, leaving a positive impression of governmental performance. And the severe rains and floods in Tennessee during May 2010 show how governmental operations can still work fairly well even when breakdowns and miscommunications occur early in the process.

In other cases, however, bureaucratic and emergent norms diverge dramatically from each other. The response process falls apart because governmental agencies are either totally unprepared, or prepared for situations that do not occur. Meanwhile, public behavior follows unusual patterns that deviate from traditional norms. In this kind of situation, nothing ties together bureaucratic procedures and the actions of disaster victims. So the gap between the two is quite wide, and the governmental response is widely considered a failure. This is exactly what occurred in Louisiana following Hurricane Katrina and in the Caribbean Islands following Hurricane Hugo.

Most disaster situations fall somewhere between these two extremes. In some instances, governmental planning seems to roughly coincide with the public's expectations. There is confusion, disarray, and disorder, but these conditions do not prevent public agencies from implementing their pre-specified emergency management plans. Disaster assistance still bubbles up through the intergovernmental system, and the relief effort proceeds fairly smoothly and effectively. North Carolina's experience with Hurricane Hugo and the response to Hurricane Georges in the Caribbean fit this pattern quite well.

Of course, in other disasters, governmental planning and human behavior are more at odds with one another, even though the system basically works as it is intended. In cases like this, a response occurs but questions arise about its effectiveness. The government reacts too slowly or inappropriately, and the public develops unrealistic expectations. This leads to widespread confusion within the intergovernmental system and intense criticism of the entire recovery effort. Florida during Hurricane Andrew and South Carolina following Hurricane Hugo are vivid examples of this latter scenario; California's situation during the recovery phase of the Loma Prieta Earthquake also fits this pattern.

Taken together, these cases show the range of governmental responses to natural disasters in the United States. But they do not comprise a *representative* sampling of governmental responses—some of these activity patterns occur more frequently than others. Consider the two most extreme kinds of situations that are examined in this study: the complete breakdown of governmental operations is, fortunately, extremely rare (G. Peterson 1992; Miskel 2008). Therefore, the two instances of the scenario considered here—the Caribbean Islands during Hurricane Hugo and Louisiana during Hurricane Katrina—represent an "oversampling" of this problem relative to other disaster responses. In contrast, the vast majority of governmental relief efforts are carried out smoothly and effectively (U.S. General Accounting Office 1991, 1993b, 2003; U.S. Government Accountability Office 2008b; U.S. House of Representatives 2008). Hence, the examples of this relatively smooth and effective governmental effort—the responses to the 1990 South Carolina floods, the 2010 Tennessee severe rains and floods, and Hurricane Georges in the Florida Keys and along the Gulf Coast—are greatly "undersampled" compared to the other disasters.[1] In summary, the governmental disaster response system works well most of the time. Problematic responses are relatively infrequent, and complete failures are very rare. But when breakdowns do occur, they can have lasting repercussions on governmental operations.

This skewed distribution of disaster response effectiveness poses a difficult dilemma for the public emergency management system. When the system operates smoothly, it does not receive much popular attention or media publicity. Emergency management officials carry out their responsibilities in a businesslike, routine manner. Therefore, their actions are simply not very interesting to the mass media and they go largely unnoticed by the general public. Most citizens are simply not aware that the governmental disaster response has been mobilized; hence they have no idea that it is operating successfully.

In a tiny minority of natural disasters, public attention focuses directly on the response process. When this occurs, that attention will almost certainly be critical in tone. The disaster response system only receives extensive media coverage when it is "news" in itself; that is, when it is operating in a manner that is contrary to prior expectations. To use the terms of this study, there is a large gap between governmental planning and human behavior. These are the kinds of situations where the effectiveness of the relief efforts is called into serious question. They are also the natural disasters that people tend to remember. As a result, large-scale disasters have long-term consequences, shaping public perceptions of the entire disaster response system as well as the more general performance and capabilities of the government.

It is tempting to assert that the success or failure of the governmental response is a direct by-product of the magnitude of the disaster. In other words, it might seem that the system can handle small disasters relatively well, but that it always experiences partial or complete failures during large, catastrophic events. However, this simple explanation does not always hold true. It is the size of the gap, rather than the size of the disaster, that determines the effectiveness of the governmental response.

There are large-scale disasters during which bureaucratic and emergent norms converge, producing a small gap. For example, the Great Flood of 1993 placed tremendous strains on many midwestern communities, as well on the nation's governmental relief system. Yet the government and the flood victims both dealt with the situation in a calm and orderly fashion. Numerous stories circulated among the media and governmental officials, relating how individual citizens worked tirelessly for days to build up levees around their homes and businesses in order to ward off the rising floodwaters (U.S. Department of Commerce 1994). Similarly, many reports described how emergency management personnel, including Federal Emergency Management Agency (FEMA) officials, went out of their way to help flood victims obtain assistance as quickly as possible (Claiborne 1993a, 1993b; Kilborn 1993). Overall, the response effort received high marks from the affected population, the general public, and the government itself (U.S. Senate 1993b, 1994a, 1994b).

On the other hand, there are cases where relatively small, isolated disasters have led to noticeable gaps between bureaucratic and emergent norms. When a tornado touched down in Plainfield, Illinois, during the summer of 1990, neither the affected population nor the individuals involved in the governmental relief system seemed to know how to handle the situation. No warnings were issued about the possibility of a tornado hazard; consequently, precautionary steps were not taken to protect residents, homes, and businesses. The twister struck suddenly, but violently, killing twenty-five people and injuring several hundred more. It knocked out telephone and electrical services and made transportation into and within Plainfield virtually impossible. Local residents reacted to the situation with disbelief, despair, and fear. Because of the initial confusion, Illinois Governor James R. Thompson sent National Guard troops into the affected areas to patrol against looters and to reassure disaster victims (Schmidt 1990).

There have been other, more recent instances where a noticeable gap develops between emergent and bureaucratic norms. On October 18, 2007, a strong low-pressure system moved up through the central part of the United States into much of the southern areas of Michigan. The system produced heavy rain, wind gusts between 120 and 130 miles per hour, and at least thirty-five tornadoes. One of the tornadoes touched down in the city of Williamston, Michigan, where it was responsible for two deaths and extensive property damage. The tornado overturned cars and trucks along the interstate, toppled trees, tore apart homes, and knocked out power to hundreds of people. Some local residents were caught off guard by the timing of the storm. Tornado watches and warnings had been issued for the area throughout most of the afternoon and evening hours. Almost everyone in the affected area was shocked at how much destruction the tornado caused in such a short time. Tree limbs and power lines cluttered almost every street: the entire community was in disarray (Bouffard 2007). As a result, town officials became concerned about how to ensure the safety and security of local citizens. So they issued a strict curfew, allowing only residents to enter and leave the affected areas.

By objective standards, both the Plainfield and Williamston tornados were small disasters. Nevertheless, in both situations, a period where the plans and actions of governmental officials did not meet the expectations and needs of the affected population clearly unfolded. This, in turn, generated a noticeable gap between the two sets of behavioral norms. Thus, the size of the gap must be considered as a factor that is distinct and separate from the size of the disaster that produces it in the first place.

Even though the size of the gap and the magnitude of the disaster are separate variables, the two are certainly related to each other. Extremely large natural disasters are definitely more likely to produce the conditions that facilitate the emergence of a large gap. Catastrophic events impose particularly severe strains on social arrangements, political institutions, and normal patterns of human interaction (Fritz 1957; Quarantelli 1966; Dynes and Quarantelli 1968; Drabek 1970, 1986; Dynes 1970; Silverstein 1992; Aguirre, Wenger, and Vigo 1998; Kreps 1998; Posner 2004; National Research Council 2006; Tierney 2006). Under such conditions, people follow courses of action that, to them, appear to be perfectly rational (Stallings and Quarantelli 1985). They often engage in behavior that is quite positive—providing help and support to those who are affected by the disaster (Dynes, Quarantelli, and Wenger 1990; Aguirre 2005).

But when viewed in the broader context of the disaster situation, these actions may actually magnify the gap between the behavior of the disaster-stricken population and government agencies. This problem arises among all of the major actors in any natural disaster situation. First, bureaucrats and public agencies want to maintain order so they retain pre-established plans and standard operating procedures. The problem is that during unusually severe disasters, administrative mechanisms are often impaired or inappropriate for the situation at hand. Since catastrophic events occur far less frequently than other types of emergencies, bureaucratic organizations are simply not as equipped or prepared to handle them. Second, elected officials have specific roles to play during emergencies that are identified in local, regional, state, and national emergency response plans. But they often do things that are not part of their standard activities in order to get relief to their constituents (Abney and Hill 1966; Mayhew 1974) or to shift the burden of responsibility to others (Arceneaux and Stein 2006; Gomez and Wilson 2008; Maestas et al. 2008; Malhotra 2008). Such actions tend to create more complication and confusion when they do so. Third, the mass media covering the disaster have direct incentives to relay the most newsworthy events. Therefore, they tend to focus on highly dramatic or unusual stories that emphasize human suffering, the personal burdens of victims, the breakdown of law and order, governmental disarray, and bureaucratic incompetence (Scanlon et al. 1985; Wenger 1985; Drabek 1986; Rogers et al. 1990; Benthall 1993; Singer and Endreny 1993; Graber 1997; Kasperson et al. 2005; Rodriquez, Trainor, and Quarantelli 2006; Tierney, Bevc, and Kuligowski 2006). But this presents an incomplete and generally misleading picture of the response and recovery processes.[2]

Fourth, disaster victims want to comprehend their own situations and obtain immediate relief. But major catastrophes impair the normal lines of communication and supply, making it extremely difficult for the affected population to rely upon traditional ways of handling the situation. Therefore, the public searches for understanding and assistance in ways that are inconsistent with traditional norms and behavior (Parr 1970; Drabek 1986).

Thus, the conditions imposed by major natural catastrophes along with the narrowly defined rational behavior of *all* relevant actors both widen the gap between human behavior and governmental planning. This, in turn, hastens the breakdown of the response and recovery process and thereby increases the likelihood of intense criticism aimed at the entire governmental disaster response system.

Nature of Success and Failure

Success and failure in disaster recovery is almost entirely a matter of public perception rather than objective reality. Sometimes the success of the governmental system is signaled by the very lack of public attention to the response process. In the vast majority of the disaster situations that occur in the United States, the government steps in, provides relief, and terminates its efforts within its own pre-established time frames. There is little fanfare, no widespread criticism of any kind, and indeed, little public notice outside of the immediately affected areas (Federal Emergency Management Agency 1993, 2008).

On a more objective level, the governmental response system is effective in dealing with many of the most violent natural upheavals—those that tend to produce vocal public criticism of the response process. Breakdowns in public order and official assistance are usually temporary and short-lived (Tierney, Lindell, and Perry 2001). Most inhabitants do return to their homes. Most local businesses and industries do resume operations. Community infrastructure is eventually rebuilt. And after a period of time, life simply returns to normal—that is, to its pre-disaster conditions.[3]

The government also distributes massive amounts of emergency assistance to help families, businesses, and entire communities respond to and recover from natural disasters (U.S. Senate 1994b; Platt 1999; Rosenbaum 2003; Lindsay and Murray 2010; Robertson 2010; M. Cooper 2011). In addition, the government devotes significant resources to hazard mitigation activities, which are designed to prevent disasters from occurring and to reduce their severity (Sylves 2007). This represents an enormous undertaking, when one considers the number and magnitude of natural catastrophes that have struck the United States over the years.[4] Thus, if one takes a broader perspective, governmental efforts in this area have been quite remarkable and successful.

It may be tempting to take an optimistic view of this situation. After all, if governmental policy failure is only perceived and not real, than it can be discounted as not posing a critical threat to the response system. But this seriously underestimates the true state of affairs. Individual citizens rarely view disaster relief through the long-term perspective required to fully appreciate the effectiveness of the system. Therefore, they cannot reasonably be expected to fully comprehend the difficulties and complexities involved in any recovery effort. Disaster victims are naturally absorbed with their own personal problems and situations. For obvious and perfectly understandable reasons, they tend to view anything short of immediate, direct, and comprehensive help as failure. This view is often picked up by the mass media and also by elected officials who use emergency management administrators as convenient scapegoats. Therefore, negative impressions of governmental activity materialize and endure.

Public perceptions of governmental failure have direct repercussions for the nation's disaster relief system. The media take a hostile stance, and other governmental agencies take a skeptical view of emergency management officials. Legislative oversight committees assume a more critical tone; funding levels for disaster assistance decline. The public develops a cynical outlook toward disaster response officials that seriously undermines their credibility and authority during the very times when they are most essential.

Negative impressions of governmental activity during natural disasters can also have longer-range consequences for the broader political system. Public perceptions play an extremely important role in American politics and policymaking. They have a direct impact on the ways that social problems gain access to the governmental agenda and on the ability of public institutions to address important public problems (Eyestone 1978; Cobb and Elder 1983a; Kingdon 1994; Baumgartner and Jones 1993). They can also affect the overall level of confidence that citizens have in political institutions. If citizens are dissatisfied with governmental activity in one policy area, these sentiments can carry over to broader assessments of the overall performance of political leaders and public institutions (Jones 2003, 2007; AP/Ipsos 2005a, 2006a, 2006b).

We know that the public pays close attention to natural disaster situations (Birkland 2007). Indeed, Americans are more likely to follow stories about disasters than any other type of policy issue or problem (Pew Research Center 1997, 2007). This is particularly the case for large-scale, catastrophic events. For example, over 70 percent of the respondents to a Pew Public Interest Survey in October 2005 indicated that they carefully monitored what was happening during the Hurricane Katrina and Rita disasters (Pew Research Center 2005).

We also know that the American public is quite willing to evaluate the performance of governmental officials and agencies in emergency situations. During the Hurricane

Katrina disaster, a large number of public opinion surveys were conducted to obtain information about citizens' reactions to the governmental response and recovery efforts. These surveys produced a set of fairly consistent findings. A majority of Americans are dissatisfied with the governmental response to Hurricane Katrina (Pew Research Center 2005b); they are particularly critical of how President Bush and FEMA handled the situation (AP/Ipsos 2005b, 2006b; CBS News 2005; Fletcher and Morin 2005; J. Jones and Carroll 2005); and they are skeptical about the government's ability to handle the next natural emergency (AP/Ipsos 2005a; CBS News 2007; Frankovic 2007). Overall, bureaucratic breakdowns—like what happened during Hurricane Katrina—produce a lasting image of governmental incompetence and failure (Rozario 2007). Such negative impressions are extremely difficult to dislodge or change. And they can be generalized to broader assessments of governmental performance (McClam 2005; Public Broadcasting System 2005; Malhotra 2008). After all, if governmental organizations cannot handle the situations generated by natural disasters, how are they going to deal with other societal problems and conditions? Thus, public perceptions of policy failure cannot be dismissed; they have serious, long-term, detrimental effects on governmental activity.

The importance of perception creates a paradox for public policymaking in the area of emergency management and disaster relief. Most of the time, people are completely unaware that the government is responding to a natural disaster. Yet these are precisely the situations in which the process runs smoothly, effectively, and successfully. The general public only learns about governmental relief activities when there are problems, difficulties, or breakdowns. These latter situations generate a lasting, negative impression among the general public. If the government wants to change this impression, it faces an interesting dilemma. To restore public confidence in its activities, it must fix the problems that have developed in only a very few disaster situations, but problems that nevertheless have attracted widespread attention. At the same time, the government must retain the components of the system that seem to work well in the vast majority of natural disaster situations, but go largely unnoticed by the media and the general public.[5] Accomplishing these two objectives simultaneously has proven to be extremely difficult.

Over the last couple of decades, the government has made a number of major changes to the nation's disaster response system. During the 1990s, the Federal Emergency Management Agency was "reinvented" in order to improve the agency's self-image, internal operations, and external relations with other participants in the process. As a result of these internal changes, FEMA was able to clarify and refocus its own operations, and it was also able to enhance its interactions with the many public and private agencies involved in emergency response at the federal, state, and local levels. And FEMA's internal transformation helped to strengthen the nation's entire disaster response management system. As we saw in Chapter Eleven, governmental agencies responded fairly quickly and smoothly when Hurricane Georges struck Puerto Rico, the Florida Keys, and the northern Gulf Coast in September 1998. Bureaucratic actions corresponded to public expectations, producing positive impressions of governmental performance. Compared to its earlier record with several large-scale events, including Hurricane Hugo, Hurricane Andrew, and the Loma Prieta Earthquake, the U.S. disaster relief system operated much more effectively. The reinvention of FEMA, which began several years prior to Hurricane Georges, played a key role in enhancing the nation's entire emergency management and response capabilities during this period (S. Schneider 1998).

Then, following the terrorist attacks of September 11, 2001, the nation's disaster response system was reorganized and refocused to handle a broader array of emergency situations. A cabinet-level Department of Homeland Security was created, a new response plan was developed to identify the national government's role in this process, and new standard operating procedures were formulated to guide the actions of emergency response organizations. A major part of this change involved moving FEMA into the Department of Homeland Security where it lost its status as an independent agency, but gained closer ties to other federal agencies that were also involved in emergency relief.

Hurricane Katrina was the first real test of the nation's redesigned response framework. Unfortunately, serious breakdowns occurred in governmental operations at the local, state, and national levels. A noticeable gap developed between public expectations and bureaucratic behavior. The governmental response to Hurricane Katrina was widely criticized and the entire relief effort was viewed by the American public as a catastrophic failure.

Once again, the government was unable to handle a major natural disaster. In turn, this produced a large number of commentaries about, and investigations into what went wrong during Hurricane Katrina. It also led to more changes in the nation's disaster response framework. The Post-Katrina Emergency Management Reform Act of 2006 returned several important emergency management responsibilities to FEMA, although it left the agency within the Department of Homeland Security; it established new offices to facilitate better communication between public and private agencies; and it created a host of new provisions designed to clarify and extend the government's disaster response operations. Unquestionably, Hurricane Katrina triggered a national debate about the roles and responsibilities of governmental agencies during *major* natural disasters. It also raised an even broader question: How can we improve governmental performance in crisis situations?

Notes

1. This analysis has focused on major natural disasters—that is, those that the president declares to be severe enough to require the resources of the national government. It is important to keep in mind that in addition to these situations, hundreds of other minor disasters occur every year in the United States, including tornadoes in the Midwest, ice storms in the Northeast, and mudslides in the West. These minor disasters are handled by individual citizens, private organizations, and local emergency management agencies, and they never escalate to the state or national governmental levels.

2. The role of the media in disasters is not restricted to natural phenomena. For more information on the media's coverage of other types of crisis situations—such as technological mishaps, riots, health care epidemics, environmental problems, and so forth—see Wilkins

(1987); J. Brown (1990); Fensch (1990); Benthall (1993); Rochefort and Cobb (1994); Dynes and Quarantelli (2007); and Scanlon (2008).

3. There are notable exceptions to this return to normalcy. Some disaster victims do experience long-term psychological trauma as a result of their ordeal. And some homes and businesses are never rebuilt after a devastating earthquake or hurricane. But remarkably, most disaster-stricken populations and communities do recover from their experiences (Webb, Tierney, and Dahlamer 2000; Alesch et al. 2001; Kendra and Wachtendorf 2003; and Tierney and Webb 2006). For additional discussion of the societal impacts of disasters, see Dacy and Kunreuther (1969); Haas, Kates, and Bowden (1977); Rossi, Wright, and Weber-Burdin (1978); Friesema et al. (1979); Wright, Rossi, Wright, and Weber-Burdin (1979); May (1985b); Drabek (1986); Kreps (1989); Albala-Bertrand (1993); DeVoe (1997); Mileti (1999); Tierney, Lindell and Perry (2001); Nakagawa and Shaw (2004); G. Smith (2004); National Research Council (2006); Tierney and Webb (2006); Drabek (2007); and Webb (2007).

4. This has led some critics to argue that the government is too generous in providing disaster relief. The argument is made that disaster assistance may actually make people too complacent and less conscientious about taking the necessary precautions to mitigate against and prepare for natural catastrophes. For additional discussions of how citizens might react in such a fashion to disasters, see Berry (1994); Platt (1999); R. Kasperson (2005); and Kasperson, Golding, and Tuler (2005).

5. This same dilemma occurs in other public policy areas as well. For example, the public hears more about problems in the administration of public assistance—for example, welfare fraud, corruption in the food stamp program, and inefficiency in the social security system—than it does about the positive benefits of governmental aid.

15

Considering Recommendations for Change

A number of recommendations have been presented for improving the governmental response to natural disasters in the United States. These proposals cover a wide range of possibilities. They originate from a variety of sources, including the mass media, disaster research scholars, legislative oversight committees, governmental investigatory agencies, and the emergency management community itself. The content varies widely, from proposals for overhauling the entire system, to plans that entail only modest adjustments to existing policies and procedures. Some of these ideas are quite old, pre-dating the current disaster response system itself. Others are of more recent vintage. But all of these recommendations have certainly received their share of attention, particularly after a major, catastrophic event occurs.

Theoretically, the existing disaster response system could be abolished and a new framework for addressing disasters could be created. One possibility would be to privatize the nation's emergency preparedness and relief operations. This would mean getting the government out of the disaster relief business entirely, by shifting all emergency response activities to the private sector (Sobel and Leeson 2006). At the other end of the continuum, the basic intergovernmental structure of the disaster relief process could be changed: the national government could be placed in charge of addressing all disaster situations, no matter when or where they occur; or alternatively, the process could be decentralized so that state and local governments take complete responsibility for emergency management activities within their respective jurisdictions. Although such changes have been proposed at various times, they do not receive serious, sustained attention. They would involve major reallocations of resources, new designations of lines of authority, and significant changes in the relationships between the public and private sectors as well as between various levels of government. Moreover, they would probably not be received very favorably by politicians and administrators, who depend upon disaster assistance programs for money, employment, and support (Platt 1999; Sylves 2008).

A complete overhaul of the governmental response process is also incompatible with the American public's impressions of how emergency relief should be implemented. Most citizens believe that the government should play a major role in addressing emergency situations (Schneider, Jacoby, Lewis 2011), and that responsibility for disaster assistance should be shared by all three levels of government (S. Schneider 2008b). They do not think that the private sector should take the lead in this area or that any one level of government should have total responsibility for addressing natural disasters. In fact, the public's view of emergency management closely parallels the current intergovernmental structure of disaster assistance (S. Schneider 2008b).

Furthermore, if the basic framework of emergency assistance is substantially altered, it might hinder the government's ability to handle the vast majority of disasters that occur every year. The current process was created with this wide range of disasters in mind. It was designed so that public organizations could handle any type of emergency situation, no matter when or where it occurred. So it naturally focuses on those events that happen the most frequently. And the governmental response process works fairly well during such situations.

At a more realistic level, five suggestions for building a more effective emergency management system in the United States are frequently mentioned: (1) placing the military in charge of the system; (2) centralizing the disaster response process and giving national-level civilian agencies more responsibility during extreme, catastrophic circumstances; (3) creating a new federal agency to lead the governmental response process; (4) removing the Federal Emergency Management Agency (FEMA) from the Department of Homeland Security and reinstating it as the nation's chief disaster response agency; and (5) keeping the current framework, but developing and expanding the use of network models across the entire emergency management system. All of these recommendations build upon currently existing institutional arrangements. Therefore, they represent viable alternatives, worthy of serious consideration.

Placing the Military in Charge of Disaster Relief

One of the most popular recommendations is to strengthen the role of the military in relief operations. This idea almost always surfaces in the mass media following major catastrophic events (Lippman 1992b; Moniz 1992; Benjamin 2005; Bumiller 2005; Sanger 2005; U.S. House of Representatives 2006; U.S. Senate 2006c). During recent disaster situations, the military has often appeared to be the only governmental institution capable of responding in a timely and effective manner. Moreover, many policymakers, and even members of the public, feel that finding domestic roles for the armed forces when international conflicts get scaled back is desirable. Therefore, why not give the military a larger role in the nation's disaster response process? Why not place the military in charge of the entire system?

Superficially, military organizations do seem to be well-equipped to handle emergencies (U.S. General Accounting Office 1993a; U.S. House of Representatives 2005). They are structured in a fairly rigid, hierarchical manner, which simplifies decision making and expedites policy implementation during crisis situations (Benjamin 2005). They have experience handling a wide variety of emergencies, ranging from international terrorism to feeding the starving masses in Somalia and Rwanda. They have individuals within their ranks who are well-trained and well-versed in emergency management practices and procedures. They have the equipment, such as tents and electric generators, and resources to provide relief to the victims of natural catastrophes. They have the authority to enforce their own actions and to support the efforts of other relief workers. And they have extensive expertise with "command and control" systems, which are promoted as the best way to organize, mobilize, and distribute disaster assistance. Taken together, these attributes seem to make the military the perfect emergency management organization.

Several of the disasters discussed in this book demonstrate just how effective military organizations can be in actual disaster situations. For example, the U.S. Army, with help from the U.S. Navy, the U.S. Air Force, the Federal Bureau of Investigation, and the U.S. Marshal's Office, restored law and order to the Virgin Islands following Hurricane Hugo (Branigin 1989a, 1989b; G. Peterson 1989; York 1989). Military involvement was also essential to the response efforts in south Florida after Hurricane Andrew: both the Florida National Guard and the U.S. military, which included personnel from the army, the navy, the air force, and the marine corps, helped stabilize local conditions, airlifted food and supplies into the damaged communities, created temporary shelter, such as tent cities, dispensed needed medical care to storm victims, and removed tons of hurricane debris (U.S. General Accounting Office 1993a).

More recently, the military played a key role during the governmental response to Hurricane Katrina. The U.S. Northern Command (NORTHCOM) quickly established a Joint Task Force of military units from all of the armed services, which placed the activities of a large number of organizations under the command of a single officer (Miskel 2008). This enabled military officials to distribute relief more quickly and efficiently, particularly in comparison to the other federal agencies involved in the relief effort (Scavo, Kearney, and Kilroy 2007).

But it was the U.S. Coast Guard that emerged as one the most effective and responsive organizations involved in the Hurricane Katrina relief operations (Brinkley 2006). The Coast Guard rescued about 33,500 people and provided essential support to repair maritime commerce in the area (U.S. Government Accountability Office 2006c). To many Americans, the Coast Guard was the one positive face of the recovery effort (Morris, Morris, and Jones 2007).

Clearly, the military can perform essential activities during a disaster situation. But there are several major reasons why disaster relief should remain a civilian undertaking in the United States. First, the military's primary mission is to maintain the country's defense capabilities during international conflicts and wars (Sylves 2007). Responding to natural disasters is, at best, a secondary concern. If a natural catastrophe occurs at the same time as an international incident, the military must focus on the latter, not the former. Who would then mobilize and lead the governmental response to the natural disaster?

Second, it would be extremely costly to place the military in charge of responding to all natural disasters. At present, the military does *not* become involved in the vast majority of emergencies that occur in the United States (Miskel 2008). Most are handled by civilian organizations. Even when the military does become involved during these situations, their role is often quite limited to specific operations—such as maintaining law and order, mobilizing search and rescue operations, organizing evacuation procedures, and so forth. The military would need significantly more personnel and resources to be able to respond to all natural disasters in a comprehensive fashion.

Third, putting the military in charge just does not address many of the nation's emergency management problems. The current disaster response system operates on the basis of intergovernmental cooperation. Local, state, and national authorities must work together to provide the most efficient utilization of governmental resources during a natural disaster. It is assumed that subnational governments will handle many situations without the help of the national government. Even when a major disaster strikes, state and local governments must still coordinate and direct the flow of federal assistance into the affected areas (National Governor Association 2009). The national government does not have the knowledge or the ability to take control of an entire relief effort. Instead, it must work with state and local governments throughout the entire process (Graham 2005). As several of the case studies presented in this book demonstrate, problems can and do occur at the state and local levels. When this happens, the intergovernmental response stalls and in some situations completely breaks down. Placing the military in charge of disaster relief simply does not fix this problem. It will not prevent breakdowns from occurring in the intergovernmental response process.

Fourth, a more fundamental caution about involving the military in this policy area exists. According to a long-standing constitutional principle in the United States, the responsibility for public policymaking remains firmly in the hands of civilian agencies and organizations (Associated Press 2005). Placing the military in control of disaster relief operations would directly contradict this central component of American democracy. A civilian-run disaster response system was created and developed precisely because it reflects the ideal of civilian control over governmental operations (Popkin 1990; Bowman and Gorman 2005; Rubin 2007; Sylves 2008). Clearly, the military can play an important role in this process, but it must remain subordinate to higher *civilian* authorities (G. Peterson 1992; U.S. House of Representatives 2005; Witt 2006; Miskel 2008; National Governors Association 2009). It would be a dangerous precedent to initiate a system where the military has the power to tell civilian agencies what to do.[1] This is true, even though disaster situations—where such military control would be asserted—occur only infrequently and over limited periods of time. Thus, placing the military in control of the nation's disaster response system is not really a viable option (Waugh and Streib 2006)

Centralizing the Process, Giving the National—Civilian—Government More Responsibility

Most observers and analysts of disaster relief openly acknowledge that the governmental response to natural disasters has been quite variable and, at times, woefully inadequate. However, they don't believe that the military control is the answer. Instead, they want to strengthen the mechanisms that will enable civilian agencies within the national government to respond more quickly and effectively to *catastrophic* events, that is, those that go far beyond normal disasters. After all, these latter situations have clearly proven to be the most troublesome for the current intergovernmental system to handle.

Over the years, a variety of scholars, practitioners, and politicians have advocated some variant of this approach. Following the breakdown of governmental operations during Hurricane Andrew, the National Academy of Public Administration (1993), the U.S. General Accounting Office (1993b), and the Federal Emergency Management Agency (1993) recommended that the role of the national government in disaster response needed to be strengthened. But these reports and analyses did not advocate massive changes in the structure of the system or a dramatic shift in power toward the federal government. Instead, the proposals focused on how FEMA could be turned into a more reliable, effective, and respected agency. In undergoing such a transformation, FEMA would be able to coordinate the federal government's response efforts and provide the leadership that is needed to develop a more cooperative intergovernmental system of emergency management (National Academy of Public Administration 1993).

The September 11, 2001, attacks on the Pentagon and the World Trade Center renewed the discussion about the federal government's involvement during emergency situations. The 9/11 attacks were a major shock to the U.S. political system (Kettl 2004): they revealed the vulnerabilities and inadequacies of the existing emergency management system. They also pushed the issues of terrorism and homeland security to the top of the national agenda. They opened a "policy window" that would trigger major change in governmental activities (Kingdon 1994).

A political consensus emerged that a major overhaul of the nation's emergency management system was necessary. As a result, one of the most significant reorganizations of the U.S. federal bureaucracy occurred. A new cabinet-level Department of Homeland Security (DHS) was created out of twenty-two existing agencies, bureaus, and units. DHS was placed in charge of the federal government's emergency management activities, and it was given greater authority to coordinate the government's disaster response operations.

The new department was also instructed to develop a process to guide the national government's operations during unusually severe disaster situations. Consequently, the Department of Homeland Security issued guidelines that gave the national government the authority to assume a proactive leadership role when an extremely rare, catastrophic event—an incident of national significance—occurs. Hence, the general process to initiate a top-down response—led and organized by the federal government—was officially inserted into the nation's disaster response plan. The basic rationale for creating such a response was straightforward. The 9/11 terrorist attacks revealed fundamental weaknesses in the existing bottom-up response apparatus. It is simply unrealistic to expect that state and local authorities will be able to carry out their pre-established duties when chaos and extreme disruption permeate the environment. In such situations, it would be better to develop a mechanism that allows the federal government to assume a proactive, leadership role in the process. A more immediate and aggressive federal presence is justified for extreme, catastrophic disaster situations, but it would not be needed during the more routine situations that arise from the vast majority of disasters in the United States.

The general strategy of strengthening the federal government's role in disaster management has advantages. First, it leaves the rest of the intergovernmental framework of the current emergency management system intact. Public agencies at the local, state, and national levels would still compose the basic infrastructure of the response system. Thus, there would be very few resources expended on reorganization activities below the national government.

Second, this approach preserves certain fundamental tenets of American politics. It is still based on civilian control over the nation's disaster response system. It also conforms to the values of federalism by dividing important policy responsibilities between the local, state, and national authorities. Routine disasters would be dealt with by local and state governments with federal assistance; extremely disruptive events would be handled more directly by the national government.

Third, this approach reflects the realities of the contemporary policymaking process by giving the national government greater authority and control during extreme crisis situations. Clear imbalances exist in resources, power, and expertise across the three levels of government. This causes problems and breakdowns in the current system due to misperceptions and over-reliance on higher-level authorities. Under the current structure, the federal government's position would be used to greater advantage. It could step in quickly, taking preemptive steps to prevent situations from becoming even more disruptive and chaotic. By doing so, it could short-circuit the criticisms and problems that have developed in the past when the traditional, bottom-up framework is used for catastrophic disasters.

However, there are a number of problems with the implementation of this strategy. First, natural disasters do not receive the same level of attention and resources as do other types of emergencies. Under the current organizational configuration, the Department of Homeland Security is at the top of the nation's emergency management system. DHS is a large organization with broad objectives: it is responsible for a wide variety of other activities—including airline security, border patrols, counterterrorism, and so forth. Although hazard mitigation and emergency response fall under its jurisdiction, the department devotes fewer resources toward natural disaster preparation than it does toward other operations. For example, three-fourths of the federal preparedness grants that DHS distributed prior to Hurricane Katrina were directed toward counterterrorism, rather than toward natural disaster preparedness and response activities (Glasser and White 2005). Funds that are directed to counterterrorism activities are simply not available for natural hazard mitigation, preparedness, response, or relief (Steinhauer and Lipton 2006). After Hurricane Katrina, additional resources were added to the hazard mitigation operations of the Department of Homeland Security. But natural disasters still receive a relatively small proportion of the Department's budget (Sylves 2008).

Second, the reorganization of the federal government's disaster response operations has had a negative impact on emergency management personnel. DHS employees have been criticized as being more interested in other activities, such as developing counterterrorism procedures, investigating fraud and abuse, and so forth, than in dealing with natural disaster issues. During the Hurricane Katrina response there were numerous complaints that DHS personnel did not care about, and in some cases appeared unable to even recognize, the problems faced by the Gulf Coast residents (Shane, Lipton, and Drew 2005). And yet, government workers simply cannot ignore their other responsibilities even during major disasters.

Third, the federal government's responsibilities during different types of disasters have not been carefully or clearly delineated. Since 2003, the national government has had the ability to take a more proactive role during extreme, catastrophic situations. But such responsibilities were certainly not well known or well understood when Hurricane Katrina struck the U.S. coast in 2005. And even today, five years after Katrina, the proactive federal role remains an underdeveloped element of national disaster response operations. The criteria for determining when a major, catastrophic even has occurred, or is occurring, are still unclear, as are the procedures that the federal government is supposed to follow during such circumstances. Emergency management officials are much more familiar with the types of disasters that occur more regularly; hence, they are better equipped to handle them (Schneider 2008a). In contrast, catastrophic events occur far less frequently, so disaster relief personnel are less knowledgeable about how to prepare for and respond to them.

Finally, this approach places too much emphasis on *governmental* actions (Boaz 2005; McNeill 2010). Certainly, public organizations play an extremely important role in the process. But the government is not solely responsible for the way the system operates. As this study has shown, it is the degree of discrepancy or consistency between governmental actions and human behavior that accounts for the effectiveness of disaster relief efforts. Consequently, changes that focus exclusively on the government's internal organization and operations miss a key element of the process: The emergent citizen behavior that inevitably occurs in the aftermath of a natural disaster.

Of course, governmental activities can, and do, have an impact on how the affected population will react. If public officials can quickly restore communication and supply channels, then the disaster-stricken population will probably rely on traditional patterns of behavior to guide their own actions. But emergent norms inevitably occur after natural disasters and their exact nature is impossible to predict beforehand. Therefore, any governmental response system will likely not be able to fully anticipate and deal with the human behavior that follows a natural disaster. This may be even more difficult when policy responsibilities are centralized at the national level. Federal personnel may simply not be able to identify and respond to the needs of the affected population since they are less familiar with their particular problems. Hence, the gap between bureaucratic activity and citizen expectations might even be larger when a top-down, as opposed to a bottom-up, process is used.

Creating Another Federal Agency to Handle Natural Disasters

A third recommendation is to abolish FEMA and in its place create another federal response agency (Hsu 2006; U.S. House of Representatives 2006). The new agency would then have the primary responsibility of mobilizing the federal government's emergency relief operations, as well as those of the entire intergovernmental response system.

Usually, this proposal surfaces after a failed governmental response, particularly one in which the national government is unable to augment the efforts of state and local agencies, stabilize conditions, and provide assistance quickly and effectively. During such situations, people tend to blame those who are in charge of the national government's response operations for the problems they encounter. Although presidents, cabinet secretaries, and other federal officials are certainly admonished for breakdowns in the process, it is the Federal Emergency Management Agency that is held primarily responsible for governmental failures (Pew Research Centers 2005a). For example, FEMA was intensely criticized for its mishandling of its responses to Hurricane Hugo in 1989 and Hurricane Andrew in 1992 (Cook 1989; Jordan 1992a; *Andrew: Savagery from the Sea* 1992). FEMA personnel were said to be incompetent, uncaring, and derelict; the entire agency was called a political dumping ground and bureaucratic wasteland (Bandy 1989a; Lancaster 1989). Similarly, during the governmental response to Hurricane Katrina in 2005, FEMA was, once again, said to be responsible for the most serious breakdowns in the governmental relief efforts. Many observers called FEMA a "bureaucratic disaster." Critics advocated that every official in the organization should be fired (*New Orleans Times-Picayune* 2005, 15) and the entire agency should be dismantled (Bumiller and Haberman 2005; Hsu and Deane 2005). Indeed, Hurricanes Hugo, Andrew, and Katrina were clearly severe, catastrophic events; all of them caused massive disruptions that necessitated federal-level intervention. And FEMA was responsible for mobilizing and coordinating the governmental relief efforts during each of these situations.

FEMA, indeed, has been plagued with so many problems that it not able to perform its functions. Regardless of whether it is a free standing agency or a part of a larger federal department, FEMA has always been a tiny administrative unit within a massive federal bureaucracy. Since its creation in 1979, it has maintained a small staff of 2,000 to 3,000 full-time employees located in offices throughout the country. It then uses a pool of part-time reservists who are called into action when major disasters are imminent. In order to perform their duties, FEMA's small arsenal of employees must be well-trained and knowledgeable about a wide range of emergency conditions. Over the years, however, many complain that FEMA personnel are not up to the tasks at hand. This became a particular problem when FEMA lost its independent agency status and was subsumed within the larger Department of Homeland Security. A number of long-time employees left FEMA: they moved on to positions in other public and private organizations or they retired completely from government service. In the end, this had a negative impact on the caliber and expertise of FEMA personnel.

FEMA also has a relatively small operating budget to fund its day-to-day operations. For example, during the early 1990s, FEMA's annual operating budget was between $450 and $500 million. By 2005, when Hurricane Katrina struck the Gulf Coast, the agency's budget had increased to about $1 billion (U.S. Senate 2006c). But these figures are paltry by the standards of the federal government. Further, FEMA's stature and finances did not improve after its movement to the Department of Homeland Security. In fact, it has actually become more difficult to determine exactly how much money the agency receives or how FEMA allocates its funds across various activities (U.S. Government Accountability Office 2007a). Overall, though, it seems clear to many that FEMA does not possess sufficient resources to organize and mobilize effective governmental responses to major natural disasters (U.S. General Accounting Office 1993b; U.S. Department of Homeland Security 2006; U.S. Government Accountability Office 2006b).

In addition, the agency's mission is neither consistent nor clear. During the late 1980s and early 1990s, most of its planning, resources, and activities were focused on coping with the consequences of nuclear attacks against the United States (National Academy of Public Administration 1993). From 1982 to 1992, FEMA spent twelve times more money on preparing for the possibility of nuclear war, than on preparing for natural disasters such as hurricanes, earthquakes, and floods (G. Peterson 1992; Lipman and Jaspin 1993). When FEMA was moved into the Department of Homeland Security in 2003, its activities were directed even further away from natural hazard mitigation toward antiterrorism measures. Once again, FEMA's activities reflected this priority: during this time, FEMA spent a large percentage of its resources on homeland security operations—primarily antiterrorism measures—that were not directly related to preparing for and responding to natural disasters (U.S. Government Accountability Office 2007b). But the harsh reality is that natural disasters occur far more frequently than do terrorist attacks.

FEMA has also had serious leadership problems. During particular time periods, the agency has had a large number of political appointees within its ranks (Democratic Study Group 1989; Hsu 2005; *System Failure* 2005). And many of these appointees have not had disaster-related experience or training. As a result, these individuals are viewed with some skepticism by career emergency management employees (Wamsley 1993). Added to this, the political appointees' relatively short tenure in office ensured that FEMA has not always had effective leadership (Bandy 1989a; Lippman 1992c; Hsu and Glasser 2005; S. Schneider 2005).[2] In sum, FEMA has not always had leaders with the expertise, background, and capabilities to take charge of the federal response system or to provide direction and guidance during disaster response operations (U.S. Government Accountability Office 2006b).

FEMA's problems also stem, in part, from external factors. FEMA's lines of responsibility have been unclear and inconsistent. When FEMA was an independent agency it reported to twenty-five different congressional committees and subcommittees (Peterson 1989). Instead of one legislative taskmaster, FEMA had many. Numerous other independent federal agencies are accountable to many fewer oversight committees. Then, when FEMA became part of the Department of Homeland Security, its roles and responsibilities became even more uncertain. Not only did FEMA lose its status as an independent bureaucracy, but it gave up much of its jurisdiction over hazard mitigation and disaster assistance policies (Rubin 2007). These activities were parceled out to a number of other units and directorates within the Department of Homeland Security. FEMA now found that it was in competition with these other units to obtain critical resources and support for emergency management operations. Moreover, FEMA's role as the chief federal agency in charge of disaster assistance was officially transferred to the Department of Homeland Security. More specifically, the secretary of DHS (not FEMA) was given the primary responsibility for developing and implementing the nation's disaster response plans. So instead of being at the helm of the nation's emergency management system, FEMA was now in a subordinate role within the larger Department of Homeland Security.

Following Hurricane Katrina, many emergency preparedness functions were supposed to be moved back under FEMA's jurisdiction (U.S. Congress 2006, 2007). To date, however, FEMA's position in the nation's disaster response system is still uncertain: some hazard mitigation activities have still not been transferred back to FEMA, and the agency still does not have the ability to implement important elements of the nation's disaster response plan (Government Accountability Office 2008a).

Given FEMA's many internal and external problems, it may seem an expedient course of action simply to abolish the agency and create an entirely new one. Presumably, such a new entity would have its mission, powers, and responsibilities articulated more clearly and directly. It would have more direct access to the full array of resources available at the national level, and it would be in a better position to work with the many public and private agencies that operate within the intergovernmental emergency management system. But the creation of an entirely new federal agency brings its own set of problems.

Initially, a new federal disaster response agency might have more drive and more energy than the existing Federal Emergency Management Agency. The officials in such a new agency might be eager to demonstrate the effectiveness of their new organization. They would try to take bold, pathbreaking steps, and thereby bring a new sense of commitment to their activities. But this initial spurt would probably not last very long. All organizations tend to become more routinized and conservative over time (Downs 1967). New organizations quickly lose their initial burst of energy and enthusiasm; they develop standard operating procedures and policies; and they increasingly concentrate their efforts on preserving their own operations and spheres of responsibilities (Rourke 1984).[3] A new federal disaster response agency would almost certainly follow this same pattern of organizational development.

In addition, a new federal response agency would be confronted with many of the same constraints and problems that FEMA currently faces: "turf wars" with other federal agencies over policy responsibilities, competition from other federal personnel for access to the president, intense scrutiny by legislative oversight committees, and battles with appropriations committees for critical financial support. And it is quite likely that a new federal agency would possess many of the same bureaucratic characteristics and problems—for example, the obsession with paperwork, red tape, and the inability to handle non-routine situations—that have plagued almost all emergency management agencies. Thus, replacing the latter with a new organization would probably not lead to any lasting improvements in the system.

Reinstating FEMA as the Federal Government's Principal Disaster Response Organization

The failed response to Hurricane Katrina gave prominence to another suggestion for altering the governmental response process. Once again, the basic idea is to establish a federal organization that is more directly focused on hazard mitigation and disaster response (Perrow 2006). But unlike the previous proposal, FEMA would not be abolished. Instead, FEMA would be removed from the Department of Homeland Security, reinstated as an independent federal agency, and given the resources it needs so that it can mobilize and coordinate the government's relief efforts (Weitz 2006; *Government Executive* 2009). Stated simply, FEMA should be the lead agency for the governmental response to major natural disasters.

Many advocates of this perspective believe that FEMA occupied such a position in the process before it was moved into the Department of Homeland Security. During the early 1990s, FEMA became the poster child of a movement to reinvent government. As a result, the agency became more focused, better organized, more responsive, and more efficient.

FEMA's transformation began in earnest when James Witt became the agency's director in 1993. Almost immediately upon assuming his post, Witt had FEMA articulate its general, overriding mission: to provide leadership and support for "all-hazards, comprehensive emergency management" (Witt 1993, p. 1). Once the agency's focus had been clearly established, Witt implemented a number of other important reforms. First, extensive organizational and structural changes were made within the agency: new administrative units were created, the functions of the organization's existing offices were consolidated, and responsibilities were shifted between program areas. In addition, a new "rapid response unit" was established within FEMA to enable the agency to deploy teams of federal relief workers to any event within a matter of hours (Federal Emergency Management Agency 1996).

Then, several strategic goals were identified to guide the agency's day-to-day operations. One of the most important of these goals was the idea of building a stronger emergency management framework, across all levels of government and between the public and private sectors. This allowed FEMA to build stronger working relationships with other federal agencies, such as the Small Business Administration and the Department of Transportation, and with public and private agencies throughout the intergovernmental system. The agency also took steps to strengthen its public service activities by providing more accurate and timely information to disaster victims and the entire population. In turn, this enabled FEMA to inform citizens about the potential hazards of impending disasters and to sensitize them to the realities of emergency conditions.

Finally, efforts were made to change the attitudes of FEMA personnel, as well as the public's image of the agency. FEMA employees were given better training in emergency management and more responsibilities to handle disaster situations. This was done to improve the low morale of FEMA personnel and to enhance the overall reputation of the agency in the eyes of the general public, as well as to upgrade its performance in disaster situations. Overall, these reforms were designed to refocus and sharpen FEMA's mission, make the agency more consumer-oriented, streamline its operations, and establish an esprit de corps among its employees. All of these objectives are taken directly from the principles of the reinventing government movement that was popular during the 1990s.

This approach for improving the nation's response system has several obvious advantages. First, it builds upon the current intergovernmental framework. As a result, it would not require dismantling the response system and starting over anew with an entirely different structure. It expands upon the technical expertise, operating procedures, and structural relationships that already exist within the system, and it ties these elements together with tighter partnerships and cooperative, working relationships.

Second, this approach also emphasizes the need for strong direction and leadership, particularly at the national level (Peters 2009b). As the case studies in the book demonstrate, the entire governmental response operates more effectively when the federal government is more focused, better organized, and amply prepared for natural disasters. This is precisely what happened during the responses to Hurricane Georges. The storm caused major disruptions and affected thousands of lives in Puerto Rico, the Florida Keys, and along the Gulf Coast. But the governmental response process worked fairly smoothly and effectively. And there was almost no public criticism of governmental actions, personnel, or policies. But why were these operations successful? At least part of the reason is due to the role that FEMA played during these disasters. FEMA was more focused, better organized, and amply prepared; it worked in concert with other public and private agencies; it mobilized, coordinated, and implemented resources more effectively; and it responded more quickly to the needs of affected populations. In sum, it provided leadership for the response efforts.[4]

While the reinstatement and reinvigoration of FEMA as the lead federal agency seems to have promise, there are also a number of caveats that should be considered with this proposal. First, as previously discussed, sustaining organizational energy and initiative is difficult. New leaders can revitalize bureaucratic personnel, but they may serve for relatively short periods of time (Peters 2009). And new administrators may have different ideas, objectives, and approaches than their predecessors. This can create problems for a governmental system that relies upon pre-established routines and standard operating procedures to guide its day-to-day operations. In addition, broader organizational constraints can limit the scope and duration of administrative enthusiasm. Unfortunately, this is precisely what happened to FEMA when it was moved into the Department of Homeland Security. The agency slipped back into many of its old habits: it no longer had a clear mission, it lacked strong leadership, its personnel were not squarely focused on hazard mitigation, and it was not well respected within the federal bureaucracy. FEMA's placement within the Department of Homeland Security did little to bolster the agency's reputation or stature in the intergovernmental response process.

Second, the linkages between a governmental agency and the public it serves are extremely important (Niskanen 1971; Rourke 1984; Meier and Bohte 2006; Meier and O'Toole 2006). This is particularly true with emergency management institutions. Disasters are, by their very nature, unpredictable events. So the collective behavior that follows a catastrophic situation may proceed in directions that are completely unanticipated by public officials, no matter how closely the latter try to stay in touch with their constituencies. Added to this is the ongoing fact that citizens' post-disaster expectations are often at odds with the immediate capabilities of governmental institutions. Relations between response agencies and disaster victims will inevitably remain somewhat troublesome, no matter what agency is in charge of the system. Consequently, it is not possible to fix all of the problems in the governmental response process simply by putting FEMA back in charge of the nation's emergency management system.

Developing Strong Organizational Networks

All of the previous recommendations focus on the federal government's role in the emergency management process. Although they differ in terms of specifics, these proposals all advocate a stronger role for the national government. However, some scholars and analysts do not think that the centralization of emergency response activities will improve the government's performance during disasters. Instead, they believe that the entire intergovernmental framework of emergency management organizations should be strengthened, particularly the linkages among subnational governmental units.

Most of the proposals that fall within this general category are based on some type of "network model" (O'Toole 1997; Milward and Provan 2000; Agranoff and McGuire 2001; Wise 2002; Keast et al. 2004). The basic assumption is that the disaster response system comprises a network of many public, nonprofit, and private organizations. Government plays a key role in managing and guiding this network of organizations. But government does not control the other organizations in this network in a hierarchical manner. Instead, it helps them collaborate with one another and develop the capacity to be better able to address natural disaster situations (Waugh and Streib 2006; Wise 2006).

This approach rests heavily on inter-organization communication and cooperation (Comfort 2007). The organizations that are a part of the network must be able to interact with each other and work toward the achievement of a common goal. They must also be able to adjust their activities as the situations confronting them change. Hence, the actions of organizations within the network are dynamic, requiring constant adjustments as environmental conditions evolve. In this context, overall success is measured by the joint efforts of the entire network of organizations, not by the actions of any single agency or individual (Wise 2006).

The network model has been used for quite some time in the nation's disaster response system. During the 1990s, an "all-hazards" approach to emergency management became quite popular. This approach encouraged public managers to consider a much wider range of emergency situations, as well as a broader spectrum of hazard mitigation and response activities. It also expanded the number and type of organizations involved in the process. And it required a different set of skills and attributes on the part of emergency management personnel. Instead of using "command and control" type procedures, officials had to rely more on their ability to communicate, interact, and cooperate with others in the system.

As a consequence of these changes, networks of emergency management organizations developed. Some of these networks are based on mutual aid agreements, which specify the legal conditions and working relationships between different types of organizations, often within specific geographic areas. For example, a mutual aid agreement might indicate how various local organizations will cooperate with one another in order to evacuate nursing home residents (Sylves 2008) or it might outline the procedures to ensure that state and local search and rescue operations are coordinated (Waugh and Streib 2006). Other types of networks are created as agreements or compacts. These networks facilitate intergovernmental cooperation and assistance. The most prominent example of this type of arrangement is the Emergency Management Assistance Compact (EMAC). EMAC was initiated by the Southern Governors' Association in 1996; it originally committed fourteen states and territories to cooperate in the planning and implementation of emergency management assistance (Waugh 2007). Today, all fifty states belong to EMAC: it "represents a strong collective effort of the states to facilitate state-to-state mutual aid when major disasters and emergencies take place" (Sylves 2008, 146).

The network approach to disaster relief has some obvious advantages. First, it tries to tie together the multiplicity of public agencies involved in the process, and it provides a general framework to facilitate communication, cooperation, and collaboration. Without such arrangements, it would be extremely difficult to implement disaster relief across the intergovernmental system, particularly if an emergency requires resources that are beyond the capacity of any local or state government.

In addition, this approach also recognizes that governmental agencies are not the only organizations involved in emergency relief. A variety of different types of organizations—public, nonprofit, and private—play a role in the process. Therefore, it is important to identify arrangements that will link together these various types of organizations so that they can achieve a common goal. The network approach is specifically designed to accomplish this.

A third advantage of the network model is its ability to adapt to various types of disasters in different locations. Indeed, this model assumes that many organizational arrangements will emerge, with no one single structure fitting every kind of emergency situation or locale. So a network along the Gulf Coast for hurricane relief would differ from one surrounding an earthquake-prone area in California. Networks can be much more fluid in design and operation than traditional types of emergency management arrangements.

The network approach does have its weaknesses. It involves a delicate balance between planning on the one hand and spontaneity on the other. The very creation of a network of organizations requires a great deal of discussion and planning in order to ensure that participants agree on the necessary degree of cooperation and collaboration. But the successful implementation of an agreement will require organizations to adjust and adapt their operations depending upon the circumstances that they encounter. This may mean that organizations will have to abandon some pre-existing plans and routine and adopt new ones to respond more appropriately. Such modifications are not automatic or easy to achieve.

Networks provide a framework for inter-organization collaboration, but they do not ensure that cooperation will occur. The organizations that are a part of these arrangements can change, as can the personnel involved in their development and execution. Such factors can affect whether a compact is activated, as well as how quickly and effectively it is implemented. The potential variability of inter-organization networks was perhaps most apparent during the response to Hurricane Katrina. Overall, the EMAC system performed fairly well during this disaster. However, noticeable differences between Mississippi and Louisiana were seen in how well public officials understood the elements of the compacts, their willingness to activate them, and their ability to follow through on inter-organization commitments (Waugh 2007).

Combining Recommendations: A Set of Tangible Changes in the System

After carefully considering the U.S. disaster response system, its performance in a range of disaster situations, and the major proposals for changing the system, we are still left with a single overriding question. What can and should be done to strengthen the governmental disaster response system? Although each of the proposals described earlier in this chapter contains some useful, thought-provoking ideas, no single recommendation, by itself, provides an ideal solution. However, suggestions from several different proposals can be combined to produce a set of recommendations that would correct the most persistent problems.

First, the basic organizational structure of disaster assistance should be retained. The results from this study suggest that the current system has certain obvious advantages: it allows the government to handle the vast majority of natural disasters quietly, smoothly, and successfully. Consequently, the current governmental framework should not be dismantled and replaced with an entirely new structure. Putting the military in charge might facilitate faster emergency responses, but it would generate a host of other, potentially more severe problems—such as conflicts between civilian and military officials and the role of the military in long-term recovery efforts. Similarly, the abolishment of FEMA and the creation of a new federal agency to lead the response and recovery charge is also not the solution. At best, this would only delay the onset of the same bureaucratic pathologies that have hindered the performance of the existing system. At worst, this would substitute one set of organizational problems for another.

Second, it is also clear that the existing intergovernmental response process needs to be re-energized and strengthened. The quality of the entire response is a direct byproduct of local, state, and national governmental actions. Weaknesses at any level can have a negative impact on the relief effort. The results of this study clearly indicate that hazard mitigation and disaster relief need to become higher priorities throughout the governmental system. At the local level, it is simply too easy for city and county personnel to forget about their emergency management responsibilities, particularly when they are confronted with ongoing and persistent community problems. Moreover, local officials are naturally tempted to view emergency management as someone else's responsibility—usually this "someone else" is the state or national government. Hence, steps must be taken to strengthen the emergency management efforts of *local* governments across the nation, and particularly those in high-risk, disaster-prone, areas.

Significant improvements also need to be made at the state level. Statewide hazard mitigation plans need to be prepared more carefully and conscientiously; state emergency management agencies need to be given the requisite resources, that is, funding, personnel and authority, to fulfill important responsibilities; and other state-level personnel need to be better equipped to perform critical supportive emergency management functions. In sum, state governments need to take their disaster relief responsibilities more seriously.

Emergency management compacts can certainly enhance the operations of state and local governments in the disaster response system. But these arrangements need to be more fully developed and integrated across a wider array of emergency situations (U.S. Government Accountability Office 2007a). Moreover, emergency management personnel need to become more versed in what these compacts can do, when they can be activated, and how they can be implemented. Such training and preparation need to be provided on a continuing basis to ensure that changes within and across jurisdictions—in personnel, resources, training, commitment, and so forth—do not inhibit the effectiveness of these inter-organization arrangements.

Finally, the role of the federal government in natural disaster situations needs to be clarified and bolstered. To begin, the Federal Emergency Management Agency must emphasize the importance of preparing for, and responding to, natural disasters. FEMA is the lead federal agency for emergency response; therefore, it must focus its activities and operations on these events. The case studies presented in this book demonstrate the important role that FEMA plays in the process. When FEMA is squarely focused on hazard mitigation, management, and response, the entire process operates much more smoothly and efficiently. However, when FEMA's focus is redirected toward other activities, it is unable to mobilize or organize an effective disaster response.

It is also necessary to strengthen FEMA's capabilities so that it can serve as the lead agency for disaster relief. After all, how can FEMA or any federal agency mobilize and implement a credible response if it is viewed as the laughingstock of the federal bureaucracy? How can that agency provide effective leadership if it is the dumping ground for political hacks and political patronage paybacks? And how can a federal agency provide emergency relief to disaster victims in a timely and effective manner without adequate financial support from Congress and appropriate administrative support from the rest of the federal government?

The Post-Katrina Emergency Management Reform Act of 2006 contains a number of provisions designed to enhance FEMA's role as the lead federal response agency. Specifically, it consolidates emergency management functions under FEMA's jurisdiction, and it strengthens the agency's authority and status within the federal bureaucracy. The Post-Katrina Reform Act also makes changes to the agency's personnel structure and management system: it sets up new positions within the agency, and it establishes specific background and experience requirements for top FEMA administrators. In addition, the Act requires that FEMA develop a "strategic plan on human capital" that will enhance the recruitment, training, deployment, and retention of the agency's entire workforce (Bea 2006, p. 24). All of these provisions are designed to rectify shortcomings that prevented FEMA from responding to major disasters in an effective manner (U.S. General Accountability Office 2009). Hopefully, once they are fully implemented, these measures will have a direct, positive impact on FEMA's activities.

However, it is not enough to clarify and enhance FEMA's role in the emerging management process. Other changes must be made in the system in order to ensure a smoother, more effective and consistent response to natural disasters. In particular, a clear distinction must be made between the role of the national government during *catastrophic* disasters versus its role in *major,* but non-catastrophic situations (Quarantelli 2006). This would enable the federal government to develop a more straightforward set of policies and procedures specifically tailored for disasters of different magnitude.

For catastrophic events, the federal government now has the ability to assume a more proactive stance; for non-catastrophic, but major, disasters, the federal government should retain its supplementary role, stepping in when state and local resources have been exhausted. These two processes are already delineated in the current governmental response plans and policies. However, the procedures for initiating and guiding direct federal involvement during extreme, catastrophic situations are still not clearly defined, adequately developed, or widely known. Moreover, they are not given sufficient attention in the training and preparation provided to emergency management personnel.

The Post-Katrina Reform Act helped to clarify this process: it amended the Stafford Act and gave the president the ability to provide accelerated federal assistance in the absence of a specific disaster declaration (U.S. Government Accountability Office 2009). And FEMA has issued guidelines to help governors prepare a request for an emergency declaration before a disaster strikes. But complete guidelines and protocols have not been prepared to guide proactive actions by FEMA in advance of a potential disaster. Until this process is clearly explained with sufficient training given to all those who might be involved, questions will continue to surface about when and how the federal government should intervene in catastrophic situations. This widens the gap between bureaucratic actions and public expectations, leading to breakdowns in, or even a total collapse of, the governmental response process.

In sum, there are several direct, tangible modifications that can be made in the intergovernmental response system. These changes would not require a complete overhaul of the existing apparatus. If these changes were made, however, they would allow the government to respond more quickly and effectively to natural disaster situations. And they would contribute to more positive images about governmental performance in this policy area.

Final Thoughts

It is important to remember that some key aspects of the governmental response process will be difficult, and perhaps even impossible, to change. This study makes it quite clear that the components of the system that most need to be altered are relatively intangible: the perceptions, feelings, attitudes, and morale of everyone involved in the disaster response process, both private citizens and public officials. This under-scores the difficulties facing the disaster response system, precisely because effecting meaningful change in psychological orientations is hard.

Different perspectives can and often do develop within the governmental response system itself—particularly across the three levels of government. This usually takes the following form: local and state officials feel that their responsibilities have ended once they pass on the response to the national government; their feeling is that federal agencies should be in charge of the relief effort and totally responsible for its opera-tions. Conversely, federal officials do not view their role as one of taking over the responsibilities of state and local governments during the vast majority of situations Instead, they see the system as a team effort in which the three units of government have separate but clearly interdependent responsibilities. These differing role perceptions emerged in varying degrees across virtually all of the disasters discussed in this study. In the Caribbean during Hurricane Hugo and Hurricane Georges, and in Louisiana following Hurricane Katrina, local and territorial/state governments were unable to respond to the disaster, pushing the relief effort up to the federal government almost immediately. In South Carolina's response to Hugo, Florida's response to Andrew, and Mississippi's response to Katrina, state and local officials were able to start the process, but expected the federal government to take over as soon as the magnitude of the situation became clear. During the Loma Prieta Earthquake, local officials tended toward this same view; however, it was not nearly as widespread in South Carolina during Hurricane Hugo or Florida during Hurricane Andrew. During the responses to Hurricane Georges in the Florida Keys and along the Gulf Coast and the Northridge Earthquake, local, state, and federal officials all had a fairly consistent view of their responsibilities; hence, there were smaller differences in the perceptions of their roles. During Hurricane Hugo in North Carolina, Hurricane Andrew in Louisiana, the 1990 floods in South Carolina, and the 2010 severe storms/floods in Tennessee, local, state, and federal officials all had similar views of their responsibilities: differences in the perceptions of their roles were minimized.

A clear pattern has emerged in this regard. When all three governmental levels have the same view of their roles and responsibilities, the system works better. When there are differences, the disaster response produces confusion and conflict, or even complete stalemate and collapse. It is, therefore, essential that officials from each level of government understand their own duties in order to handle disasters successfully. But again, achieving this understanding will be very difficult.

Problems can also arise when other actors develop unrealistic or inappropriate expectations about governmental activity. In many of the case studies considered in this book, serious breakdowns in the system occurred precisely because nongovernmental actors and elected officials intervened in the response process. Political leaders, the media, and individual citizens all have their own reasons for circumventing standard operating procedures. Senators, governors, and presidents all want to undertake actions that benefit their own careers, and natural disasters provide excellent opportunities for doing so. Network news organizations, along with print journalists, want to report items that will appeal to the widest possible audience. Stories about unmanageable disaster conditions, bureaucratic indifference to human suffering, and the sheer human chaos produced by natural catastrophes are all attractive scenarios from a journalistic perspective. This remains true even though such images rarely convey a balanced, or even accurate, picture of a disaster's aftermath.

Finally, disaster victims naturally want to obtain essential relief for themselves and their families. Time-consuming paperwork and seemingly nonsensical administrative procedures appear merely to hinder their access to the food, shelter, and medical supplies that they require. Hence, activities that circumvent these procedures appear quite rational, even necessary to the affected population. As this study has demonstrated, such behavior is a natural byproduct of any disaster situation. Once again, however, the problem is that such actions by public or private participants can hinder the overall effectiveness of the disaster response. Thus, disaster response will probably remain a problematic element of public policymaking in the United States.

In conclusion, the governmental response to natural disasters is an important topic on several levels. From a scholarly perspective, the government's ability to respond to disasters reveals a great deal about public policymaking under extraordinarily stressful conditions. From a more practical viewpoint, it is essential that the public and governmental officials, including those not directly involved in the response process, have a clear understanding of what to expect in disaster situations. Natural disasters provide a real-world laboratory for dealing with extremely trying circumstances. If the government can improve its performance here, it may be able to do so elsewhere as well. Hopefully, this analysis will not only increase our understanding of natural disasters and the effectiveness of emergency management procedures. It should also stimulate further research on the linkages between governmental activities and human behavior in other important areas of public policymaking.

Notes

1. There are other problematic and potentially dangerous aspects of allowing the military to assume primary responsibility for disaster relief. These include the military's ability to control the release of information about disaster situations to the general public and the mass media; their ability to declare martial law, taking over the authority of civilian authorities; and their standing with respect to liability and damage issues.

2. These problems are not unique to FEMA. See Ingraham (1987) for a more general discussion of how similar internal problems, that is, political appointees, have plagued other federal agencies.

3. New organizations may also lack expertise and experience; consequently, they can also make monumental mistakes. For example, see Shaffer (1977) and Thompson (1982) for an account of OSHA's blunders during the early years of its existence.

4. FEMA was able to respond well to other disasters during its "reinvention" period in the 1990s, again because of a renewed emphasis on natural disasters, stronger leadership, better outreach, and improved communications/coordination with state and local authorities (Claiborne 1993a, 1993b; *Natural Hazards Observer* 1993; *The State* 1993; Federal Emergency Management Agency 1994a, 1994b, 1997; Franklin 1995; Sylves 1996; Ryan 1997; Schneider 1998; Daniels and Clark-Daniels 2000; Suburban Emergency Management Project 2009).

References

ABC News. 2005. "Who's to Blame for Delayed Response to Katrina?" September 6, 2005. http://ABCNEWS.go.com.

Aberbach, Joel D., Robert D. Putnam, and Bert A. Rockman. 1981. *Bureaucrats and Politicians in Western Democracies.* Cambridge, MA: Harvard University Press.

Abney, F. Glenn, and Larry B. Hill. 1966. "Natural Disasters as a Political Variable: The Effect of a Hurricane on an Urban Election." *American Political Science Review* 60 (December): 974–81.

Adams, William C. 1986. "Whose Lives Count? TV Coverage of Natural Disasters." *Journal of Communication* 36 (2): 113–122.

Adler, Jerry. 1994. "After the Quake." *Newsweek,* January 31, 25–33.

"Advance Men in Charge." 2005. *The New York Times,* September 9, Editorial. http://www.nytimes.com/2005/09/09/opinion/09fri1.html.

"After Katrina, a Deadly Nightmare." 2005. *Newsweek,* September 12.

Agranoff, Robert. 2007. *Managing in Networks: Boundary Spanning Among Public and Nongovernmental Organizations.* Washington, DC: Georgetown University Press.

Agranoff, Robert, and Michael McGuire. 2001. "Big Questions for Public Network Management Research." *Journal of Public Management Research and Theory* 11 (3): 295–327.

Aguirre, B.E. 1994. "Collective Behavior and Social Movement Theory." In *Disasters, Collective Behavior, and Social Organization,* ed. Russell R. Dynes and Kathleen J. Tierney. Newark: University of Delaware Press.

———. 2005. "Emergency Evacuations, Panic, and Social Psychology." *Psychiatry* 68 (2): 121–129.

Aguirre, B.E., Dennis Wenger, and Gabriela Vigo. 1998. "A Test of Emergent Norm Theory of Collective Behavior." *Sociological Forum* 13 (2): 301–320.

Albala-Bertrand, J.M. 1993. *The Political Economy of Large Natural Disasters.* Oxford: Clarendon Press.

Albert, Bruce. 2009. "President Bush Concedes Mistakes During Katrina, but Says Federal Action Not Slow." *The Times-Picayune,* January 12. http://www.nola.com/news/index.ssf/2009/01/bush_concedes_mistakes_during.html.

Alesch, D.J., H.N. Holly, E. Mittler, and R.A. Nagy. 2001. *Organizations at Risk: What Happens When Small Businesses and Not-for-Profits Encounter Natural Disasters.* Fairfax, VA: Public Entity Risk Institute.

Alexander, David. 2006. "Symbolic and Practical Interpretations of the Hurricane Katrina Disaster in New Orleans." *Understanding Katrina: Perspectives from the Social* Sciences. Social Science Research Council, June 11. http://understandingkatrina.ssrc.org/Alexander/.

Alexander, Keith L., and Neil Henderson. 2005. "A Trickle of Financial Relief: Katrina Survivors Must Wade Through Bureaucracy for Government Aid." *The Washington Post National Weekly Edition,* September 19–25, 31.

Alford, Robert. 1969. *Bureaucracy and Participation.* Chicago: Rand-McNally.

"An American Tragedy." 2005. *Time,* September 12.

"Anatomy of a Disaster: Five Days that Changed a Nation." 2005. *U.S. News & World Report,* September 26.

Anderson, Ed, Michael Perlstein, and Robert Travis Scott. 2005. "We'll Do What It Takes to Restore Order. *The Times-Picayune,* September 1, http://www.nola.com/newslogs/breakingtp/index.ssf?/mtlogs/nola_Times-Picayune/archives/2005_09.html.

Anderson, James. 1994. "L.A.: Long Lines, Uncertainty, Chaos." *The State,* January 19, 1A, 6A.

Anderson, W.A. 1970. "Military Organizations in Natural Disaster: Established and Emergent Norms." *American Behavioral Scientist* 13 (3): 415–422.

And Hugo Was His Name: Hurricane Hugo, A Diary of Destruction. 1989. Sun City West, AZ: C.F. Boone.

Andrew: Savagery from the Sea. 1992. Fort Lauderdale, FL: Sun-Sentinel.

Andrews, Edmund L. 1992. "Bush Sending Army to Florida amid Criticisms of Relief Effort." *The New York Times,* August 28, A1, A10.

Anton, Thomas J. 1989. *American Federalism and Public Policy.* New York: Random House.

AP/Ipsos. 2005a. "Americans Have Lost Confidence that Billions for Hurricane Recovery Effort Will Be Spent Wisely." Associated Press/Ipsos Poll, October 6.

———. 2005b. "Bush's Approval Mired at Lowest Levels of Presidency; Optimism About Nation's Direction Sinks to New Depths." Associated Press/Ipsos Poll, October 7.

———. 2005c. "Katrina Raises Voters' Doubts About Bush Priorities, Recovery Plans." Associated Press/Ipsos Poll, September 20.

———. 2006a. "A Year After Katrina, Many Don't Believe the Nation Is Ready for Another Major Disaster." Associated Press/Ipsos Poll, August 27.

———. 2006b. "Six Months After Katrina, Poll Finds Fading Confidence in Government." Associated Press/Ipsos Poll, February 22.

Apple, R.W. 1992. "Politicians Warily Gauge the Effects of Los Angeles's Rioting at the Polls." *The New York Times,* May 17, A20.

Applebome, Peter. 1989. "For Survivors of Hurricane, Relief is Giving Way to Despair." *The New York Times,* September 27, A1, A12.

Arceneaux, Kevin. 2006. "The Federal Face of Voting: Are Elected Officials Held Accountable for the Functions Relevant to Their Office?" *Political Psychology* 27 (5): 731–754.

Arceneaux, Kevin, and Robert M. Stein. 2006. "Who Is Held Responsible When Disaster Strikes: The Attribution of Responsibility for a Natural Disaster in an Urban Election." *Journal of Urban Affairs* 28 (1): 43–53.

Archea, John. 1990. "Immediate Reactions of People in Houses." In *The Loma Prieta Earthquake: Studies of Short-Term Impacts,* ed. Robert Bolin, 56–64. Boulder: University of Colorado, Institute of Behavioral Science, Program on Environment and Behavior, Monograph #50.

Arnone, Michael. 2006. "FEMA Pledges Better Disaster Relief Fund Payouts." *Federal Computer Weekly,* June 19. http://fcw.com/articles/2006/06/19/fema-pledges-better-disaster-relief-fund-payouts.aspx.

Arrow, Kenneth. 1963. *Social Choice and Individual Values.* 2nd ed. New York: Wiley.

Associated Press. 2005. "States Oppose Greater Role for Military in Disasters." November 4. http://www.Fox.News.com.

Ayres, B. Drummond, Jr. 1994. "Los Angeles Is Taking Rapid Road to Recovery." *The New York Times,* Thursday, March 17, A20.

———. 1998a. "Hurricane Falters After Thrashing Coast." *The New York Times,* September 28, A18.

———. 1998b. "A Recharged Hurricane Batters Gulf Coast with 110 MPH Winds." *The New York Times,* September 28, A1, A12.

Balz, Dan. 1994. "Clinton, Wilson Seize on Freeway as a Road to Political Popularity." *The Washington Post,* April 13, A6.

Bandy, Lee. 1989a. "Bungled Management, Disrespect, Scandal Mark Relief Agency's Past." *The State,* October 29, A1.

————. 1989b. "South Carolina Seeks Inquiry into FEMA." *The State,* October 4, B2.

————. 1990. "FEMA's Needs Outlined." *The State,* January 14, B1.

Bardach, Eugene. 1977. *The Implementation Game: What Happens After a Bill Becomes a Law.* Cambridge, MA: MIT Press.

Baratz, Morton, and Peter Bachrach. 1963. "Decisions and Non-Decisions: An Analytic Framework." *American Political Science Review* 57: 632–642.

Barbour, Haley. 2005. "Written Testimony of Governor Haley Barbour, State of Mississippi." Select Bipartisan Committee to Investigate the Preparation and Response to Hurricane Katrina." U.S. House of Representatives, December 7.

Barnett, Krystin. 2010. "Massive TN Cleanup Takes Center Stage." Disaster News Network, June 15. http://www.disasternews.net/news/article.php?articleid=4043.

Barr, Donald. 2007. *Introduction to U.S. Health Policy.* Baltimore: Johns Hopkins University Press.

Barr, Stephen. 2005. "The Blame Game Is Simple: Dealing with the Problem Is Complicated." *The Washington Post,* September 9, B2.

Barron, James. 1992a. "At Least 8 Killed—Houses Left in Splinters." *The New York Times,* August 25, A1, A12.

————. 1992b. "Hurricane Roars Across Gulf—Toll Is at 12." *The New York Times,* August 26, A1, A14.

Barsky, Lauren, Joseph Trainor, and Manuel Torres. 2006. "Disaster Realities in the Aftermath of Hurricane Katrina: Revisiting the Looting Myth." Quick Response Research Report 184. Boulder, CO: Natural Hazards Center.

Barton, Allan. 1969. *Communities in Disaster.* Garden City, NY: Anchor Doubleday Books.

Barzelay, Michael. 1992. *Breaking Through Bureaucracy: A New Vision for Managing in Government.* Berkeley: University of California Press.

Bassham, James H. 2010a. "May Storms and Flooding of 2010." Tennessee Emergency Management Agency. http://www.tnema.org/event/index.html.

————. 2010b. "Testimony of James H. Bassham, Director, Tennessee Emergency Management Agency Before the Senate Appropriations Subcommittee on Energy and Water Development." U.S. Senate, July 22.

Baum, Dan. 2006. "Deluged. When Katrina Hit, Where Were the Police?" *The New Yorker,* January 9, 50–63.

Baumgartner, Frank R. and Bryan D. Jones. 1993. *Agendas and Instability in American Politics.* Chicago: University of Chicago Press.

————. 2009. *Agendas and Instability in American Politics,* 2nd ed. Chicago: University of Chicago Press.

Bea, Keith. 2005a. *Federal Stafford Act Disaster Assistance: Presidential Declarations, Eligible Activities, and Funding.* CRS Report for Congress RL 33053. Washington, DC: Congressional Research Service. http://www.fas.org/sgp/crs/homesec/RL33053.pdf.

————. 2005b. *Organization and Mission of the Emergency Preparedness and Response Directorate: Issues and Options for the 109th Congress.* CRS Report for Congress, RL 33064. Washington, DC: Congressional Research Service. http://fpc.state.gov/documents/organization/53095.pdf.

————. 2006. "CRS Report for Congress: Federal Emergency Management Policy Changes After Hurricane Katrina: A Summary of Statutory Provisions." Washington, DC: Congressional Research Service, December 15.

————. 2007. "The Formative Years: 1950–1978." In *Emergency Management: The American Experience 1900–2005,* ed. Claire B. Rubin. Fairfax, VA: Public Entity Risk Institute.

Beckham, Tom. 1989. Deputy Director, South Carolina Emergency Preparedness Division, Office of the Adjutant General, personal interview, Columbia, SC, September 23.

Behr, R.L., and Shanto Iyengar. 1985. "Television News, Real-World Cues, and Changes in the Public Agenda." *Public Opinion Quarterly* 49: 99–114.

Benac, Nancy. 2005. "Anger Directed at FEMA Leader." *The Boston Globe*. September 8. http://www.boston.com/news/nation/articles/2005/09/08/anger_directed_at_fema_leader/?comments=all.

Benjamin, Scott. 2005. "Bigger Military Role in Disasters? Lawmakers must decide Pentagon's Role while Respecting States." CBS News/Associated Press. http://www.cbsnews.com/stories/2005/09/25/national/main883220.shtml.

Bendix, Reinhard. 1947. "Bureaucracy: The Problem and Its Setting." *American Sociological Review* 12: 493–507.

Bennett, C. Scott. 1990. *Heavy Rains, Flooding Hit Central South Carolina.* Columbia, SC: United States Department of Interior, Geological Survey.

Bennett, Lance W. 1988. *News: The Politics of Illusion.* 2nd ed. New York: Longman.

Bennis, Warren G., ed., 1970. *American Bureaucracy.* Chicago: Aldine.

Benthall, Jonathan. 1993. *Disasters, Relief, and the Media.* London: I.B. Taurus.

Benveniste, Guy. 1977. *Bureaucracy.* San Francisco: Boyd and Fraser.

Berger, P.L. and T.L. Luckmann. 1967. *The Social Construction of Reality.* New York: Aldine de Gruyter.

Berk, Richard. 1974. *Collective Behavior.* Dubuque, IA: William C. Brown.

Berry, John M. 1994. "In Case of Emergency, Call Uncle Sam." *The Washington Post National Weekly Edition,* February 7–13, 20.

Best, J. 1989. *Images of Issues: Typifying Contemporary Social Problems.* New York: Aldine de Gruyter.

Bickerstaff, Brandon M. 2005. "Dark Side: Looters Add Insult to Injury." *Sun Herald,* August 31, 3.

"Billion Dollar Disasters." 2008. The Intute Consortium. http://www.intute.ac.uk/hazards/billion.html.

Birkland, Thomas A. 1997. *After Disaster: Agenda Setting, Public Policy, and Focusing Events.* Washington, DC: Georgetown University Press.

———. 2007. *Lessons of Disaster: Policy Change After Catastrophic Events.* Washington, DC: Georgetown University Press.

Blackburn, Marsha. 2010. "Testimony by the Honorable Marsha Blackburn, Testimony Concerning Lessons from the 2010 Tennessee Flood," as Prepared for Delivery. Senate Committee on Appropriations, Subcommittee on Energy and Water Development, U.S. Senate, July 22.

Blake, Eric S., Edward N. Rappaport, and Christopher W. Landsea. 2007. "The Deadliest, Costliest, and Most Intense United States Cyclones from 1851 to 2006 (And Other Frequently Requested Hurricane Facts)." Miami, Florida: National Weather Service and National Hurricane Center. http://www.nhc.noaa.gov/pdf/NWS-TPC-5.pdf.

Blau, Peter M. 1955. *The Dynamics of Bureaucracy: A Study of Interpersonal Relationships in Two Government Agencies.* Chicago: University of Chicago Press.

Blumenthal, Ralph. 2006. "Simpler Form Created to Aid Storm Victims." *The New York Times,* October 13.

Blumer, Herbert George. 1957. "Collective Behavior." In *Review of Sociology*, ed. Joseph B. Gittler, 127–158. New York: Wiley.

Boaz, David. 2005. "Catastrophe in Big Easy Demonstrates Big Government's Failure." Cato Institute, September 19. http://www.cato.org/pub_display.php?pub_id=4819.

Boin, Arjen, Paul 't Hart, Eric Stern, and Bengt Sundelius. 2005. *The Politics of Crisis Management: Public Leadership Under Pressure.* New York: Cambridge University Press.

Bolin, Robert. 1990. "The Loma Prieta Earthquake: An Overview." In *The Loma Prieta Earthquake: Studies of Short-Term Impacts*, ed. Robert Bolin, 1–16. Boulder: University of Colorado, Institute of Behavioral Science, Program on Environment and Behavior, Monograph #50.

Bolin, Robert, and Lois Stanford. 1998. *The Northridge Earthquake: Vulnerability and Disaster.* New York: Routledge.

Bolt, Bruce. 1999. *Earthquakes.* New York: W.H. Freeman.

Bolton, Patricia. 1993. *The Loma Prieta California Earthquake of October 17, 1989: Public Response.* Washington, DC: Government Printing Office.

Booth, William. 1992a. "Hurricane Pounded 165 Square Miles of Florida into the Ground." *The Washington Post,* August 30, A1, A18.

———. 1992b. "Next Survival Test: Anger and Anomie." *The Washington Post,* September 4, A1, A18.

———. 1998. "Key West Greets Hurricane with Shrug." *The Washington Post,* September 25, A33.

Booth, William, and Mary Jordan. 1992. "As Tempers Shorten, Miamians Get Unruly." *The Washington Post,* August 27, A1, A21.

Booth, William, and Christina Sherry. 1993. "Picking Up the Pieces One Year After Andrew: Communities Are Slowly Rising from the Rubble." *The Washington Post National Weekly Edition,* August 30–September 5, 31.

Boston Globe. 1994. "Victims Forage for Food, Water, Warm Place to Sleep." January 19.

Bouffard, Karen. 2007. "Deadly Tornado Turns Couple's First Night in New Home to Tragedy." *The Detroit News,* October 20. http://www.detnews.com/apps/pbcs.dll.

Bourgin, Frank R. 1983. *A History of Federal Disaster Relief Legislation, 1950–1974.* Washington, DC: Federal Emergency Management Agency.

Bousquet, Steve, Mark Silva, and Martin Merzer. 1998. "Water, Water Everywhere; Storm Inundates Gulf Coast." *The Miami Herald,* September 28, 1A.

Bowman, Tom, and Siobhan Gorman. 2005. "Increasing Military's Role Raises Questions." *Baltimore Sun,* September 20. http://articles.baltimoresun.com/2005–09-20/news/0509200262_1_comitatus-posse-law-enforcement.

Bozeman, Barry. 2000. *Bureaucracy and Red Tape.* Upper Saddle River, NJ: Prentice Hall.

Branch, Karen. 1998. "A Strong Showing." *The Miami Herald,* September 26, 1B.

Branigin, William. 1989a. "In San Juan, Poor Still Feel Hugo's Wrath." *The Washington Post,* October 30, A1, A10.

———. 1989b. "A Slow Recovery from 12 Hours of Terror." *The Washington Post,* October 31, A1, A8.

Brinkley, Douglas. 2006. *The Great Deluge: Hurricane Katrina, New Orleans, and the Mississippi Gulf Coast.* New York: HarperCollins.

British Broadcasting Company. 1998. "World: Americas, Hurricane George Still a Threat." British Broadcasting Company Online. http://news.bbc.co.uk/2/hi/americas/175471.stm.

Brown, JoAnn. 1990. "The Social Construction of Invisible Danger: Two Historical Examples." In *Nothing to Fear,* ed. Andrew Kirby, 39–52. Tucson: University of Arizona Press.

Brown, Michael K. 2006. "Ghettos, Fiscal Federalism, and Welfare Reform." In *Race and the Politics of Welfare Reform,* ed. Sanford F. Schram, Joe Soss, and Richard C. Fording, 47–71. Ann Arbor: University of Michigan Press.

Browning, Robert X. 1986. *Politics and Social Welfare Policy in the United States.* Knoxville: University of Tennessee Press.

Bruner, Jerome. 1983. *Child's Talk: Learning to Use Language.* New York: Norton.

Bumiller, Elisabeth. 2005. "Bush Pledges Federal Role in Rebuilding Gulf Coast." *The New York Times,* September 16. http://www.nytimes.com/2005/09/16/national/nationalspecial/16bush.html.

Bumiller, Elisabeth, and Clyde Haberman. 2005. "Bush Makes Return Visit: Two Levees Secured." *The New York Times,* September 6. http://query.nytimes.com/gst/fullpage.html?res=950CE6D81531F935A3575AC0A9639C8B63.

Burdeau, Cain. 2006. "Grand Jury to Probe New Orleans Police." *The Washington Post.* January 25.

Burke, John P. 1986. *Bureaucratic Responsibility.* Baltimore: Johns Hopkins University Press.

Burke, Sheila, and Travis Loller. 2010. "Cumberland River Flooding: Death Toll Rises." *The Huffington Post,* May 10. http://www.huffingtonpost.com/2010/05/05/cumberland-river-flooding.

Burton, Keith. 2007. "Where's the Money? Residents Wonder Why Katrina Recovery Moving So Slow." *Gulf Coast Recovery News,* January 30. http://www.gulfcoastnews.com/GCNsp ecialReportWhere%27sthemoney.htm.

———. 2009a. "Governor Says Billions of Dollars Still Unspent." *Gulf Coast Recovery News,* March 5. http://www.gulfcoastnews.com/GCNnewsKatrinaRecoveryGov0305.

———. 2009b. "Housing Advocacy Group Says Mississippi Falling Behind on Katrina Recovery Spending." *Gulf Coast Recovery News,* September 1. http://www.gulfcoastnews.com/ GCNnewsKatrinaStepsReport0901009.htm.

California Governor's Office of Emergency Services. 1995. *The Northridge Earthquake of January 17, 1994: Preliminary Report of Data Collection and Analysis, Part A: Damage and Inventory Data.* Irvine and Pasadena: EQE International and Office of Emergency Services.

———. 1997. *The Northridge Earthquake of January 17, 1994: Report of Data Collection and Analysis, Part B: Analysis and Trends.* Irvine and Pasadena: EQE International and Office of Emergency Services.

Cannon, Lou, and Jessica Crosby. 1994. " 'It Was One Big Explosive Jolt.' " *The Washington Post,* January 18, A1, A8.

Carson, Kiki, and Susan MacManus. 2006. "Mandates and Management Challenges in the Trenches: The Intergovernmental Perspective on Homeland Security." *Public Administration Review* 66: 532–536.

Carter, Gary M. 2010. "Written Testimony of Mr. Gary M. Carter, Director, Hydrologic Development, National Weather Service, National Oceanic and Atmospheric Administration, U.S. Department of Commerce." Hearings on Lessons from the 2010 Tennessee Flood Before the Subcommittee on Energy and Water Development, Committee on Appropriates, U.S. Senate, July 22.

Carter, L. Fred. 1989. Special Assistant to Governor Carroll Campbell. Personal Interview, September 23.

CBS News. 2005. "Poll: Katrina Response Inadequate." CBS News Poll, September 8. http:// www.cbsnews.com/stories/2005/09/08/opinion/polls/main8245.

———. 2007. "Poll: Little Progress Seen since Katrina." CBS News Poll, August 28. http:// www.cbsnews.com/stories/2007/08/28/opinion/polls/main321.

———. 2010. "Tennesseans Clean Up from Fatal Floods." May 8. http://www.cbsnews.com/ stories/2010/08/national/main6469250.shtml.

Centers for Disease Control. 1998. "Deaths Associated with Hurricane Georges—Puerto Rico, September 1998." October 30, 1998. http://www.cdc.gov/mmwr/preview/mmwrhtml/00055476.htm.

Christian, Cora L.E. 1992. *Hurricane Hugo's Impact on the Virgin Islands.* Boulder: University of Colorado, National Hazards Research and Applications Information Center, Institute of Behavior Science, Working Paper #73.

Chubb, John E. 1985. "Federalism and the Bias for Centralization." In *The New Direction in American Politics,* ed. John E. Chubb and Paul E. Peterson. Washington, DC: Brookings Institution.

Church, Christian. 2010. "Obama Administration Responds Decisively to Tennessee Flooding." *American Chronicle,* May 16. http://www.americanchronicle.com/articles/view/156704.

Cigler, Beverly A. 1988. "Current Policy Issues in Mitigation." In *Managing Disaster,* ed. Louise K. Comfort, 39–52. Durham, NC: Duke University Press.

Claiborne, William. 1992a. "After Storms and Controversy, What's in Store for FEMA?" *The Washington Post,* October 6.

———. 1992b. "Paperwork Slows Storm Relief; Complaints Called Overstated." *The Washington Post,* September 7, A11.

———. 1993a. "FEMA Cleaned Up Its Act While Cleaning up the Midwest." *The Washington Post National Weekly Edition*, August 23–29, 33.

———. 1993b. "More Welcome Than Disaster: For Once—in Midwest—FEMA Is Relatively Well Received." *The Washington Post,* August 13, A23.

———. 1994a. "Around the Campfires, Cisneros Comforts Frightened Quake Victims." *The Washington Post,* January 22, A4.

———. 1994b. "Doling Out Praise, FEMA Critic Presses for Reform at Hearing." *The Washington Post*, March 25.

———. 1994c. "FEMA Centers Open amid Tension over Quake Aid." *The Washington Post,* January 21.

———. 1994d. "FEMA to Stay in L.A. Until 'Needs Are Met.'" *The Washington Post,* January 19, A15.

Clary, Bruce B. 1985. "The Evolution and Structure of Natural Hazard Policies." *Public Administration Review* 45 (January): 20–28.

CNN. 2005. "A Disturbing View from Inside FEMA." September 17. http://www.cnn.com/2005/US/09/20050903.html.

———. 2010. "21 Dead in Tennessee Flooding." May 6. http://news.blogs.cnn.com/2010/05/06/21-dead-in-tennessee-flooding-governor-says.

Cobb, Roger W., and Charles D. Elder. 1983a. *Participation in American Politics: The Dynamics of Agenda-Building.* 2nd ed. Baltimore: Johns Hopkins University Press.

———. 1983b. *The Political Uses of Symbols.* New York: Longman.

Cochrane, Hal. 1975. *Natural Disasters and Their Distributive Effects.* Boulder: University of Colorado, Institute of Behavioral Science, Program on Environment, Technology and Man, Monograph #NSF-RA-E-75–003.

———. 1990. "A Preliminary Analysis of Damages and Economic Dislocations." In *The Loma Prieta Earthquake: Studies of Short-Term Impacts,* ed. Robert Bolin, 25–32. Boulder: University of Colorado, Institute of Behavioral Science, Program on Environment and Behavior, Monograph #50.

Cocking, Susan. 1998. "Church Offers Victims 'Good' Fare." *The Miami Herald,* September 30, 5B.

Cohn, Jonathan. 2007. *Sick: The Untold Story of America's Health Care Crisis.* New York: HarperCollins.

Col, Jeanne-Marie. 2007. "Managing Disasters: The Role of Local Government." *Public Administration Review* 67 (Special Supplementary Issue on Administrative Failure in the Wake of Hurricane Katrina): 114–124.

Colon, Yves. 1998. "South Florida Comes to Aid of Haitians." *The Miami Herald,* October 1, 3B.

Comfort, Louis K. 1985. "Integrating Organizational Action in Emergency Management; Strategies for Change." *Public Administration Review* 45 (Special Issue, January): 155–164.

———. 1988. "Designing Policy for Action: The Emergency Management System." In *Managing Disaster*, ed. Louis K. Comfort, 3–21. Durham NC: Duke University Press.

———. 2007. "Crisis Management in Hindsight: Cognition, Communication, Coordination, and Control." *Public Administration Review* 67 (Special Supplementary Issue on Administrative Failure in the Wake of Hurricane Katrina): 189–197.

Conlan, Timothy. 1988. *New Federalism: Intergovernmental Reform from Nixon to Reagan.* Washington, DC: Brookings Institution.

Conlan, Timothy, and Paul Posner, eds. 2008. *Intergovernmental Management for the 21st Century.* Washington, DC: Brookings Institution.

Connolly, Cecil. 2005. "Top New Orleans Police Official to Retire." *The Washington Post*, September 28, A06.

Cook, Michael L. 1989. "FEMA: Bureaucratic Disaster Area." *The State*, November 1.

Cooper, Christopher, and Robert Block. 2006. *Disaster: Hurricane Katrina and the Failure of Homeland Security.* New York: Times Books.

Cooper, Jim. 2010a. "Cooper Blasts Corps Decision on Flood." June 18. http://cooper.house.gov/index.php?option=com_content&task=view&id=384&Itemid=73.

———. 2010b. "Cooper Critical of Corps' Preliminary Flood Report." July 21. http://www.cooper.house.gov/index.php?option=com_content&task=.

———. 2010c. "Testimony of Rep. Jim Cooper." Energy and Water Subcommittee, Appropriations Committee, U.S. Senate, July 22.

Cooper, Michael. 2011. "Reconstruction Lifts Economy After Disasters." *The New York Times,* June 1, A1, A17.

Cottingham, Phoebe H., and David T. Ellwood. 1989. *Welfare Policy for the 1990s.* Cambridge: Harvard University Press.

Couch, Carl J. 1968. "Collective Behavior: An Examination of Some Stereotypes." *Social Problems* 15: 310–322.

———. 1970. "Dimensions of Association in Collective Behavior Episodes." *Sociometry* 33: 457–471.

Couch, S.R. 2000. "The Cultural Science of Disasters: Conceptualizing the Field of Disasters and Popular Culture." *International Journal of Mass Emergencies and Disasters* 18 (1): 21–38.

Cousins, Juanita. 2010. "Tennessee Flooding Kills 5." *Tennessean,* May 2. http://www.tennessean.com/article/20100502/NEWS01/5020355/Tennessee-flooding-kills-5.

Covington, Dennis. 1992. "Holding On and Praying on Bayou at World's End." *The New York Times,* August 29, 8.

Cowin, Brian, Michael Mahoney, and Stephen A. Mahin. 2000. *Directory of Northridge Earthquake Research.* Darby, PA: Diane Publishing Company.

Crosby, Jessica. 1994. "An Upbeat Outlook: 'Californians Are a Resilient Bunch.'" *The Washington Post,* January 18, A9.

Crozier, Michael. 1964. *The Bureaucratic Phenomenon.* Chicago: University of Chicago Press.

Dacy, D.C., and H. Kunreuther. 1969. *The Economics of Natural Disasters.* New York: Free Press.

Daniels, R. Steven, and Carolyn L. Clark-Daniels. 2000. "Transforming Government: The Renewal and Revitalization of the Federal Emergency Management Agency." The PricewaterhouseCoopers Endowment for The Business of Government, 2000 Presidential Transition Series, April.

Dao, James, and N.R. Kleinfield. 2005. "More Troops and Aid Reach New Orleans; Bush Visits Area; Chaotic Exodus Continues." *The New York Times,* September 3.

Davis. Bob. 1992a. "Federal Relief Agency Is Slowed by Infighting, Patronage, Regulations." *The Wall Street Journal,* August 31, A1, A12.

———. 1992b. "Federal Response to Hurricane Andrew to Be Costly, Critical to Bush Campaign." *The Wall Street Journal,* August 28, A2.

Davis, Christopher, David Obey, and TheCapitol.Net. 2009. *Economic Policy Crisis and the Stimulus.* TheCapitol.Net. Washington, DC.

Davis, Tom. 2005. "Opening Statement, Select Bipartisan Committee to Investigate the Preparation for and Response to Hurricane Katrina, Hearing on Preparedness and Response by the State of Mississippi." U.S. House of Representatives, December 7.

deLeon, Peter, and Linda deLeon. 2002. "What Ever Happened to Policy Implementation? An Alternative Approach." *Journal of Public Administration Research and Theory* 12 (4): 467–492.

Democratic Study Group. 1989. "Short-Handed at FEMA: Fighting Disasters Without Leaders." Washington, DC: U.S. House of Representatives.

De Neufville, Judith I., and Stephen E. Barton. 1987. "Myths and the Definition of Policy Problems: An Exploration of Home Ownership and Public-Private Partnerships." *Policy Sciences* 20: 181–206.

De Nies, Yunju, and Hanna Siegel. 2010. "Nashville Flooding: At Least 29 Dead from Record Rains in Mid-South." ABC News, May 4. http://abcnews.go.com/WN/nashville-flooding-29-dead-flash-flooding-south/story?id=10555626.

Deppa, Joan. 1993. *The Media and Disasters: Pan Am 103*. New York: New York University Press.

Derthick, Martha. 2007. "Where Federalism Didn't Fail." *Public Administration Review* 67 (Special Supplementary Issue on Administrative Failure in the Wake of Hurricane Katrina): 36–48.

Deslatte, Melinda. 2006. "Blanco Says FEMA Rules Delay Rebuilding." *The Washington Post*, January 25.

DeVoe, R.F., Jr., 1997. "The Natural Disaster Boom Theory: Or Window-Breaking Our Way to Prosperity." In *Economic Consequences of Earthquakes*, ed. B.G. Jones, 181–188. Buffalo: State University of New York at Buffalo.

Dewan, Shaila. 2006a. "FEMA Halts Evictions from Trailers in Mississippi." *The New York Times*, June 22.

———. 2006b. "FEMA Not Required to Restore Aid to Evacuees, Court Rules." *The New York Times*, December 23.

———. 2006c. "FEMA Ordered to Restore Evacuees' Housing Aid." *The New York Times*, November 30.

———. 2006d. "Gulf Hurricane Evacuees Remain in the Grip of Uncertainty." *The New York Times*, December 6.

———. 2006e. "Storm Evacuees Remain in Grip of Uncertainty." *The New York Times*, December 6.

———. 2007a. "Hurricane Aid Is Extended for Some." *The New York Times*, July 24.

———. 2007b. "Road to New Life After Katrina is Closed to Many." *The New York Times*, July 12.

———. 2008. "Out of FEMA Park, Clinging to a Fraying Lifeline." *The New York Times*, August 4.

———. 2009. "Katrina Victims Will Not Have to Vacate Their Trailers." *The New York Times*, June 4.

DiIulio, John J., Jr., Gerald Garvey, and Donald F. Kettl. 1993. *Improving Government Performance: An Owner's Manual*. Washington, DC: Brookings Institution.

Dinan, John, and Shama Gamkhar. 2009. "The State of American Federalism, 2008–2009: The Presidential Election, The Economic Downturn, and the Consequences of Federalism." *Publius: The Journal of Federalism* 39: 369–407.

Dodd, D. Aileen. 1998. "Camp Setup Delay Leaves Homeless in Dilemma." *The Miami Herald*, September 28, 2B.

Donahue, Amy K., and Sean O'Keefe. 2007. "Universal Lessons from Unique Events: Perspectives from Columbia and Katrina." *Public Administration Review* (Special Issue): 77–81.

Donahue, John D. 1989. *The Privatization Decision*. New York: Basic Books.

Dowd, Maureen. 2005. "United States of Shame." *The New York Times*, September 3, A21.

Downs, Anthony. 1957. *An Economic Theory of Democracy*. New York: Harper and Row.

———. 1967. *Inside Bureaucracy*. Boston: Little, Brown. (Reissued by Waveland Press, Prospect Heights, IL, 1994).

———. 1972. "Up and Down with Ecology: The Issue Attention Cycle." *Public Interest* 28: 38–50.

Drabek, Thomas. 1968. *Disaster in Isle 13*. Columbus: Disaster Research Center, Ohio State University.

———. 1970. "Methodology of Studying Disasters." *American Behavioral Scientist* 13: 331–43.

———. 1984. *Some Emerging Issues in Emergency Management*. Emmitsburg, Maryland: National Emergency Training Center, Federal Emergency Management Agency.

————. 1985. "Managing the Emergency Response." *Public Administration Review* 45: 85–92.

————. 1986. *Human System Responses to Disasters.* New York: Springer-Verlag.

————. 2007. "Community Processes: Communication." In *Handbook of Disaster Research,* ed. Havidan Rodriquez, Enrico L. Quarantelli, and Russell R. Dynes, 217–234. New York: Springer.

Drabek, Thomas, and Gerald Hoetmer, eds. 1991. *Emergency Management: Principles and Practice for Local Government.* Washington, DC: International City Management Association.

Drabek, Thomas, and John Stephenson. 1971. "When Disaster Strikes." *Journal of Applied Social Psychology* 1: 187–203.

Driscoll, Amy. 1998. "Keys: Uprooted; Water Unsafe, Power Out for Many Going Home." *The Miami Herald,* September 27, 1A.

Driscoll, Amy, Phil Long, and Martin Mercer. 1998. "In Georges' Wake." *The Miami Herald,* September 26, 1A.

Driscoll, Amy, Marika Lynch, and Michael Browning. 1998. "Monroe Picks Up the Pieces." *The Miami Herald,* September 28, 1A.

Durkheim, Emile. 1895. *The Rules of Sociological Method.* New York: Free Press.

————. 1915. *The Elementary Forms of Religious Life.* Trans. Joseph Ward Swain. New York: Macmillan.

Dynes, Russell R. 1970. *Organized Behavior in Disasters.* Lexington, MA: Heath Lexington Books.

Dynes, Russell R., and E.L. Quarantelli. 1968. "Group Behavior Under Stress: A Required Convergence of Organizational and Collective Behavior Perspectives." *Sociology and Social Research* 52 (July): 416–429.

————. 1977. "Organizational Communications and Decision Making in Crises." Report Series #17. Columbus, Ohio: Disaster Research Center.

————. 2007. "Finding and Framing Katrina: The Social Construction of Disaster." In *The Sociology of Katrina*, ed. David Brunsma, David Overfelt, and J. Steven Picou. Lanham, MD: Rowman and Littlefield.

Dynes, Russell R., E.L. Quarantelli, and Dennis Wenger. 1990. *Individual and Organizational Response to the 1985 Earthquake in Mexico City, Mexico.* Newark: University of Delaware, Disaster Research Center, Book and Monograph Series No. 24.

Dynes, Russell R., and Kathleen Tierney, eds. 1994. *Disasters, Collective Behavior and Social Organization.* Newark: University of Delaware Press.

Earthquake Museum. 2009. "The 1994 Northridge Earthquake." http://www.olympus.net/personal/gofamily/quake/famous/northridge.html.

Eaton, Leslie. 2006a. "Report Finds New Problems in FEMA Aid Distribution." *The New York Times,* December 6.

————. 2006b. "Slow Home Grants Stall Progress in New Orleans." *The New York Times*, November 11.

————. 2007a "Critics Cite Red Tape in Rebuilding of Louisiana Public Works." *The New York Times,* November 6.

————. 2007b. "Some 3,000 Louisiana Families to Leave FEMA Trailers." *The New York Times,* November 29.

————. 2008. "FEMA Vows New Effort on Trailers Posing Risk." *The New York Times*, February 15.

Echterling, Lennis G., and Mary Lou Wylie. 1999. "In the Public Arena: Disaster as a Socially Constructed Problem." In *Response to Disaster: Psychosocial, Community, and Ecological Approaches*, ed. Richard Gist and Bernard Lubin, 327–346. Philadelphia: Taylor and Francis.

Edelman, Murray. 1964. *The Symbolic Uses of Politics.* Champaign: University of Illinois Press.

————. 1977. *Political Language: Words That Succeed and Policies That Fail.* New York: Academic Press.

————. 1989. *Constructing the Political Spectacle.* Chicago: University of Chicago Press.

Edwards, George C., III. 1980. *Implementing Public Policy.* Washington, DC: Congressional Quarterly Press.

Eichel, Henry. 1989. "Relief Effort Faulted: Experts Say South Carolina System Lacked Co-ordination." *The State,* October 22, A1, A17.

Elazar, Daniel. 1962. *The American Partnership: Intergovernmental Cooperation in the Nineteenth-Century United States.* Chicago: University of Chicago Press.

Elmore, Richard F. 1979. "Backward Mapping: Implementation Research and Policy Decisions." *Political Science Quarterly* 94: 601–616.

Enos, Gary. 1993. "Disaster Response Improves." *City and State,* December 6, 23.

EQE International. 1992. *Hurricanes Andrew and Iniki, 1992.* San Francisco, CA: EQE International.

————. 1994. "The January 17, 1994, Northridge California Earthquake." http://www.lafire.com/famous_fires/1994-117_NorthridgeEarthquake/quake/00_EQE_contents.htm.

Erickson, Erick. 2010. "Screw the Gulf Coast. White House Staff Plays Beer Pong & Water Guns." *RedState.com: Conservative Blog and News.* June 7. www.redstate.com/erick/2010/06/07/screw-the-gulf-coast-lets-play-beer-pong/.

Erikson, Robert S, Michael B. MacKuen, and James A. Stimson. 2002. *The Macro Policy.* Cambridge: Cambridge University Press.

Etheart, Pascale. 1998. "People Prepare Early After Andrew." *The Miami Herald,* September 27, 3.

Evans, Ben. 2010. "Feds Defend Response to Tennessee Flooding." *Memphis Daily News,* July 23.

Eyestone, Robert. 1978. *From Social Issues to Public Policy.* New York: John Wiley and Sons.

Fairweather, V. 1990. "The Next Earthquake." *Civil Engineering,* March: 54–57.

Farmer, Blake, 2010. "Could Tennessee's Flooding Have Been Prevented?" National Public Radio, May 13. http://www.npr.org/templates/story/story.php?storyId=126791955.

Faust, Roland. 1989. Federal Emergency Management Agency, Region IV. Phone Interview, November 12.

Federal Emergency Management Agency. 1988. *Federal Catastrophic Earthquake Response Plan.* Washington, DC: U.S. Government Printing Office.

————. 1989a. *Interagency Hazard Mitigation Team Report.* Prepared by the Region IV Interagency Hazard Mitigation Team in Response to the September 22, 1989, Disaster Declaration, State of South Carolina (FEMA-843-DR-SC).

————. 1989b. *When Disaster Strikes.* Washington, DC: Office of Public Affairs, Federal Emergency Management Agency.

————. 1990a. *Interagency Hazard Mitigation Team Report.* Prepared by the Region IV Interagency Hazard Mitigation Team in Response to the October 22, 1990, Disaster Declaration, State of South Carolina (FEMA-881-DR-SC).

————. 1990b. Public Information Office. Phone Interview.

————. 1992a. *Briefing Reports on Recent Disaster Activity.* Washington, DC: Federal Emergency Management Agency.

————. 1992b. *Federal Response Plan: For Public Law 93–288, As Amended.* Washington, DC: Federal Emergency Management Agency.

————. 1993. *FEMA's Disaster Management Program: A Performance Audit After Hurricane Andrew.* Washington, DC: Office of Inspector General.

————. 1994a. *Reinventing Disaster Response 1994: Northridge Earthquake—The First Five Weeks.* Washington, DC: U.S. Government Printing Office.

————. 1994b. *Renewal of Emergency Management: The FEMA One-Year Report, April 1993–April 1994.* Washington, DC: FEMA.

————. 1996. *Status Report of FEMA's Activities.* Washington, DC: Federal Emergency Management Agency, December 26.

———. 1998a. "FEMA, Caribbean Islands Continue Preparations as Hurricane Georges Bears Down: Disaster Declarations Already Submitted." Washington, DC, September 21.

———. 1998b. "FEMA Disaster Housing Aid in Puerto Rico Surpasses $200 Million." Washington, DC, November 17.

———. 1998c. "FEMA: Federal Response Activities Related to Hurricane Georges." Washington, DC, September 25.

———. 1998d. "FEMA Prepares as a Strengthened Hurricane Georges Threatens States Throughout the U.S. Gulf Coast." Washington, DC, September 25.

———. 1998e. "Hurricane Georges Marches Towards Gulf States; FEMA Puerto Rican Recovery Effort Intensifies." Washington, DC, September 25.

———. 1998f. "Hurricane Georges Sunday Update." Washington, DC, September 27.

———. 1998g. "Hurricane Georges Surpasses Hurricane Andrew in Total Number of Disaster Applicant Registrations." Washington, DC, October 17.

———. 1998h. "President Orders Emergency Aid for Florida Hurricane Victims." Washington, DC, September 25.

———. 1998i. "Time Period for FEMA Assistance Expanded." Washington, DC, November 25.

———. 1999. "FEMA Disaster Housing Aid to Puerto Rico Tops $400 Million." Washington, DC: January 20.

———. 2003. "The 1993 Great Midwest Flood: Voices Ten Years Later." Washington, DC. http://www.fema.gov/business/nfip/voices.shtm, last updated/modified August 11, 2010.

———. 2004. *National Incident Management System.* Washington, DC: U.S. Department of Homeland Security. http:www.fema.gove/pdf/emergency/nims/nims_doc_full.pdf.

———. 2005a. "Assistance Continues to Areas Impacted by Hurricane Katrina." Washington, DC, August 29.

———. 2005b. "Critical Commodities Continue into Disaster Areas while Government Responds to Challenges of Most Catastrophic Disaster in U.S. History." Washington, DC, September 2.

———. 2005c. "Disaster Application Deadline Extended to March 11 for Mississippi Affects All Gulf Coast Katrina and Rita Victims." Washington, DC, December 30.

———. 2005d. "Disaster Recovery Centers Open in Ocean Springs and Pascagoula." Washington, DC, September 5.

———. 2005e. "Disaster Update: FEMA/State Housing Assistance Tops $1 Billion." Washington, DC, September 20.

———. 2005f. "Emergency Aid Authorized for Hurricane Katrina Emergency Response in Louisiana." Washington, DC, August 27.

———. 2005g. "Federal Gulf Coast Responses to Hurricanes Katrina and Rita." Washington, DC, October 6.

———. 2005h. "FEMA Expands Assistance to Help Mississippi Rebuild Hurricane-Ravaged Infrastructure." Washington, DC, September 13.

———. 2005i. "First Responders Urged Not to Respond to Hurricane Impact Areas Unless Dispatched by State, Local Authorities." Washington, DC, August 29.

———. 2005j. "FEMA Urges Patience While Search Continues for Stranded Victims and Supplies Stream In." Washington, DC, September 2.

———. 2005k. "Katrina Response Update for Mississippi." Washington, DC, October 8.

———. 2005l. "Homeland Security Prepping for Dangerous Hurricane Katrina." Washington, DC, August 28.

———. 2005m. "Hurricane Katrina: One Year Anniversary Mississippi by the Numbers." Washington, DC, August 17.

———. 2005n. "Mississippi, Alabama, Louisiana Establish Hotlines to Coordinate Donations for Victims of Katrina." Washington, DC, September 11.

——— 2005o. "Mississippi/FEMA Expedited Assistance." Washington, DC, September 9.

————. 2005p. "Mississippians Now Have Until January 11 to Apply for Individual Disaster Assistance." Washington, DC, October 22.

————. 2005q. "More Counties Eligible for Disaster Assistance for Damage from Katrina." Washington, DC, September 7.

————. 2005r. "More Than 5,000 Families Now Housed in FEMA Travel Trailers." Washington, DC, October 12.

————. 2005s. "More Than 8,700 Families out of Shelters and into Temporary Housing." Washington, DC, October 23.

————. 2005t. "More Than 35,000 Displaced Mississippians Now in FEMA Travel Trailers or Mobile Homes." Washington, DC, October 31.

————. 2005u. "More Than $2 Billion in Federal Assistance Pours into Mississippi in First Two Months After Katrina." Washington, DC, October 29.

————. 2005v. "More Than $760 Million in Federal Dollars to Help Louisiana." Washington, DC, September 26.

————. 2005w. "National Urban Search and Rescue Teams Deployed." Washington, DC, September 3.

————. 2005x. "Nearly $690 Million in Assistance Helping More than 330,000 Families Displaced by Katrina." Washington, DC, September 10.

————. 2005y. "President Bush Extends 100% Funding for Debris Removal in Five Louisiana Parishes." Washington, DC, June 30.

————. 2005z. "President Bush Increases Relief Funds." Washington, DC, October 23.

————. 2005aa. "President Declares Major Disaster for Louisiana." Washington, DC, August 29.

————. 2005bb. "President Declares Major Disaster for Mississippi." Washington, DC, August 29.

————. 2005–2010. "Hurricane Rita News Releases." Washington, DC: U.S. Department of Homeland Security. http://www.fema.gov/news/ritanews.fema.

————. 2006a. "The First Year After Katrina: What the Federal Government Did." Washington, DC: U.S. Department of Homeland Security. http://www.dhs.gov/xfoia/archives/gc_1157649340100.shtm.

————. 2006b. "Mississippians Now Have Until January 11 to Apply for Individual Disaster Assistance." Washington, DC, October 22.

————. 2007. "Response Operations and Multi-Hazard Catastrophic Disaster Planning in the New FEMA: Charting a Course for the New FEMA." National Academies Disaster Roundtable Workshop, June 28.

————. 2008. "Gulf Coast Recovery Three Years Later." Washington, DC, August 26.

————. 2009a. "Hurricane Katrina by the Numbers: Four Years of Rebuilding a Better Mississippi." Washington, DC, August 25.

————. 2009b. "Overview of Stafford Act Support to the States." http://www.fema.gov/pdf/emergency/nrf/nrf-stafford.pdf.

————. 2010a. "Additional Counties Designated for Disaster Assistance." Washington, DC: U.S. Department of Homeland Security, May 20 and May 27. http://www.fema.gov/news/newsrelease.fema?id=51544; www.fema.gov/news/newsrelease.fema?id=51642.

————. 2010b. "Brownsville Disaster Recovery Center Transitions to Disaster Loan Outreach Center." Washington, DC: U.S. Department of Homeland Security, June 10. http://www.fema.gov/news/newsrelease.fema?id=51780.

————. 2010c. "Communities Form Long-Term Recovery Teams." Washington, DC: U.S. Department of Homeland Security, August 12. http://www.fema.gov/news/newsrelease.fema?id=52358.

————. 2010d. "Designated Counties for Tennessee Severe Storms, Flooding, Straight-Line Words, and Tornadoes." Washington, DC: U.S. Department of Homeland Security, May 4. http://www.fema.gov/news/eventcounties.fema?id=12789.

————. 2010e. "Disaster Applicants Urged to Take Charge of Their Recovery." Washington, DC: U.S. Department of Homeland Security, June 5. http://www.fema.gov/news/newsrelease.fema?id=51718.

————. 2010f. "Earthquakes in the United States" Washington, DC. http://www.fema.gov/hazard/earthquake/usquakes.shtm.

————. 2010g. "Federal Aid Programs for Tennessee Disaster Recovery." Washington, DC: U.S. Department of Homeland Security, May 4. http://www.fema.gov/news/newsrelease.fema?id=51252.

————. 2010h. "FEMA Continues Response Efforts in Tennessee." U.S. Department of Homeland Security, May 6. http://www.fema.gov/news/newsrelease.fema?id=51283.

————. 2010i. "FEMA Declares Major Disaster for Tennessee." U.S. Department of Homeland Security, May 4. http://www.fema.gov/news/newsrelease.fema?id=51251.

————. 2010j. *The Federal Emergency Management Agency*. Washington, DC: U.S. Department of Homeland Security. http://www.fema.gov/pdf/about/pub1.pdf.

————. 2010k. "FEMA Staff on the Job in Tennessee." Washington, DC: U.S. Department of Homeland Security, May 6. http://www.fema.gov/news/newsrlease.fema?id=51276.

————. 2010l. "Flood Recovery Is the Business of Tennessee's Private Sector." Washington, DC: U.S. Department of Homeland Security, July 13. http://www.fema.gov/news/newsrelease.fema?id=52125.

————. 2010m. "Getting to the Point: FEMA Provides Points-of-Distribution Training in Tennessee." Washington, DC: U.S. Department of Homeland Security, August 16. http://www.fema.gov/news/newsrelease.fema?id=5238.

————. 2010n. "Katrina/Rita: The 5th Commemoration." Washington, DC: U.S. Department of Homeland Security, September 24. http://www.fema.gov/pdf/hazard/hurricane/2005katrina/5th_comm_book.pdf.

————. 2010o. "Mobile Disaster Recovery Centers Open in Middle Tennessee." May 16. Washington, DC. http://www.fema.gov/news/newsrelease.fema?id=51435.

————. 2010p. "Most Expensive Presidentially-Declared Disasters." http://www.fema.gov/hazard/hurricane/top10hu.shtm.

————. 2010q. "President Declares Major Disaster for Tennessee." May 4. Washington, DC:.

————. 2010r. "Strong Inter-Faith Effort Characterizes Tennessee Flood Recovery." Washington, DC: U.S. Department of Homeland Security, September 2. http://www.fema.gov/news/newsrelease.fema?id=52571.

————. 2010s. "Tennesseans Affected by Severe Spring Storms and Flooding Can Apply for Disaster Assistance." Washington, DC: U.S. Department of Homeland Security, May 6. http://www.fema.gov/news/newsrelease.fema?id=51275.

————. 2010t. "Tennesseans from 17 Counties Trained as Disaster Recovery Case Managers." Washington, DC: U.S. Department of Homeland Security, October 5. http://www.fema.gov/news/newsrelease.fema?id=52938.

————. 2010u. "Tennesseans Make Steady Progress Toward Recovery: FEMA Commitment Remains Strong." Washington, DC: U.S. Department of Homeland Security, November 9. http://www.fema.gov/news/newsrelease.fema?id=53225.

————. 2010v. "Top Ten Natural Disasters: Ranked by FEMA Relief Costs." Washington, DC: U.S. Department of Homeland Security. http://www.fema.gov/hazard/topten.shtm, last modified August 11, 2010.

————. 2010w. "Wilson County Disaster Recovery Center Transitions to Disaster Loan Outreach Center." Washington, DC: U.S. Department of Homeland Security, June 10. http://www.fema.gov/news/newsrelease.fema?id=51781.

————. 2010x. "2010 in Review: FEMA Helping Tennesseans Move Forward." U.S. Department of Homeland Security, December 20. http://www.fema.gov/news/newsrelease.fema?id=55399.

———. 2011a. "About FEMA." Washington, DC, http://www.fema.gov/about/index.

———. 2011b. "Declared Disasters by Year or State." Washington, DC: U.S. Department of Homeland Security. http://www.fema.gov/news/disaster_totals_annual.fema, last modified May 20, 2011.

———. 2011c. "Federal Dollars Continue to Assist New Orleans' Recovery." February 15. http://www.fema.gov/news/newsrelease.fema?id=53717.

———. 2011d. "FEMA Fact Sheet." http://www.fema.gov/pdf/media/factsheets/2009/cdp.pdf, last modified April 21, 2011.

———. 2011e. "FEMA: FEMA Grants and Assistance Programs." http://www.fema.gov/government/grant/index.shtm, last modified April 21, 2011.

———. 2011f "FEMA History." Washington, DC, http://www.fema.gov/about/history.shtm.

———. 2011g. "The Declaration Process." Washington, DC: U.S. Department of Homeland Security. http://www.fema.gov/rebuild/recover/dec_guide.shtm, last modified April 21, 2011.

———. 2011h. "The Disaster Process and Disaster Aid Programs." Washington, DC: U.S. Department of Homeland Security. http://www.fema.gov/hazard/dproc.shtm, last modified April 21, 2011.

———. 2011i. "What We Do." Washington, DC: U.S. Department of Homeland Security. http://www.fema.gov/about/what.shtm, last modified April 21, 2011.

FEMA Law Associates. 2006. "DHS Appropriations Bill—Amendments to the Robert T. Stafford Act." In *Flash Newsletter*, Volume 1, Issue 3, October. Washington, DC: FEMA Law Associates.

Fenno, Richard F., Jr. 1978. *Home Style: House Members in Their Districts.* Boston: Little, Brown.

Fensch, Thomas. 1990. *Associated Press Coverage of a Major Disaster: The Crash of Flight 1141.* Hillsdale, NJ: Lawrence Erlbaum.

Fesler, James W., and Donald F. Kettl, 1991. *The Politics of the Administrative Process.* Chatham, NJ: Chatham House.

Fiedler, Tom, and Peter Slevin. 1992. "Military Comes to Florida's Aid." *The Charlotte Observer,* August 29, A1.

Finley, Jeremy. 2010a. "Corps, NWS Defend Water Release Response." WSMV, May 20. http://www.wsmv.com/weather/23626569/detail.html.

———. 2010b. "No One Alerted Dam Was Open During Flooding." WSVM, May 10. http://www.wsmv.com/weather/23511402/detail.html.

"Fire Every FEMA Official!" 2005. *New Orleans Times-Picayune,* September 4.

Fitzpatrick, Colleen, and Dennis S. Mileti. 1990. "Perception and Response to Aftershock Warnings During the Emergency Period." In *The Loma Prieta Earthquake: Studies of Short-Term Impacts,* ed. Robert Bolin, 75–83. Boulder: University of Colorado, Institute of Behavioral Science.

Fletcher, Michael A. 2010. "Uneven Katrina Recovery Efforts Often Offered the Most Help to the Most Affluent." *The Washington Post,* August 27. http://www.washingtonpost.com/wp-dyn/content/article/2010.

Fletcher, Michael A., and Richard Morin. 2005. "Bush's Approval Rating Drops to New Low in Wake of Storm." *The Washington Post,* September 13. http://pqasb.pqarchiver.com/washingtonpost/access/895223841.html.

Fleury, Maureen K. 2009. "Top Ten U.S. Natural Disasters: Tragedies in America Caused by Forces of Nature." http://naturaldisasters.suite101.com/article.cfm/top_ten_us_natural_disasters.

Forman, Sally. 2007. *Eye of the Storm: Inside City Hall During Katrina.* Bloomington, IN: AuthorHouse.

Fountain, John W. 1998. "Hurricane Georges Settles In to Inundate the Gulf Coast." *The Washington Post,* September 29, A3.

Fountain, John W., and Susan Saulny. 1998. "Hurricane-Seasoned Gulf Coast Prepares for Georges' Worst." *The Washington Post,* September 27, A18.

Fournier, Ron. 2006. "Analysis: Video Shows Leaders' Dissonance." *The Washington Post,* March 3.

Fox, Gerald C. 1990. "Evaluation of FEMA's Performance in Responding to Hurricane Hugo in N.C." Testimony Before the Subcommittee on Investigations and Oversight, Committee on Public Works and Transportation, U.S. House of Representatives. May 2.

FOX News. 2010. "Record Flood Threatens Nashville After Violent Storms Kill At Least 19." May 3, http://www.foxnews.com/us/2010/05/02/possible-tornados-kill-mississippi/.

Frankovic, Kathy. 2007. "Polls Show Skepticism of Katrina Recovery." CBS News, August 29. http://www.cbsnews.com/stories/2007/08/29/opinion/pollpositions/main3216082.shtml?tag=mncol;lst;8.

Franklin, Daniel. 1995. "The FEMA Phoenix: How One Federal Agency Rose from the Ashes to Become a Symbol of What Government Can Do." *The Washington Monthly,* July/August, pp. 38–42.

Free Republic. 2010. "Tennessee Governor Meets with (One Administrator from) FEMA on Flooding." May 4. http://www.freerepublic.com/focus/f-news/2506714/posts?page=9.

Fretwell, Sammy. 1989a. "Frustration Rises as Victims Await Help." *The State,* October 23, A1, A4.

———. 1989b. "S.C. Homeless in FEMA Limbo." *The State,* October 12, A1, A8.

Friedmann, Louis. 2010. "Emergency Communications Success During the Tennessee Floods." Washington, DC: Office of Emergency Communications, U.S. Department of Homeland Security. http://www.ntia.doc.gov/psic/Tennessee%20Floods%20Success.pdf.

Friesema, H. Paul, James Caporaso, Gerald Goldstein, Robert Lineberry, and Richard McCleary. 1979. *Aftermath: Communities After Natural Disasters.* Beverly Hills, CA: Sage.

Fritsch, Jane. 1994. "U.S. Is Setting Up Tent Cities as Nerves Fray After Quake." *New York Times,* January 22, A1, A24.

Fritz, Charles. 1957. "Disasters Compared in Six American Communities." *Human Organization* 16 (Summer): 6–9.

———. 1961. "Disaster." In *Contemporary Social Problems: An Introduction to the Sociology of Deviant Behavior and Social Organizations*, ed. Robert K. Merton and Robert A. Nisbet, 651–694. New York: Harcourt, Brace and World.

Gall, Melanie, and Susan L. Cutter. 2007. "2005 Events and Outcomes: Hurricane Katrina and Beyond." *Emergency Management: The American Experience, 1900–2005*, ed. Claire B. Rubin, 185–206. Fairfax, VA: Public Entity Risk Institute.

Gawthrop, Louis. 1969. *Bureaucratic Behavior in the Executive Branch: An Analysis of Organizational Change.* New York: Free Press.

"Georges Becomes Category 4 Hurricane." 1998. *The Washington Post,* September 20, A24.

"Georges Plows into Puerto Rico." 1998. *The State,* September 22, A3.

Gibbs, Robert. 2010. "On the Ground Before the Raindrops Started Falling." *The White House Blog*, May 6. http://www.whitehouse.gov/blog/2010/05/06/ground-raindrops-started-falling.

Gillespie, D.F. 1991. "Coordinating Community Resources." In *Emergency Management: Principles and Practices for Local Government,* ed. T.E. Drabek and G.J. Hoetmer, 55–78. Washington, DC: International City Management Association.

Gillespie, D.F., Dennis Mileti, and Ronald W. Perry. 1976. *Organizational Response to Changing Community Systems.* Mishawaka, IN: Better World Books.

Gilliam, Frank D., and Shanto Iyengar. 2000. "Prime Suspects: The Influence of Local Television News on the Viewing Public." *American Journal of Political Science* 44: 560–573.

Ginsberg, Benjamin. 1976. "Elections and Public Policy." *American Political Science Review* 70 (March): 41–49.

Gitlin, T. 1989. "Gauging the Aftershocks of Disaster Coverage." *The New York Times*, November 11.

Giuffrida, Louis O. 1983. *Emergency Management: The National Perspective*. Emmitsburg, MD: National Emergency Training Center.

———. 1985. "FEMA: Its Mission, Its Partners." *Public Administration Review* 45 (Special Issue, January): 2.

Glasser, Susan B., and Michael Grunwald. 2005. "The Steady Buildup to a City's Chaos." *The Washington Post*, September 11. http://www.washingtonpost.com/wp-dyn/content/article/2005/09/10/AR2005091001529.html.

Glasser, Susan B., and Josh White. 2005. "Storm Exposed Disarray at the Top" *The Washington Post*, September 4, A1, A31. http://www.washingtonpost.com/wp-dyn/content/article/2005/09/03/AR2005090301653.html.

Goggin, Malcolm L., Ann O'M. Bowman, James P. Lester, and Laurence J. O'Toole, Jr. 1990. *Implementation Theory and Practice: Toward a Third Generation.* Glenview, IL: Scott, Foresman/Little, Brown Higher Education.

Goldman, Kevin, and Patrick Reilly. 1992. "Untold Story: Media's Slow Grasp of Hurricane's Impact Helped Delay Response." *The Wall Street Journal*, September 10, A1, A9.

Goltz, James D. 1984. "Are the News Media Responsible for the Disaster Myths? A Content Analysis of Emergency Response Imagery." *International Journal of Mass Emergencies and Disasters* 2: 345–368.

———. 1994. *The Northridge, California, Earthquake of January 17, 1994: General Reconnaissance Report,* Technical Report. NCEER-94–0005. Buffalo, NY: National Center for Earthquake Engineering Research.

Gomez, Brad T., and J. Matthew Wilson. 2008. "Political Sophistication and Attribution of Blame in the Wake of Hurricane Katrina." *Publius: The Journal of Federalism* 38 (4): 633–650.

Goodnough, Abby. 2006. "Chertoff Pushes for More Hurricane Readiness." *The New York Times,* April 13.

Goodsell, Charles. 2004. *The Case for Bureaucracy.* 4th ed. Washington, DC: CQ Press.

Gore, Rick. 1993. "Andrew Aftermath." *National Geographic*, April.

Gormley, William. 1989. *Taming the Bureaucracy: Muscles, Prayers, and Other Strategies.* Princeton: Princeton University Press.

Gormley, William, and Steven J. Balla. 2008. *Bureaucracy and Democracy: Accountability and Performance.* Washington, DC: CQ Press.

Government Executive. 2009. "Louisiana Senator Endorses FEMA Independence." December 11. http://www.govexec.com/dailyfed/1208/121108cdam3.htm?oref=rellink.

"Governor Meets with FEMA on Flooding." 2010. *WKRN-TV Nashville*, May 4. http://www.wkrn.com/story/12424068/governor-meets-with-fema-on-flooding?redirected=true.

Governor's Disaster Planning and Response Review Committee. 1993. Tallahassee, FL: Governor's Disaster Planning and Response Review Committee.

Graber, Doris A. 1997. *Mass Media and American Politics.* Washington, DC: CQ Press.

Graham, Bradley. 2005. "Some Urge Greater Use of Troops in Major Disasters." *The Washington Post*, September 9, A15.

Grodzins, Morton. 1966. *The American System: A New View of Government in the United States.* Chicago, IL: Rand McNally.

Grogger, Jeffrey, and Lynn A. Karoly. 2006. *Welfare Reform: Effects of a Decade of Change.* Cambridge, MA: Harvard University Press.

Gross, Jane. 1990. "Pressured Agencies Alter Post-Quake Relief Policy." *The New York Times*, March 6.

———. 1994. "Los Angeles Drivers Try New Ways on Old Roads." *The New York Times,* March 1, A16.

Grunwald, Michael, and Susan Glasser. 2005. "The Slow Drowning of New Orleans." *The Wash-

ington Post, October 9. http://www.washingtonpost.com/wp-dyn/content/article/2005/10/08/AR2005100801458_pf.html.

Gugliotta, Guy, and Peter Whoriskey. 2005. "Floods Ravage New Orleans, Two Levees Give Way." *The Washington Post,* August 31, A.

Guider, E. 1989. "Stations Networks Ponder Lessons Learned in Quake." *Victory* (October 25–31): 45–46.

Guiliana, Rudolph. 2007. *Leadership.* New York: Miramax.

Gulf Coast News. 2006. "$280 Million Awarded for Mississippi 'Katrina Cottage' Program." *Gulf Coast News*, December 21. http://www.gulfcoastnews.com/GCNarchive/2006–2005/GCNnewsKatrina.

———. 2007a. "GCN Recovery News Report." January 26. http://www.gulfcoastnews.com/Katrina/GCN_Local_News-Update.htm.

———. 2007b. "GCN Recovery News Report." February 23. http://www.gulfcoastnews.com/Katrina/GCN_Local_News-Update.htm.

———. 2008a. "GCN Recovery News Report." January 19. http://www.gulfcoastnews.com/Katrina/GCN_Local_News-Update.htm.

———. 2008b. "GCN Recovery News Report." November 23. http://www.gulfcoastnews.com/Katrina/GCN_Local_News-Update.htm.

———. 2009a. "GCN Recovery News Report." September 18. http://www.gulfcoastnews.com/Katrina/GCN_Local_News-Update.htm.

———. 2009b. "Hurricane Katrina by the Numbers: Four Years of Rebuilding a Better Mississippi." September 25, 2009. http://www.gulfcoastnews.com/Katrina/GCN_Local_News-Update.htm.

Gulick, Luther, and L. Urwick. 1937. *Papers on the Science of Administration.* New York: Institute of Public Administration.

Haas, Eugene, Robert W. Kates, and Martyn J. Bowden, eds. 1977. *Reconstruction Following Disaster.* Cambridge, MA: MIT Press.

Haddow, George D., and Jane A. Bullock. 2006. *Introduction to Emergency Management.* 2nd ed. Boston: Elsevier, Butterworth-Heinemann.

Haider-Markel, Donald P., William Delehanty, and Matthew Beverlin. 2007. "Media Framing and Racial Attitudes in the Aftermath of Katrina." *Policy Studies Journal* 35 (4): 587–605.

Hall, Kristin M. 2010a. "Corps of Engineers Defends Actions During Tennessee Flooding." May 11. http://www.nola.com/politics/index.ssf/2010/05/corps_of_engineers_defends_act.html.

———. 2010b. "Nashville Residents Return Home to Devastation: 'My While Life Was Gone.'" *Huffington Post,* May 6. http://www.huffingtonpost.com/2010/05/06/nashville-residents-retur_n_566456.html.

Hall, Kristin M., and Sheila Burke. 2010. "Nashville Floodwaters Recede, Crews Search for Bodies." *Huffington Post*, May 4, http:huffingtonpost.com2010/05/04/Nashville-floodwaters-recede.

Hall, Paul. 1989. Federal Coordinating Officer for Hurricane Hugo in the Carolinas, Federal Emergency Management Agency, Personal Interview, December 15.

Hamilton, Dane, and Gregory S. Johnson. 1992. "Hurricane Aid Proves Logistical Nightmare." *The Journal of Commerce,* September 2, 1A, 3A.

Hamilton, William. 1994. "L.A.'s Unspoken Rule: Positively No Pessimists Allowed." *The Washington Post,* January 27, A1.

Hamilton, William, and Christine Spolar. 1994. "Los Angeles Quake Toll Rises to 44: Clinton, Other Politicians Assure City of Assistance." *The Washington Post,* January 19, A1, A13.

Hamman, Henry. 2005. "Economic Losses Set to Exceed $100 Billion." *Financial Times,* September 3.

Hamner, Thomas. 1990. Federal Coordinating Officer for the Loma Prieta Response, Federal Emergency Management Agency, Phone Interview, January 31.

Hancock, David, and Anthony Faiola. 1992. "Bigger, Stronger, Closer: South Florida Bracing for Hurricane Andrew." *The Miami Herald*, August 23, 1A, 19A.

Hannity, Sean. 2010. *FOX News' Hannity*, May 6. http://www.hannity.com/show/2010/05/06.

Hansen, Gladys, and Condon, Emmet. 1989. *Denial of Disaster: The Untold Story and Photographs of the San Francisco Earthquake and Fire of 1906*. San Francisco: Cameron and Co.

Harless, Bill. 2010. "Army Corps Is Criticized for Actions in Flood." *The New York Times*, May 20. http://www.nytimes.com/2010/05/21/us21flood.html.

Harrald, John R. 2006. "Agility and Discipline: Critical Success Factors for Disaster Response." In *Shelter from the Storm: Repairing the National Emergency Management System After Hurricane Katrina*. Special Issue of *The Annals of the American Academy of Political and Social Science* 604 (March): 256–272.

———. 2007. "Emergency Management Restructured: Intended and Unintended Outcomes of Actions Taken Since 9/11." In *Emergency Management: The American Experience 1900–2005*, ed. Claire B. Rubin. Fairfax, VA: Public Entity Risk Institute.

Harrison, Carlos. 1989. "St. Croix Collapses in Hugo's Wake." *The State*, September 20, A9.

Harvey, Carol D.H., and Howard M. Bahr. 1980. *The Sunshine Widows: Adapting to Sudden Bereavement*. Toronto: Lexington Books.

Haygood, Wil, and Ann Scott Tyson. 2005. "Living Hell: In the Convention Center, Anarchy Ruled while Helpless Victims Languished." *The Washington Post National Weekly Edition*, September 19–25, 7–9.

Heclo, Hugh. 1978. "Issue Networks in the Executive Establishment." In *The New American Political System*, ed. Anthony King. Washington, DC: American Enterprise Institute.

Heflin, Frank. 1990. "FEMA Finally Gets Relief." *The State*, March 17, A1, A4.

Hill, Larry B. 1992. "Taking Bureaucracy Seriously." In *The State of Public Bureaucracy*, ed. Larry B. Hill, 15–58. New York: M.E. Sharpe.

Hodgkinson, Peter E., and Michael Stewart. 1990. *Coping with Catastrophe: A Handbook of Disaster Management*. New York: Routledge.

Honig, Meredith I, ed. 2006. *New Directions in Education Policy Implementation: Confronting Complexity*. Albany: State University of New York Press.

Horne, Jed. 2005. "Help Us, Please: After the Disaster, Chaos and Lawlessness Rule the Streets." *New Orleans Times-Picayune*, September 2, A1.

———. 2006. *Breach of Faith: Hurricane Katrina and the Near Death of a Great American City*. New York: Random House.

Hsu, Spencer S. 2005. "Leaders Lacking Disaster Experience; 'Brain Drain' at Agency Cited." *The Washington Post*, September 9, A1.

———. 2006. "First the Flood, Now the Fight: Critics Say FEMA Is Impeding Efforts to Rebuild on the Gulf Coast." *The Washington Post National Weekly Edition*, September 4–10, 6–7.

———. 2007. "FEMA Taking Hit on Sale of Surplus Trailers." *The Washington Post*, March 8, A01.

———. 2008. "Hazardous Haste: The Rush to House Katrina Victims Resulted in Trailers that Endanger Health." *The Washington Post National Weekly Edition*, June, 6–7.

Hsu, Spencer S., and Daniela Deane. 2005. "Embattled FEMA Director Michael Brown Resigns." *The Washington Post*, September 12.

Hsu, Spencer S., and Susan B. Glasser. 2005. "FEMA Director Singled Out by Response Critics." *The Washington Post*, September 6. http://www.washingtonpost.com/wp-dyn/content/article/2005/09/05/AR2005090501590.html.

Hugo. 1990. Columbia, SC: The State Publishing Company.

Hurricane Disasters Live. 2008. *Hurricane Georges 1998*. http://www.hurricanedisasterslive.com/HURRICANE-GEORGES-1–1998.html.

Hurricane Hugo: Storm of the Century. 1990. Mount Pleasant, SC: BD Publishing.

Hy, Ronald, and William Waugh, 1990. "The Function of Emergency Management." In *Handbook of Emergency Management,* ed. Ronald Hy and William Waugh, 11–26. New York: Greenwood Press.

Hyneman, Charles S. 1950. *Bureaucracy in a Democracy.* New York: Harper.

Ibarra, P.R., and J.I. Kitsuse. 1993. "Vernacular Constituents of Moral Discourse: An Interactionist Proposal for the Study of Social Problems." In *Contructionist Controversies: Issues in Social Problems Theory,* ed. G. Milller and J.A. Holstein, 21–54. New York: Aldine de Gruyter.

Ingraham, Patricia. 1987. "Building Bridges or Burning Them? The President, the Appointees, and the Bureaucracy." *Public Administration Review* 47 (September/October): 425–435.

Ingwerson, Marshall. 1993. "FEMA Is 'Not Waiting' for the Winds to Die Down." *The Christian Science Monitor,* Wednesday, September 1, 6.

Iyengar, Shanto. 1991. *Is Anyone Responsible? How Television Frames Political Issues.* Chicago: University of Chicago Press.

Iyengar, Shanto, and Donald R. Kinder. 1987. *News That Matters.* Chicago: University of Chicago Press.

Iyengar, Shanto, and Jennifer A. McGrady. 2007. *Media Politics.* New York: W.W. Norton and Company.

Jadacki, Matt. 2010. Statement Before the Subcommittee on Economic Development, Public Buildings, and Emergency Management, Committee on Transportation and Infrastructure, U.S. House of Representatives, Office of Inspector General, U.S. Department of Homeland Security, September 22.

Jervis, Rick. 1998. "Near-Hit Leaves Minor Sweep-Up for South Florida; FPP&L Restores Power Quickly to Most Homes." *The Miami Herald,* September 27, 2B.

Johnson, Haynes, and David Broder. 1997. *The System: The American Way of Politics at the Breaking Point.* New York: Hachette Book Group.

Johnson, N.R. 1987. "Panic and the Breakdown of Social Order: Popular Myth, Social Theory, Empirical Evidence." *Sociological Focus* 20 (3): 171–183.

Jones, Bryan D., and Frank R. Baumgartner. 2005. *The Politics of Attention: How Government Prioritizes Problems.* Chicago: University of Chicago Press.

Jones, Charisse. 1994. "Quake Refugees Ponder the Unthinkable." *The New York Times,* January 20.

Jones, Jeffrey M. 2003. "Issues Facing State, Local Governments Affect Public Trust." Gallup News Service. http://www.gallup.com/poll/9487/Issues-Facing-State-Local-Governments-Affect-Public-Trust.aspx.

———. 2007. "Low Trust in Federal Government Rivals Watergate Era Levels." http://www.gallup.com/poll/28795/Low-Trust-Federal-Government-Rivals-Watergate-Era-Levels.aspx.

Jones, Jeffrey M., and Joseph Carroll. 2005. "Hurricane Victims' Views Vary on Government's Response." Gallup News Service. http://www.gallup.com/poll/19276/Hurricane-Victims-Views-Vary-Governments-Response.aspx.

Jordan, Mary. 1992a. "After Andrew: Protecting What's Left and Wondering Why." *The Washington Post,* August 30, A18.

———. 1992b. "Local Relief Officials Fault Federal Response to Hurricane." *The Washington Post,* August 28, A1, A14.

Jurkiewicz, Carole J. 2007. "Special Supplementary Issue, Administrative Failure in the Wake of Katrina." *Public Administration Review* 67, Supplement.

Kaiser Family Foundation. 2010. *New Orleans Five Year After the Storm.* Henry J. Kaiser Family Foundation, August.

Kaniewski, Daniel J. 2009. "PKEMRA Implementation: An Examination of FEMA's Preparedness and Response Mission." Statement Before the U.S. House of Representatives, Subcommittee on Emergency Communications, Preparedness, and Response, Committee on Homeland Security, March 17.

Kartez, J.D., and M.K. Lindell. 1990. "Adaptive Planning for Community Disaster Response." In *Cities and Disaster: North American Studies in Emergency Management,* ed. Richard T. Sylves and W.L. Waugh, 5–31. Springfield, IL: Charles C. Thomas.

Kasper, Kennard. 2006. "Hurricane Wilma in the Florida Keys." National Oceanic and Atmospheric Administration. http://www.srh.noaa.gov/media/key/Research/wilma.pdf.

Kasperson, Jeanne X., and Roger E. Kasperson. 2005a. "Hidden Hazards." In *The Social Contours of Risk.* ed. Jeanne X. Kasperson and Roger E. Kasperson, 115–132. Sterling, VA: Earthscan.

Kasperson, Jeanne X., and Roger E. Kasperson, eds. 2005b. *The Social Contours of Risk.* Sterling, VA: Earthscan.

Kasperson, Jeanne X., Roger E. Kasperson, Betty Jean Perkins, Ortwin Renn, and Allen L. White. 2005. "Media Risk Signals and the Proposed Yucca Mountain Nuclear Waste Repository, 1985–1989." In *The Social Contours of Risk,* ed. Jeanne X. Kasperson and Roger E. Kasperson, 133–160. Sterling, VA: Earthscan.

Kasperson, Roger E. 2005. "Six Propositions on Public Participation and Their Relevance for Risk Communication." In *The Social Contours of Risk,* ed. Jeanne X. Kasperson and Roger E. Kasperson, 19–28. Sterling, VA: Earthscan.

Kasperson, Roger E., Dominic Golding, and Jeanne X. Kasperson. 2005. "Risk, Trust, and Democratic Theory." In *The Social Contours of Risk,* ed. Jeanne X. Kasperson and Roger E. Kasperson, 181–201. Sterling, VA: Earthscan.

Kasperson, Roger E., Dominic Golding, and Seth Tuler. 2005. "Social Distrust as a Factor in Siting Hazardous Facilities and Communicating Risks." In *The Social Contours of Risk,* ed. Jeanne X. Kasperson and Roger E. Kasperson, 29–50. London, Earthscan.

Kasperson, Roger E., and K. David Pijawka. 1985. "Societal Response to Hazards and Major Hazard Events: Comparing Natural and Technological Hazards." *Public Administration Review* 45 (January): 7–19.

"Katrina." 2005. *The New Republic.* September 19.

"Katrina: Four Years Later." 2009. Progress Report on Recovery, Rebuilding, and Renewal, Governor Haley Barbour.

"Katrina: Why It Became a Man-Made Disaster." 2005. *National Geographic.* Special Edition, December 26.

Katz, Daniel, and Robert L. Kahn. 1978. *The Social Psychology of Organizations.* 2nd ed. New York: Wiley.

Katz, Michael B. 1989. *The Undeserving Poor.* New York: Pantheon Books.

Kaufman, Herbert. 1969. "Administrative Decentralization and Political Power." *Public Administration Review* 29 (January/February): 3–15.

———. 1981. "Fear of Bureaucracy: A Raging Pandemic." *Public Administration Review* 41: 1–10.

Keast, Robyn, Myrna Mandell, Kerry Brown, and Geoffrey Woolcock. 2004. "Network Structures: Working Differently and Changing Expectations." *Public Administration Review* 64 (3): 364–71.

Kendra, J., and T. Wachtendorf. 2003. "Elements of Community Resilience in the World Trace Center Attack." *Disasters* 27 (1): 37–53.

Kerr, Gail. 2010. "Flood Recovery Brought Nashville Communities Closer Together: Disaster Put City's Strength on Display for World." *Tennessean,* November 7. http://www.tennessean.com/apps/pbcs.dll/article?AID=201011070360.

Kettl, Donald F. 2004. *System Under Stress: Homeland Security and American Politics.* Washington, DC: CQ Press.

———. 2006. "Is The Worst Yet to Come?" In *Shelter from the Storm: Repairing the National Emergency Management System After Hurricane Katrina.* Special Issue of *The Annals of the American Academy of Political and Social Science* 604 (March): 273–287.

Key, V.O. 1961. *Public Opinion in American Democracy.* New York: Knopf.

Kilborn, Peter T. 1992. "Snarl of Red Tape Keeps U.S. Checks from Storm Areas." *The New York Times,* September 6, A1, A13.
————. 1993. "Flood Victims Find Tortuous Path to U.S. Relief Agency Money." *New York Times,* August 9, A10.
Killian, Lewis M. 1994. "Are Social Movements Irrational or Are They Collective Behavior?" In *Disasters: Collective Behavior and Social Organization,* ed. Russell Dynes and Kathleen Tierney, 273–280. Newark: University of Delaware Press.
Kingdon, John. 1994. *Agendas, Alternatives, and Public Policies.* 2nd ed. Boston: Little, Brown.
Kirby, Andrew, ed. 1990. *Nothing to Fear.* Tucson: University of Arizona Press.
Klein, Allison. 1998. "Puerto Rico Must Wait for Water, Power: 'We Will Suffer Until Then.'" *The Miami Herald,* September 28, 23A.
Kosar, Kevin. 2005. *Failing Grades: The Federal Politics of Education Standards.* New York: Lynne Rienner.
Kovaleski, Serge F. 1998a. "Hurricane Georges Bears Down on Northern Caribbean Islands." *The Washington Post,* September 21, A17.
————. 1998b. "Hurricane Hammers Puerto Rico." *The Washington Post,* September 23, A1.
————. 1998c. "Hurricane Takes Aim at Florida Keys." *The Washington Post,* September 25, A1.
Krause, Monika. 2006. "New Orleans: The Public Sphere of the Disaster." Social Science Research Council, June 11.
Kreimer, Alcira, and Mohan Munasinghe. 1990. "Managing Environmental Degradation and Natural Disasters." In *Managing Natural Disasters and the Environment,* ed. Alcira Kreimer and Mohan Munasinghe, 31–51. Washington, DC: World Bank.
Kreps, Gary A. 1989. *Structure and Disaster.* Newark: University of Delaware Press.
————. 1991. "Organizing for Emergency Management." In *Emergency Management: Principles and Practice for Local Government,* ed. T.S. Drabek and G.J. Hoetmer, 30–54. Washington, DC: International City/County Management Association.
————. 1998. "Disaster as Systemic Event and Social Catalyst." In *What Is a Disaster? A Dozen Perspectives on the Question,* ed. E.E. Quarantelli, 32–55. New York: Routledge.
Krosnick, John A., and Donald R. Kinder. 1990. "Altering the Foundations of Support for the President Through Priming." *American Political Science Review* 87: 963–978.
Kurtz, Howard. 2010. "Howard Kurtz Explores How Oil Spill, Bombing News Trumped Nashville Flood." *The Washington Post,* May 17. http://www.washingtonpost.com/wp-dyn/content/article/2010/05/16/AR2010051603282.html.
Lancaster, John. 1989. "The Storm After the Hurricane: South Carolinians Say Federal Relief Is Too Slow." *The Washington Post National Weekly Edition,* October 9–15, 32.
————. 1994. "San Fernando Valley Reeling; U.S. Team Sent." *The Washington Post,* January 18, A1, A12.
Landy, Marc. 2008. "Mega-Disasters and Federalism." *Public Administration Review,* Special Issue: S187–S198.
Lang, K., and G.E. Lang. 1961. *Collective Dynamics.* New York: Thomas Y. Crowell.
Larson, Lee W. 1993. "The Great Midwest Flood of 1993." *Natural Disaster Survey Report.* Kansas City, MO: National Weather Service.
Latham, Robert. 2005. "Testimony Before the House Select Bipartisan Committee to Investigate the Preparation for and Response to Hurricane Katrina." House Select Bipartisan Committee to Investigate the Preparation for and Response to Hurricane Katrina, December 7.
Lee, Spike. 2006. *When the Levees Broke: A Requiem in Four Acts.* HBO Documentary Films Event.
Lee, Trymaine. 2010. "Rumor to Fact in Tales of Post-Katrina Violence." *The New York Times,* August 26. http://www.nytimes.com/2010/08/27/us/27racial.html?ref=hurricane_katrina.

Leff, Lisa. 1994. "Boulevard of Broken Glass: 'Inevitable' Looters Cause Some Damage." *The Washington Post,* January 18, A8.

Lester, William, and Daniel Krejci. 2007. "Business 'Not' as Usual: The National Incident Management System, Federalism, and Leadership." *Public Administration Review* 67 (Special Supplementary Issue on Administrative Failure in the Wake of Hurricane Katrina): 84–93.

Lewin, Tamar. 2010. "Many States Adopt National Standards for Their Schools." *The New York Times,* July 21. http://www.nytimes.com/2010/07/21/education/21standards.html.

Lewis, Michael. 1989. "Some Disaster Victims Can't Get Federal Help." *The State,* September 28, B5.

Lewis, Ralph G. 1988. "Management Issues in Emergency Response." In *Managing Disaster,* ed. Louis Comfort, 163–179. Durham, NC: Duke University Press.

Light, Paul C. 1982. *The President's Agenda.* Baltimore: Johns Hopkins University Press.

Limbaugh, Rush. 2010. *The Rush Limbaugh Show.* May 7. (Courtesy of MediaMatters for America). http://mediamatters.org/mmtv/201005070028.

Lindell, M.K., and R.W. Perry 1992. *Behavioral Foundations of Community Emergency Management.* Washington, DC: Hemisphere Publishing Corporation.

———. 1996. "Assessing Gaps in Environmental Emergency Planning." *Journal of Environmental Planning and Management* 39: 541–545.

Lindblom, Charles E. 1959. "The Science of 'Muddling Through.' " *Public Administration Review* 19: 79–88.

Lindsay, Bruce R., and Justin Murray. 2010. "Disaster Relief Funding and Emergency Supplemental Appropriations." Washington, DC: Congressional Research Service, May 24.

Lipman, Larry, and Elliott Jaspin. 1993. "Top-Secret Obsession Slows FEMA." *The State,* February 22, A1, A8.

Lippman, Thomas W. 1992a. "Hurricane May Have Exposed Flaws in New Disaster Relief Plan." *The Washington Post,* September 3, A21.

———. 1992b. "One Disaster Followed by Another?" *The Washington Post National Weekly Edition,* September 7–13, 31.

———. 1992c. "Wounded Agency Hopes to Heal Itself by Helping Hurricane Victims." *The Washington Post,* August 28, A21.

Lipsky, Michael. 1978. "Standing the Study of Policy Implementation on Its Head." In *American Politics and Public Policy,* ed. Walter D. Burnham and Martha W. Weinberg. Cambridge, MA: MIT Press.

Lipton, Eric. 2006a. " 'Breathtaking' Waste and Fraud in Hurricane Aid." *The New York Times.* June 27.

———. 2006b. "Report Finds New Problems in FEMA Aid Distribution." *The New York Times,* December 6.

Lipton, Eric, Christopher Drew, Scott Shane, and David Rohde. 2005. "Breakdowns Marked Path from Hurricane to Anarchy." *The New York Times,* September 11, A1, A28.

Livingston, Mike. 1989. "FEMA Documents Swallow Small Staff." *The State,* October 7, 1B, 4B.

Lofland, John. 1981. "Collective Behavior: The Elementary Forms." In *Social Psychology,* ed. Morris Rosenberg and Ralph H. Turner, 411–446. New York: Basic Books.

———. 1985. *Protest: Studies of Collective Behavior and Social Movements.* New Brunswick, NJ: Transaction Books.

Loller, Travis, and Kristin M. Hall. 2010. "Cumberland River Flooding Forces Evacuation in Downtown Nashville, Tennessee: Storms Kill 12." *Huffington Post,* May 3. http://www.huffingtonpost.com/2010/05/03/cumberland-river-flooding_n_561129.html.

Lowi, Theodore. 1979. *The End of Liberalism.* 2nd ed. New York: Norton.

Lozano, Juan A. 2005. "FEMA Under Fire Again, Now for Rita Effort." *The New York Times,* September 28.

Luo, Michael. 2005. "The Embattled Leader of a State Immersed in Crisis." *The New York Times,* September 8.

Maestas, Cherie, Lonna Atkeson, Thomas Croom, and Lisa Bryant. 2008. "Shifting the Blame: Federalism, Media, and Public Assignment of Blame Following Hurricane Katrina." *Publius: The Journal of Federalism* 38 (4): 609–632.

Magnuson, Ed. 1989. "Earthquake." *Time,* October 30, 29–40.

Majone, Giandomenico. 1989. *Evidence, Argument, and Persuasion in the Policy Process.* New Haven, CT: Yale University Press.

Makata, John K., Charles E. Meyer, Howard G. Wilshire, John C. Tinsley, William S. Updegrove, D.M. Peterson, Stephen D. Ellen, Ralph A. Haugerud, Robert J. McLaughlin, G. Reid Fisher, and Michael F. Diggles. 1999. "The October 17, 1989, Loma Prieta, California, Earthquake." U.S. Geological Society. http://pubs.usgs.gov/dds/dds-29.

Malhotra, Neil. 2008. "Partisan Polarization and Blame Attribution in a Federal System: The Case of Hurricane Katrina." *Publius: The Journal of Federalism* 38 (4): 651–670.

Malhotra, Neil, and Alexander G. Kuo. 2008. "Attributing Blame: The Public's Response to Hurricane Katrina." *Journal of Politics* 70 (1): 120–135.

Manegold, Catherine. S. 1992a. "Amid Wreckage, Survivors Tell Their Stories." *The New York Times,* August 25, A1, A13.

———. 1992b. "In Migrant Labor Camp, Relief is Slow and Chaotic." *The New York Times,* September 1, A8.

———. 1992c. "Restoring Power After Storm to Take Months and Millions." *The New York Times,* September 5, A1, A6.

———. 1992d. "What Was Once Home Is Foreign Landscape." *The New York Times,* August 31, A1, A9.

Maraniss, David. 1992a. "As Hurricane Crosses Gulf, Pounds at Louisiana." *The Washington Post,* August 26, A1, A26.

———. 1992b. "Dwindling Andrew Partly Pulls Punch Along Gulf Cost." *The Washington Post,* August 27, A1, A21.

March, James G., and Johan P. Olsen. 1989. *Rediscovering Institutions: The Organizational Basis of Politics.* New York: Free Press.

Marcus, Frances Frank. 1992. "Louisianians Calm About Storm but Fear Their Turn May Come." *New York Times,* August 25, A12.

Marvick, Dwaine. 1954. *Career Perspectives in a Bureaucratic Setting.* Ann Arbor: University of Michigan Press.

Masel-Walters, Lynne, Lee Wilkins, and Tim Walters. 1989. *Bad Tidings: Communication and Catastrophe.* Hillsdale, NJ: Lawrence Erlbaum.

Mathews, Tom, 1992. "The Siege of L.A." *Newsweek,* May 11, 30–38.

Mathews, Tom, Peter Katel, Todd Barrett, Douglas Waller, Clara Bingham, Melinda Liu, Steven Waldman, and Ginny Carroll. 1992. "What Went Wrong?" *Newsweek,* September 7, 22–27.

Matland, Richard E. 1995. "Synthesizing the Implementation Literature: The Ambiguity-Conflict Model of Policy Implementation." *Journal of Public Administration Research and Theory* 5(2): 145–174.

May, Peter J. 1985a. "FEMA's Role in Emergency Management: Recent Experience." *Public Administration Review* 45 (Special Issue, January): 40–48.

———. 1985b. *Recovering from Catastrophes: Federal Disaster Relief Policy and Politics.* Westport, CT: Greenwood Press.

May, Peter J., and Walter Williams. 1986. *Disaster Policy Implementation: Managing Programs Under Shared Governance.* New York: Plenum Press.

Mayer, Matt A., Richard Weitz, and Diem Nguyen. 2008. "The Local Role in Disaster Response: Lessons from Katrina and the California Wildfires." Heritage Foundation. http://www.heritage.org/Research/HomelandDefense/bg2141.cfm.

Mayhew, David R. 1974. *Congress: The Electoral Connection.* New Haven, CT: Yale University Press.

Mazmanian, Daniel A., and Paul A. Sabatier. 1983. *Implementation and Public Policy.* Glenview, IL: Scott, Foresman.

McAda, William. 1989. Public Information Officer. Federal Emergency Management Agency. Personal Interview, November 9.

———. 1990. Public Information Officer. Federal Emergency Management Agency. Phone Interview, January 13.

McClam, Erin. 2005. "Poll: Storm Changed Americans' Attitudes." CNN Report. http://cnn. netscape.cnn.com/news/story.jsp?idq=/ff/story.

McEntire, David A. 2007. "Local Emergency Management Organization."In *Handbook of Disaster Research,* ed. Havidan Rodriquez, Enrico L. Quarantelli, and Russell R. Dynes, 168–182. New York: Springer.

McFadden, Robert, and Ralph Blumenthal. 2005. "Bush Sees Long Recovery for New Orleans." *The New York Times,* September 1, A1.

McGill, Kevin. 2005. "Officials Throw Up Hands as Looters Ransack City." *Times-Picayune,* August 31. http://www.nola.com/newslogs/breakingtp/index.ssf?/mtlogs/nola_Times-Picayune/archives/2005_05.html.

McKay, John. 1992. Federal Emergency Management Agency. Personal Interview, December 27.

McLoughlin. David, 1985. "A Framework for Integrated Emergency Management." *Public Administration Review* 45 (Special Issue, January): 163–172.

McNair, James. 1998. "50,000 in Keys Face Power Loss for Week, Outages are Scattered Farther North." *The Miami Herald,* September 26, 19A.

McNeill, Jena Baker. 2010. "More Than Lip Service: Why Private Sector Engagement Is Essential." August 25. *The Heritage Foundation.* http://www.heritage.org/Research/ Reports/2010/08/More-Than-Lip-Service-Why-Private-Sector-Engagement-Is-Essential.

McPhail, Clark. 1991. *The Myth of the Madding Crowd.* New York: Aldine de Gruyter.

Mead, George Herbert. 1936. "The Problem of Society." In *Movements of Thought in the Nineteenth Century,* ed. Merritt H. Moore, 360–385. Chicago: University of Chicago Press.

MediaMatters. 2010a. "CNN's Erickson Falsely Suggested Obama Ignored Tennessee Flooding." June 7. http://mediamatters.org/research/201006070040.

———. 2010b. "Hannity Falsely Suggests Obama Has Ignored Tennessee Floods." May 6. http://mediamaters.org/research/201005060052.

Medsger, B. 1989. "Earthquake Shakes Four Newspapers." *Washington Journalism Review,* December, 18–20.

Meier, Kenneth J. 2000. *Politics and the Bureaucracy.* 4th ed. Forth Worth, TX: Harcourt College Publishers.

Meier, Kenneth J., and John Bohte. 2006. *Politics and the Bureaucracy,* 5th ed. New York: Wadsworth.

Meier, Kenneth J., and Laurence J. O'Toole, Jr. 2006. *Bureaucracy in a Democratic State.* Baltimore: Johns Hopkins University Press.

Merton, Robert K. 1940. "Bureaucratic Structure and Personality." *Social Forces* 18: 560–568.

———. 1957. *Social Theory and Social Structure.* New York: Free Press.

Miami Herald. 1998a. "Across Miami-Dade, a Big Sigh of Relief, Veterans of Andrew Prepared for Worst." September 26, 25A.

———. 1998b. "Getting Ready; Evacuations and Readiness Around Florida." September 26, 20A.

———. 1998c. "It's Alarming That Dominicans Weren't Prepared." October 2, 28A.

———. 1998d. "Some Best-Laid Plans Inspired by Georges." September 28, 1B.

———. 2005–2010. Articles about Hurricane Wilma. www.miamiherald.com.

Miles, Michelle, and Duke W. Austin. 2007. "The Colors of Crisis." In *Racing the Storm: Racial Implications and Lessons Learned from Hurricane Katrina,* ed. Hillary Potter, 33–50. Lanham, MD: Lexington Books.

Mileti, David S. 1999. *Disasters by Design.* Washington, DC: Joseph Henry Press.
Mileti, David S., J. Sorenson, and P. O'Brien. 1992. "Towards an Explanation of Mass Care Shelter Use in Evacuations." *International Journal of Mass Emergencies and Disasters* 10: 45–42.
Miller, Dan, Robert Hintz, and Carl Couch. 1975. "The Structure of Openings." *Sociological Quarterly* 16: 479–499.
Miller, Jeff. 1989a. "FEMA Shuns Hurricane Drills." *The State,* November 6, B1.
———. 1989b. "Storm Surge: Mass of Aid Requests Overwhelmed FEMA." *The State,* October 23, A1, A4.
———. 1992. "Emergency Agency Tries to Aid Itself." *The State,* November 24, 1B, 3B.
Miller, J.M., and John Krosnick. 2000. "News Media Impact on the Ingredients of Presidential Evaluations: Politically Knowledgeable Citizens Are Guided by a Trusted Source." *American Journal of Political Science* 44: 295–309.
Milward, H. Brinton, and Keith G. Provan. 2000. "How Networks Are Governed." In *Governance and Performance: New Perspectives,* ed. Carolyn J. Heinrich and Laurence E. Lynn. Washington, DC: Georgetown University Press.
Mintron, Michael. 2000. *Policy Entrepreneurs and School Choice.* Washington, DC: Georgetown University Press.
Mischen, Pamela A. 2007. "Intraorganizational Policy Implementation Research: Theory and Method." *Journal of Public Administration Research and Theory* 17 (4): 553–556.
Mischen, Pamela, A., Thomas A.P. Sinclair. 2009. "Making Implementation More Democratic Through Action Implementation Research." *Journal of Public Administration Research and Theory* 19: 145–164.
Miskel, James F. 2008. *Disaster Response and Homeland Security: What Works, What Doesn't.* Stanford, CA: Stanford University Press.
Mittler, Elliott. 1988. "Agenda-Setting in Nonstructural Hazard Mitigation Policy." In *Managing Disaster,* ed. Louise K. Comfort, 86–107. Durham, NC: Duke University Press.
Moe, Ronald D. 1994. "The 'Reinventing Government' Exercise: Misinterpreting the Problem, Misjudging the Consequences." *Public Administration Review* 54 (March/April): 111–122.
Molotch, Harvey. 2006. "Death on the Roof: Race and Bureaucratic Failure." Social Science Research Council, June 11.
Moniz, Dave. 1992. "Military of '90s May Fight Domestic Battles." *The State,* September 13, 1A, 6A.
Morgan, Curtis, and Phil Long. 1998. "Exhaustion, Frustration Linger in Keys." *The Miami Herald,* September 30, 9A.
Morganthau, Tom, and Karen Springen. 1992. "Storm Warnings." *Newsweek,* September 14, 24–28.
Morrill, Jim, Paige Williams, and John York. 1989. "Carolinians Line Up for Aid." *The Charlotte Observer,* October 1, A1.
Morris, J., E. Morris, and D. Jones. 2007. "Reaching for the Philosopher's Stone: Contingent Coordination and the Military's Response to Hurricane Katrina." *Public Administration Review* 67: 94–106.
Morrison, Jan. 2010. "Why Nashville's Flood Didn't Make National Headlines." http://www.lovell.com/blog?p=1033.
Mosco, Frank. 1989. Public Information Officer, Federal Emergency Management Agency. Personal interview, North Charleston, SC, November 7.
Moss, Mitchell, Charles Schellhamer, and David A. Berman. 2009. "The Stafford Act and Priorities for Reform." *Journal of Homeland Security and Emergency Management* 6 (1): Article 13.
Mushkatel, Alvin, and Louis F. Weschler. 1985. "Emergency Management and the Intergovernmental System." *Public Administration Review* 45 (January): 47–58.

Mydans, Seth. 1994a. "Angry Crowds Besiege U.S. Agency for Quake Aid." *The New York Times,* January 21, A1, A18.

———. 1994b. "President Tours Quake Area and Feels the Earth Rumble." *The New York Times,* January 20, A19.

———. 1994c. "Tallying Losses from Quake, Los Angeles Stirs and Hopes." *The New York Times,* January 19, A1, A16.

Nakagawa, Y., and R. Shaw. 2004. "Social Capital: A Missing Link to Disaster Recovery." *International Journal of Mass Emergencies and Disasters* 22 (1): 5–34.

Nakamura, Robert T., and Frank Smallwood. 1980. *The Politics of Policy Implementation.* New York: St. Martin's Press.

Nathan, Richard P. 1993. "The Role of the States in American Federalism." In *The State of the States,* ed. Carl E. Van Horn, 15–30. Washington, DC: Congressional Quarterly Press.

National Academy of Public Administration. 1993. *Coping with Catastrophe: Building an Emergency Management System to Meet People's Needs in Natural and Manmade Disasters.* Washington, DC: National Academy of Public Administration.

———. 2009. "Department of Homeland Security, Administrator, Federal Emergency Management Agency (FEMA)." Washington, DC: PrunesOnline, A Service of the National Academy of Public Administration. http://www.excellenceintransition.org/prune/prunedetail. cfm?ItemNumber=10784.

National Emergency Management Association. 2004. *2004 NEMA Biennial Report: Organizations, Operations and Funding for State Emergency Management and Homeland Security.* Lexington, KY: The Council of State Governments.

———. 2006. *NEMA 2006 Biennial Report: Organizations, Operations, and Funding for State Emergency Management and Homeland Security.* Lexington, KY: The Council of State Governments.

———. 2008a. "A Selective History of Emergency Management." Presentation by the National Emergency Management Association. Norman, OK: National Oceanic and Atmospheric Administration Weather Partners. http://www.norman.noaa.gov/NSWW2008/Ashwood.pdf.

———. 2008b. *NEMA Profile of State Emergency Management Directors and Their Agencies.* Lexington, KY: National Emergency Management Association.

National Geographic Channel. 2006. *Inside Hurricane Katrina.* http://channel.nationalgeographic .com/episode/inside-hurricane-katrina-2710/Overview.

National Geographic Society. 2005. "Video in the News: The Wrath of Hurricane Wilma." http:// news.nationalgeographic.com/news/2005/10/1028_051028_wilma_video.html.

National Governor's Association. 2007. *A Governor's Guide to Homeland Security.* http:// www.nga.com.

———. 2009. "Letter to the U.S. Senate Committee on Armed Services." August 20. http:// www.nga.org/portal/site/nga/menuitem.cb6e7818b34088d18a278110501010a0/?vgnextoi d=61a9bfdc14833210VgnVCM1000005e00100aRCRD.

National Hazards Center. 2010. "15 Minutes Lost: Disaster Media Disses Tennessee Flooding." Disaster Research 547, University of Colorado, May 20. http://www.colorado.edu/hazards/ dr/archives/dr547.html.

National Hazards Observer. 1993. "Witt Reinvents FEMA." 18 (Number 2, November): 3.

National Performance Review, Executive Office of the President. 1993. *From Red Tape to Results: Creating a Government That Works Better and Costs Less.* Washington, DC: U.S. Government Printing Office.

National Research Council. 1991. *Reducing the Impacts of Natural Disasters.* Washington, DC: National Academy Press.

———. 1994. *Hurricane Hugo: Puerto Rico, the U.S. Virgin Islands, and South Carolina, September 17–22, 1989.* Washington, DC: National Academy of Sciences.

———. 2006. *Facing Hazards and Disasters: Understanding Human Dimensions.* Washington, DC: National Academy Press.

Neal, D.M. 1997. "Reconsidering the Phases of Disaster." *International Journal of Mass Emergencies and Disasters* 15 (2): 239–264.

Neal, D.M., and B.D. Phillips. 1995. "Effective Bureaucratic Management: Reconsidering the Bureaucratic Approach." *Disasters* 19: 327–337.

New Orleans Five Years After the Storm: A New Disaster amid Recovery. 2010. The Henry J. Kaiser Family Foundation, August.

New Orleans Times-Picayune. 2005. "An Open Letter to the President." Editorial Opinion. September 4, p. 15.

———. 2010a. "Storm Toll Rises to 30 with Report of Fatality in Memphis." May 6. http://www.nola.com/weather/index.ssf/2010/05/storm_toll_rises_to_30_with_ne.html.

———. 2010b. "Tennessee Officials Fear Discovering More Bodies as Floodwaters Recede." May 4. http://www.nola.com/weather/index.ssf/2010/05/nashville-flood.html.

New York Times. 1998. "Hurricane Roils Gulf After Hitting Florida." September 27, A1, A22.

New York Times. 2005. " 'The Great City Will Rise Again,' Bush Promises." September 26.

Nicely, Gerald. 2010. "TDOT Flood Response." Tennessee Department of Transportation. June 3.http:// www.clarksvilleonline.com/2010/06/03/tdot-flood/response/.

Nigg, Joanne. 1998. *The Loma Prieta, California, Earthquake of October 17, 1989: Recovery, Mitigation, and Reconstruction.* Denver, CO: U.S. Geological Society.

Nimmo, Dan, and James E. Combs. 1985. *Nightly Horrors: Crisis Coverage by Television Network News.* Knoxville: University of Tennessee Press.

Niskanen, William. 1971. *Bureaucracy and Representative Government.* Chicago: Aldine/Atherton.

Nixon, Ron. 2007. "Agency Erred in Canceling Loans to 8,000 Along Gulf, Audit Finds." *The New York Times,* July 25.

Nixon, Ron, and Leslie Eaton. 2007. "Accusations of Agency Error in Disaster Loans." *The New York Times,* February 27.

Norris, Pipppa, Marion Just, and Montague Kern. 2003. *Framing Terrorism: The News Media, the Government, and the Public.* London: Routledge.

Northcutt, H.C. 1992. *Aging in Alberta: Rhetoric and Reality.* Calgary, Alberta: Detselif Enterprises.

Nossiter, Adam. 2007. "Louisiana Governor Won't Seek 2nd Term." *The New York Times,* March 21.

Office of the President. 2008. *Budget of the United States Government: Historical Tables 2008.* http://www.gpoaccess.gov/usbudget/fy08/hist.html.

O'Keefe, Ed. 2010. "Director W. Craig Fugate Refocusing a Chastened FEMA." *The Washington Post,* August 25 http://www.washingtonpost.com/wp-dyn/content/article/2010.

O'Keefe, Sean. 2007. "Looking Back, Moving Forward." *Public Administration Review* 67 (Special Supplementary Issue on Administrative Failure in the Wake of Hurricane Katrina): 5–21.

Olson, Mancur. 1965. *The Logic of Collective Action.* Cambridge: Harvard University Press.

Olson, R.S., and A.C. Drury. 1997. "Un-Therapeutic Communities: A Cross-National Analysis of Post-Disaster Political Unrest." *International Journal of Mass Emergencies and Disasters* 15 (2): 221–238.

One Year After Katrina. 2006. Office of Governor Haley Barbour. August 29.

Osborne, David, and Ted Gaebler. 1992. *Reinventing Government: How the Entrepreneurial Spirit Is Transforming the Public Sector from Schoolhouse to State House, City Hall to Pentagon.* Reading, MA: Addison-Wesley.

O'Toole, Laurence J. 1993. *American Intergovernmental Relations.* 2nd ed. Washington, DC: Congressional Quarterly Press.

———. 1997. "Treating Networks Seriously: Practical and Research-Based Agendas in Public Administration." *Public Administration Review* 57 (1): 45–51.

―――. 2000. "American Intergovernmental Relations: An Overview." In *American Intergovernmental Relations*, 3rd ed., ed. Laurence J. O'Toole, 1–32. Washington, DC: CQ Press.

―――. 2006. "American Intergovernmental Relations: An Overview." In *American Intergovernmental Relations,* 4th ed., ed. Laurence J. O'Toole, 1–32. Washington, DC: CQ Press.

Pacific Earthquake Engineering Research Center. 2005. "Northridge." University of California at Berkeley. http://nisee.berkeley.edu/northridge/.

Page, Benjamin I., and Robert Y. Shapiro. 1983. "Effects of Public Opinion on Policy." *American Political Science Review* 77 (March): 315–325.

Page, Robert A., Peter A. Stauffer, and James W. Hendley II. 1999. "Progress Toward a Safer Future since the 1989 Earthquake." Menlo Park, CA: U.S. Geological Survey Fact Sheet 151–199. http://pubs.usgs.gov/fs/1999/fs151-99/.

Paine, Anne. 2010a. "Communications Breakdowns Led to Confusion on Severity of Nashville Flooding." *The Tennessean,* October 17. http://www.tennessean.com/article/20101017/NEWS01/10170364/Communications-breakdowns-led-to-confusion-on-severity-of-Nashville-flooding.

―――. 2010b. "Nashville Flood's Lessons Learned, Corps Says." *The Tennessean,* November 24. http://www.tennessean.com/article/20101124/NEWS01/11240357/Nashville-flood-s-lessons-learned-Corps-says.

Palank, Jacqueline. 2007. "FEMA Faulted on Response to Risks in Trailers." *The New York Times,* July 20.

Palm, Risa, Michael Hodgson, R. Denise Blanchard, and Donald Lyons. 1990. *Earthquake Insurance in California: Environmental Policy and Individual Decision Making.* Boulder, CO: Westview Press.

Palumbo, Dennis, and Donald J. Calista. 1990. *Implementation and the Policy Process: Opening Up the Black Box.* New York: Greenwood Press.

Panetta, Leon E. 1990. "Testimony Before the Subcommittee on Investigations and Oversight Regarding the Response of FEMA Following the Loma Prieta Earthquake." U.S. House of Representatives. 101st Congress, May 1.

Parker, Laura, 1989. "Hugo's Swirl of Paperwork." *The Washington Post,* October 29, A1, A24.

Parr, A.R. 1970. "Organizational Response to Community Crises and Group Emergency." *American Behavior Scientist* 13: 424–427.

Peabody, John. 2010. "Statement on Lessons from the 2010 Tennessee Floods Before the Subcommittee on Energy and Water Development," U.S. Senate, Committee on Appropriations, Washington, DC, July 22.

Pear, Robert. 1992. "Clinton, in Attack on President, Ties Riots to Neglect." *The New York Times,* May 6, A1.

Perrow, Charles. 2006. "Using Organizations: The Case of FEMA." *Understanding Katrina,* Social Science Research Council. http://understandingkatrina.ssrc.org/perrow.

Perry, Ronald W., and Alvin H. Mushkatel. 1984. *Disaster Management: Warning Response and Community Relocation.* Westport, CT: Quorum Books.

Perry, Ronald W., and Marjorie Greene. 1983. *Citizen Response to Volcanic Eruptions.* New York: Irvington.

Perry, Ronald W., and Joanne M. Nigg. 1985. "Emergency Management Strategies for Communicating Hazard Information." *Public Administration Review* 45 (Special Issue, January): 72–76.

Petak, William J. 1985. "Emergency Management: A Challenge for Public Administration." *Public Administration Review* 45 (Special Issue, January): 3–7.

Petak, William J., and A. Atkisson. 1982. *Natural Hazard Risk Assessment and Public Policy: Anticipating the Unexpected.* New York: Springer-Verlag.

Petak, William J., and Shirin Elahi. 2000. "The Northridge Earthquake, USA, and Its Economic and Social Impacts." Presented at the Euroconference on Global Change and Catastrophic Risk Management, Laxenburg, Austria, July 6–9.

Peters, B. Guy. 1981. "The Problems of Bureaucratic Government." *Journal of Politics* 43 (February): 65–66.

———. 2009a. *American Public Policy: Promise and Performance.* 8th ed. Chatham, NJ: Chatham House.

———. 2009b. *The Politics of Bureaucracy,* 6th ed. London: Routledge.

Peters, B. Guy, and Brian W. Hogwood. 1985. "In Search of the Issue Attention Cycle." *Journal of Politics* 47 (February): 238–253.

Peters, Katherine McIntire. 2009. "Moving FEMA Out of Homeland Security Could Pose Risks." *Government Executive,* February 17. http://www.govexec.com/dailyfed/0209/021709kp1.htm.

Peterson, Grant C. 1989. Associate Director, State and Local Program and Support Agency, Federal Emergency Management Agency. Personal Interview, December 7.

———. 1992. Associate Director, State and Local Program and Support Agency, Federal Emergency Management Agency. Personal Interview, December 27.

Peterson, Paul E. 1981. *City Limits.* Chicago: University of Chicago Press.

Peterson, Paul E., and Mark C. Rom. 1990. *Welfare Magnets: A New Case for a National Standard.* Washington, DC: Brookings Institution Press.

Pew Research Center. 1997. "Ten Years of the Pew News Interest Index." The Pew Research Center for the People and the Press, May 17. http://people-press.org/1997/05/17/ten-years-of-the-pew-news-interest-index.

———. 2005a. "Katrina Relief Effort Raises Concern over Excessive Spending, Waste." The Pew Research Center for the People and the Press, October 19. http://people-press.org/2005/10/19/katrina-relief-effort-raises-concern-over-excessive-spending-waste/

———. 2005b. "Two-in-Three Critical of Bush's Relief Efforts." The Pew Research Center for the People and the Press, September 8. http://www.people-press.org/report/display/php3?ReportID=255.

———. 2007. "California Wildfires Draw Large Audience." The Pew Research Center for the People and the Press, November 1. http://people-press.org/2007/11/01/california-wildfires-draw-large-audience/

Philbin, Walt. 2005. "Widespread Looting Hits Abandoned Businesses." *Times-Picayune,* August 30. http://www.nola.com/newslogs/breakingtp/index.ssf?/mtlogs/nola_Times-Picayune/archives/2005_08.html.

Phillips, B.D. 1993. "Cultural Diversity in Disasters: Sheltering, Housing, and Long Term Recovery." *International Journal of Mass Emergencies and Disasters* 11: 99–110.

Phillips, B.D., and Mark Rom. 1990. *Welfare Magnets: A New Case for a National Standard.* Washington, DC: Brookings Institution Press.

Piacente, Steve, 1989. "In the Eye of the Storm." *Government Executive* 21 (December): 24–33.

Pierre-Pierre, Garry. 1998. "After the False Alarms, Haitians Fail to Prepare." *The New York Times,* September 29, A12.

Platt, Rutherford H. 1999. *Disasters and Democracy: The Politics of Extreme Natural Events.* Washington, DC: Island Press.

Ploughman, P. 1995. "The American Print News Media 'Construction' of Five Natural Disasters." *Disasters* 19 (4): 308–326.

Popkin, Roy S. 1990. "The History and Politics of Disaster Management in the United States." In *Nothing to Fear,* ed. Andrew Kirby, 101–129. Tucson: University of Arizona Press.

Porfiriev, Boris N. 1998. "Issues in the Definition and Delineation of Disasters and Disasters Areas." In *What Is a Disaster: A Dozen Perspectives on the Question?* ed. E.E. Quarantelli, 56–72. New York: Routledge.

Posner, Richard A. 2004. *Catastrophe: Risk and Response.* New York: Oxford University Press.

Potter, Hillary, 2007. "Reframing Crime in a Disaster." In *Racing the Storm,* ed. Hillary Potter, 51–65. Lanham, MD: Lexington Books.

Pressman, Jeffrey L., and Aaron Wildavsky. 1973. *Implementation*. Berkeley: University of California Press.
———. 1984. *Implementation*, 2nd ed. Berkeley: University of California Press.
Public Broadcasting Service. 2005. "Public Opinion After Katrina." *PBS Online News Hour,* September 9. http://www.pbs.org/newshour/bb/politics/july-dec05/opinion_9-09.html.
———. 2006. *The Storm.* PBS Home Video.
Quarantelli, E.L. 1966. "Organization Under Stress." In *Symposium on Emergency Operations,* ed. R. Brictson. Santa Monica, CA: Rand Corporation.
———. 1983. *Emergent Citizen Groups in Disaster Preparedness and Recovery Activities.* Columbus: Ohio Disaster Research Center.
———. 1988. "Local Emergency Management Agencies: Research Findings on Their Progress and Problems in the Last Two Decades." Newark: University of Delaware, Disaster Research Center, Preliminary Paper #126.
———. 1991a. "Different Types of Disasters and Planning Implications." Newark: University of Delaware, Disaster Research Center, Preliminary Paper #169.
———. 1991b. "Disaster Response: Generic or Agent-Specific." In *Managing Natural Disasters and the Environment,* ed. Alcira Kreimer and Mohan Munasinghe, 97–105. Washington, DC: World Bank.
———. 1991c. "The Mass Media in Disasters in the United States." In *Proceedings of the IDNDR International Conference 1990.* Tokyo: Japanese Government Headquarters for the IDNDR.
———. 1995. "What Is a Disaster?" *International Journal of Mass Emergencies and Disasters* 13: 221–229.
———. 2006. "Catastrophes Are Different from Disasters: Some Implications for Crisis Planning and Managing drawn from Katrina." *Understanding Katrina.* Social Science Research Council. http://understandingkatrina.ssrc.org.
Quarantellli, E.L., and Russell R. Dynes. 1972. "When Disaster Strikes (It Isn't Much Like What You've Heard and Read About)." *Psychology Today* 5 (February): 67–70.
———. 1977. "Response to Social Crisis and Disaster." *Annual Review of Sociology* 3: 23–49.
———. 1991. *Lessons from Research: Findings on Mass Communication System Behavior in the Pre, Trans, and Post Impact Periods of Disasters.* Newark: University of Delaware, Disaster Research Center, Preliminary Paper 160.
Ravitch, Diane. 1995. *National Standards in American Education.* Washington, DC: Brookings Institution Press.
Reed, Mack. 1994. "Federal Officials Tour Simi Valley Wreckage, Offer Assurances: Local Victims Receive the High-Level Assistance They Have Sought." *Los Angeles Times,* January 29.
Reicher, S.D. 1984. "The St. Paul's Riot: An Explanation of the Limits of Crowd Action in Terms of a Social Identity Model." *European Journal of Social Psychology* 19: 1–21.
Reuters. 2010. "Flooding hits Tennessee, Nearby States." May 3. http://www.reuters.com/article/idUSTRE6412Y620100503.
Riad, J.K., F.H. Norris, and R.B. Ruback. 1999. "Predicting Evacuation in Two Major Disasters: Risk Perception, Social Influence, and Access to Resources." *Journal of Applied Social Psychology* 29: 918–934.
Riccucci, Norma M. 2005. *How Management Matters: Street-level Bureaucrats and Welfare Reform.* Washington, DC: Georgetown University Press.
Riker, William. 1986. *The Art of Political Manipulation.* New Haven, CT: Yale University Press.
Riley, Joseph P. 1989. Mayor of the City of Charleston, Personal Interview, November 7.
Ripley, Amanda. 2008. *The Unthinkable: Who Survives When Disaster Strikes—and Why.* New York: Crown Publishers.
Ripley, Randall B., and Grace A. Franklin. 1991. *Bureaucracy and Policy Implementation.* Homewood, IL: Dorsey Press.
Rivera, Carla. 1994a. "Earthquake: The Long Road Back. Agencies Acted Fast, Still Overwhelmed." *Los Angeles Times,* January 31, 16.

————. 1994b. "FEMA Discontinues Unrequested Quake Checks." *Los Angeles Times,* February 4, A20.

————. 1994c. "Hundreds Get Unrequested Quake Funds from FEMA Aid." *Los Angeles Times,* February 3.

Rivlin, Alice M. 1992. *Reviving the American Dream: The Economy, the States, and the Federal Government.* Washington, DC: Brookings Institution Press.

Roberts, Michelle. 2006. "New Orleanians Wrestle Bureaucracy, Fear." *The Washington Post,* February 12.

Robertson, Campbell. 2009. "New Orleans Police Face Swarm of Inquiries." *The New York Times,* October 9.

————. 2010. "New Orleans Mayor Had a Full Plate Even Before the Spill." *The New York Times,* July 13. http://www.nytimes.com/2010/07/14/us/14landrieu.html?ref=mitchlandrieu.

Robichau, Robbine Walter, and Laurence E. Lynn, Jr. 2009. "The Implementation of Public Policy: Still the Missing Link." *Policy Studies Journal* 37: 21–37.

Robinson, Eugene. 2005. "Where the Good Times Haven't Rolled." *The Washington Post,* September 2.

Robles, Frances. 1998a. "Helicopter Shortage Slows Relief Effort." *The Miami Herald,* September 30, 9A.

————. 1998b. "A Village Swallowed: By Storm or Mistake?" *The Miami Herald,* September 29, 1A.

Rochefort, David A., and Roger W. Cobb. 1994. "Problem Definition: An Emerging Perspective." In *The Politics of Problem Definition,* ed. Rochefort and Cobb, 1–31. Lawrence: University Press of Kansas.

Rockman, Bert A. 1992. "Bureaucracy, Power, Policy, and the State." In *The State of Public Bureaucracy,* ed. Larry B. Hill, 141–170. Armonk, NY: M.E. Sharpe.

Rodgers, Harrell R. Jr. 2006. *American Poverty in a New Era of Reform.* New York: M.E. Sharpe.

Rodriguez, Havidan, and Russell Dynes. 2006. "Finding and Framing Katrina: The Social Construction of Disaster." Social Science Research Council, June 11.

Rodriquez, Havidan, Enrico L. Quarantelli, and Russell Dynes. 2006. *Handbook of Disaster Research.* New York: Springer.

Rodriguez, Havidan, Joseph Trainor, and Enrico L. Quarantelli. 2006. "Rising to the Challenges of a Catastrophe: The Emergent and Prosocial Behavior Following Hurricane Katrina." In *Shelter from the Storm: Repairing the National Emergency Management System After Hurricane Katrina.* Special Issue of *The Annals of the American Academy of Political and Social Science* 604 (March): 82–101.

Rogers, Evertt M., Matthew Berndt, John Harris, and John Minzer. 1990. "Accuracy in Mass Media Coverage." In *The Loma Prieta Earthquake: Studies of Short-Term Impacts,* ed. Robert Bolin, 44–55. Boulder: University of Colorado, Institute of Behavioral Science.

Rohter, Larry. 1992a. "As Army Gears Up, Floridians Rely on Private Relief." *The New York Times,* August 30, A1, A12.

————. 1992b. "A Million Are Told to Flee Hurricane in South Florida." *The New York Times,* August 24, A1, A8.

————. 1992c. "President Pledges Money to Rebuild in South Florida." *The New York Times,* September 2, A1, A11.

————. 1992d. "Rumors Abound of Storm Deaths Going Untallied." *The New York Times,* September 5, A6.

————. 1992e. "Survey Shows Bush Weak in Republican Stronghold." *The New York Times,* September 17, A1, A10.

————. 1998a. "Hurricane Damage Exceeds $1 Billion." *The New York Times,* September 22, A1, A16.

———. 1998b. "Hurricane Hits Cuba After Leaving at Least 60 Dead Elsewhere." *The New York Times,* September 23, A12.

———. 1998c. "Killer Hurricane Takes Property, But Apparently No Lives, in Keys." *The New York Times,* September 25, A1, A8.

———. 1998d. "Puerto Rico and Nearby Islands Brace for Big Hurricane." *The New York Times,* September 20, A10.

———. 1998e. "With Almost 200 Dead in Caribbean, Storm Heads Toward Florida Keys." *The New York Times,* September 24, A14.

Roig-Franzia, Manuel, and Spencer Hsu. 2005. "Many Evacuated, But Thousands Still Waiting." *The Washington Post,* September 4, A1, A24.

Romano, Andrew. 2010. "Why the Media Ignored the Nashville Flood." *Newsweek,* May 6. http://www.newsweek.com/blogs-the-gaggle/2010/05/06/why-the-media-ignored-the-nashville-flood.html.

Rosenbaum, David E. 2003. "The Nation: Help! Disaster Aid: The Mix of Mercy and Politics." *The New York Times,* November 2. http://www.nytimes.com/gst/fullpage.html?res=950CE0DB1330F93.

Rossi, Peter H., James D. Wright, and Eleanor Weber-Burdin. 1978. "Are There Long Term Effects of American Natural Disasters?" *Mass Emergencies* 3: 117–132.

———. 1982. *Natural Hazards and Public Choice: The State and Local Politics of Hazards Mitigation.* New York: Academic Press.

Rourke, Francis E. 1984. *Bureaucracy, Politics, and Public Policy.* 3rd ed. Boston: Little Brown.

Rozario, Kevin. 2007. *The Culture of Calamity: Disaster and the Making of Modern America.* Chicago: University of Chicago Press.

Rubin, Claire B, 2007. "An Introduction to a Century of Disaster Response and Emergency Management, From Galveston to New Orleans." In *Emergency Management: The American Experience 1900–2005,* ed. Claire B. Rubin. Fairfax, VA: Public Entity Risk Institute.

Rubin, Claire B, and Daniel G. Barbee. 1985. "Disaster Recovery and Hazard Mitigation: Bridging the Intergovernmental Gap." *Public Administration Review* 45 (Special Issue, January): 59–63.

Rubin, Claire B, and Roy Popkin. 1990. *Disaster Recovery After Hurricane Hugo in South Carolina.* Final Report to the National Science Foundation. Washington, DC: George Washington University.

Rubin, Claire B, Martin D. Saperstein, and Daniel G. Barbee. 1985. *Community Recovery from a Major Disaster.* University of Colorado: Institute of Behavioral Sciences.

Ryan, Richard A. 1997. "Politics of Disaster Relief: Reformed Agency Improves Assistance as it Reaps Benefits of 'Buying Votes.'" *The Detroit News,* July 13.

Saad, Lydia. 2005. "Trust in Federal Government Not Shaken by Katrina." Gallup Poll, September 28. www.gallup.com/poll/18835/Trust-Federal-Government-Shaken-Katrina.aspx.

Sabatier, Paul A. 1986. "Top-Down and Bottom-Up Approaches to Implementation Research: A Critical Analysis and Suggested Synthesis." *Journal of Public Policy* 6: 31–48.

Sabatier, Paul A., and Hank Jenkins-Smith. 1993. "The Dynamics of Policy-Oriented Learning. In *Policy Change and Learning,* ed. Paul A. Sabatier and Hank C. Jenkins-Smith, 41–56. Boulder, CO: Westview Press.

Sabatier, Paul A., and Daniel Mazmanian. 1980. "The Implementation of Public Policy: A Framework of Analysis." *Policy Studies Journal* (Special Issue 2): 538–60.

Sanchez, Rene. 1992. "Tough Times in the Bayou 'Nothing New for the Cajun People.'" *The Washington Post,* August 28, A14.

Sanger, David. 2005. "Bush Wants to Consider Broadening of Military's Powers During Natural Disasters." *The New York Times,* September 27.

Sattler, David N., and Charles F. Kaiser. 2000. "Hurricane: A Multinational Study Examining Preparedness, Resource Loss, and Psychological Distress in the U.S. Virgin Islands, Puerto

Rico, Dominican Republic, and the United States." Boulder, CO: Natural Hazards Center, Quick Response Report #127.

Savas, E.S. 1982. *Privatizing the Public Sector.* Chatham, NJ: Chatham House.

———. 1987. *Privatization: The Key to Better Government.* Chatham, NJ: Chatham House.

———. 2000. *Privatization and Public-Private Partnerships.* New York: Seven Bridges Press.

Scallan, Matt. 2005. "Jeff President Broussard Says 'Hell Doesn't Look so Bad.'" *New Orleans Times-Picayune,* September 6, 5.

Scanlon, Joseph T. 1977. "Post-Disaster Rumor Chains: A Case Study." *Mass Emergencies* 2: 121–126.

———. 2008. "Unwelcome Irritant or Useful Ally? The Mass Media in Emergencies." In *Handbook of Disaster Research,* ed. Havidan Rodriquez, Enrico L. Quarantelli, and Russell R. Dynes, 413–429. New York: Springer.

Scanlon, Joseph T., Suzanne Alldred, Al Farrell, and Angela Prawzick. 1985. "Coping with the Media in Disasters: Some Predictable Problems." *Public Administration Review* 45 (Special Issue, January): 123–133.

Scavo, Carmine, Richard C. Kearney, and Richard J. Kilroy, Jr. 2007. "Challenges to Federalism: Homeland Security and Disaster Response." *Publius: The Journal of Federalism* 38: 81–110.

Schaff, Jason. 2004. "The Quake: Nicely Back from the Brink." *San Fernando Valley Business Journal,* January 5.

Schattschneider, E.E. 1960. *The Semisovereign People.* New York: Holt, Rinehart and Winston.

Scheberle, Denise. 2004. *Federalism and Environmental Policy: Trust and the Politics of Implementation.* Washington, DC: Georgetown University Press.

Schmidt, William E. 1990. "Cleanup Begins at Tornado Site Where 25 Died." *The New York Times,* August 30, A18.

Schneider, Ann, and Helen Ingraham. 1993. "Social Construction of Target Populations: Implications for Politics and Policy." *American Political Science Review* 87: 334–347.

Schneider, Mark, Paul Teske, and Michael Mintrom. 1995. *Public Entrepreneurs: Agents for Change in American Government.* Princeton: Princeton University Press.

Schneider, Saundra K. 1989. "South Carolina, FEMA, and the Response to Hurricane Hugo." *The South Carolina Forum* (April–June). Columbia: Institute of Public Affairs, University of South Carolina.

———. 1990. "FEMA, Federalism, Hugo, and 'Frisco." *Publius: The Journal of Federalism* 20 (Summer): 97–116.

———. 1992. "Governmental Response to Disasters: The Conflict Between Bureaucratic Procedures and Emergent Norms." *Public Administration Review* 52 (March/April): 135–145.

———. 1998. "Reinventing Public Administration: A Case Study of the Federal Emergency Management Agency." *Public Administration Quarterly* 22 (1): 35–58.

———. 2005. "Administrative Breakdowns in the Governmental Response to Hurricane Katrina." *Public Administration Review* 65: 515–517.

———. 2008a. "The Disastrous Response to Hurricane Katrina: Blame It on the Bureaucracy?" In *Emergency Management in Higher Education,* ed. Jessica A. Hubbard. Fairfax, VA: Public Entity Risk Institute, 113–131.

———. 2008b. "Who's to Blame? (Mis)perceptions of the Intergovernmental Response to Disasters." *Publius: The Journal of Federalism* 38: 715–738.

Schneider, Saundra K., William G. Jacoby, and Daniel C. Lewis. 2011. "Public Opinion Toward Intergovernmental Policy Responsibilities." *Publius: The Journal of Federalism* 41 (1): 1–30.

Schneider, William. 2005. "Catastrophic Failure." *National Journal,* September 20.

Schoettler, Jim. 1992. "The Cheers Turned to Tears at Jeanerette Gym." *The Florida Times-Union,* August 27, A9.

Schon, Donald A., and Martin Rein. 1994. *Frame Reflections: Toward the Resolution of Intractable Policy Controversies.* New York: Basic Books.

Schwada, John. 1994. "To Deal with the Crush of Relief Applicants, FEMA Plans to Open Two New Disaster Centers Today, Raising the Total to 15." *Los Angeles Times,* January 24.

"Secretary Napolitano Visits Areas Affected by Flooding in Tennessee." 2010. *Media Newswire.* http://media-newswire.com/release_1118975.html.

Seidman, Harold, and Robert Gilmour. 1986. *Politics, Position, and Power: From the Positive to the Regulatory State.* 4th ed. New York: Oxford University Press.

Selznick, Peter. 1943. "An Approach to a Theory of Bureaucracy." *American Sociological Review* 8: 47–54.

Shaffer, Helen. B. 1977. "Job Health and Safety." In *Earth, Energy and Environment,* 189–208. Washington, DC: Congressional Quarterly Press.

Shane, Scott, Eric Lipton, and Christopher Drew. 2005. "After Failures, Officials Play Blame Game." *The New York Times,* September 5, A1, A14.

"Shattered." 1994. *Newsweek.* Special Report After the L.A. Earthquake, January 31, 16–37.

Sheppard, Noel. 2010. "Newsweek Offers Offensive Explanation for Why Media Ignored Nashville Flood." http://www.newsbusters.org/blogs/noel-sheppard/2010/05/07/newseek.

Sherif, Muzafer. 1936. *The Psychology of Social Norms.* New York: Harper.

Silva, Mark, Steve Bousquet, and Tyler Bridges. 1998. "Georges' Remnants Saturate South." *The Miami Herald,* September 30, 8A.

Silverstein, Martin E. 1992. *Disasters: Your Right to Survive.* Riverside, NJ: Macmillan.

Simao, Paul, and Michael Christie. 2005. "Qualifications of FEMA Director Questioned." *The Washington Post,* September 9.

Similie, C. 1995. "Disaster Settings and Mobilization for Contentious Collection Action: Case Studies of Hurricane Hugo and the Loma Prieta Earthquake." Doctoral dissertation. Newark: Department of Sociology and Criminal Justice, University of Delaware.

Simon, Herbert. 1976. *Administrative Behavior.* 3rd ed. New York: Free Press.

Simon, Richard, and Myron Levin. 1995. "Nearly a Year After Quake, U.S. Aid Exceeds $5 Billion Recovery: More than 500,000 People and Businesses have Received Funds. But Billions in Damage Remain." *Los Angeles Times,* January 8, 1.

Sinclair, Barbara D. 1977. "Party Realignment and the Transformation of the Political Agenda." *American Political Science Review* 71 (September): 940–953.

Singer, Eleanor. 1993. *Reporting on Risk: How the Mass Media Portray Accidents, Disease, Disaster, and Other Hazards.* New York: Russell Sage Foundation.

Singer, Eleanor, and Phyllis M. Endreny. 1993. *Reporting on Risk.* New York: Russell Sage Foundation.

Skocpol, Theda, and Edwin Amenta. 1986. "States and Social Policies." *Annual Review of Sociology* 12.

Smelser, Neil. 1963. *Theory of Collective Behavior.* New York: Free Press.

———. 1964. "Theoretical Issues of Scope and Problems." *Sociological Quarterly* 5: 116–121.

Smith, G. 2004. "Holistic Disaster Recovery." Washington, DC: Federal Emergency Management Institute, Higher Education Project.

Smith, Steve. 1990. "Severe Storms Hit, Injuring Four and Destroying Houses." *The State,* October 23, 1B, 2B.

Smith, Taiya. 2007. "Rudy Giuliani: The Man and His Moment." John F. Kennedy School of Government, Case Studies in Public Policy and Management. Boston, MA: Harvard University.

Sobel, Russell S., and Peter T. Leeson. 2006. "Government's Response to Hurricane Katrina: A Public Choice Analysis." *Public Choice* 127: 55–73.

"Some Best-Laid Plans Inspired By Georges." 1998. *The Miami Herald,* September 28, 1B.

Sontag, Deborah, 1992. "Life on Fringes of Ruin Makes Cautious Comeback." *The New York Times,* September 7, A1, A7.

South Carolina Emergency Preparedness Division. 1985. *The South Carolina Comprehensive Emergency Preparedness Plan.* Columbia, SC: Office of the Adjutant General, March.

Southern California Earthquake Center. n.d. "Northridge Earthquake." http://www.data.scec.org/chrono_index/northreq.html.

Spolar, Christine. 1994. "Night and Day, L.A. Freeway Rises." *The Washington Post,* April 2, A3.

Spolar, Christine, and William Claiborne. 1994. "Quake Aid Checks Dispatched as FEMA Mobilizes More Staff and Rain Holds Off." *The Washington Post,* January 24, A5.

Spolar, Christine, and Lynne Duke. 1994. "Strain Begins to Tear at Weary Californians." *The Washington Post,* January 21, A1, A20.

Sponhour, Michael. 1989a. "Coastal South Carolina Gears Up for Hugo." *The State,* September 20, B5.

———. 1989b. "Federal Red Tape Hinders Aid Distribution in Charleston." *The State,* September 28, B1.

———. 1989c. "Forgotten Residents Fend for Themselves." *The State,* October 29, A1, A4.

Stallings, Robert. 1998. "Disaster and the Theory of Social Order. In *What is a Disaster: Perspectives on the Question,* ed. E. L. Quarantelli, 127-145. New York: Routledge.

Stallings, Robert A., and E.L. Quarantelli. 1985. "Emergent Citizen Groups and Emergency Management." *Public Administration Review* 45 (Special Issue, January): 93–100.

Stanley, Harold W., and Richard G. Niemi. 1994. *Vital Statistics on American Politics.* 4th ed. Washington, DC: Congressional Quarterly Press.

The State. 1989. "Task of Pulling Survivors from Debris Creating New Class of Heroes." October 19, 10A.

———. 1993. "In Flooded Midwest, FEMA Gets High Marks, for a Change." August 14, 5A.

———. 1994. "Quake Victims Turn to Tents for Shelter." January 23, 3A.

"State of Shock." 1994. *Time* (Special Report), January 31, 26–46.

State of Tennessee. 2010a. *Executive Order Number 65: An Emergency Order Suspending Provisions of Certain Laws and Rules to Provide Necessary Relief to Victims of Recent Storms and Flooding.*

———. 2010b. *Executive Order 66: An Emergency Order Suspending Provisions of a Certain Law and Rules Related to the Provision of Security Services in Order to Provide Necessary Relief to Victims of Recent Storms and Flooding.*

———. 2010c. *Executive Order 67: An Emergency Order Amending Certain Provisions of Executive Order No. 65 Related to Emergency Relief.*

Steinhauer, Jennifer, and Eric Lipton. 2005. "FEMA, Slow to the Rescue, Now Stumbles in Aid Effort." *The New York Times,* September 17, A1, A14.

Stephens, G. Ross, and Nelson Wickstrom. 2006. *American Intergovernmental Relations: A Fragmented Federal Polity.* New York: Oxford University Press.

Stevenson, Jennifer L, Kaylois Henry, and David Barstow. 1992. "We're Lucky—It Could Have Been Like Florida." *St. Petersburg Times,* August 27, 1A, 2A.

Stevenson, Richard W., and Anne E. Kornblut. 2005. "Director of FEMA Stripped of Role as Relief Leader." *The New York Times,* September 10, A1, A14.

Stillman, Richard J., II. 1987. *The American Bureaucracy.* Chicago: Nelson-Hall.

Stimson, James A. 2004. *Tides of Consent: How Public Opinion Shapes American Politics.* Cambridge: Cambridge University Press.

Stone, Deborah A. 2002. *Policy Paradox: The Art of Political Decision Making.* Rev. ed. New York: W.W. Norton.

Strategic Risk. 2009. "Top Ten U.S. Natural Disasters." November 23. http://www.strategicrisk. co.uk/story.asp?sectioncode=23&storycode=381341&c=1.

Stratton, Ruth M. 1989. *Disaster Relief.* Lanham, MD: University Press of America.

Strolovitch, Dara, Dorian Warren, and Paul Frymer. 2006. "Katrina's Political Roots and Divisions: Race, Class, and Federalism in American Politics." Social Science Research Council, June 11.

Suburban Emergency Management Project. 2008. "The Incredible Expanding FEMA." September 15. http://www.semp.us/publications/biot-reader.php?BiotID=537.

———. 2009. "James Lee Witt: Twelfth FEMA Director: Part II: 1993–2001" http://www. semp.us/publications/biot_reader.php?BiotID=587.

Sugiman, Toshio, and Jyuji Misumi. 1988. "Development of a New Evacuation Methodology for Emergencies: Control of Collective Behavior by Emergent Small Groups." *Journal of Applied Psychology* 73 (February): 3–11.

Suleiman, Ezra. 1974. *Politics, Power, and Bureaucracy in France: The Administrative Elite.* Princeton: Princeton University Press.

Sullivan, Brian K. 2010. "Tennessee Floods Kill at Least 11, Drive Thousands from Homes." *Bloomberg Businessweek,* December 5. http://www.businessweek.com/news/2010–05–03/ tennessee-floods-ill-at-least-11.

Sullivan, Eileen, and Brent Kallestad. 2009. "Craig Fugate: O'Bama's FEMA Director." *Huff-Post Politics*, March 4. http://www.huffingtonpost.com/2009/03/04/craig-fugate-obamas-fema_n_171837.html.

Sundquist, James L. (with David W. Davis). 1969. *Making Federalism Work.* Washington, DC: Brookings Institution Press.

Sun Herald. 2005. "Help Us Now! We Need Relief." September 1.

Sun Sentinental. 2005–2010. "Sun Sentinental—Articles About Hurricane Wilma." http:// articles.sun-sentinel.com/keyword/hurricane-wilma.

Suro, Robert. 1992a. "Despite the Devastation, Louisianians Feel Lucky." *The New York Times,* August 28, A11.

———. 1992b. "When Storm Got Tough, the Women Got Tougher." *The New York Times,* September 10, A8.

Sylves, Richard T. 1996. "Redesigning and Administering Federal Emergency Management." In *Disaster Management in the U.S. and Canada*, ed. Richard T. Sylves and William L. Waugh, Jr., 5–25. Springfield, IL: Charles C. Thomas.

———. 2006. "President Bush and Hurricane Katrina: A Presidential Leadership Study." In *Shelter from the Storm: Repairing the National Emergency Management System After Hurricane Katrina*. Special Issue of *The Annals of the American Academy of Political and Social Science* 604 (March): 26–56.

———. 2007. "Federal Emergency Management Comes of Age." In *Emergency Management: The American Experience, 1900–2005*, ed. Claire B. Rubin, 111–160. Fairfax, VA: Public Entity Risk Institute.

———. 2008. *Disaster Policy and Politics: Emergency Management and Homeland Security.* Washington, DC: CQ Press.

"System Failure." 2005. *Time,* September 19.

Taylor, Frederick W. 1911. *Principles of Scientific Management.* New York: Harper and Row.

Telegraph. 2010. "Tennessee Flooding Kills 18." May 4. http://www.telegraph.co.uk/earth/ earthnews/7679502/Tennessee-flooding-kills-18.html.

The Big One: Hurricane Andrew. 1992. Kansas City, MO: Andrews and McNeal.

The October 17, 1989, Loma Prieta Earthquake. 1989. San Francisco, CA: EQE Engineering.

Thompson, Frank J. 1982. "Deregulation by the Bureaucracy: OSHA and the Augean Quest for Error Correction." *Public Administration Review* 42: 202–212.

Thompson, Victor A. 1961. *Modern Organizations: A General Theory.* New York: Alfred A. Knopf.

Three Years After Recovery. Governor Haley Barbour Progress Report. www.govenorbarbour. com/Recovery.

Thrift, Ashley. 1989. Advisor to Senator Hollings. Personal Interview. Office of Senator Ernest F. Hollings, Washington, DC.

Tierney, Kathleen. 1980. "Emergent Norm Theory as 'Theory': An Analysis and Critique of Turner's Formulation." In *Collective Behavior: A Source Book,* ed. Meredith Pugh, 42–53. St. Paul, MN: West.

———. 2006. "Social Inequality, Hazards, and Disasters." In *On Risk and Disaster: Lessons from Hurricane Katrina,* ed. Ronald J. Daniels, Donald F. Kettl, and Howard Kunreuther, 109–128. Philadelphia: University of Pennsylvania Press.

Tierney, Kathleen, Christine Bevc, and Erica Kuligowski. 2006. "Metaphors Matter: Disaster Myths, Media Frames, and Their Consequences in Hurricane Katrina." In *Shelter from the Storm: Repairing the National Emergency Management System After Hurricane Katrina.* Special Issue of *The Annals of the American Academy of Political and Social Science* 604 (March): 57–81.

Tierney, Kathleen, Michael K. Lindell, and Ronald W. Perry. 2001. *Facing the Unexpected: Disaster Preparedness and Response in the United States.* Washington, DC: Joseph Henry Press.

Tierney, Kathleen, and G.R. Webb. 2006. "Business Vulnerability to Earthquakes and Other Disasters." In *Earthquakes,* ed. E. Rossi and C.M. Rodriquez. New York: Routledge.

Tilly, Charles. 1978. *From Mobilization to Revolution.* Reading, MA: Addison-Wesley.

Toulmin, Llewellyn M., Charles J. Givans, and Deborah L. Steel. 1989. "The Impact of Intergovernmental Distance on Disaster Communications." *International Journal of Mass Emergencies and Disasters* 7 (August): 116–132.

Townsend, Frances Fragos. 2006. *The Federal Response to Hurricane Katrina: Lessons Learned.* Washington, DC: White House.

Treaster, Joseph B. 1992a. "Price Gouging Is Widely Cited in Storm Region." *The New York Times,* August 30, A1, A11.

———. 1992b. "Troops Begin Work in Storm-Hit Area, But Misery Mounts." *The New York Times,* August 31, A1, A8.

———. 1998. "In Dominican Republic, Sun Dries Much but Not All Tears." *The New York Times,* September 30, A11.

Treaster, Joseph B., and N.R. Kleinfield. 2005. "New Orleans Is Inundated as 2 Levees Fail: Much of Gulf Coast Is Crippled, Toll Rises." *The New York Times* August 31, A1.

Treaster, Joseph B., and Deborah Sontag. 2005. "Despair and Lawlessness Grip New Orleans as Thousands Remain Stranded in Squalor." *The New York Times.* September 2, A1. http://www.nytimes.com/2005/09/02/national/nationalspecial/02storm.html?pagewanted=2.

Tubbesing, Susan K. 1994. *The Loma Prieta Earthquake, California, of October 17, 1989: Loss Estimation and Procedures.* Washington, DC: U.S. Government Printing Office.

Turner, Barry A. 1976. "The Organizational and Interorganizational Development of Disasters." *Administrative Science Quarterly* 21 (September): 378–397.

Turner, Ralph H. 1986. *Waiting for Disaster.* Berkeley: University of California Press.

Turner, Ralph H., and Lewis Killian. 1972. *Collective Behavior.* 2nd ed. Englewood Cliffs, NJ: Prentice-Hall.

———. 1987. *Collective Behavior.* 3rd ed. Englewood Cliffs: Prentice-Hall.

Tuten, Jan. 1989. "Some Victims Still Await Help." *The State,* November 24, 1B.

———. 1990. "City Could Have Avoided Flood Deaths, Expert Says." *The State,* October 23, 2B.

Tversky, A., and D. Kahneman. 1981. "The Framing of Decisions and the Psychology of Choice." *Science* 211: 453–458.

U.S. Army Corps of Engineers. 1998. "Hurricane Georges." Hydrology and Hydraulics Branch, September.

USA Today. 1998. "Hurricane Georges' Damage Reports." http://www.usatoday/com/weather/huricane/1998/wgregedmg.htm.

U.S. Congress. 1974. *The Disaster Relief Act Amendments of 1974.* 93rd Congress. Public Law 93–288.

―――. 1988. *The Robert T. Stafford Disaster Relief and Emergency Assistance Act.* 100th Congress. Public Law 100–707.

―――. 2006. *Post-Katrina Emergency Reform Act.* 109th Congress. Public Law 109–295.

―――. 2007. *The Robert T. Stafford Disaster Relief and Emergency Assistance Act, as Amended, and Related Authorities.* 110th Congress. Public Law 93–288, as amended 42 U.S.C. 5121–5207.

U.S. Department of Commerce. 1972. *A Study of Earthquake Losses in the San Francisco Bay Area—Data and Analysis, A Report Prepared for the Office of Emergency Preparedness: U.S. Department of Commerce.* Washington, DC: National Oceanic and Atmospheric Administration.

―――. 1993. *Some Devastating North Atlantic Hurricanes of the 20th Century.* Washington, DC: U.S. Department of Commerce.

―――. 1994. *The Great Flood of 1993.* Rockville, Maryland: National Oceanic and Atmospheric Administration, and the National Weather Service.

―――. 1998. "Hurricane History: Hurricane Andrew." National Weather Service, National Hurricane Center, http://www.nhc.noaa.gov/1992andrew.html, last updated December 28, 1998.

―――. 1999. "Georges Pummels Caribbean, Florida Keys, and U.S. Gulf Coast." National Oceanic and Atmospheric Administration, National Climatic Data Center. April 12. http://lwf.ncdc.noaa.gov/oa/reports/georges/georges.html, last updated April 12, 1999.

―――. 2005a. "Hurricane Katrina." National Oceanic and Atmospheric Administration, National Climatic Data Center. http://www.ncdc.noaa.gov/special-reports/katrina.html, updated December 29, 2005.

―――. 2005b. "Hurricane Katrina: A Climatological Perspective." National Oceanic and Atmospheric Administration. National Climatic Data Center, October (updated August 2006). http://www.ncdc.noaa.gov/oa/reports/tech-report-200501z.pdf.

―――. 2005c. "Hurricane Rita." U.S. Department of Commerce, National Oceanic and Atmospheric Administration. http://www.ncdc.noaa.gov/special-reports/rita.html.

―――. 2006a. "Hurricane History: Addendum, Hurricane Andrew, 16–28 August, 1992." National Oceanic and Atmospheric Administration, National Climatic Data Center. http://www.nhc.noaa.gov/1992andrew_add.html, last updated January 5, 2006.

―――. 2006b. "Special Assessment: Hurricane Katrina, August 23–31, 2005. National Oceanic and Atmospheric Administration, National Climatic Data Center. http://www.nws.noaa.gov/os/assessments/pdfs/Katrina.pdf.

―――. 2007. "Hurricane Wilma." National Oceanic and Atmospheric Administration, National Climatic Data Center. http://www.ncdc.noaa.gov/special-reports/wilma.html.

―――. 2010a. "Deepwater Horizon/BP Oil Spill Response." National Oceanic and Atmospheric Administration. http://response.restoration.noaa.gov/dwh.php?entry_id=809.

―――. 2010b. "Hurricane Hugo: 20th Anniversary, September 21–22, 1989." National Oceanic and Atmospheric Administration, National Weather Service, http://www.erh.noaa.gov/chs/events/hugo.shtml.

―――. 2011. "Billion Dollar U.S. Weather Disasters: 1980–2010." U.S. Department of Commerce, National Oceanic and Atmospheric Administration. http://www.ncdc.noaa.gov/oa/reports/billionz.html.

U.S. Department of Homeland Security. 2004a. *National Response Plan.* Washington, DC: Department of Homeland Security. http://www.iir.com/Information_Sharing/global/resources/fusioncenter/NRPbaseplan.pdf.

―――. 2004b. "Strategic Plan—Securing Our Homeland." Washington, DC: Department of Homeland Security. http://www.masgc.org/gmrp/plans/DHS.pdf.

―――. 2006. *A Performance Review of FEMA's Disaster Management Activities in Response to Hurricane Katrina.* Office of Inspector General, OIG-0602, March.

———. 2007. *The National Strategy for Homeland Security.* Washington, DC: Department of Homeland Security, October. http://www.dhs.gov/xlibrary/assets/nat_strat_homeland-security_2007.pdf.

———. 2008a. "Implementation of the Post-Katrina Emergency Management Reform Act and Other Organizational Changes." Washington, DC: Department of Homeland Security, October 8. http://cipbook.infracritical.com/book3/chapter3/ch3ref4.pdf.

———. 2008b. *National Response Framework.* Washington, DC: Department of Homeland Security. January. http://www.fema.gov/pdf/emergency/nrf/nrf-core.pdf.

———. 2008c. *Overview: ESF and Support Annexes Coordinating Federal Assistance in Support of the National Response Framework.* http://www.fema.gov/pdf/emergency/nrf/nrf-overview.pdf.

———. 2008d. "What's New in the National Response Framework." Washington, DC: Department of Homeland Security, January 22.

———. 2010. "Secretary Napolitano Visits Areas Affected by Flooding in Tennessee." May 8. Office of the Press Secretary. http://www.dhs.gov/ynews/releases/pr_1273494259172.shtm.

———. 2011. "Department Subcomponents and Agencies." Washington, DC: Department of Homeland Security. http://www.dhs.gov/xabout/structure.

U.S. General Accounting Office. 1989. *Disaster Assistance: Timeliness and Other Issues Involving the Major Disaster Declaration Process.* Washington, DC: General Accounting Office.

———. 1991. *Disaster Assistance: Federal, State, and Local Responses to Natural Disasters Need Improvement.* Washington, DC: General Accounting Office.

———. 1993a. *Disaster Assistance: DOD's Support for Hurricanes Andrew and Iniki and Typhoon Omar.* Washington, DC: General Accounting Office.

———. 1993b. *Disaster Management: Recent Disasters Demonstrate the Need to Improve the Nation's Response Strategy.* Washington, DC: General Accounting Office.

———. 1993c. *Disaster Relief Fund: Actions Still Needed to Prevent Recurrence of Funding Shortfall.* Washington, DC: General Accounting Office.

———. 1993d. *Management Reform: GAO's Comments on the National Performance Review Recommendations.* Washington, DC: General Accounting Office.

———. 1994. *Los Angeles Earthquake: Opinions of Officials on Federal Impediments to Rebuilding.* Washington, DC: General Accounting Office.

———. 2003. *Major Management Challenges and Program Risks: Federal Emergency Management Agency.* Washington, DC: General Accounting Office.

U.S. Geological Survey. 1990. "The Loma Prieta, California, Earthquake: An Anticipated Event." *Science* 247: 286–293.

———. 2005. USGS *Response to an Urban Earthquake: Northridge '94.* Open File Report 96–263. http://pubs.usgs.gov/of/1996/ofr-96-0263.

———. 2009a. "The Great 1906 San Francisco Earthquake." http://earthquake.usgs.gov/regional/nca/1906/18april/index.php.

———. 2009b. "Historic Earthquakes: Northridge, California." http://earthquake.usgs.gov/earthquakes/states/events/1994_01_17.php.

———. 2010. "October 17, 1989 Loma Prieta Earthquake." http://earthquake.usgs.gov/regional/nca/1989/.

U.S. Government Accountability Office. 2005. *Hurricane Katrina: Providing Oversight of the Nation's Preparedness, Response, and Recovery Activities.* Washington, DC: Government Accountability Office. September 28.

———. 2006a. *Expedited Assistance for Victims of Hurricanes Katrina and Rita: FEMA's Control Weaknesses Exposed the Government to Significant Fraud and Abuse.* Washington, DC: Government Accountability Office, February 13.

———. 2006b. *Federal Emergency Management Agency: Factors for Future Success and Issues to Consider for Organizational Placement.* Washington, DC: Government Accountability Office, May 9.

———. 2006c. *Hurricane Katrina: GAO's Preliminary Observations Regarding Preparedness, Response, and Recovery.* Washington, DC: Government Accountability Office, March 8.

———. 2006d. *Hurricane Katrina and Rita Disaster Relief: Improper and Potentially Fraudulent Individual Assistance Payments Estimated to be Between $600 Million and $1.4 Billion.* Washington, DC: Government Accountability Office. http://www.gao.gov/new.items/d06844t.pdf.

———. 2007a. *Budget Issues: FEMA Needs Adequate Data, Plans, and Systems to Effectively Manage Resources for Day-to-Day Operations.* Washington, DC: Government Accountability Office, January.

———. 2007b. *Emergency Management Assistance Compact: Enhancing EMAC's Collaborative and Administrative Capacity Should Improve National Disaster Response.* Washington, DC: Government Accountability Office, June.

———. 2007c. *Homeland Security: Observations on DHS and FEMA Efforts to Prepare for and Respond to Major and Catastrophic Disasters and Address Related Recommendations and Legislation.* Washington, DC: Government Accountability Office, May 15.

———. 2007d. *Homeland Security: Preparing for and Responding to Disasters.* Washington, DC: Government Accountability Office, March 9.

———. 2008a. *Actions Taken to Implement the Post-Katrina Emergency Management Act of 2006.* Washington, DC: Government Accountability Office, November 21.

———. 2008b. *Disaster Recovery: Past Experiences offer Insights for Recovering from Hurricanes Ike and Gustav and Other Recent Natural Disasters.* Washington, DC: Government Accountability Office, September.

———. 2008c. *Emergency Management: Observations on DHS's Preparedness for Catastrophic Disasters.* Washington, DC: Government Accountability Office, June 11.

———. 2009. *Emergency Management: Actions to Implement Select Provisions of the Post-Katrina Emergency Management Reform Act.* Washington, DC: Government Accountability Office.

———. 2010a. *Disaster Response: Criteria for Developing and Validating Effective Response Plans.* Washington, DC: Government Accountability Office, September 22.

———. 2010b. *Hurricane Recovery: Federal Government Provided a Range of Assistance to Nonprofits Following Hurricanes Katrina and Rita.* Washington, DC: Government Accountability Office, July.

———. 2011. *Measuring Disaster Preparedness: FEMA Has Made Limited Progress in Assessing National Capabilities.* Washington, DC: Government Accountability Office, March 17.

U.S. House of Representatives. 1989. Hearing Before the Subcommittee on Science, Research, and Technology, Committee on Science, Space, and Technology. *The Loma Prieta Earthquake: Lessons Learned.* 101st Congress, 1st Session, December 4.

———. 1990. Hearing Before the Subcommittee on Investigations and Oversight, Committee on Public Works and Transportation. *The Federal Emergency Management Agency's (FEMA) Response to Natural Disasters.* 101st Congress, 2nd Session, May 1 and 2.

———. 1993. Hearing Before the Subcommittee on Investigations and Oversight, Committee on Public Works and Transportation. *Federal Emergency Management Agency's Disaster Assistance Program.* 103rd Congress, 1st Session, March 2.

———. 1994. Hearing Before the Committee on Science, Space, and Technology. *Lessons Learned from the Northridge Earthquake.* 103rd Congress, 2nd Session, March 2.

———. 1996. Hearing Before the Subcommittee on Government Management, Information, and Technology, Committee on Government Reform and Oversight. *The Government Response to the Northridge Earthquake.* 104th Congress, 2nd Session, January 19.

———. 2005. Joint Hearing Before the Subcommittee on Emergency Preparedness, Science and Technology, Committee on Homeland Security with the Subcommittee on Terrorism, Unconventional Threats, and Capabilities, Committee on Armed Services. *Responding to Catastrophic Events: The Role of the Military and National Guard in Disaster Response.* 109th Congress, 1st Session, November 9.

———. 2006. *A Failure of Initiative. Final Report of the Select Bipartisan Committee to Investigate the Preparation for and Response to Hurricane Katrina.* 109th Congress, 2nd Session. Report 109–377. http://www.gpoaccess.gov/congress/index.html.

———. 2007. Hearing Before the Committee on the Budget. *Hurricanes Katrina and Rita: What Will Be the Long Term Effect on the Federal Budget.* 110th Congress, 1st Session, August 2.

———. 2008. Hearing Before the Subcommittee on Emergency Communications, Preparedness and Response, Committee on Homeland Security. *Moving Beyond the First Five Years: Ensuring FEMA's Ability to Respond and Recover in the Wake of a National Catastrophe.* 110th Congress, 2nd Session, April 9.

U.S. Office of Management and Budget. 2009. *Historical Tables: Budget of the United States Government, Fiscal Year 2009.* Executive Office of the President.

U.S. Senate. 1988. Hearing Before the Committee on Environment and Public Works. *Report on the Disaster Relief Act Amendments of 1988.* 100th Congress, 2nd Session.

———. 1993a. Hearing Before the Committee on Agriculture, Nutrition, and Forestry. *Flood and Disaster Relief in the Midwest.* 103rd Congress, 1st Session, July 16.

———. 1993b. Hearing Before the Committee on Governmental Affairs. *Rebuilding FEMA: Preparing for the Next Disaster.* 103rd Congress, 1st Session, May 18.

———. 1993c. Hearing Before the Subcommittee on Toxic Substances, Research and Development, Committee on Environment and Public Works. *Lessons Learned from Hurricane Andrew.* 103rd Congress, 1st Session, April 19.

———. 1993d. Hearing Before the Subcommittee on VA Hud-Independent Agencies. 103rd Congress, 1st Session, January 27.

———. 1994a. Hearing Before the Committee on Environment and Public Works. *Federal Response to the Midwest Floods of 1993.* 103rd Congress, 1st Session, November 9.

———. 1994b. Hearing Before the Committee on Environment and Public Works. *Response to the California Earthquake.* 103rd Congress, 2nd Session, January 27.

———. 2006a. Hearing Before the Committee on Homeland Security and Governmental Affairs. *Hurricane Katrina: The Defense Department's Role in the Response.* 109th Congress, 2nd Session. February 9.

———. 2006b. Hearing Before the Committee on Homeland Security and Governmental Affairs. *National Emergency Management: Where Does FEMA Belong?* 109th Congress, 2nd Session, June 8.

———. 2006c. *Hurricane Katrina: A Nation Still Unprepared.* Committee on Homeland Security and Government Affairs. http://www.gpoaccess.gov/serialset/creports/katrinanation.html.

———. 2006d. *Hurricane Katrina: The Role of the Governors in Managing the Catastrophe.* Committee on Homeland Security and Government Affairs. 109th Congress, 2nd Session, February 2. http://hsgac.senate.gov/public/index.cfm?FuseAction=Hearings.Hearing&Hearing_ID=d3da7aa3-104d-41f6-9e6d-314c1e0fa62a.

VandeHei, Jim. 2005. "Katrina Darkens the Outlook for Incumbents; Public Dismay Could Shape 2006 Elections." *The Washington Post,* September 11. http://pqasb.pqarchiver.com/washingtonpost/access/894496942.html.

VandeHei, Jim, and Peter Baker. 2005. "Bush Pledges Historic Effort to Help Gulf Coast Recover." *The Washington Post,* September 16.

Van Heerden, Ivor L.I. 2006. "The Failure of the New Orleans Levee System Following Hurricane Katrina and the Pathway Forward." *Public Administration Review* 67 (Special Supplementary Issue on Administrative Failure in the Wake of Hurricane Katrina): 24–35.

Van Heerden, Ivor, and Mike Bryan. 2006. *The Storm.* New York: Penguin.

Van Meter, Carl E., and Donald S. Van Horn. 1976. "The Implementation of Intergovernmental Policy." In *Public Policy-Making in a Federal System,* ed. Charles Jones and Robert Thomas. Beverly Hills, CA: Sage.

Vedantam, Shankar, and Dean Starkman. 2005. "Lack of Cohesion Bedevils Recovery." *The Washington Post,* September 15.

Vig, Norman J., and Michael E. Kraft. 2009. *Environmental Policy: New Directions for the Twenty-first Century.* Washington, DC: CQ Press.

Von Mises, Ludwig. 1944. *Bureaucracy.* New Haven, CT: Yale University Press.

Wagar, Linda, 1990. "Hugo and the Earthquake: Lessons Learned." *The Council of State Governments* 33: 11–33.

Walden, Richard M. 1992. "The Disaster After the Disaster." *The New York Times,* August 28, A15.

Waldo, Dwight. 1961. "Organization Theory: An Elephantine Problem." *Public Administration Review* 21: 210–225.

Walker, Jack L. 1977. "The Diffusion of Innovations Among the American States." *American Political Science Review* 68 (September): 880–899.

Walters, Jonathan, and Donald Kettl. 2005. "The Katrina Breakdown." *Governing.* December: 20–25.

Wamsley, Gary L. 1993. "The Pathologies of Trying to Control Bureaucracy and Policy: The Case of F.E.M.A. and Emergency Management." Blacksburg: Virginia Polytechnic Institute and State University, Center of Public Administration and Policy.

Ward, Robert, and Gary Wamsley. 2007. "From a Painful Past to an Uncertain Future." In *Emergency Management: The American Experience 1990–2005,* ed. Claire B. Rubin, 207–241. Fairfax, VA: Public Entity Risk Institute.

Warr, Brent. 2005. "Written Testimony Before the House Select Bipartisan Committee on Preparation and Response to Hurricane Katrina." U.S. House of Representatives, December 7.

Warwick, Donald P. 1973. *A Theory of Public Bureaucracy: Politics, Personality and Organization in the State Department.* Cambridge, MA: Harvard University Press.

Washburn, Mark, and George Haj. 1998. "Largest Evacuation a Success." *The Miami Herald,* September 27, 27A.

Washburn, Mark, and Tyler Bridges. 1998. "Mandatory Evacuation is a Record for Florida." *The Miami Herald*, September 26, 20A.

Washington Post-ABC News. 2005. "Response to Hurricane Katrina." September 2.

Waugh, William L., Jr. 1988. "States, Counties, and the Question of Trust and Capacity." *Publius: The Journal of Federalism* 18 (1): 189–198.

———. 1990. "Emergency Management and State and Local Government Capacity." In *Cities and Disaster*, ed. Richard T. Sylves and William L. Waugh, 221–238. Springfield, IL: Charles C. Thomas.

———. 1994. "Regionalizing Emergency Management: Counties as State and Local Government." *Public Administration Review* 54 (May/June): 253–258.

———. 2000. *Living with Hazards, Dealing with Disasters: An Introduction to Emergency Management.* Armonk, NY: M.E. Sharpe.

———. 2006a. "The Political Costs of Failure in the Katrina and Rita Disasters." In *Shelter from the Storm: Repairing the National Emergency Management System After Hurricane Katrina.* Special Issue of *The Annals of the American Academy of Political and Social Science* 604: 10–25.

———. 2006b. *Shelter from the Storm: Repairing the National Emergency Management System After Hurricane Katrina,* ed. William L. Waugh. Annals of the American Academy of Political and Social Science, Volume 604, March. Thousand Oaks, CA: Sage.

———. 2007. "EMAC, Katrina, and the Governors of Louisiana and Mississippi." *Public*

Administration Review 67 (Special Supplementary Issue on Administrative Failure in the Wake of Hurricane Katrina): 107–113.

Waugh, William L., Jr., and Gregory Streib. 2006. "Collaboration and Leadership for Effective Emergency Management." *Public Administration Review* 66: 131–40.

Waxman, J.J. 1973. "Local Broadcast Gatekeeping During Natural Disasters." *Journalism Quarterly:* 751–758.

Webb, Gary R. 2007. "The Popular Culture of Disaster: Exploring a New Dimension of Disaster Research." In *Handbook of Disaster Research,* ed. Havidan Rodriquez, Enrico L. Quarantelli, and Russell R. Dynes, 430–440. New York: Springer.

Webb, Gary. R., Kathleen H. Tierney, and J.M. Dahlhamer. 2000. "Businesses and Disasters: Empirical Patterns and Unanswered Questions." *Natural Hazards Review* 1: 83–90.

Weber, Max. 1958. *From Max Weber: Essays in Sociology.* Trans. H.H. Gerth and C. Wright Mills. New York: Oxford University Press.

Weible, Christopher, Paul Sabatier, and Mark Lubell. 2004. "A Comparison of a Collaborative and a Top-Down Approach to the use of Science in Policy: Establishing Marine Protected Areas in California." *Policy Studies Journal* 32 (2): 187–207.

Weiss, Janet A. 1989. "The Powers of Problem Definition: The Case of Government Paperwork." *Policy Sciences* 22: 97–121.

Weitz, Richard. 2006. "FEMA, DHS, and Katrina: Managing Domestic Catastrophes Better." Hudson Institute, Panel on "Homeland Security: Coping with Natural and Man-Made Disasters." Potomac Institute for Policy Studies, November 21, 2005.

Weller, Jack, and Enrico L. Quarantelli. 1973. "Neglected Characteristics of Collective Behavior." *American Journal of Sociology* 79 (November): 665–686.

Wenger, Dennis E. 1978. "Community Response to Disaster: Functional and Structural Alternations." In *Disasters, Theory and Research,* ed. E.L. Quarantelli, 18–47. London: Sage.

———. 1985. "Mass Media and Disasters." Newark: University of Delaware, Disaster Research Center, Preliminary Paper No. 98.

———. 1987. "Collective Behavior and Disaster Research." In *Sociology of Disasters,* ed. R.R. Dynes, B. DeMarche, and C. Pelanda, 213–239. Milano, Italy: Franco Angelo.

Wenger, Dennis E. and E.L. Quarantelli. 1989. *Local Mass Media Operations, Problems, and Products in Disasters.* Newark: University of Delaware, Disaster Research Center, Report Series No. 19.

West, Darrell M., and Marion Orr. 2007. "Race, Gender, and Communications in Natural Disasters." *Policy Studies Journal,* 35 (4): 569–586.

White, Josh, and Peter Whoriskey. 2005. "Planning, Response Are Faulted." *Washington Post,* September 2. http://www.washingtonpost.com/wp-dyn/content/article/2005/09/01/AR2005090102428.html.

White House. 2003. "Homeland Security Presidential Directive/HSPD-5." http:www.whitehouse.gove/news/releases/2003/02/20030228–9.html.

———. 2010a. "President Obama Signs Tennessee Disaster Declaration." Office of the Press Secretary, May 4. http://www.whitehouse.gov/the-press-office/president-obama-signs-tennessee-disaster-declaration.

———. 2010b. "Statement by the Press Secretary on the President's Southeastern Flooding Briefing." Office of the Press Secretary, May 6. http://www.whitehouse.gov/the-press-office/statement-press-secretary-presidents-southeastern-flooding-briefing.

White House Blog. 2010. "On the Ground Before the Raindrops Started Falling." http://www.whitehouse.gov/blog/2010/05/06/ground-raindrops-started-falling.

Wildavsky, Aaron. 1964. *The Politics of the Budgetary Process.* Boston: Little, Brown.

Wilkerson, Isabel. 1992. "Giant Worries Are Stalking Hurricane's Smallest Victims." *The New York Times,* September 4, A1, A8.

Wilkins, Lee. 1987. *Shared Vulnerability: The Media and American Perceptions of the Bhopal Disaster.* New York: Greenwood.

Williams, Walter. 1980. *The Implementation Perspective.* Berkeley: University of California Press.

Wilmer, L. 1958. "Toward a Definition of the Therapeutic Community." *American Journal of Psychiatry* 114: 824–834.

Wilson, James Q. 1989. *Bureaucracy: What Government Agencies Do and Why They Do It.* New York: Basic Books.

Wines, Michael. 1992. "President to View U.S. Relief Efforts in Storm-Hit Areas." *The New York Times,* September 1, A1, A10.

Winston, Pamela. 2002. *Welfare Policymaking in the States: The Devil in Devolution.* Washington, DC: Georgetown University Press.

Wise, Charles. 2002. "Organizing for Homeland Security." *Public Administration Review* 62 (2): 131–144.

———. 2006. "Organizing for Homeland Security After Katrina: Is Adaptive Management What's Missing?" *Public Administration Review* 66 (3): 302–318.

Witt, James L. 1993. "Foundations of the Future." *National Hazards Observer* 17 (No. 6, July): 1–3.

———. 2006. "Military Role in Natural Disaster Response." *Disaster Preparedness,* Volume 1, Issue I (Summer). Center for Defense and Security Policy, Wilburforce University. http://www.wilberforce.edu/cdsp/cdsp_art2_01.html.

Witte, Griff, and Robert O'Harrow, Jr. 2005. "Short-Staffed FEMA Farms Out Procurement." *The Washington Post,* September 17. http://www.washingtonpost.com/wp-dyn/content/article/2005/09/16/AR2005091601833.html.

Wolensky, Robert, and Edward Miller. 1981. "The Everyday Versus the Disaster Role of Local Officials." *Urban Affairs Quarterly* 16 (June): 483–504.

Wolensky, Robert, and Kenneth C. Wolensky. 1991. "American Local Government and the Disaster Management Problem." *Local Government Studies* (March/April): 15–32.

Wolf, Charles. 1988. *Markets or Governments: Choosing Between Imperfect Alternatives.* Cambridge, MA: MIT Press.

Woll, Peter. 1963. *American Bureaucracy.* New York: Norton.

Woolsey, Matt. 2007. "In Pictures: America's Most Expensive Natural Disasters." *Forbes,* October 29. http://www.forbes.com/2008/09/15/property-disaster-hurricane-forbeslife-cx_mw_0915disaster_slide_2.html?thisSpeed=15000.

———. 2008. "America's Most Expensive Natural Disasters." *Forbes,* September 13. http://www.forbes.com/2007/10/29/property-disaster-hurricane-forbeslife-cx_mw_1029disaster.html.

World Bank. 2004. "Natural Disasters: Counting the Cost." http://web.worldbank.org/WBSITE/EXTERNAL/NEWS/0,,contentMDK:20169861~menuPK:34457~pagePK:34.

Wright, Deil S. 1988. "Models of National, State, and Local Relationships." In *Understanding Intergovernmental Relations,* ed. Deil S. Wright. Pacific Grove, CA: Brooks/Cole.

Wright, Gerald C., Robert S. Erikson, and John P. McIver. 1987. "Public Opinion and Policy Liberalism in the American States." *American Journal of Political Science* 31: 980–1001.

Wright, James, and Peter Rossi. 1981. *Social Science and Natural Hazards.* North Scituate, MA: Duxbury Press.

Wright, James D., Peter H. Rossi, Joseph A. Pereira, and Eleanor Weber-Burdin. 1983. *Victims of the Environment: Loss from Natural Hazards in the United States, 1970–1980.* New York: Springer Press.

Wright, James, Peter Rossi, S.R. Wright, and E. Weber-Burdin. 1979. *After the Clean-Up: Long Range Effects of Natural Disasters.* Beverly Hills, CA: Sage.

Wright, Sam. 1978. *Crowds and Riots: A Study in Social Organization.* Beverly Hills, CA: Sage.

WSMV. 2010. "Corps Defends Actions During Tenn. Flooding." May 11. http://www.wsmv.com/weather/23523580/detail.html.

Yates, Douglas. 1982. *Bureaucratic Democracy: The Search for Democracy and Efficiency in American Government.* Cambridge, MA: Harvard University Press.

York, Michael. 1989. "Making Sense Out of St. Croix: Why Did Order Collapse Completely After Hugo?" *The Washington Post National Weekly Edition,* October 9–15, 32–33.

Zaneski, Cyril T. 1998. "Georges May Take Toll on U.S. 1 Plan." *The Miami Herald,* September 28, 5B.

Zensinger, Larry. 1992. Program Coordinator, Federal Emergency Management Agency. Personal Interview. Washington, DC, December 27.

Index

Page numbers in *italics* indicate illustrations and figures

About the Author

Saundra K. Schneider is a professor and director of the Master of Public Policy Program in the Department of Political Science at Michigan State University. Her general research interests focus on the role of administrative factors in public policy development. Her articles have appeared in *Political Analysis*; the *British Journal of Political Science*; the *Journal of Politics*; *Publius: The Journal of Federalism*; the *Journal of Public Administrative Research and Theory*; *Public Administration Review*; *Comparative Politics*; *Policy Studies Journal*; *State Politics and Policy Quarterly;* and *Public Administration Quarterly*.

*9 7 8 0 7 6 5 6 2 2 4 3 3 *

An environmentally friendly book printed and bound in England by www.printondemand-worldwide.com

PEFC Certified

This product is
from sustainably
managed forests
and controlled
sources

PEFC™

www.pefc.org

PEFC/16-33-415

This book is made of chain-of-custody materials; FSC materials for the cover and PEFC materials for the text pages.

#0243 - 250116 - C0 - 229/152/17 - PB - 9780765622433